FAITH AND FIRE

The flames of hell-fire surround those who have offended by covetousness, gluttony, lust and other mortal sins. Woodcut in *Auslegung des Lebens Jesu Christi* (Ulm, *c.* 1478).

FAITH AND FIRE

POPULAR AND UNPOPULAR RELIGION
1350 – 1600

MARGARET ASTON

THE HAMBLEDON PRESS
LONDON AND RIO GRANDE

Published by The Hambledon Press 1993
102 Gloucester Avenue, London NW1 8HX (U.K.)
P.O. Box 162, Rio Grande, Ohio 45674 (U.S.A.)

ISBN 1 85285 073 6

A description of this book is available from
the British Library and from the Library of Congress

Typeset by York House Typographic Ltd., London.
Printed on acid-free paper and bound in
Great Britain by Cambridge University Press

Contents

In memory of T.H.A.
who died 17 October 1985
having had his three score but not the ten
he thought we all need
for things undone

Acknowledgements

All but one of the chapters in this book were originally published elsewhere and are reprinted by the kind permission of the original editors and publishers.

1   *The Christian World: A Social and Cultural History of Christianity*, ed. Geoffrey Barraclough (Thames and Hudson, London, 1981), pp. 157-70.

2   *From Ockham to Wyclif*, ed. Anne Hudson and Michael Wilks, *Studies in Church History*, Subsidia 5 (Oxford, 1987), pp. 281-330, by permission of the editor and committee of the Ecclesiastical History Society.

4   *The Church, Politics and Patronage in the Fifteenth Century*, ed. Barrie Dobson (Alan Sutton, Gloucester & St. Martin's Press, New York, 1984), pp. 45-81.

5   *Medievalia et Humanistica*, new series, 9 (1979), pp. 1-24.

6   *The Meaning of the Renaissance and Reformation*, ed. Richard L. DeMolen (Houghton Mifflin, Boston and London, 1974), pp. 71-129.

7   *The Church and Wealth*, ed. W.J. Sheils and Diana Wood, *Studies in Church History*, 24 (1987), pp. 189-207, by permission of the editor and committee of the Ecclesiastical History Society.

8   *Journal of Ecclesiastical History*, 40 (1989), pp. 524-52.

9   *Iconoclasm vs. Art and Drama*, ed. Clifford Davidson and Ann Eljenholm Nichols, Early Drama, Art, and Music Monograph Series, 11 (Kalamazoo, MI, Medieval Institute Publications, 1989), pp. 47-91.

10 *Bilder und Bildersturm im Spätmittelalter und in der frühen Neuzeit*, ed. Bob Scribner and Martin Warnke, Wolfenbütteler Forschungen, Bd. 46 (Wiesbaden, 1990), pp. 175-202.

List of Illustrations

Plates between pp. 110-11

Foreword

Most of the chapters in this book are 'command papers', written by invitation between 1974 and 1986 on defined themes for particular books or occasions. All but one have been published before, and I have taken the opportunity to do a certain amount of revising and updating, or to add annotation where there was none. The pieces on Popular Religious Movements and the Northern Renaissance were general surveys that formed part of two widely ranging books on the Christian World and Europe in the period of Renaissance and Reformation. Also fairly general in scope is the essay on Huizinga, commissioned as an assessment of the legacy of *The Waning of the Middle Ages* in England fifty years on (a kind of jubilee piece of the late 1970s that marks a phase of English fifteenth-century historiography). Three more narrowly focused chapters (those on Wycliffe, Caim's Castles, and the last, on Fire) started life as lectures to historical conferences. 'Bishops and Heresy', one of three pieces on the Lollard movement, is a somewhat expanded and revised version of an address, previously unpublished, delivered at the Annual General Meeting of the Canterbury and York Society in October 1986. The essays on Gold and Rickmansworth reflect greater personal initiative; in the latter case much of that coming from two friends who set the ball rolling and kept it in motion. These, like the last two chapters, are closely connected with my book on iconoclasm, developing ideas that occurred in work on that subject.

Starting to write at someone else's request rather than off one's own bat naturally makes a difference to the task in hand. Nevertheless certain themes run through the book – I hope to its advantage. If we are all fearful we may be spending our lives walking round one idea, we necessarily delude ourselves into thinking it has to be a good one. Rereading oneself is as good a way as any for discovering *idées fixes* and there is certainly plenty about images and the role of imagery in religion scattered through this book. I make no apology for that, though I have to admit that it took me a long time to grasp the subconscious imperative behind an examination question I proposed for a General Paper decades ago – 'Image-worship is the beginning and ending of religion'; one of those impossible 'Discuss' questions. (Was any candidate rash enough to attempt it?)

My subtitle – which comes with apologies to Christopher and Rosalind Brooke and Patrick Collinson, to mention no others – may seem to beg too many questions. What is 'popular religion'? Is the term too categorical to be useful, itself unrealistic, better – as has been suggested – avoided altogether? Historians have become wary, conscious of their inability to reach the realities of the commonplace or effectively to tap the seepage of ideas that could move, as they still do, from streets on to pages as well as the other way round. If we have suffered from a tendency to love heretics as well as rebels, it may be a fallacy to think we can learn from them about the people at large. Yet heretical developments in England can tell us something of the relationship between the religious beliefs of learned and unlearned. Late medieval understanding of the eucharist existed on at least two levels; the history of Lollardy helps us to see something of the differences of these two worlds, clerical and lay, as Latin theology was translated into the vernacular of market-place and village tavern.

Heretics might be of the people but they were not popular. They endangered not only their own souls, but the spiritual health of their community and society. Neighbours as well as inquisitors feared the fatality of that infection. There is a historiographical paradox, itself instructive for historians, in the slogan used today to entice visitors to the dark hills and fortresses of Langue-doc – 'Visitez Limoux - Pays Cathare'. Heretics nowadays are a tourist attraction. In the twelfth century some Cathars were burned by crowds despite the efforts of clergy to save them. In the pilgrimage centre of Saint-Gilles, in Provence, outraged townspeople saw to it that Peter de Bruys, who had challenged the need for church buildings and the veneration of the cross, perished in 1140 on one of his own bonfires. It was no different in sixteenth-century England. Heretics were cold-shouldered in early Tudor London; in Exeter people threw sticks and gorse on to the fire that was burning a heretic in 1533.

Listening too much to dissidents distorts the past. The truly 'popular' may be the most conventional and mundane and ordinary, that which is likely to be the least recorded part of the past, as of all lives. Of course, since heresy could be defined as an opinion founded in Scripture, contrary to the opinion of the church, learning about heresy may help to show ways in which the church was developing, or suggest pointers to the future. If we adopt this viewpoint we are ourselves perpetuating a historiographical tradition, for it was reformers of the sixteenth century, zealously seeking to reconvert the mass of believers, who exaggerated the enthusiasm of the people for this biblical salvation.

Working on both sides of the Reformation divide has its advantages, and may promote a longer perspective. Fire has a place in this credal continuity, for in the seventeenth century, as in the thirteenth, hell-fire and the flames that would engulf the world at its final consummation were present realities. Fire, annihilating and life-giving, the means to purge the impure and to translate the irredeemable to perdition and eternal punishment, was annexed to Christian belief. It is an element of history.

I am grateful to all those who have promoted the chapters in this book in one way or another and have kindly allowed them to reappear in this form. I also thank for various kinds of aid, inspiration and encouragement John Bossy, Barrie Dobson, Anne Hudson, Alison McHardy, Ann Nichols, Derek Plumb, Colin Richmond and Bob Scribner. Sophie Buxton has been a great help reading the proofs. My biggest debt is to Martin Sheppard for spending so much time on the book, patiently and cheerfully, as editor and publisher.

It is an heretic that makes the fire,
Not she which burns in't.

William Shakespeare, *The Winter's Tale*, II:iii

Abbreviations

AFH	*Archivum Franciscanum Historicum*
Allen, ed.	*Opus epistolarum Des. Erasmi Roterodami*, ed. P.S. Allen and H.M. Allen (Oxford, 1906-58)
ARG	*Archiv für Reformationsgeschichte*
BIHR	*Bulletin of the Institute of Historical Research*
BL	British Library
BM	British Museum
CCR	*Calendar of Close Rolls*
CFR	*Calendar of Fine Rolls*
CHB	*Cambridge History of the Bible*
CMH	*Cambridge Medieval History*
CPL	*Calendar of Papal Letters*
CPR	*Calendar of Patent Rolls*
CS	Camden Society
CSPD	*Calendar of State Papers Domestic*
CWE	*Collected Works of Erasmus* (Toronto University Press, 1974-)
CYS	Canterbury and York Society
DNB	*Dictionary of National Biography*
EETS	Early English Text Society
EHR	*English Historical Review*

Emden (C)	A.B. Emden, *Biographical Register of the University of Cambridge* (Cambridge, 1963)
Emden (O)	A.B. Emden, *Biographical Register of the University of Oxford* (Oxford, 1957-9, 1974)
EWW	*English Works of Wyclif*, ed. F.D. Matthew (EETS, 74, 1880)
Foxe, *A&M*	John Foxe, *Acts and Monuments*, ed. J. Pratt (London, 1853-8, 1877)
FZ	*Fasciculi zizaniorum*, ed. W.W. Shirley (RS, London, 1858)
HRO	Hertfordshire Record Office
JEH	*Journal of Ecclesiastical History*
JTS	*Journal of Theological Studies*
LP	*Letters and Papers . . . of the Reign of Henry VIII*
MED	*Middle English Dictionary* (Ann Arbor, MI, 1952-)
ODCC	*Oxford Dictionary of the Christian Church*
PBA	*Proceedings of the British Academy*
PRO	Public Record Office
PS	Parker Society
Rot. Parl.	*Rotuli Parliamentorum* (London, 1767-77)
RS	Rolls Series
SCH	*Studies in Church History*
SEW	*Select English Works of John Wyclif*, ed. T. Arnold (Oxford, 1869-71)
SR	*Statutes of the Realm*
STC	*Short-Title Catalogue of Books printed in England . . . 1475-1640*, ed. W.A. Jackson, F.S. Ferguson and K.F. Pantzer (London, 1976-86)
TRHS	*Transactions of the Royal Historical Society*
Wilkins, *Concilia*	*Concilia Magnae Britanniae et Hiberniae*, ed. D. Wilkins (London, 1737)
WS	Wyclif Society

1

Popular Religious Movements in the Middle Ages

The religion of the people belongs to the unscripted history of the church. It is true of Christianity in all periods that, as well as the church forming the people, the people also form the church. If an institution is to remain alive there has to be a continuous process of interaction (what one might call a dialectical relationship) between its forms and formulas and the beliefs of its members. They must contribute to each other's existence. This dialectical process was particularly evident in the late medieval church, which, having reached a high point of doctrinal and institutional definition in the thirteenth century, was confronted by a rising tide of devotional activity among believers. It represented a challenge that tested the limits of the organized church. While Christianity tended to become more and more clerical, lay society, in becoming more religious, generated an increasing number of spiritual initiatives. The religion of the people always amounted to a great deal more than a vulgarized reflection of the clerical elite, and the fact that some of these initiatives were declared heretical tells more of weakened church structures than it does of the nature of popular piety.

There was a tension, latent or explicit, between the church defined as ecclesiastical hierarchy and the church defined as community of faithful believers. Or, to put it differently, there was potential alienation, or at least divergence, between the knowing and the unknowing. The religion of the learned and the religion of the people were expressed in different ways of thinking and doing, each with its own momentum, though it would be quite wrong to think of them as belonging to separate worlds.

In the strictest sense, the religion of the people is impenetrable. It remains a forever closed book by virtue of the fact that it was so largely remote from books. Deprived of the oral communications of the past, we can only see the beliefs of the illiterate refracted through the writings of the literate, whose religious understanding was professedly of a different order. Since so much popular religion existed in the life of the spoken word, vanished passages of pulpit oratory and the transient flight of speech constitute a very large loss. Nor can the visual arts, for all their importance, bridge this gap. Not only is their survival and coverage at best patchy; as reporters they belong in the main to

1

the same world as literary sources. We are, therefore, distanced by the nature of the records, as well as by the passage of time, from direct knowledge of the religion of the people, and all that we can say of the religious mentality of the humblest believers amounts, in effect, to deduction.

While the hierarchy mobilized the people, the people could mobilize the hierarchy. The church, which in one sense undeniably was the people, also had to beware of the people. Since those who were capable of guiding and instructing the mass of believers were always a tiny minority, and clerical education in fact always lagged far behind theory, the more actively the laity concerned themselves with doctrine, the greater the danger. Wherever and whenever there was a quickening of the intellectual tempo, a stirring of thought in the shape of new ideas and more people coming into contact with learning (not necessarily through direct contact with books, but through hearing about the world of books), there was the greater likelihood that error would arise. The devotions of the illiterate posed almost insuperable problems of control, and there was almost no spiritual activity that was not open to misinterpretation and misuse. The veneration of images could turn back into something resembling pagan idolatry, and the perverse inversion of image-worship was the manipulation of images for magical purposes. Mass pilgrimages might result in anticlerical demonstrations, like that which attended the apocalyptic preaching of the shepherd, Hans Böhm at Niklashausen in 1476.[1] Self-imposed penance could give way to displays that seemed to suggest an alternative to the ministry of the church. The ideals of holy poverty and chastity, withdrawn from clerical supervision and imitated by the laity, were capable of building what seemed like heretical counter-churches in the hands of Cathars and Waldensians.

The religious movements of the later middle ages reflect the interactions of two worlds: the literate clerical and the illiterate secular. Some took their beginnings from an inspired leader in the literate world, whose ideas were translated from academic hall to street corner, thereby undergoing a sea-change. Others started with leadership that was itself of the people, or else arose at the prompting not of an individual but of catastrophic events. What we might call the folkways of devotional piety included various forms of traditional group activity that could spring into larger life under the stress of circumstance without any guiding hand. Penitential pilgrimage and corporate associations for the service of the dead lent themselves to spontaneous demonstrations of fervour at times of common need. Individuals were mutually bonded in more ways and groups than are dreamt of in our cellular society.

A great part of popular piety amounted to an endeavour to live with the inexplicable and intolerable. God and the saints (specially the latter) bore the

---

[1] Norman Cohn, *The Pursuit of the Millennium* (London, 1962), pp. 241-9; Richard Kieck-hefer, *Repression of Heresy in Medieval Germany* (Liverpool, 1979), pp. 98-99.

Fig. 1 The relics of St. Alban, in a rich shrine, being carried to a new chapel by a procession of monks. Two cripples implore the saint's aid as they pass.

consequences of the general incomprehension of natural phenomena. The religion of the people was deeply impregnated by ancient peasant fears of natural forces. Those who had no inkling of scientific laws, who suffered many mortal and crippling diseases, found their own laws of explanation in healing and punishing saints. Surrounded by mysterious powers and unaccountable events, people sought aid in formulaic expressions of word or deed. God dwelt in some places more than others and the habitations of saints were geographically dispersed. Holiness in this age was very much located. Through chosen people, particular places and special objects one found access to spiritual controls. It was on the move, in pursuit of these mediatory powers, that the people's religion was most in evidence – whether the movement was that of groups of laymen taking to the roads and leaving home, or gatherings of large numbers mobilized in their own locality by some religious visitor.

The habit of pilgrimage has suffered from the jibes of critics, but it was among the oldest devotional practices of the church and its popularity in the thirteenth, fourteenth and fifteenth centuries shows that it answered widely felt needs. Whether or not the pilgrim could say his paternoster or the creed, he believed that the appropriate prayer or offering rendered to his saint might secure the desired material or spiritual benefit. Though the most famous pilgrimage centres were the most distant – Jerusalem, Rome and Santiago de Compostela – and pilgrims travelled singly and in groups to all these places, it is a mistake to think only, or even first, of them. For every well-placed pilgrim, like the fifteenth-century travellers Felix Fabri (a Dominican of Ulm who went twice to the Holy Land), or Margery Kempe (wife of a Norfolk burgess who went to Rome, Jerusalem, Compostela, Canterbury and Wilsnack), both of whom wrote up their experiences,[2] there were countless others whose similar, less distant journeyings, went unrecorded. The great bulk of the pilgrim traffic was formed by cults that remained as they started, relatively local. For most people a journey of any kind was a luxury; a journey to Jerusalem or Rome almost as unthinkable as a trip to the moon still is today. But that did not mean that the spiritual hopes that fastened on a pilgrim road were closed to those peasants and labourers and lesser mortals who formed perhaps 80 per cent of the population. On the contrary, as time went on the probability increased that a holy man, or a miraculous event would present itself within the walking range and work round of such people. When these workers and wives downed tools and left their hearths for several days' journey to a local shrine, it was irrelevant to them whether or not the holy place or saintly person had received an official stamp of approval. They had their own understanding of the holy, which had nothing to do with canonists and records and the proprieties of Rome.

Popular belief attached itself to the concrete and the seen, not because the faith of the people was materialistic, but because for them matter was an expression of spiritual forces. Holiness was real because one could see its effects. A peasant of Sabarthès believed that the harvests had been less good since the Cathar 'perfect' had left the area. Likewise it seemed that the arrival in Hereford of the bones of Thomas Cantilupe had brought more abundant crops. One looked to divine powers for prodigious physical results. Such attitudes – orthodox or otherwise – sometimes seemed shocking, even at the time. 'Don't you see how stupid, foolish and senseless are these people who wish to see me?' complained Dauphine de Signe (1284-1360) in 1353, when a crowd of blind, epileptic and other diseased people gathered from a wide area to wait outside her house in hopes of a miraculous cure. 'Why do they come to me, who am neither Christ nor Peter nor Paul, but a stinking body, food for worms and heap of iniquities? They ask for signs, they want prodigies, miracles!' She stressed the need to place trust in God above hope in creatures.

---

[2] *The Wanderings of Felix Fabri*, trans. A. Stewart, 2 vols. (Palestine Pilgrims Text Society, vii, ix, 1897); *The Book of Margery Kempe*, ed. S.B. Meech and H.E. Allen (EETS, 212, 1940, rep. 1982), modern version by B.A. Windeatt (Harmondsworth, 1985); see also Clarissa W. Atkinson, *Mystic and Pilgrim: The Book and the World of Margery Kempe* (Ithaca and London, 1983); Rosalind and Christopher Brooke, *Popular Regligion in the Middle Ages: Western Europe, 1000-1300* (London, 1984), pp. 14-30; M. Aston, *The Fifteenth Century* (London, 1968), pp. 85-102.

One should confess and do penance for one's sins before taking requests to the saints.[3]

Too often the priorities were reversed. The saints were cultivated at the expense of the sacraments. And suppliants frequently appeared to invoke saints for specific remedies in a manner suggestive of a contract: 'If I . . . may it please you to . . .' People endangered by shipwreck would vow an offering to the Virgin (*stella maris*, patroness of the sea) if they were spared. Those threatened by plague made promises to St. Roch. One of the commonest forms of offering at pilgrimage shrines was a wax votive, either in the shape of candles or trindles measured according to the height or breadth of the suppliant, or else a model of the limb for which a cure was sought. These objects were both numerous and sometimes very large (and wax was a valuable commodity). In 1307 the objects at Bishop Cantilupe's tomb included 1,200 wax images of parts of the body and limbs. The process of canonization of Dauphine revealed that the bishop of Avignon had promised a candle of twelve pounds if one of his friends recovered from a wound, and the abbess of Ste-Croix at Apt offered a wax bullock if the holy woman's intercession led to the recovery of a lost herd of oxen. Conditional promises of this kind (and they were made by all classes of society), accompanied by appropriate acts of piety, constituted 86 per cent of the 221 miracles attributed to Louis of Anjou in the *Liber miraculorum*, drawn up soon after his death in 1297 (the majority of which, 199 cases, were concerned with human cures).[4]

For most medieval believers sainthood was a vital link in the chain attaching them to God, and the establishment of new saints and new pilgrimage centres owed much to popular enthusiasm. An illuminating example of the interweaving of high-level diplomacy and popular devotion that went into making a new saint is the process by which Thomas Cantilupe was canonized. This bishop of Hereford, who died in 1282 and was canonized by papal bull in 1320, was one of the last to achieve official sainthood in medieval England. The irony is that by the time he did so his cult was in decline. Although Cantilupe's remains had been honourably interred in the Lady Chapel at Hereford not many months after his death (which took place in Italy), it was five years before any miraculous cure was attributed to him. Coincidentally, but surely not accidentally, this happened on 3 April 1287, the very day on which Thomas's successor in the see, Bishop Swinfield, moved the bones into a new tomb in the north transept. Once launched, the new cult moved off on a wave of popular local devotion. There was a spontaneous burst of miracles among the visitors to the

---

[3] A. Vauchez, 'La religion populaire dans la France méridionale au XIVe siècle d'après les procès de canonisation', and 'Conclusion', in *La religion populaire en Languedoc du XIIIe siècle à la moitié du XIVe siècle* (Cahiers de Fanjeaux, 11, 1976) ed. E. Privat, introd. M.-H. Vicaire, pp. 102-3, 436-7.

[4] Jonathan Sumption, *Pilgrimage: An Image of Mediaeval Religion* (London, 1975), pp. 138-40; Ronald C. Finucane, *Miracles and Pilgrims: Popular Beliefs in Medieval England* (London, 1977), pp. 95-99; Jacques Paul, 'Miracles et mentalité religieuse populaire à Marseille au début du XIVe siècle', in *Religion populaire*, ed. Privat, pp. 61-70, cf. 99.

new shrine, most of whom were humble local people living in the vicinity of Hereford. Of the total of some 470 miracles attributed to Cantilupe in the extremely lengthy process of canonization, about two-fifths (194) took place in the first two years. In 1307, when the papal process of enquiry finally started, the tale of miracles was petering out and the flood of local pilgrims abating. By the time that Cantilupe's relics were translated into a still more splendid new shrine in 1348, the popular enthusiasm on which the whole process rested had faded away and Cantilupe, though doubtless cherished as a local father of the church of Hereford, was no longer the wonder-worker he had been.[5]

The great preachers of the fifteenth century show us another form of popular piety on the move. The most famous of them were itinerant apostles, who not only took the word to many places, gathering vast congregations of auditors as they went, but also in some cases attracted trains of followers. St. Vincent Ferrer (d. 1419) reached the ears of millions during his twenty years' preaching through Provence, Savoy, Dauphiné, Castile, Aragon, Catalonia, Normandy and Brittany. His call to repentance was responded to with scenes of communal flagellation. Apocalyptic messages, the news that the reign of Antichrist was about to begin, fell on willing ears in all parts of western Christendom. The Dominican Manfredi of Vercelli, preaching this word in Lombardy in the same period, soon found that he had a following of up to a thousand *simplices*, a large proportion of them women who had left their husbands in the holy cause. The potential sect was dispersed by Pope Martin V, who summoned Manfredi to Rome in 1424.[6]

The anxieties and enthusiasms of lay people were readily galvanized into action by the electric powers of pulpit orators. St. Bernardino, the greatest preacher of his age, managed to reach the ears of countless auditors in Italy without passing the bounds of orthodoxy, though he, like Vincent Ferrer and Manfredi of Vercelli, had to explain himself in the highest quarters. Bernardino, magnetic in his down-to-earth vernacular passion, brought believers in their thousands to mass repentance and self-flagellation, but it was his popularization of the cult of the Name of Jesus, making the monogram of the Holy Name familiar in the piazzas of northern Italy, that brought charges of heresy and idolatry against him. His name was cleared, and the church's eventual endorsement of the cult that St. Bernardino did so much to extend is an outstanding example of a popular devotion reaching liturgical use. An ancient devotion, encouraged by both Cistercians and Franciscans, gained currency from mass homiletics and arrived, before the end of the fifteenth century, with

---

[5] Finucane, *Miracles and Pilgrims*, pp. 173-88; A. Vauchez, *La sainteté en occident aux derniers siècles du moyen age d'après les procès de canonisation et les documents hagiographiques* (Rome, 1981), p. 257ff; *St. Thomas Cantilupe, Bishop of Hereford*, ed. M. Jancey (Hereford, 1982).

[6] E. Delaruelle, E.-R. Labande and P. Ourliac, *L'église au temps du Grand Schisme et de la crise concilaire (1378-1449)* (Paris, 1962), ii, pp. 636-56.

Fig. 2a, b St. Bernardino, in a print made ten years after his death in 1444, holding the sacred monogram IHS. Above, the foolish preacher inciting people to violence, as satirized in Sebastian Brant's *Ship of Fools* (1494).

its own office and mass. In the sixteenth century the Franciscans gained official recognition for the feast of the Name of Jesus.[7]

The treatment of the dead shows the currents of influence moving in the reverse direction. We can see here how official dogma promoted a welter of foundations that affected the whole of society from top to bottom, clerical and lay alike, across the whole of Europe. The pursuit of the security of souls was perhaps the most common and binding passion of western Christendom in the later middle ages, and it owed a great deal to ecclesiastical formulation. The doctrine of purgatory, though itself provocative of anxiety, also offered a means of relief to the living, who could both hope for the ultimate redemption of endangered souls and themselves assist that end. The church's teaching on this topic, evolving from the patristic period, was not defined until the Council of Lyons (1274). The concept of a treasury of merits which could be unlocked and spent on behalf of the suffering souls of the dead held the living thereafter in a terrible grip, for it seemed obvious that the more one could provide for one's own soul, or for the souls of others one cared for, the less the agonies of

---

[7] Iris Origo, *The World of San Bernardino* (New York, 1962), pp. 117-30; L. McAodha, 'The Holy Name of Jesus in the Preaching of St. Bernardine of Siena', *Franciscan Studies*, 29 (1969), pp. 37-65; R.W. Pfaff, *New Liturgical Feasts in Later Medieval England* (Oxford, 1970), pp. 62-83.

Fig. 3 Holy dying: devils, faced by the crucifix, lose the deathbed contest as the last rites are given to the dying man and his soul is received by angels.

posthumous redemption in purgatory, where (according to St. Thomas) the smallest pain was greater than the greatest on earth.[8]

Purgatory both consoled and terrified. Michel Magot, a revered lay brother who died in 1334, was able to comfort the Franciscans of Toulouse when one of their members died before completing his confession and receiving the last rites. There was no need to worry, said Magot (to whom prophetic powers were attributed for his words at this emotional moment), God had taken into account the deceased's intention to confess. 'So he is really in the way of salvation?' asked the superior anxiously. 'Yes he is', Magot was able to reply reassuringly. The brother had escaped the danger of damnation, 'but he suffers great purgatorial pains'.[9]

To provide for the souls of the dead was just as important as provision for the living, and (in a period that remembered obits more than birthdays) this was an assumption common to all classes. When Sir John Bosville killed Thomas del Hill and Robert de Derley, it seemed right in 1367 that 30 of the 160 marks he provided as compensation should be spent on masses for the souls of his

[8] Jacques Le Goff, *The Birth of Purgatory*, trans. A. Goldhammer (Chicago and London, 1984; orig. French edn. Paris, 1981).

[9] H. Dedieu, 'Quelques traces de religion populaire autour des frères mineurs de la province d'Aquitaine', in *Religion populaire*, ed. Privat, pp. 235-8.

victims – half the amount that went to dependants of the slain.[10] Fears and worries over the souls of the dead (shriven and unshriven) produced, particularly from the fourteenth century, an enormous number of foundations, large and small, by which the living and dying provided intercessory prayers. Confraternities, which were established with regional variations all over Europe, existed, among a variety of other purposes, to maintain obsequies and prayers for their members. They were to be found in small villages as well as in towns, and people of all kinds belonged. By means of joining a confraternity even quite humble persons, including those who were too poor to pay the entry fees and dues, could provide themselves with a form of spiritual security. Whereas cathedrals were the monuments to the piety of an earlier age, the foundations typical of this period were the countless confraternity and chantry chapels constructed for the most part inside existing churches. Lay piety, in invading the church, turned inwards. The forms of spiritual self-help were multiplying.

The sheer popularity and proliferation of some of these devotional forms is indicative of instability. The late medieval church was caught up in an inflationary spiral of a dangerous kind. Its pieties were subject to multiplication of the sort that inescapably leads to devaluation and to the disquieting effects with which we are all familiar. The fewer the higher, the more the lower was an observable law, even then, and was seen to apply to people, to practices and to things.

The enormous numbers of people who were admitted to lower clerical orders, many of whom never reached or aspired to the priesthood, meant that the percentage of clergy to people was seemingly ever on the increase (in a manner somewhat analogous to government bureaucrats today). It also had the effect of bringing into the clerical estate many men who were indistinguishable from laymen. The fact that one could join the ranks of the church and receive its distinctive mark of the tonsure without abandoning secular life or marriage, indeed without any kind of meaningful commitment, reflected back on popular views of the priestly calling. It was not altogether surprising, given the large numbers of most unpriestly persons who had received the first tonsure for the most worldly reasons, if there was not always a clear understanding of the precise requirements of a spiritual vocation, or if ordination failed to command due respect. Schoolboy choristers might be tonsured at the age of seven years, and this purely technical ceremony could serve unworthy purposes in later life, if it became convenient to claim benefit of clergy. Ignatius Loyola, tonsured in his early years, used this device to escape the consequences of a youthful crime of violence.[11] The fact that a provincial

---

[10] *Testamenta Eboracensia*, ed. J. Raine, i (Surtees Society, 4, 1836), p. 84.

[11] James Brodrick, *Saint Ignatius Loyola: The Pilgrim Years* (London, 1956), pp. 30-31, 45-7; cf. Richard de Bury, *Philobiblon*, trans. E.C. Thomas, ed. M. Maclagan (Oxford, 1970), pp. 36-41 on youthful tonsure and its exploitation to escape punishment for crime.

synod at Paris, in 1429, found it necessary to remind candidates for the order of subdeacon that this involved a vow of celibacy shows the perennial problem of the supposed line between major and minor orders – a line that Innocent III redrew, in 1207, when he made the subdeacon, hitherto a minor order (not involving continence), into a major one. Early sixteenth-century reformers who drew attention to this damaging state of affairs may have exaggerated in seeing the minor clerical orders as an 'asylum for scoundrels', but their consensus of criticism indicates the conspicuousness of the problem.[12] The fact that so many lesser clergy were of the people in everything but name affected the nature of all popular religious movements, which were never purely lay, and ensured that the anticlericalism they so often expressed was always in part a reflection of the church's intramural divisions. Also, which was more important, disrespect for the clergy undermined their ministry, informing views like those of heretical villagers in the diocese of Pamiers in the 1320s, who parodied the elevation of the host, calling the sacrament a slice of turnip, and questioned the value of all this 'singing of clerks and chaplains', who 'shout "ho, ho, ho" for all they are worth'. The church's final sanction, excommunication, was presented as an invention for clerical domination: 'Excommunication doesn't hole your hide' – words to comfort a wretched man who had been under ecclesiastical ban for three years for failure to pay a minor debt.[13]

Sainthood, like clerical orders, might be cheapened by proximity. This, too, was suggested by contemporaries, who thought that too many saints were being canonized. On one historian's count, 211 individuals who lived between 1300 and 1500 were canonized or beatified either then or later. This figure does not include the many more who were advanced for this honour and failed to reach it. Increasing numbers of ordinary people, laymen and laywomen, lived with the feeling that sainthood (or beatitiude) might lie just round the corner of daily experience. Many believed they had seen it, and a sizeable proportion of those for whom claims of sanctity were made remained relatively unknown outside the areas that venerated them. Such for example were Thomas de la Hale, a monk of Dover murdered in 1295, Douceline de Digne, who was the centre of an early fourteenth-century cult at Hyères and Marseille, and Dorothy of Montau, revered at several places in Prussia besides Marienwerder, where she died in 1395.[14]

---

[12] Denys Hay, *Europe in the Fourteenth and Fifteenth Centuries* (London, 1970), p. 304; *ODCC*, p. 919; *The Catholic Reformation: Savonarola to Ignatius Loyola*, ed. John C. Olin (New York and London, 1969), p. 102 (Contarini's *De officio episcopi*, 1516).

[13] *Le registre d'inquisition de Jacques Fournier evêque de Pamiers (1318-1325)*, ed. J. Duvernoy (Toulouse, 1965), ii, pp. 109, 318; iii, p. 457; cited *Religion populaire*, ed. Privat, Gabriel de Llobet, 'Variété de croyances populaires au Comté de Foix au début du XIVe siècle d'après les enquêtes de Jacques Fournier', pp. 116-17.

[14] Hay, *Europe*, p. 316; Claude Carozzi, 'Douceline et les autres', in *Religion populaire*, ed. Privat, pp. 251- 67; idem, 'Une béguine joachimite: Douceline, soeur d'Hugues de Digne', in *Cahiers de Fanjeaux*, 10 (1975), pp. 169-201; E.W. Kemp, *Canonization and Authority in the Western Church* (Oxford, 1948), pp. 123, 132.

There were surely as many failed saints in this period as successful ones and the numbers of both must greatly have exceeded the total of the previous two hundred years. Successful canonization depended on papal authority, but the faithful believed in more saints and miracles than ever came to be inscribed in official catalogues. In England alone one can set beside the nine successful processes of canonization between 1198 and 1500 another ten that failed. Technical failure, as everyone knew, did not prevent celebration, witness the image of 'St. Richard' that stood to commemorate Richard Rolle in the chapel at Hampole, and the pilgrimages that were made to the remains of Henry VI in the abbey of Chertsey.[15]

Ecclesiastical and popular canonization had never entirely coincided, and by 1500 they were dangerously at variance. Here, as elsewhere, there was an all too obvious discrepancy between official theory and popular reality. Endorsement by the church was certainly no bar to enthusiasm, but it could also be disillusioning. 'Good woman, do you believe this king's son has so quickly been made a saint?' a middle-aged woman caustically asked her cousin, who was offering a candle at the Franciscan church in Marseille. The latter was giving thanks for a cure to St. Louis of Anjou (son of Charles II), who, having died in 1297 aged twenty-three, after a meteoric career as Franciscan and bishop of Toulouse, was canonized in 1317. 'The Friars Minor', continued this critic 'say it and preach it to get the profits of wax.' New saints by no means necessarily contributed to the lustre of the church. 'The other saints who are in paradise won't have much to do now, seeing that St. Louis takes care of everything', jeered a stonemason of Marseille, meeting a crowd of people processing one Sunday with candles and images to honour the saint.[16]

These local scoffers (whose blasphemies were miraculously punished) expressed doubts that were related to the worries of elevated church reformers. There were dangers in making too many modern saints. The canonization in 1391 of a widowed mother of eight, who had died less than twenty years earlier, greatly troubled Henry of Langenstein and John Gerson. Gerson was not alone in thinking the widely circulated *Revelations* of St. Bridget of Sweden unsuitable hagiographic material. The case was reopened at the Councils of Constance and Basel and St. Bridget's *Revelations* were supported by papal theologians, but questioning of this kind did the church no good.[17]

---

[15] Kemp, *Canonization*, pp. 133, 135, 176-7.

[16] From the 'Processus canonizationis et legendae variae Sancti Ludovici OFM', in *Analecta Franciscana*, vii (Florence, 1851), pp. 233, 236; cited Paul, 'Miracles' (above, n. 4) in *Religion populaire*, ed. Privat, pp. 84-5; M.R. Toynbee, *S. Louis of Toulouse and the Process of Canonisation in the Fourteenth Century* (Manchester 1929); *Saints and their Cults: Studies in Religious Sociology, Folklore and History*, ed. Stephen Wilson (Cambridge, 1983), pp. 7, 31-3, 172-3. Of course these scoffers only got into the record because their doubts were miraculously punished.

[17] Kemp, *Canonization*, pp. 128-30; J.L. Connolly, *John Gerson: Reformer and Mystic* (Louvain, 1928), pp. 180, 238-40; Delaruelle, *L'église*, ii, pp. 510-11, 789, 826-7, 1147.

The same divergence between theology and popular practice is observable in the use of religious images. The church's sanction of the plastic arts moved far between Gregory the Great's endorsement of 'laymen's books' (imagery as instruction for the illiterate) and the treatment of this question by Thomas Aquinas in the thirteenth century. It was not only that the images in churches (paintings, stained glass, statuary, crucifixes) changed in kind and became more common. There was also a continuous tendency for people to use imagery in ways other than the church intended. Images expressed, as well as informed, popular theology and in doing so were capable of anticipating (or by-passing) official doctrine. There were saints who owed their existence to popular misreadings of art, as well as artistic conventions that derived from misreadings of texts. St. Wilgefortis or Uncumber (said to have been supplicated by English women who hoped to be relieved of their husbands) apparently originated in early crucifixes that portrayed a long-haired, bearded Christ, robed to the ankles.[18] Artists followed (and catered for) the conventions of the people, as well as the dictates of patrons. It was objected that Catherine of Siena (d. 1380) had been widely depicted 'in the manner of those blessed by the church' before her canonization, which took place in 1461. These images – to be found as far afield as Poland, Dalmatia and Slavonia – were of all kinds, tablets and cards and on cloth as well as in books and on walls.[19] It is clear that the lost evidence of the religious life of the people includes a large amount of portable domestic imagery, which antedated cheap woodcut (and later printed) reproductions. There were also enormous numbers of religious representations in many other secular settings: in streets, on bridges, or at country cross-roads – where one might find, for instance, a huge image of St. Christopher to satisfy the belief that the day one caught sight of it one would be protected from sudden death.

Imagery proliferated like a natural growth, thanks as much to believers' enthusiasm as to clerical sponsoring. Bernard of Angers, who, in the early eleventh century, was amazed at the almost pagan veneration of images of saints he discovered in Auvergne, tells of this accelerating process. 'For it is an old practice and ancient custom', he wrote of this area, 'to erect a statue of their saint of gold or silver or whatever metal they can . . . ', which initially shocked him, as being contrary to Christian law.[20]

The church, like Bernard, was converted by its members. The testimony of its acceptance was the intricate theory of image-worship expounded by high medieval theologians: the idea that the honour given to the image passed to its prototype, and the concept of different kinds of worship. The terms *latria*,

[18] D.H. Farmer, *Oxford Dictionary of Saints*, 2nd edn. (Oxford, 1987), pp. 437-8; Jean Gessler, *La légende de sainte Wilgeforte ou Ontcommer: La Vierge miraculeusement barbue* (Brussels and Paris, 1938); G.G. Coulton, *Five Centuries of Religion* (Cambridge, 1923), i, pp. 546-51. On St. Uncumber see below p. 280.

[19] Delaruelle, *L'église*, ii, pp. 783-4, 790.

[20] *Liber miraculorum Sancte Fidis,* ed. A. Bouillet (Paris, 1897), pp. 46-7; M. Aston, *England's Iconoclasts*, i, (Oxford, 1988), p. 25.

Fig. 4 St. Anthony, in the black robes, with Tau cross and bells of a Hospitaller, surrounded by supplicants and votive offerings. The saint was sought specially by sufferers from ergotism, 'St. Anthony's Fire'.

dulia and *hyperdulia*, learnedly explained by Aquinas and others, remained as remote to most worshippers who lit candles before images as the theory of electricity is to most of us when we switch on the light. For the unsophisticated believer who knelt before a statue there existed a practical identity between the image and the saint. The sculpture of Our Lady at Rocamadour or at Walsingham *was* the Virgin in that it spoke directly to the pilgrim's needs and answered his or her prayers. The Virgin of Impruneta was the Florentines' *Nostra Donna* who came to the city's aid to bring or stop the rain. An image was an instrument of holiness through which believers reached towards God, and pilgrims expected to 'see' their saints.[21]

Not surprisingly, holy icons grew in number, far beyond the powers of ecclesiastical control. Certainly there were efforts to put a stop to burgeoning local cults, such as the steps taken by the archbishop of York, in 1313, to prevent the 'great concourse of simple people' who were visiting an image of the Virgin 'newly placed' in the church of Foston; or the bishop of Lincoln's enquiry, in 1386, into the complaint that in the parish of Rippingale 'many of our subjects have made for themselves a pretended statue', to which people were thronging and reporting miracles. In this instance local initiative (abetted

---

[21] R.C. Trexler, 'Florentine Religious Experience: The Sacred Image', *Studies in the Renaissance*, xix (1972), pp. 7-41; Aston, *England's Iconoclasts*, i, pp. 20-34.

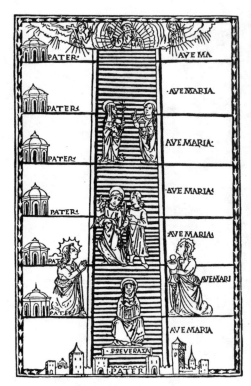

Fig. 5 The ladder of salvation: Italian woodcut of 1512. The multiplication of prayer, like the Pater Nosters and Ave Marias of the Rosary, was part of late medieval spiritual inflation.

by the rector) was such that it thwarted episcopal condemnation by gaining papal licence to found a new chapel for this – purportedly hundred-year-old – holy cross.[22] Despite some attempted restraints, the increase of imagery continued and sometimes seems more geometrical than arithmetic.

Some contemporaries were worried, as they were over new saints, about the cheapening of respect. It was a point made by Bishop Pecock, who went out of his way to defend church imagery against the attacks of the Lollards. Images, he wrote, should 'not be multiplied so widely that an image should be set at every church, every chapel, every street's end, or every hedge's end in the country', for then undoubtedly they would be 'of little repute, and would be unesteemed because of the great number of them'. 'Plenty is no dainty' – which was another way of saying that you can have too much of a good thing.[23]

Lastly, one may notice how this arithmetical piety affected the salvation of souls. Thanks to the reckless rivalry of popes, religious orders and pilgrimage towns competing for the alms of the faithful, grants of indulgence multiplied. The numerous crusades preached by the popes and antipopes of Rome and Avignon made indulgences notorious. Plenary indulgences, once restricted to

[22] D.M. Owen, 'Bacon and Eggs: Bishop Buckingham and Superstition in Lincolnshire', *SCH*, 8 (1972), pp. 141-2; Aston, *England's Iconoclasts*, i, p. 23.

[23] Reginald Pecock, *The Repressor of Over Much Blaming of the Clergy*, ed. C. Babington (RS, 1860), i, pp. 183-4.

a crusade, were now given for pilgrimaging to Roman basilicas during years of jubilee (which also increased in frequency); famous relic collections could offer indulgence to those who came to their displays. Flurries of investment produced absurd numbers of indulgences and masses. The great were able to buy masses in thousands to secure a near-infinity of release. Cardinal Albrecht of Brandenburg managed to amass more than 39,000,000 years of indulgence in Halle, and Henry VIII, England's first iconoclastic monarch, who had much to atone for, ordered daily masses to be said for as long as the world should endure. The church positively encouraged anxious belief in the quantitative value of such prayers. Do not imagine, said Archbishop Pecham in 1281, that one mass said devoutly for a thousand people procures them the same benefit as a thousand individual masses said with equal devotion.[24] Ordinary mortals could not aspire to these astronomical sums, and in this period of numerical devotion they might well have agonized. They did their best. Hence the growing number of confraternities, so many that some towns may have reached saturation point in the fifteenth century. There were too many such foundations, thought Nicholas of Cusa, and John Gerson indicated the superstition of totting up indulgences till they reached 20,000 years.

Among the most dramatic manifestations of popular piety on the move were the spontaneous demonstrations that took place in the face of the terrible mortality of the Black Death. Flagellants, groups of men and even women who inflicted penance on themselves in public, scourging their bodies till they drew blood, appeared in various parts of Europe in 1349. Flagellation (a gestural imitation of Christ) was itself neither new nor scandalous. It was a recognized monastic practice, and Franciscan piety expressed itself in this kind of sacred exhibition. Enacting as well as meditating on Christ's scourging was an acceptable Christian devotion. Why then should anyone have been alarmed at the spectacle of bands of devout lay people practising such public penance to appease the wrath of God evinced in the plague, calling all sinners to repentance? An eye-witness description of Flagellants in Verona in 1396 shows that they were not disorderly: 'six hundred people, going two by two, beating flails made of iron chains through the city, making a procession with crosses and habited priests, doing their penance and bearing the body of Our Lord', their faces covered save for the eyes, and 'singing, as they beat themselves, one song together'.[25]

The church, alarmed, saw a double threat in the Flagellants, who were formally proscribed by Clement VI in 1349. Firstly, there was the fact that

---

[24] F. Rapp, *L'église et la vie religieuse en occident à la fin du moyen âge* (Paris, 1971), pp. 322-3; B. Moeller, 'Piety in Germany around 1500', in *The Reformation in Medieval Perspective*, ed. S.E. Ozment (Chicago, 1971), p. 55; K.L. Wood-Legh, *Perpetual Chantries in Britain* (Cambridge, 1965), p. 308.

[25] E. Delaruelle, *L'église*, ii, pp. 678-9, cf. 828-9; idem, *La piété populaire au moyen age* (Turin, 1975), pp. 277-313 (at 295), 403-4.

these penitents seemed in some cases like a sect with its own organized rules, discipline and habit. Secondly, there was an appearance of doctrinal error in that flagellation, instead of being simply an ascetic practice, looked like dispensing with sacramental penance, rivalling, if not despising, part of the church's ministry; the fervent participants seemed to be both aping the church and detracting from it. The Flagellants, in the Low Countries and Germany in 1349-50, and elsewhere thereafter, presented a challenge that was always fearful to church authorities and urban rulers alike; they were the lower orders – 'the multitude of simple men' – on the move. The dynamic potential of the people lay in their ability to take themselves and their ideas into towns and areas where they were not known, disappearing into the dangerous anonymity of the urban world in which individuals could easily attract followings. In a country where he is unknown, ran a satirical Czech verse of about 1360, the heretic remains hidden for two or three years and finds supporters.[26]

As mistrust increased towards the claims of wealth and office, the entitlements of rank and parchment formulas, so the poor correspondingly gained new respect. Poverty had its own dignity. It had been sanctified by Christ, who in himself and in his words made it a spiritual pattern. This perennial Christian message gained fresh momentum in this period. The revulsion that it was natural to feel from above towards the tawdry masses of the rude people was turned to new account. The sense of Christian mission was pointed towards 'poor folk in hovels, burdened with children and chief lord's rent', those 'halt old men and maimed, who all day and night cower continually before the altars, and in the crypts; and such folk as wear old mantles and old tattered frocks, and naked folk and shoeless, and covered with sores, perishing of hunger and thirst, and of cold, and of little ease'.[27] It came to seem in certain quarters that the only authentic religious experience was to be found among such people. The conviction that 'none are sooner saved or firmer in their faith, than ploughmen and shepherds and poor common people' was not confined to *Piers Plowman*'s visionary gloss on St. Augustine.[28] God still spoke to the present age, but his words were only heard by the humble – the 'poor men', the 'simple priests' and self-disciplined mendicant 'perfects'. These were all contemporary self-descriptions used by those whose choice of life (the imitation of Christ) ended in some kind of separation from the church. Of course, when voiced by those who were themselves inexorably poor, there was an inevitable note of social criticism in popular insistence that the clergy should live in voluntary poverty. But the larger view of the evangelical vocation went beyond the carping of the jealous. It was believed that divine

[26] J. Gonnet and A. Molnár, *Les Vaudois au moyen âge* (Turin, 1974), p. 145.

[27] *Piers Plowman by William Langland*, C Text. ed. Derek Pearsall (London, 1978), passus ix, line 73, p. 164; Finucane, *Miracles and Pilgrims*, p. 150.

[28] *Piers Plowman*, ed. W.W. Skeat (Oxford, 1886), i, p. 323. On this subject see Michel Mollat, *The Poor in the Middle Ages: An Essay in Social History*, trans. A. Goldhammer (New Haven and London, 1986; orig. French edn. 1978).

truths were vouchsafed to the simplest hearers – and they were gospel, not theological. Their immediacy was that of experience, not learning.

The example of one man had an enormous influence on this idea of poverty. The unaffected simplicity of Francesco Bernardone, after his dramatic wedding of himself to 'Lady Poverty', caught the imagination of contemporaries and met with a wide response. But the practical difficulties encountered by St. Francis and the Franciscans in attempting to imitate Christ, reflect the paradox of the later medieval church: the more popular and successful the pursuit of evangelical life, the greater the likelihood of a condemnation for heresy.

The issue seems simple enough. Christ forsook possessions and expected his disciples to forsake all: renunciation of goods was part of the imitation of Christ. Such was the assumption of St. Francis, and his way of life was premised on it. But the more Franciscans there were the more impossible it became to live with undefined beliefs, and between the death of Francis in 1226 and the death of Pope John XXII in 1334 numbers of people, including the pope himself, came to be charged with heresy for their view of what Christian contempt for temporal goods should amount to.

The main friction was that between the two wings of the Franciscan friars: the Conventuals and the Spirituals. There was much basic agreement between them, for they both started from the belief that Franciscan poverty uniquely exemplified the poverty of Christ, and both regarded the complete renunciation of all dominion, whether corporate or individual, as essential to evangelical life. Beyond that agreement, however, started critical differences about the nature of usufruct and the rights involved in the use of consumables – points that may now seem like legal quibbles but which concerned basic day-to-day practicalities and which ran into important points of doctrine. Was it possible to deny dominion (some right of property) over things consumed by use? Could the Franciscans' claim that they enjoyed only a bare use (*nudus usus*) in their goods, by virtue of the ownership of them being vested in the Holy See, be other than a legal fiction?[29]

The question became clouded by the conspicuous acquisition of buildings and funds by the Franciscan order in the late thirteenth and early fourteenth century, which made the denial of property rights seem the most blatant artifice. The fact remained that, despite the self-evident difficulties of establishing an order which could maintain the hand-to-mouth existence implied in absolute poverty (living on alms, having no settled abode), this was an ideal that continued to have a tremendous appeal. Perhaps it was the very non-institutional (if not anti-institutional) aspect of the call that made it so powerful. This sort of abnegation implied the renunciation of office and governance, as well as of taking thought for the morrow. The fact that it could not be institutionalized enhanced its vitality, as well as its danger. The very call to regenerate Christian life in this way was a challenge to the church, which

---

[29] M.D. Lambert, *Franciscan Poverty: The Doctrine of the Absolute Poverty of Christ and the Apostles in the Franciscan Order, 1210-1323* (London, 1961).

could only control it by transforming it. Absolute poverty, in short, revealed the inherent contradiction between church and gospel, scripture and tradition. To be too faithful to Christ was to question the organized church.

It is no accident, therefore, that in varying ways and degrees the *imitatio Christi* ended in charges of heresy. It had done so already in the twelfth century, after a rich merchant of Lyons, called Valdes, inspired by hearing the story of St. Alexius, abandoned his wealth and property to take up a life of evangelical poverty. He wanted both to know Christ and to follow Christ and commissioned translations of scripture so that he could himself learn and preach the Word of God. Others were eager to do the same and soon the voluntary mendicant attracted followers and had the beginnings of a movement. But was it right to teach the Word of God publicly to the people without the authority of the church? Members of the clergy certainly thought not. Valdes's followers took their case to the Third Lateran Council in 1179, where Alexander III endorsed their ideal of evangelical poverty but placed the activity of preaching firmly under clerical supervision. It was not long before fidelity to the call to preach took Valdes's disciples into excommunication and schism.

If there was always a grey zone between orthodoxy and dissent, the situation was changing fast between the renunciations of Valdes and Francis. The determination of the border that separated the heretic from the body of the faithful, subject at the best of times to the accidents of ecclesiastical politics, was affected by the church's preparedness and expectations. In 1200 Innocent III was still prepared to allow the third order of the *Humiliati*, with their artisans and humble lay members, the right to pious exhortation under episcopal supervision.[30] Such a breaching of the fundamental principle that preaching belonged exclusively to those in orders became increasingly unthinkable after 1215, with the issue of the ban on the founding of new religious orders. In the twelfth century a popular heretical movement (as opposed to individual heretics) had been a new phenomenon. The early years of the thirteenth century produced a proliferation of new religious groups and, above all, saw the spread of Catharism in Lombardy and Languedoc. By the 1230s the church had developed institutional forms specifically designed to deal with a heretical movement. The Inquisition never operated as effectively in northern Europe as it did in the south, but the fact of its existence had an enormous effect on the climate of heretical expectation. The grey zone had, as it were, been institutionalized.

Not all heresy was popular, but it became increasingly likely that a popular religious movement would be declared heretical, increasingly difficult for aspiring laymen and laywomen to lead a life dedicated to holiness while still living in, or only half withdrawn from the world. To be too ascetic might be dangerous. 'Hear me, my lords! I am no heretic: for I have a wife and cohabit

[30] R.I. Moore, *The Origins of European Dissent* (London, 1977), pp. 226-31; Brenda Bolton, 'Innocent III's Treatment of the *Humiliati*', *SCH*, 8 (1972), pp. 73- 82.

with her and have children; and I eat flesh and lie and swear and am a faithful Christian.'[31] In this manner a thirteenth-century suspect hoped to convince the inquisitors of his orthodoxy. Once popular heresy was recognized, it became possible, like a new species, to find it anywhere. Thus the censuring of the writings of Petrus Johannis Olivi in 1283 was largely influenced by the fear that his humble followers in Provence (where the call of the Spiritual Franciscans had such success) would start another sect of poor men, as Valdes's preaching had done a hundred years earlier. Zealots of this kind, estimable though their intentions might be, constituted a threat to order. John XXII therefore condemned the doctrine of absolute poverty and moved firmly against the Spiritual Franciscans, four of whom were burned in Marseille in 1318.

The bull *Cum inter nonnullos,* issued in November 1323, condemned as heretical the belief that Christ and the apostles had owned nothing, and also the assertion that they had held no rights over the goods they used.

> Since it is the case that among various men of learning it is often doubted whether the persistent assertion – that our redeemer and lord Jesus Christ and his apostles did not have anything, either privately or in common – should be deemed heretical . . . we . . . declare by this everlasting edict that a persistent assertion of this kind shall henceforth be deemed erroneous and heretical, since it expressly contradicts Holy Scripture, which in a number of places asserts that they did have some things . . .[32]

It was a declaration that dealt decisively with the immediate troubles in the Franciscan order, but it could not shut the door on further controversies of this kind. William of Ockham was one of the men of learning who acted on his conviction that the pope's own edict was heretical. Just as important – perhaps more so – were the various other quite unlearned people who in subsequent years preferred the word of scripture to papal arbitration on the life of Christ and the disciples.

There was one remarkable movement in this period that managed to promote the shared evangelical existence without falling foul of the law. This community, less easily defined than some others (though it had a contemporary title), reflected the widespread desire, evident in all classes, to escape the frustrating world of externals for internal religion. A quiet meditative life, combining communal work with devotion, untrammelled by formal rules and regulations, became possible for groups of lay people in the Low Countries. 'Christ is our rule; his life and doctrine are our breviary for life . . . This is the Book of Hours common to clerks and laymen.'[33] Thanks to Jan van Ruysbroeck, who wrote these words (d. 1381, at Groenendaël, where his small apostolic community had come together), and to Gerard Groote (d. 1384, at Deventer, where he had turned his house into a refuge for pious women), there

---

[31] Cecil Roth, *The Spanish Inquisition*, (New York, 1964; orig. pub. London, 1937), p. 90.

[32] Lambert, *Franciscan Poverty*, p. 235; idem, *Medieval Heresy: Popular Movements from Bogomil to Hus* (London, 1977), pp. 199-203.

[33] Delaruelle, *L'église*, ii, p. 920.

Fig. 6 Title-page woodcut from the English edition of *c.* 1518–19 of *The Imitation of Christ*, with a border of the instruments and symbols of the Passion.

began a movement that enabled people of both sexes to lead a shared devotional life without transgressing either the prohibition of 1215 against new orders, or the ruling of 1323. What became known as the *Devotio Moderna* consisted of groups of men and women who lived together in poverty and obedience, but without formal vows, and their ability to do so depended on the ruling that in thus following evangelical precept they were not forming a new order. Ordinary working people thereby found new opportunities for their religious aspirations. The number of houses grew under the direction of Florentius Radewyns and his successors, recruiting clerks as well as lay people, some of them humble peasants and brewers. Among such *pauperes* in the fraternity at Deventer was the son of a blacksmith, Thomas à Kempis, who wrote in *The Imitation of Christ,* 'associate with the humble and simple'.[34]

In other movements evangelical fidelity caused a breach with the church. This divide between scripture and tradition lay behind the two major heretical movements that appeared in the late fourteenth and early fifteenth century. Both were popular movements, attracting much support among ordinary trades and work people as well as lower clergy. In both cases the initiative, and

[34] Thomas à Kempis, *The Imitation of Christ*, trans. L. Sherley-Price (Harmondsworth, 1952), bk I, c. 8, p. 35; 'cum humilibus et simplicibus, cum devotis et morigeratis sociare . . . '

initial fears of heresy, started in academic circles and intellectual theology, but it was the currents of belief and agitation that ran through the people that attracted such attention. Although their personalities, lives and deaths were very different, John Wycliffe (d. 1384) and John Hus (d. 1415) shared a fierce concern for moral regeneration, an impassioned desire to redeem contemporary Christendom, and both took scripture as their starting-point in redefining what was meant by the church. From these learned Latinate beginnings grew the popular followings of Lollards and Hussites, owing their success and survival to lively vernacular preaching and a corpus of vernacular writings that made popular theology, as well as much scriptural learning, available to humble (often self-educated) Christians. In England, though the sect went on through the fifteenth century, it relapsed – as did the Waldensian following in Germany – into a sort of sectarian underground, of sporadic strength. In Bohemia, where there was an ongoing tradition of moral reform, as well as a more conspicuous background of political upheaval and uncertainty, heresy advanced to the point of schism and counter-church.

The Bohemians' biblical enthusiasm and millennial eschatology combined to produce the remarkable phenomenon of Tabor and other hilltop religious communities consciously modelled on apostolic Christian example. Owing to the skills of their military leaders (specially Žižka and Procop), as well as to the peculiar unsettlement of Bohemia and the contemporary papacy, the Hussites managed to do something that had never been done before in the history of the church. They reached the point of negotiating with the leaders of the church for their own religious platform. After a series of crusades had been launched unsuccessfully against the heretics, a combination of conservative forces finally defeated the Hussite radicals at the battle of Lipany in 1434. This defeat helped to bring about the agreement between the Bohemians and the Council of Basel on the basis of the so-called Compactata. It was the first time a popular heretical movement had reached such a level of power: the first time that a split in observance received formal recognition.

The Compactata, a form of the earlier programme of the Four Articles of Prague, represented the minimum demands of the Hussites. These four articles, which tell us a good deal about the movement, return us to our starting-point, for they reflect that dialectical bond between popular religion (or popular heresy) and the church structure. The first point, utraquism, was the right of all believers to communicate in both kinds (bread and wine), *sub utraque specie*. This was fundamental to the Bohemian reform which from its beginnings had produced demands for more frequent communion, and which led among the Taborite radicals to congregational celebrations on open hilltops. The other three points were free preaching of the Word of God; the call for all priests from the pope downwards to give up their 'pomp, avarice and improper lordship'; and the correction of public mortal sins.[35] At best it was a

---

[35] H. Kaminsky, *A History of the Hussite Revolution* (Berkeley and Los Angeles, 1967), pp. 369–83; Lambert, *Medieval Heresy*, p. 320.

partial programme that summarized aspects of the tremendous surge of activity that transformed the Bohemian church in this period, doing away with monasteries and religious foundations (including the archbishopric of Prague, which was forcedly vacant between 1431 and 1516), destroying many images and relics of saints, killing religious, and everywhere making the cult of the Word prominent, whether in great preaching like that of Hus in the Bethlehem Chapel, or in vernacular writings like those of the laymen Thomas of Štitny and Peter Chelčicky.

Lollardy, imperative though it sometimes sounded and programmatic though it sometimes was, never commanded this extraordinary influence on ecclesiastical affairs. But if we compare this movement's aims with those of the Hussites, we can see something of the various strands of which popular heresy was compounded. The question of the eucharist was as important in England as in Bohemia. Though a consensus on this matter is hard to arrive at, Lollards – often in earthy rural terms – followed Wycliffe in finding difficulties in the doctrine of transubstantiation, and the denial of this doctrine was one of the ways in which adherence to the sect could be determined. 'God made man, and not man God, as the carpenter doth make the house and not the house the carpenter',[36] was a crude way of saying something like what Wycliffe was thought to have said; that the consecrated host was not corporeally Christ and could not be an accident without a substance; that the words of administration could not miraculously annihilate the substance of the bread. The Hussites who gave the cup to the laity and the Lollards who denied transubstantiation were both, in effect, rejecting the distancing of sacrament from people, brought about by previous centuries. Scholastic logic applied to the doctrine of the eucharist enhanced the miracle of this sacrament and helped to make it an ever more remote and clerical rite; the congregation was expected to participate by seeing, not by understanding, and the layman's role in the eucharist was of a completely different order from that of the ministering priest. The heretical call in both cases amounted to a demand for greater participation, a refusal of the people to remain passive spectators at sacramental celebrations. While both English and Bohemian heretics refused to accept this clerical arrogation of the rite, they did so in quite different ways. Hussite utraquism was an expression of moral reforming ardour, and celebration in both kinds, though it involved no doctrinal unorthodoxy, constituted a demonstration of religious independence. Yet the Bohemians were here linked with many reformers of contemporary Europe, who shared this eucharistic fervour, and, to the extent that it answered devotional needs, Hussite utraquism was swallowed up as time went on by other reforming developments. In England, meanwhile, where the moral drive was weaker, eucharistic heresy remained more negative and lacked the initiative to build a new ceremonial.

[36] John A.F. Thomson, *The Later Lollards, 1414-1520* (Oxford, 1965), p. 112, cf. p. 48; Anne Hudson, *The Premature Reformation: Wycliffite Texts and Lollard History* (Oxford, 1988), p. 285. See also below Chapter 2.

The free preaching of the Word was a matter on which agreement was total. This was where Hus and Wycliffe had their greatest effect. Lollards and Hussites alike saw the church as the ministry of the Word and believed that the duty and freedom to preach was the essence of priesthood. Commitment to this call as a Gospel command that overrode all ecclesiastical powers helped to send Hus to the stake and promoted the idea that men and women of virtuous life were more truly priests than any ordained by the church. 'I held and affirmed that every true man and woman being in charity is a priest',[37] confessed a fifteenth-century English heretic, and there were plenty of humble people of both sexes at this time who were busy studying and teaching the Word of God. It was preaching, and the writings, handbooks and translations that served the task of evangelization, that attracted congregation after congregation and turned ideas into movements. This was an age in which many people yearned to hear as well as to see. The preacher (whether a St. Bernardino or a Hus) could gratify an appetite that could not be satisfied by going to church to kneel before a Virgin or to watch a mass: the appetite to understand.

Dissatisfaction with the church stemmed from spiritual angers, as well as from spiritual hungers. Where the Hussites sacked monasteries and killed monks, the Lollards hoped and sometimes planned, but without results. Many words were spoken and much ink used in castigating the pomp and pride of churchmen, with their extensive properties and excessive trains of horses and servants. Anticlericalism was always a strain of heresy, and the signs of it were clear to read, in England as in Bohemia. 'I trusted to God to see no church standing nor priest living within three years', said a Lollard.[38] Millennial eschatology could make the most unreal of dreams seem reachable, and though such beliefs were less in evidence in England than elsewhere, aims of massive destruction were in the air. The idea of making priests' heads, like sheep's heads, three a penny, floated among the jetsam of proletarian gossip, occasionally resulting in radical action. It attached itself easily to that other ancient argument, 'when Adam delved and Eve span, who was then a gentleman?',[39] premised on the idea of a golden age of paradisal equality. Though their world was far from paradisal, the Hussite radicals at Tabor, with their pooling of resources in common chests and their belief that 'there is nothing mine and nothing yours',[40] got nearest to making a new, more biblically just society.

Popular heresy was thus an expression of hostility towards the clerical church. At the same time it turned against the forms of popular piety. Lollards

---

[37] M. Aston, 'Lollard Women priests?', in *Lollards and Reformers: Images and Literacy in Late Medieval Religion* (London, 1984), p. 60.

[38] Thomson, *Later Lollards*, p. 50; Hudson, *Premature Reformation*, p. 469 n. 129.

[39] G.R. Owst, *Literature and Pulpit in Medieval England* (Oxford, 1961), pp. 290-1.

[40] H. Kaminsky, 'Chiliasm and the Hussite Revolution', in *Change in Medieval Society*, ed. Sylvia Thrupp (London, 1965), p. 265.

who talked jeeringly of the 'witch of Lincoln' or the 'lefdy [lady] of Walsingham', and Prague labourers who pawned their crucifixes, were ready to
jettison the whole apparatus of image-worship and pilgrimage. They rejected
both the famous Marian shrines cultivated by late medieval pilgrims, and even
the worship of the crucifix, the central Christian image. Our Lady of Willesden, said Elizabeth Sampson in 1508, 'was a burnt arsed elf and a burnt arsed
stock; and if she might have helped men and women which go to her on
pilgrimage she would not have suffered her tail to have been burnt'.[41] 'If you
want to see the true cross of Christ', the wife of a Norfolk village wright told a
Norwich housewife, 'I'd like to show it to you here in your own house.' She did
so, stretching out her arms. 'This is the true cross of Christ, and this cross you
can and ought to see and worship every day here in your own house, and so you
labour in vain when you go to churches to worship or pray to any images or
dead crosses.' It was the same message that had been taught more than a
century earlier by Cathar perfects in Pyrenean villages: 'Do you believe these
bits of wood can perform miracles?' Farmers were given a lesson that could
well have come from Isaiah. 'You carved with your own axes the statues of
saints in the "house of idols" and then you worship them!'[42]

Where ecclesiastical reformers were worried and tentative (admitting abuse
and suggesting the need for more instruction) popular heretical movements
pointed to radical solutions. Iconoclasm, the erasure of imagery as offensive to
Christianity, was a feature of all the main medieval heretical movements,
which broke and burnt crucifixes and images of the Virgin and saints. The idea
that art and Christian religion were inherently contradictory, that visual and
other sensory aids to worship either (at best) detracted from the spiritual or (at
worst) induced idolatry, was confined in the later middle ages to the sphere of
popular heresy. Lollards here went beyond Wycliffe, Hussites beyond Hus. To
be sure, there were also plenty of heretics whose criticisms of church art were
more moderate, who suggested that the historical criterion of imitating Christ
should apply to representation as much as to life. Kept within such limits,
depicting Christ and the saints in the poverty in which they had lived, 'not
wantonly or falsely adorned' in such a way as to seduce and mislead believers,
imagery might be tolerable. There was also the social argument claiming then
(as it still does) that Christian art is a denial of Christian charity. Feeding the
hungry and clothing the naked should take precedence over gilding statues and
decorating walls. The only true image of Christ was man himself and the only
true form of pilgrimage was that 'to poor men'.[43]

---

[41] Aston, *England's Iconoclasts*, i, pp. 107, 133, 136, and see below, p. 304, n. 34 on the
aspersions in this last remark.

[42] *Heresy Trials in the Diocese of Norwich, 1428-31*, ed. N.P. Tanner (Camden Fourth Series,
20, 1977), p. 44; E. Le Roy Ladurie, *Montaillou*, trans. B. Bray (London, 1978), p. 318.

[43] Aston, *England's Iconoclasts*, i, pp. 124-9.

In a variety of ways, through the pious expressions and foundations of the orthodox, and in the clamorous demands of the unorthodox, by retreating from the world, and by trying to take it over, the lay people in the later middle ages made themselves and their religious needs more known. It was very much an age of the laity. It was also an age in which the *menu peuple,* the humble anonymous Christians, made an unprecedented mark on the church through popular movements of which the hierarchy could not fail to take cognizance, even when it failed to lead and control them.

The renewal of the church, the call to evangelical regeneration that is the essence of the Christian faith, was expressed in this period from below. The voice of secular men and women, commanding attention, demanding instruction and spiritual assurance, becomes audible as never before in the fourteenth and fifteenth centuries. At the centre of all religion of the people lies the search for direct spiritual experience. It may be the miraculous or the practically pious; seen or heard, acted or received. In every case the reality of the experience is more important than ecclesiastical or clerical forms. A great deal of the piety of the people remained devoutly orthodox, whether enlarging ever more vertiginously the numerical devotions sponsored by the church, or making for the retreats of individual, internal religion. The advance of the people in education, aspiration and enthusiasm, coinciding unfortunately with the church's marked lack of institutional resilience, allowed them to play a disproportionate part in the development and counter-development of Christianity and its culture. Both the making of saints and the representing of saints reflected popular pressures. The multiplication of images, the enormous growth of the arts of the church, like the proliferation of persons blessed by popular esteem, show the appetites of believers outdistancing ecclesiastical provisions.

Ordinary believers also found for themselves a spiritual independence that was remote from the ecclesiastical hierarchy. Evangelical knowledge (derived directly from the page or otherwise) yielded remarkable initiatives and experiments, whether on the material level of redistributing church property, or the spiritual level of giving ordinary men and women an active share in the ministry of the Word. Women found in heresy a recognition of ability, and opportunities for religious enterprise that were hard to find within orthodox forms, and we may see in these beginnings a contribution to that long, still ongoing quest for sexual equality that has gathered strength from the Christian ethic.

Christianity, the religion of a book of singular diversity, began in this age the earnest exploration of its sources that was to prove so problematical. The Christian call to renewal centres on scripture, but, whatever the concentration on the evangelical law, that could not be taken alone: it was necessary to reconcile the requirements of the old law with the new, to strike a balance between the two Testaments. Though it was not till later that Christendom divided over the interpretation of its sources, the popular movements of the later middle ages (followed, quite differently but just as importantly, by

Humanist scholars) had embarked on that fresh pursuit of biblical patterns. And already there were hints of the potential conflict stemming from the Christian graft on Judaic roots.

The survival – and the vitality – of the Christian faith has always rested on more than the institutions of the church. In all periods (including our own) in which the faith has seemed at risk, the responsibility for recovery lies as much with the community as with the hierarchy. Salvation, the starting-point of the faith, comes back to the individual, and there were many individuals among the people in this period who aspired to the redemption of the church, as well as of themselves.

Christianity will exist as long as there are believers. As Dante put it: 'The form of the church is nothing other than the life of Christ, understood in both words and deeds. For his life was both the conception and the pattern of the militant church.'[44] Though it was once highly dangerous to say so, the structured hierarchy is dispensable, and it sometimes seems as if the church is most alive when that hierarchy, subject to gospel appraisal, is most in question. Whether or not one thinks that the Christian message is itself social, giving a sense of community, dignity and equality to the humble, it was the movements from below that did the most to widen the Christian horizons of this age. Granted – and the history of the times proved it – a purely popular religious movement could not change ecclesiastical forms, but there is a sense in which popular religion both made and unmade the church. We can see in the later middle ages the power of the Christian mission to revitalize society, as well as the power of society to revitalize the church. Much of the best that remains to us from that time derives from this fruitful dialectic.

---

[44] 'Forma autem ecclesie nichil aliud est quam vita Christi, tam in dictis quam in factis comprehensa'; Dante Alighieri, *De monarchia libri III*, ed. L. Bertalot (Friedrichsdorf, Frankfurt, 1918), iii, 15, pp. 105-6.

2

Wycliffe and the Vernacular*

> . . . laudo Deum qui me liberavit ab isto scandaloso et derisibili errore de quidditate huius sacramenti.[1]
>
> *De eucharistia*

> . . . Gog . . . statuit sibi unam transsubstanciacionem quam eciam Magog fatetur se non posse intelligere; quomodo igitur informaret simplices in hac fide?[2]
>
> *De apostasia*

People began celebrating Wycliffe long before they began celebrating centenaries. Though we have failed to make our celebration in the correct calendar year, 1984 did not pass without some appropriate manifestations. They included the suspicions, in some quarters, that it was divine displeasure at the threat of heresy in the present-day Church of England that caused lightning to strike York Minister on 9 July. What then, was to be made of the fact that ten days later large parts of the country were shaken by the most severe earthquake for many years?[3] There could once have been little doubt.

> for þei put an heresye vpon Crist and seyntes in heuyne, wherefore þe erthe tremblide, fayland mannus voys ansueride for God, als it dide in tyme of his passione, whan he was dampnyde to bodely deth.[4]

* I am grateful to Dr. Colin Richmond for his comments on this essay, to Professor W.L. Warren and Dr. Anne Hudson for the loan of microfilms, and to the staff of the library of Queen's University, Belfast, for their help. My thanks also to Professor Robert E. Lewis for answering enquiries and sending information about forthcoming entries in the *Middle English Dictionary*, and to Dr. A. I. Doyle and Dr. C. Kightly for allowing me to cite their unpublished works.

[1] *De euch.*, p. 199.

[2] *De apos.*, p. 144.

[3] *The Times*, 10 July 1984; *The Guardian*, 20 July and 27 Sept. 1984. There does seem to be some sort of analogy here for, as I understand it, the bishop of Durham's case for reinterpreting the doctrines of the resurrection and the virgin birth rests, as did Wycliffe's reinterpretation of the eucharist, on a fresh understanding of the figurative sense of scripture.

[4] *Selections from English Wycliffite Writings*, ed. A. Hudson (Cambridge, 1978), p. 18. In *The Image of Both Churches* Bale took this earthquake as a leading illustration of that which occurred at the opening of the sixth seal in Rev. 6:12. *Select Works of John Bale,* ed. H. Christmas, PS (Cambridge, 1849), p. 326.

In starting with this quotation, which comes from the second vernacular confession on the eucharist attributed to Wycliffe, I am anticipating. For though it is certain (for instance, from several references in the *Trialogus*)[5] that Wycliffe regarded the 1382 earthquake as divine judgement on the decisions of the Blackfriars Council, my objective here is to consider the grounds for believing that he wrote these, or other words in the English vernacular.

A hundred years ago this would have appeared a quite pointless, if not extraordinary exercise. The centenary year of 1884 produced a sizeable crop of books on Wycliffe, in which his vernacular achievements stood high. At that time, it is worth remembering, only two of the Wyclif Society's publications had appeared; the first instalment being the *Polemical Works*, edited by the Leipzig scholar Rudolf Buddensieg, who wrote somewhat tartly in his introduction about England's ingratitude towards one of her greatest sons. Oxford, whose university press had turned down this pioneering edition, had much to answer for – as indeed, in the following years, had English scholars who were prepared to leave so much of the editorial burden of the Wyclif Society to their continental colleagues. Buddensieg himself, who insisted that 'the only way to understand him [Wycliffe] is to read him, not to read about him',[6] presumably thought he was contributing to that end by producing a small quincentenary volume aimed at the general reader, on *John Wyclif Patriot and Reformer: Life and Writings*, the second part of which consisted of an anthology of texts from English and Latin sources.[7]

---

[5] *Trial.*, pp. 339, 374-7, 445, 447 and cf. below, p. 69. W.R. Thomson, *The Latin Writings of John Wyclif* (Toronto, 1983), pp. 79-80, 82-3 n. 22, dating the *Trialogus* late 1382 to early 1383, seems to take too little account of the place of these references near the end of the work, where Wycliffe retraces some ground he had already covered earlier in book IV (notably on the eucharist). His treatment and increasingly polemical tone towards the end, combined with the allusion (*Trial.*, p. 374) to the friars' poisonous activity generally 'during 1382 recently and particularly in their earthquake council in London', show clearly, I think, that Wycliffe was already at work on and had completed a large part of the *Trialogus* before May 1382, though we may agree that the turn of 1382-3 saw its possible completion.

[6] *Polemical Works*, i, preface, p. v; cf. p. vi and introduction, pp. iv-vi (rather more outspoken in the *Vorwort*, p. x, and *Einleitung*, pp. v-vi, of the 1883 Leipzig edition) on Buddensieg's failed efforts to persuade the Delegates of the Oxford University Press to publish his work – a failure that was in marked contrast with the reception given to the publication of the English works, proposed in 1865 by W. W. Shirley, Regius Professor of Ecclesiastical History (who died aged thirty-eight in 1866). W. W. Shirley, *A Catalogue of the Original Works of John Wyclif* (Oxford, 1865), p. v; *Select English Works of John Wyclif*, ed. T. Arnold (Oxford, 1869-71), i, p. i. See also J. P. Whitney, 'A Note on the Work of the Wyclif Society', *Essays in History presented to Reginald Lane Poole*, ed. H. W. C. Davis (Oxford, 1927), pp. 98-114. In 1884 appeared *De compositione hominis*, ed. R. Beer (London & Vienna).

[7] R. Buddensieg, *John Wyclif Patriot and Reformer: Life and Writings* (London, 1884). The preface, p. 5 expresses the aim 'to recall to the memory of England one of her greatest sons, and to press home the thought of how much she owes to the advocate of her political and religious freedom, the translator of her Bible, and the maker of her language'. The texts (all in English) in book II, pp. 83-164 were taken from *De veritate sacre scripture*, *Trialogus*, *Wickliffe's Wicket* and *Tracts and Treatises of John de Wycliffe, D.D.*, edited by R. Vaughan (London, 1845) for the

Fig. 7 The first Wycliffe Society in the 1840s saw Wycliffe as a light of Protestant nonconformity, thanks to the Congregational divine, Professor Robert Vaughan.

The claims Buddensieg staked for Wycliffe seem unlimited. 'England owes to him her Bible, her present language, the reformation of the Church, her religious and, to a very large degree, her political liberty.' Despite the durability of old clichés, nobody (even a television producer) is likely to say as much today. But the first part of this eulogy still deserves reappraisal – that which concerns Wycliffe's relationship with the corpus of vernacular Wycliffite writings. What can be said now of the 1884 picture of how Wycliffe 'appealed to the nation at large'?

In the tongue of the people tract after tract on the Eucharist, the Friars, the Prelates, the Pope, the crusade to Flanders, were issued with amazing rapidity. He had addressed his academical hearers in Latin. This he now set aside . . . He stepped in at Chaucer's side as the father of later English prose, and brought about by these tracts, in which the speech of the peasant and the trader of the day is embodied, a new epoch in the history of the English language . . . [8]

Wycliffe Society, which had been founded in 1843 to reprint tracts and treatises of earlier reformers, puritans and nonconformists.

[8] Buddensieg, *John Wyclif*, pp. 13, 51. For a cheerful endorsement of Wyclif's vernacular influence see G. P. Krapp, *The Rise of English Literary Prose* (New York & London, 1915), p. xi. 'If English Prose must have a father, no one is so worthy of this title of respect as Wiclif' – to whom Chapter II of the book is devoted; see p. 43 and thereafter on how 'Wiclif wrote abundantly in English . . . .' See also R. W. Chambers, *On the Continuity of English Prose from Alfred to More and his School* (EETS, 186, 1932), pp. lvii, lxxxix, ciii, cvii, clxvii.

Have we tended to over-react in reversing that judgement? 'That he ever wrote anything in the vernacular is open to question', wrote McFarlane, adding: 'his Latin works can in any case have left him with time for little else'. And the more recent verdict of Anne Hudson is that 'None of the English texts can certainly be ascribed to Wyclif himself, despite the desire of modern critics to associate him directly with many of them.'[9]

I have no intention here of trying to go over the whole of this ground. Where the Bible is concerned we have to leave a question mark over Wycliffe's possible role, remembering that it was not until 1411 that Archbishop Arundel told the pope of Wycliffe having 'devised the expedient' of scriptural translation, and that Henry Knighton's earlier remarks related not to the whole Bible, but to the gospels. It is surely (as I am not the first to stress) essential to bear in mind that limitation, both when we are listening to what Wycliffe himself had to say about vernacular scripture, and when we hypothesise about what may have been going on in Queen's College, Oxford, about 1375, when John Trevisa, Nicholas Hereford and Wycliffe were all in residence.[10] Wycliffe's familiarity with the recently translated gospels is evident from his remarks on the ability of secular lords to study them, and on the horror of bishops and friars at this achievement.[11] It seems unwise to go further than that. As regards the English sermon cycle we await the completion of Anne Hudson's magisterial edition. This has already made clear the problematical relationship of the English sermons to the Latin ones, examples of close dependence of the former on the latter being rare, whatever the overall proximity of outlook.[12]

It might be argued – *pace* many earlier editors – that the ascription of authorship is not automatically of importance in itself. It *is* significant though, from the point of view of dating and doctrinal development, and that matters a good deal when we are trying to probe the elusive question of a popular heresy growing out of an academic one. The problem of Wycliffe's relationship with the vernacular is central to the development of his influence. It may yet be soluble, for the materials exist, many of them in print, on which to focus scrutiny of the derivation or divergence of the vernacular texts from Wycliffe's

---

[9] K.B. McFarlane, *John Wycliffe and the Beginnings of English Nonconformity* (London, 1952), p. 118; *Selections*, p. 10.

[10] *Snappe's Formulary*, ed. H. E. Salter, OHS, 80 (1924), p. 134; M. Wilks, 'Misleading Manuscripts: Wyclif and the Non-Wycliffite Bible', *SCH*, 11 (1975), pp. 147-61; H. Hargreaves, 'The Marginal Glosses to the Wycliffite New Testament', *Studia neophilologica*, 33 (1961), pp. 293-4, 296- 300; idem, *CHB*, ii, pp. 387-415; D.C. Fowler, 'John Trevisa and the English Bible', *Modern Philology*, 58 (1960), pp. 81-98; idem, *The Bible in Early English Literature* (London, 1977), pp. 154-9; J.R. Magrath, *The Queen's College*, i (Oxford, 1921), pp. 105-29.

[11] *Opera Minora*, p. 378; *Opus Evang.*, iii, p. 36-7, 115; *Polemical Works*, i, p. 126, cf. p. 168 and *Trial.*, p. 240.

[12] *English Wycliffite Sermons*, i, ed. A. Hudson, (Oxford, 1983), p. 159 n. 3; cf. pp. 9-13, 50.

Latin writings.[13] This is not an easy task. Wycliffe was prone to repeating, alluding to, and citing from himself, so that the interrelationship of the Latin works is itself complex. It is as well to start with the assumption that a vernacular text could be related in just as complex a way to its Latin sources, though there are of course examples of more or less direct translations.

Leaving aside then those parts of the vernacular Wycliffite heritage which may reasonably be considered central, I want here to concentrate on a particular topic at a particularly critical moment. The topic is that which Buddensieg put first when writing about Wycliffe's appeal to the nation in 'tract after tract': the eucharist. The moment is the period between 1380 and 1382, culminating in the proceedings of the 'earthquake council' at Blackfriars, when Wycliffe was making known his views on the doctrine of the eucharist and turning erstwhile friends and allies into opponents, if not enemies. How did the use of the vernacular affect the dramatic changes of this time in the careers of Wycliffe and leading Wycliffites?

Before addressing this topic some preliminary observations: first, concerning Wycliffe's use of the vernacular, and second on how prevailing views may have affected initial responses to the Wycliffites.

During Wycliffe's lifetime no single writing by him, as opposed to tenets propounded by him, was condemned by name. The eighteen points condemned by Pope Gregory XI in May 1377 were drawn from the text of *De civili dominio*, but this, though doubtless self-evident to those in the know, was left unstated. It is no easy task to correlate the twenty-four heresies and errors condemned at Blackfriars in May 1382 with Wycliffe's writings, and perhaps the search is itself to some degree misguided.[14] For already in 1377, and still more so in 1382, the statements that were proscribed were singled out for the very reason that they were thought to have left the page and the relatively safe covers of books and walls of university lecture-rooms. In both the papal letters of 1377 (which named Wycliffe), and the archbishop of Canterbury's orders of 1382 (which did not), there was mention of the public preaching of the

---

[13] It was of course a misfortune that the publication of English Wycliffite texts, including *The English Works of Wyclif Hitherto Unprinted,* ed. F. D. Matthew (EETS, 74, 1880), antedated the Wyclif Society – but not the printing of the *Trialogus,* which may have been a specially important source. Shirley (*Catalogue,* pp. viii-ix) had already sounded a caution, stressing the very doubtful ascription of the vernacular tracts ('mentioned in no catalogue earlier than that of Bale'), as compared with the Latin works. 'I believe we shall never arrive at any satisfactory conclusion as to the genuineness of many of the English tracts, until some considerable portion of the confessedly genuine works has been printed, and opportunity given for a large and careful comparison' – an opportunity that has yet to be fully exploited.

[14] J. H. Dahmus, *The Prosecution of John Wyclyf* (New Haven & London, 1952), pp. 49-54 (taking the number of points condemned as 19); 93-8; H. B. Workman, *John Wyclif* (Oxford, 1926), i, pp. 297-9; ii, pp. 266-8, 416-17; McFarlane, *John Wycliffe,* pp. 79-81, 106-7; A. Gwynn, *The English Austin Friars in the Time of Wyclif* (Oxford, 1940), pp. 232-3, 249.

erroneous and heretical propositions.[15] Wycliffe became suspect because he was seen to have gone public. His views had been made known outside the schools and were thought to be attracting a secular audience. The question is: what degree of responsibility can be attributed to him as this process gathered momentum?

That Wycliffe was a forceful and effective preacher in the vernacular is clear from what happened in London during the last months of Edward III's reign. Though it did little to help his own career, he certainly made a stir and gained the kind of attention that gladdens the hearts of radicals more than any office-holding. Walsingham (whose reporting suggests access to some good source) stressed the effect Wycliffe's novel opinions on excommunication and temporalities had on simple auditors. Running from one city church to another, his preaching attracted (or, to the chronicler's thinking, deluded) many ordinary London citizens, as well as those lordly patrons responsible for this tour of the pulpits.[16].

We may connect this civic outing with Wycliffe's first known excursion into the written vernacular. Though no English text has been identified that would fit, there seems no doubt that it was about this time (anyway before the spring of 1378), that Wycliffe published a vernacular address that focused on the abuses of church endowments of which he had spoken in London. We do have the Latin version of this tract. The *Thirty-Three Conclusions* (also called *De paupertate Christi*) were a comeback – one of many! – on the topic of church possessions, which can be seen as amounting to a digest of *De civili dominio*. Wycliffe himself in *De officio regis* alluded to the last conclusion for his

---

[15] *Chronicon Angliae*, ed. E.M. Thompson, RS (London, 1874), pp. 174-5, cf. 176-7, 178; *Historia Anglicana*, ed. H.T. Riley, RS (London, 1863-4), i, pp. 346-53; *Fasciculi zizaniorum* (henceforward *FZ*), ed. W.W. Shirley, RS (London, 1858), pp. 275-6; cf. 309-10 for the order of 12 June 1382 for the twenty-four conclusions to be publicly condemned in St. Mary's church, Oxford, in both English and Latin, and forbidding their teaching *in scholis aut extra*. In this context it is worth considering the list of nine bishops who attended the Blackfriars Council (*FZ*, p. 286; Workman, *John Wyclif*, ii, pp. 254-60; Dahmus, *Prosecution*, p. 92). Of these William Bottisham was suffragan to the bishop of Winchester and John Fordham, recently promoted to Durham may (Workman suggested) have participated as archdeacon of Canterbury: cf. I.J. Churchill, *Canterbury Administration* (London, 1933), i, p. 48. All the remaining seven came from the south of England and we can point to events in the dioceses of Exeter, Salisbury and Winchester, as well as London and Lincoln, that might have made the presence of five of these diocesans specially desirable. See A.K. McHardy, 'Bishop Buckingham and the Lollards of Lincoln Diocese', *SCH*, 9 (1972), p. 131 and below, pp. 38, 39, and nn. 20, 32.

[16] *Chronicon Angliae*, pp. 115-16, 189-90; cf. *Historia Anglicana*, i, ppp. 324-5, 363. *The Anonimalle Chronicle 1333 to 1381*, ed. V.H. Galbraith (Manchester, 1927) p. 103. Walsingham, who stresses Wycliffe's effect on *simplices auditores . . . simplices quosdam Londoniensium cives . . .* says Wycliffe referred to William Rufus in support of his argument that king and lords could remove temporalities from sinful churchmen. For the use of this example in *De civili dominio* see E.C. Tatnall, 'John Wyclif and *Ecclesia Anglicana*', *JEH*, 20 (1969), p. 33. On Wycliffe's popular preaching see A. Hudson, 'Lollardy: The English Heresy?', *SCH*, 18 (1982), p. 271; G. Holmes, *The Good Parliament* (Oxford, 1975), pp. 166-7, 189-91, 197-8; McFarlane, *John Wycliffe*, p. 70; Workman, *John Wyclif*, i, pp. 278-89.

summary of the duty of king and temporal lords to defend the gospel law. In another reference in *De veritate sacre scripture*, in the course of a truculent advertisement of his own confidence, Wycliffe tells of the English version of this text. I am quite ready, he said, to recognize the Roman church as part of Christ's church, though it may be that the pope is ignorant of scripture and that the English church is more distinguished for catholic truth. My own deeds, he claims, have made clear that I cannot be accused of fearfulness over my conclusions, 'since I despatched them through a great part of England and Christendom and also as far as the Roman curia'. The point was driven home with these words.

> Whence, because I wished the material to be communicated to clerks and laymen, I collected and communicated thirty-three conclusions on this matter in two languages [*in lingwa duplici*].[17]

The vernacular was itself a mixed medium. We shall never know exactly what Wycliffe told his London audiences, and the lost flight of the spoken word affects us in two ways: through our inability to recover it and through the way in which contemporaries treated it. The fact that, as a Wycliffite sermon put it, 'the words passen away anon when we have spoken them',[18] delimited reactions to the ripples caused by words that were only uttered.

Some sixty years later Reginald Pecock commented on the degree of tolerance that still attached to the spoken word.

> And also weel y wote and in experience y haue it knowun þat þouȝ a man preche in þe comoun peplis language to þe comoun as hiȝe and sutil maters as ben in þe bifore

---

[17] *De ver. sac. scrip.*, c. 14, pp. 349-50: 'Unde quia volui materiam communicatam clericis et laicis, collegi et communicavi triginta tres conclusiones illius materie in li[n]gwa duplici': (cf. *Trial.*, p. 341, 'Dixi alias in lingua multiplici'; *Polemical Works,* i, p. 168, 'evangelium in lingwa triplici exaratum'); *De off. reg.* pp. 78-9: 'Et patet sentencia quam dixi in xxxiii conclusione abbreviata'. For verbal parallels between the thirty-three conclusions and *De civ. dom.*, see *Opera minora,* p. viii: S.H. Thomson, 'Three Unprinted Opuscula of John Wyclif', *Speculum,* 3 (1928), p. 252, and for the text of the conclusions *Opera minora,* pp. 19-73. On the dating and relationship of these texts see Thomson, *Latin Writings,* pp. 257-8, and see pp. 56, 60-61 for the dates of March-April 1378 for c. 14 of *De veritate sacre scripture* and mid 1379 for *De officio regis* (which grew out of these arguments).

[18] *English Wycliffite Sermons,* i, p. 348. For the possibility that seven of Wycliffe's *Sermones Quadraginta* (*Sermones,* iv, nos. 59, 55-7, 62, 60, 23) forming a Sunday series from 19 Oct. to 30 Nov. 1376, may have been part of these London addresses see W. Mallard, 'Dating the *Sermones Quadraginta* of John Wyclif', *Medievalia et humanistica,* 17 (1966), pp. 98-101; G.A. Benrath, *Wyclifs Bibelkommentar* (Berlin, 1966), pp. 380-2, 386. In addition to a reference to London (*Sermones,* iv, p. 460), these sermons include various observations on the abuses of temporal possessions, business fraud (p. 484) and debt (p. 198), and some remarks about funeral pomp and Christian knighthood (pp. 433-4) which, on 26 October, only three weeks after the solemn burial at Canterbury of the Black Prince (who had lain in state at Westminster since June), would have been extraordinarily pointed.

named bokis, he schal not be þerfore blamed but it schal be þouȝt þus: who may take, take he.[19]

In view of the self-evident anxieties about the dangers of vernacular preaching during the previous half-century this statement may seem surprising. But if one takes it to refer to the overall potential of spoken sermon or text, there seems something to it: a preacher's words might cause trouble if they produced certain effects among his auditors; if not, they could evaporate without trace. The same words, written, themselves became informants, capable of convincing or converting. One eccentric sermon would not start a summons.

But attitudes changed as the vernacular changed. By the time Pecock wrote these words in the 1440s it seemed natural to compare the error-potential of popular preaching with that of vernacular books. If we project ourselves back to, say 1370, it would have been most unnatural to think along these lines, for the kind of vernacular theology which Pecock read and wrote was itself inconceivable. In 1370 it might have seemed far-fetched to the point of insanity to suppose that a glover or skinner in the town of Beccles in Suffolk had from reading or hearing texts come to believe 'that no priest hath power to make God's body in the sacrament of the altar, and that after the sacramental words said of a priest at mass there remaineth nothing but only a cake of material bread'.[20] It was unthinkable for two reasons: first, because no clerk in his right

---

[19] *The Rule of Crysten Religioun*, ed. W.C. Greet (EETS, 171, 1927), p. 21, cf. p. 99. (Pecock commends the ability he has found among *gentil men* of the laity to understand high matters, even when given little help on 'the terms or words'. Pecock himself invented words, some of which seem to have remained solely his coinage; e.g. *endal, endalli, menal, menali, knouingal, knoual*; see entries under these headings in *Middle English Dictionary*, ed. H. Kurath and S.M. Kuhn (Ann Arbor, 1954-). He also englished theological terminology, for example *rememoratijf signes* for *signa recordativa*.

[20] *Heresy Trials in the Diocese of Norwich, 1428-31*, ed. N.P. Tanner (CS, 4th ser. 20, 1977), pp. 111, 121. To refer to the eucharistic bread as 'Christ in a cake' was not at all disrespectful in itself; see *Legends of the Holy Rood*, ed. R. Morris (EETS, 46, 1871), p. 211; cf. p. 220, and for a discussion (citing this) of how the sacrament of the altar was 'often spoken of as a kind of banquet which had its beginning on Christmas Day', see V.A. Kolve, *The Play Called Corpus Christi* (Stanford, 1966), p. 165. There is an interesting precedent for later eucharistic heresy in the diocese of Exeter, where in March 1355 Bishop Grandisson tried to bring to book Ralph Tremur, sometime (1331-4) rector of Warleggan in Cornwall. Temur was an M.A., described as skilled in grammar and four languages (Latin, French, English and Cornish/Breton), and had licences to study 1331-4. He was acused of asserting 'that the bread and wine were not substantially transformed (*substancialiter non transire*) into the flesh and blood of our lord Jesus Christ by the consecration of the words'. He attached this denial (as did Wycliffites) to the adoration of the host, reportedly saying 'you are absurdly worshipping the work of your hands, for what does a priest do except gape and blow on a little bread?' Tremur, who challenged the law as well as doctrine, was said to have stolen a pyx from church, taken it home, and thrown the sacrament into the fire. Grandisson, inspired to flights of rhetoric in his worry over this case and believing that Tremur had been spreading his views into other dioceses, wrote anxiously to the bishop of London about these events, as well as ordering denunciation of the offender in the vernacular in every parish of the diocese of Exeter. Tremur had taught his erroneous theology in the vernacular and led simple and unlearned people into error; 'quosdam simplices et indoctos et theologie veritatis ignaros vel ad heresim pronos obtinuit sibi in errore tam execrabili secrecius adherere'. But there is no

mind would speak let alone write thus of this topic in English; second, because simple laymen did not discuss such theology. What was unthinkable in 1370 had happened by 1430 – long before – and the authorities had come to terms with this new phenomenon: an unorthodoxy with the capacity to produce and circulate English theological writings for lay consumption.

The novelty of the circumstances makes it understandable that there was a time-lag between the beginnings of this vernacular textual activity, and the formulation of counter-measures to control it. It was taken for granted at the outset, that if the people were learning false doctrine, they were learning it from preachers.[21] It was only natural, when Wycliffite errors were found to be spreading, that preachers and the control of preaching received the first attention. And since the authorities acted on their normal assumption that popular errors must stem from the spoken word, it was some years before the textual bases of Lollardy began to be exposed.[22] Vernacular theology of this kind was quite new. It took churchmen by surprise.

Of course books had always been potential breeders of error. Gregory XI's bull mentioned Marsilio of Padua and John of Jandun as sources of Wycliffe's opinions.[23] But the deviations of academic theologians were one thing; those of the people another. It is not until 1388 that we find the first official notice of

suggestion that he committed his suspect views to writing. It was his speech and all too fluent preaching that caused his bishop such anguish: (*O detestabilis lingua . . . verborum loquacitate . . . garrulus et disertus*). Despite these efforts Tremur seems to have evaded arrest and nothing is known of him after this. Nothing seems to be known of Tremur's university career either, but his case should not be forgotten when considering later Oxford evangelists, specially the Cornishmen Lawrence Bedeman (below, p. 38): for (a) Grandisson's counter-action must have made Tremur's case notorious in Exeter diocese (b) the rectory of Lifton, Devon, which Bedeman held from 1383 to his death in 1423, had been served in 1329 by Tremur's uncle. *The Register of John de Grandisson, Bishop of Exeter (A.D. 1327-1369)*, ed. F.C. Hingeston-Randolph (Exeter, 1894-9), ii, pp. 1147-9, 1179-81; cf. pp. 621-2, 627, 660, 715; iii, pp. lxxiii-lxxvi, 1285, 1303; B.L. Manning, *The People's Faith in the Time of Wyclif* (Cambridge, 1919), p. 70. Emden, (O), iii, pp. 1895-6 mentions only John Tremur, Ralph's uncle, though both were described as M.A.

[21] 'Christianity in the fourteenth century was still an oral religion'; Manning, *People's Faith*, p. 1 – above all, one might add, in the expectations clerks had of lay learning, which meant that 'preaching was considered the fundamental didactic tool for reaching a wide audience'; R.M. Haines, 'Education in English Ecclesiastical Legislation of the Later Middle Ages': *SCH*, 7 (1971), pp. 161-75 (cited at p. 173); V. Gillespie, '*Doctrina* and *Predicacio*: The Design and Function of Some Pastoral Manuals', *Leeds Studies in English,* new series 11 (1980), pp. 36-50.

[22] See Hudson, 'English Heresy?', p. 265 for the argument that 'it was only very slowly that the authorities of the established church came to see that the vernacular lay at the root of the trouble'. I am here suggesting that this statement might be qualified by distinguishing between awareness of new dangers in the *spoken* vernacular, and awareness that the *written* vernacular was being put to new uses. The former seems to have become clear by 1381-2; the latter not until later. On the colophon in the *Speculum Vite* (an English poem, composed after 1349, derived from the French *Somme le Roi*) purportedly recording inspection and approval of the text in Cambridge in 1384, see Anne Hudson, *The Premature Reformation* (Oxford, 1988), p. 416.

[23] *Chronicon Angliae*, pp. 174, 176, 178; G. Leff, *Heresy in the Later Middle Ages* (Manchester, 1967) ii, p. 560; S.H. Thomson, 'The Philosophical Basis of Wyclif's Theology', *Journal of Religion* 11 (1931), p. 109.

any vernacular writings by Wycliffe. The royal commissions appointed from March that year were ordered to search out, confiscate and transmit to the council any books, booklets, schedules and quires which had been compiled, published, communicated and written either in English or Latin (*tam in Anglico quam in Latino*) by John Wycliffe (during his lifetime), Nicholas Hereford and John Aston.[24] But there was still no mention of any specific work. Only eleven years after Wycliffe's death, when in 1395 his followers presented flagrant evidence of their vernacular quarrying of the *Trialogus*, were the wheels for the first time set in motion for a grand process of posthumous public refutation, centred on a particular named book.[25]

Let us turn to the critical changes that were taking place during the last four years of Wycliffe's life.

It has long been recognized that Wycliffe's views on the eucharist were his undoing. His denial of transubstantiation raised the alarm at Oxford, and caused the loss of supporters, clerical and lay. John of Gaunt is said to have made a flying visit to Oxford to warn Wycliffe against further speech on this topic, and Repton and Hereford were likewise to find themselves repulsed by the duke of Lancaster when he understood the drift of their sacramental teaching.[26] It is worth looking carefully into what caused this sense of shock.

Obviously the scandal started in the schools. The reaction there is clearly reflected by the Carmelite compiler of the *Fasciculi zizaniorum*, who listed the erroneous conclusions Wycliffe had reached by the summer of 1381, including the assertion (maintained in a public determination) that the bread and wine

---

[24] *Chronicon Henrici Knighton,* ed. J.R. Lumby, RS (London, 1889-95), ii, pp. 264-5; *CPR, 1385-1389* (London, 1900), pp. 427, 430, 448, 536, 550 (the commissions differ in the authors specified, some including Purvey, others naming only Wycliffe and Hereford); Hudson, 'English Heresy?', p. 270.

[25] The fourth of the twelve conclusions of 1395 cited the *Doctor Evangelicus* in the *Trialogus* on the 'feigned miracle of the sacrament of bread' for his authority (given in Latin) *quod panis materialis est habitudinaliter corpus Christi* (*Selections*, p. 25). This seems to be a reading of, rather than a quotation from the *Trialogus,* pp. 267, 272 (where one notices the lack of the troublesome words *panis materialis,* on which see below). Several of the other conclusions (though this was the only reference to this authority) could be related to the *Trialogus,* for the first three and the ninth all dealt with points raised there, and the remarks on general versus special prayer in Book IV, c. 38 are treated by Netter together with conclusion seven; *Doctrinale antiquitatum fidei catholicae ecclesiae,* ed. B. Blanciotti (Venice, 1757- 9), ii, c. 107, cols. 677-8, 680 (citing *Trialogus,* p. 381), 681. The batteries directed against the *Trialogus* from the summer of 1395 undoubtedly owed much to this vernacular publicity, and the royal orders of 18 July to the chancellor and university of Oxford to have the book searched for heresy, specifically mentioned the king's discovery that it contained heresy on the sacrament, the publication of which would spread unsound doctrine among the people. *CCR, 1392-1396* (London, 1925), pp. 437-8.

[26] *FZ,* pp. 114, 318; McFarlane, *John Wycliffe,* pp. 98, 110. According to the *Fasciculi,* the duke's message to Wycliffe after the sentence of the chancellor of Oxford was *quod de cetero non loqueretur de ista materia* – the emphasis being on making his views known by speech, just as the Oxford sentence stressed public teaching.

remained after the words of consecration.[27] Whatever Wycliffe might say about recalling the church from its idolatry, this was enough for men like the Austin Adam Stockton to transform the 'venerable doctor' into the 'execrable seducer'.[28] And worse was being said (and written) for, in the heat of his conviction that nothing could be more debased than an accident without a subject, Wycliffe horrified his contemporaries, who blushed to report such words, by going so far as to say repeatedly that the church's teaching made the visible consecrated host more abject in nature than the basest matter: less than horse bread, rat bread, rat's dung, or a tortoise.[29]

This was bad enough. But it was not all. For appalling statements about the nature of the eucharist were not confined to the lecture-room and the medium of Latin. The doctrine of the sacrament was also being discussed in English and this move into the vernacular introduced an entirely fresh dimension of reproach and consternation. It was quite wrong and a complete break with accepted convention to involve the laity in the quiddities of sacramental theology. To do so by apparently denying the central mystery of the eucharist was unspeakable.

When did the vernacular preaching against transubstantiation begin, and who was responsible? The sentence issued by the chancellor of Oxford, William Barton, probably in the winter of 1380-81, which took Wycliffe aback when he was told of it in the middle of a lecture, makes clear that already at this time the topic was being aired outside the university. The two dangerously heretical assertions concerning the eucharist that Barton condemned had, he reported, been 'publicly taught, both in this university and outside'. As chancellor his jurisdiction extended only to what went on inside the university,

---

[27] *FZ*, pp. 104-6. The date of these lectures is controversial, but the summer of 1380 seems to fit best – the *De eucharistia* probably being the outcome of them. Thomson, *Latin Writings*, pp. 67-70; F.D. Matthew, 'The Date of Wyclif's Attack on Transubstantiation', *EHR*, 5 (1890), pp. 328-30; Gwynn, *Austin Friars*, pp. 258-9; B.L. Manning, 'Wyclif', in *CMH*, 7 (1932), pp. 492, 501; cf. Workman, *John Wyclif*, ii, pp. 140ff, 408-9.

[28] Gwynn, *Austin Friars*, pp. 239, 254-5.

[29] Wycliffe used a variety of analogies to emphasize the offensiveness of the doctrine 'quod sacramentum non sit nisi accidens abiectum'; *De euch.*, p. 114; cf. p. 129: 'Non enim pinsavit Deus unam pastam monstruosam accidencium per se existencium . . . '; p. 186, making the host a bundle of accidents makes it more abject in nature 'quam aliqua vilis substancia corporea assignanda'; p. 284, conventionally comparing the host with manna. The language of *De apostasia* becomes more extreme and specific; see pp. 106, 121, 127, 205, 235; cf. pp. 80, 81, 95, 107-8, 129, 242, 245; *Trial.*, p. 269. For shocked reactions see *FZ*, pp. 108, 158; *Eulogium historiarum*, ed. F.S. Haydon, RS (London 1858-63), iii, p. 350; Netter, *Doctrinale*, ii, cols. 383, 386 c. 63; col. 278, c. 44; for William Woodford on this 'horrible' conclusion see *Fasciculus rerum expetendarum & fugiendarum,* ed. O. Gratius rev. E. Brown (London, 1690), i, p. 200; cf. p. 193 on Wycliffe's 'great temerity' in not only challenging the doctrine that the accidents remained without substance, but in asserting that this was heresy.

and it was there, both inside the schools and outside them, that this teaching was prohibited.[30]

As far as extramural developments were concerned, other events took over and superseded all other interests in the summer of 1381. When the ecclesiastical authorities (under new dynamic leadership) finally mobilized themselves after the hiatus of the rising, a number of culprits stood charged of this sacramental offence, though in no case can we be sure of the exact time at which their teaching against transubstantiation had started. Philip Repton (or Repingdon), before his inception in the summer of 1382, had reportedly preached Wycliffe's view of the sacrament of the altar at Brackley in Northamptonshire, where he had converted his auditors.[31] Other Oxford men who took the same message to English hearers were Nicholas Hereford, John Aston, Robert Alington and Lawrence Bedeman. They were all accused by the bishop of Winchester in May 1382 of having publicly preached and taught errors at Odiham (Hants.) and elsewhere in the diocese, views on the eucharist coming top of the list though no details were given. One of these men, Lawrence Bedeman or Steven of Cornwall, whose preaching was also the object of enquiry in the diocese of Exeter, seems to have thought fit to pull out of Oxford (where he was fellow and rector of Exeter College) in mid-April 1380.[32]

In trying to reconstruct these events and disentangle the chronology, we are hampered by the difficulty that the contemporaries on whom we must largely depend wrote with a retrospective view that was tinctured by *post hoc, propter*

---

[30] *FZ*, pp. 109-13; note the phrases 'et tam in ista universitate quam extra publice dogmatizant' (110); 'in scholis vel extra scholis in hac universitate' (112). See also n. 15 above. Gwynn, *Austin Friars*, p. 260 suggests that Wycliffe's lecturing in the house of the Austins at the time of this announcement is an indication of their support up to this time.

[31] *FZ*, pp. 296-7 (Brackley being a living appropriated to Repton's own Augustinian house at Leicester; McFarlane, *John Wycliffe*, pp. 102-3); see also pp. 299-300, 306-7 and *Historia Anglicana*, ii, p. 60 for Repton's Corpus Christi day sermon at St. Frideswide's (5 June 1382) in which he defended Wycliffe's eucharistic teaching, while indicating the need to keep his lips sealed over this until the clergy became more enlightened – words which might seem to echo Wycliffe's (below p. 69).

[32] *Wykeham's Register*, ed. T.F. Kirby, *Hampshire Record Society* (1896-9), ii, pp. 337-8, 342-3 (the orders were dated at Southwark on 21 May, at the conclusion of the first critical meeting of the Blackfriars Council); A.K. McHardy, 'The Dissemination of Wyclif's Ideas', *SCH*, Subsidia 5, *From Ockham to Wyclif* (1987), pp. 361-8. For Alington, see below n. 102. On Bedeman, see *The Register of Thomas de Brantyngham, Bishop of Exeter (A.D. 1370-1394)*, ed. F.C. Hingeston-Randolph (Exeter, 1901-6), i, pp. 158, 480-1; *Registrum Collegii Exoniensis,* ed. C.W. Boase, *Oxford Historical Society,* 27 (1894), pp. lxv-lxvii; Emden (O), iii, p. 1772; Workman, *John Wyclif*, ii, pp. 139, 252, 287; McFarlane, *John Wycliffe*, pp. 102, 109, 112; *DNB*. Brantingham's (undated) commission of enquiry was prompted by the Blackfriars decision which (in the formulaic words of his letter) had brought Bedeman's preaching to the bishop's attention. Workman and Emden place this preaching tour *after* the Winchester proceedings, but it would make just as good sense to place it *before*, given the fact that Bedeman made his submission to the bishop of Winchester and the lack of any secure evidence that he actually went to the west country between May and October 1382. (Wykeham's 1382 letter calls him 'Lawrence Bedeman of Cornwall').

hoc convictions. Theirs was a syllogistic understanding of events: preaching led to revolt; Wycliffites had been preaching; *ergo* Wycliffites caused revolt. In some cases we can catch them out. For instance it is highly suspicious that the alleged confession of John Ball, who was executed in July 1381, seems based on knowledge of the activity of several Wycliffites that only became public in the spring of 1382, and that the Carmelite chronicler produces it (with apologies for earlier omission) in the context of those later revelations.[33] Henry Knighton, the compiler of the *Fasciculi zizaniorum*, and the continuator of the *Eulogium historiarum*, all wrote their narratives of the early 1380s with the benefit of more than ten years' hindsight. It is hard not to suspect that their interpretation of the events of 1381 owed something to their knowledge of 1382.

Nevertheless it must be noted that independent reporters agreed in placing the extramural spread of Wycliffe's sacramental errors *before* the 1381 revolt. The *Eulogium* writer who, as a Franciscan, had reason to be in the know since members of his order (one of whom he referred to) were refuting Wycliffe on this score in 1381, showed himself well versed in the eucharistic dispute. 'John Wycliffe determined in Oxford that the sacrament of the eucharist is bread . . .' This introduction (under the year 1381) is followed by quite an accurate summary of Wycliffe's arguments, concluding with the following observations: 'His disciples preached and spread this teaching throughout England, seducing many laymen, even nobles and great lords who supported these false preachers . . . The archbishop of Canterbury did not seem much bothered by this'.[34]

Walsingham makes the same point with one of his characteristically vivid stories. It comes at the beginning of his report on 1381 (again, before the account of the rising). Wycliffe, says Walsingham, better called Wykbileve (and other appropriate insults) was leading Christians into the abyss by maintaining that the bread and wine remained in the sacrament after consecration and that it was wrong to worship the host. Such ravings had seduced many. 'Whence a certain knight of Wiltshire, near Salisbury', Sir Lawrence of Saint Martin, misled in a similar fashion had committed a terrible sacrilege. At Easter (which fell on 14 April 1381), when he should have received the sacrament, he had persuaded his priest to let him communicate on the eve of the feast. But instead of eating the host he had taken it in his hand and sped

---

[33] *FZ*, pp. 273-4; the names of Wycliffe's alleged *comitiva* being Nicholas Hereford, John Aston and Lawrence Bedeman, who appear together in this connection in 1382 (see previous note and *FZ*, p. 310); R.B. Dobson, *The Peasants' Revolt of 1381* (London, 1970), pp. 372-8. Of course we cannot rule out the possibility that Ball, in the hopes of a temporary reprieve through ecclesiastical intervention, did claim a Wycliffite association – a claim that would have gained credibility in a context of rumours of eucharistic deviation.

[34] *Eulogium historiarum*, iii, pp. 350-1; J.I. Catto, 'An Alleged Great Council of 1374', *EHR*, 82 (1967), pp. 764-71, at p. 766; A. Gransden, *Historical Writing in England*, ii (London 1982), p. 158 n. 5. The chronicler refers to the refutation of Wycliffe by the Franciscan regent John Tissington (see below p. 52). Another Franciscan who wrote at length against Wycliffe on the eucharist was William Woodford (n. 59 below).

home with it. The priest, reckoning the knight must have gone out of his mind, followed in hot pursuit, beseeching him to beware – but to no avail. Sir Lawrence shut out his pursuer and proceeded to eat his consecrated host in three portions, with his oysters, his onions and his wine, asserting that it was on a par with any other bread. His householders, gasping at the scandal, noted and reported every detail. Sir Lawrence was duly cited before Bishop Erghum of Salisbury, who treated him considerately, since he was a man of standing in those parts, and suggested that the knight should take counsel on the eucharist with his clerks. This he did, and returned to confess his error. The penance enjoined on him is interesting, and one befitting a man of means. He was to erect in a public place in Salisbury a stone cross sculpted with representations of his misdeed, and to confess his offence there weekly for the rest of his life.[35]

Walsingham, we should observe, was quite candid about this tale. He does not say that Sir Lawrence of Saint Martin's eccentric stunt resulted from Wycliffe's teaching. He says the knight was 'similarly misled' (*non dissimiliter seductus*), and was to be taken as an example of the terrible evils Wycliffe was sowing. From our point of view it is worth noting that at least some of the chronicler's facts can be corroborated. Sir Lawrence of Saint Martin, who died in 1384, was a fairly substantial landowner in Wiltshire, and represented the county in parliament in January 1380. In October that year he was appointed sheriff of Wiltshire, but on the following 6 May 1381, he was apparently relieved of his office and Hugh Cheyne nominated instead. At this point what had previously been an ordinary county career of a local knight seems to have halted.[36] What rumours, we may wonder, about Wycliffe and speculations on the eucharist may have been circulating in London, and further afield, in 1380 and the spring of 1381?

---

[35] *Chronicon Angliae*, pp. 281-3; cf. *Historia Anglicana*, i, pp. 450-1; 'crucem lapideam, in qua per ordinem tota series hujus rei sculpteretur'. The suggestion seems to be that Sir Lawrence imitated priestly fraction in his domestic celebration; perhaps too (though Walsingham does not say so) the significance of Easter Eve was that this was a *supper*. It should be noted also that the penance was to be performed at the cross on Fridays (cf. Workman, *John Wyclif*, ii, p. 255, who misreads this as 'six market days'). It seems more likely that Saint Martin was thinking in terms of the Last Supper than the Passover, as Workman suggested, and there is no reason to identify this Sir Lawrence with the man of the same name who appears in the London *domus coversorum* at this time. Gransden, *Historical Writing*, ii, p. 132 regards this tale as an example of Walsingham treating Lollardy (*sic*) 'with apparent humour'. If the John de la Mare (M.P. for Wiltshire in the Good Parliament) who served on local commissions in Wiltshire with Saint Martin, was related to Thomas de la Mare, abbot of St. Albans (whose family the *DNB* reports as connected with the earl of Salisbury) we could postulate a source for this story.

[36] *CCR, 1377-1381* (London, 1914), pp. 350, 356; *CPR, 1377-1381* (London, 1895), pp. 38, 47, 473, 510, 512, 568; *CFR, 1377-1383* (London, 1926), pp. 143, 220; *CFR, 1383-1391* (London, 1929), pp. 127-8, 133-4, 143; *CCR, 1385-1389* (London, 1921), p. 137. *Members of Parliament* (House of Commons, 1878), vol. 62, pt. i, p. 205, cf. pp. 168, 185, 187. See also C. Kightly, 'The Early Lollards: A Survey of Popular Lollard Activity in England, 1382-1428' (unpublished D.Phil. thesis, York, 1975), pp. 311-13 on this incident and Sir Lawrence's career, including the facts that he was born in 1319 and fought at Crécy.

Though it is difficult to answer that question, the events that took place in May 1382, show that Archbishop Courtenay (making up for his predecessor's inertia), was concerned to give the maximum publicity to combating eucharistic deviations. The publication of the tenets condemned at Blackfriars seems to reflect fears of the spread of popular sacramental error. The assembled bishops and doctors reached their verdict on the twenty-four heresies and errors (headed by three eucharistic heresies) on Wednesday 21 May. On Friday the following week, 30 May, their decision was given the utmost notice, with a solemn procession through the city of London, attended by both laity and clergy, and a sermon preached at (most probably) Paul's Cross. It is of some interest that the speaker chosen for this occasion was the Carmelite, John Kenningham. He was exceptionally well equipped to understand the theological issues, having been engaged in friendly (and latterly less cordial) controversy with Wycliffe for about ten years, as well as sitting on the Blackfriars Council.[37]

The day after the sermon produced a dramatic sequel. Knighton told the story of how a man who had followed Wycliffe into thinking that the material bread remained in the sacrament of the altar, heard Kenningham preach, and the next day was amazed to see the consecrated host bleeding before his very eyes as he watched the celebration by a Dominican at Blackfriars. The highly opportune Saturday conversion was fully exploited the next day, in another public occasion. On 1 June, at Paul's Cross, the sermon for Trinity Sunday was preached by the friar whose mass had produced the happy result, while the convert, Sir Cornelius Cloune, stood by to endorse the tale and reaffirm his acceptance of orthodox belief in the real presence.[38] Whatever one thinks of the authenticity of this event, its exploitation, if not stage-management, certainly argues for contemporary worry about the extension of Wycliffe's eucharistic heresy.

Those on whom suspicion fell went out of their way to enhance these anxieties. Hereford, Repton and Aston all took particular pains to publish their eucharistic opinions in the vernacular right in the middle of their trial by Archbishop Courtenay. On 18 June all three men appeared for examination before the archbishop at Blackfriars. They were treated somewhat differently. Hereford and Repton, both doctors of theology, were given copies of the conclusions and ordered to reply in writing. Aston, not yet a bachelor of theology, was asked if he wanted to be given a day to reply but refused, and

---

[37] *Knighton*, ii, pp. 162-3; Workman, *John Wyclif*, ii, pp. 266-7, 272 and on Kenningham pp. 120-2; Gwynn, *Austin Friars*, pp. 228-31; Emden (O), ii, p. 1077 under Kynyngham. Kenningham became confessor to John of Gaunt before 28 May 1392 (*FZ*, pp. 3, 357) though it is not clear when. If he already held this position he might be presumed to have had some part in the duke's cooling relations with the Wycliffites. See *De apos.*, pp. 60-1 for an attack on friars who, as confessors of kings and lords, failed to reach truth about the eucharist.

[38] *Knighton*, ii, pp. 163-4; Workman, *John Wyclif*, ii, pp. 272-3 (on the grants given to this Irish knight).

offered to do so at once. His answer was suspect, and he was admonished not to preach and told to reappear on Friday 20 June.[39]

The day after their examination, on 19 June, all three did something utterly unorthodox. They issued English statements of their beliefs about the eucharist, publishing their answers to the archbishop's questions. Hereford and Repton made a joint address to 'all Christian men', ending with a request for support and prayers from all reached by this confession. Aston's statement, which specifically dealt with the proposition that 'Material bread remains in the sacrament after the consecration', was worded differently, though it likewise concluded with an appeal to 'all men and all women to whom this confession comes' to bear witness for him. According to the *Fasciculi*, which included a Latin version of Aston's address, he wrote it in both English and Latin and circulated copies of it in the streets and squares of London.[40]

Aston's offence proved worse than that of the other two. He seems to have been imprisoned. The content of his English schedule might seem innocuous enough. 'I acknowledge that the same bread that the priest holds in his hands is made through virtue of the sacramental words verily the same Christ's body.'[41] But Aston offended both in his prevarications under examination, and in the deceptions and omissions of his English bill. It was what he refused to say, more than what he said, that was fatal. He had failed to commit himself to the reality of Christ's presence as understood in the miracle of transubstantiation.

So troubled were the examiners by Aston's subterfuge, that they took the extraordinary, perhaps ill-advised step, of answering in kind, with their own

---

[39] Wilkins, iii, pp. 160-1: *FZ*, pp. 289-90, 318-19ff. Hereford and Repton both incepted as doctors of theology this year. Aston was an M.A. and Emden says probably mistakenly called bachelor of theology in Courtenay's register. Emden (O), i, p. 67; ii, p. 913; iii, p. 1566.

[40] The English versions of these addresses (both of which bear the marks of being copies) survive in *Knighton*, ii, pp. 170-2, and MS Bodley 647, fo. 70 r.-v. (the latter being a Wycliffite collection). Comparison of the two suggests Knighton's general accuracy, though loyalty to his house caused him to omit Repton's name from the former document. It is to be noted that Aston (not the other two) 'was required specially to say what I felt of this proposition *Material bread remains in the sacrament after the consecration*'. The Latin text in *FZ*, pp. 329-30 reads in the main as a faithful version of the English, but there is one interesting and critical difference. In Bodley 647 after Aston's protestation 'that the matter and the speculation thereof passes in height my understanding', we have 'and therefore as mickle *as holy church* tells openly for to believe in this matter I believe'. Knighton here omits 'as holy church' and *FZ* has 'et ideo quantum *de illa scriptura sacra* docet expresse credendum est, credo' (my italics). In the context of the preceding and succeeding allusions to holy writ, which is indicated as having priority over the determinations of the church, it seems probable that the Latin here represents the correct version. See Appendix below; also *FZ*, pp. 331-3 for the 'confession' Aston submitted to Courtenay six months later, which, while yielding, quoted scripture at the archbishop and cited no authority later than Bede in support of church teaching on the sacrament (and did not mention transubstantiation).

[41] MS Bodley 647, fo. 70 v. *FZ*, pp. 329-30 says the archbishop had placed Aston in secular custody, and that the accused presented his appeal as 'confessio pauperis incarcerati'; Dahmus, *Prosecution*, p. 117. Aston may have been imprisoned for some months after 20 June (McFarlane, *John Wycliffe*, p. 111), and it is possible (see Appendix n. 3) that Hereford and Repton were on remand 19-20 June.

counter-propaganda. A bill, briefly explaining the reason for John Aston's condemnation, was distributed by the clergy in London streets and churches. He was (reported this document) condemned as a heretic not for what he had stated about Christ's presence by virtue of the words of consecration, but because (1) he refused to accept the church's teaching that Christ was identically present in bodily form, and (2) because he held that the substance of material bread and wine remained after consecration. The *Fasciculi zizaniorum*, which includes this remarkable statement, does not say what language it was in. Could it really have been in English, as Professor Dahmus assumed?[42] Naturally it would not have had the same impact in Latin, but if the prosecution really took this plunge into the vernacular it would have been a quite extraordinary concession to the other side. For it was the use of – or from the church's point of view, descent into – the vernacular that was here on trial.

John Aston, who was rash enough to act out his convictions on this score before the archbishop himself, shows clearly what was at stake. When he returned for examination on 20 June (this being the fourth session of the Blackfriars Council), Aston was questioned further on the first of the twenty-four conclusions: namely that the substance of material bread and wine remains after consecration in the sacrament of the altar. In view of his university standing it was to be assumed that the examination would proceed in Latin. But instead the accused insisted on replying in English, 'shouting', as the trial record puts it, 'frivolous, abusive and most disgraceful words, apparently in an effort to arouse and excite the people against the archbishop of Canterbury'. This was not simply a matter of playing to the gallery. It was making an issue of something that Aston and others had already shown they regarded as of critical importance. The defendant stuck to his guns, replying to questions on various articles in the vernacular and 'saying often and expressly, as a layman, that it was sufficient for him to believe as holy church did'. The archbishop repeatedly rebuked him for this behaviour, telling him he ought to reply in Latin, 'on account of the laymen who were present'. We do not know the number or persons of these lay witnesses, but one can imagine Courtenay's sense of shame and embarrassment when in answer to questions about the sacrament of the altar, this Oxford theologian kept on repeating that the matter was too difficult for him, and he could say no more. Finally, pressed on the question of the material bread of the host, Aston remarked with dangerous playfulness of the word *materialis*; 'you put this in your bag if you've got one', at which the archbishop lost patience and terminated the proceedings.[43]

This incident points up the critical nature of the language question. Aston's obstinate stand against the conventional Latin of the schools, sacraments and church courts, was a challenge to clerical traditions. When applied to the

---

[42] *FZ*, p. 331; Dahmus, *Prosecution*, pp. 117-18.

[43] Wilkins, iii, pp. 163-4; McFarlane, *John Wycliffe*, p. 111; Workman, *John Wyclif*, ii, p. 284. The following November (*FZ*, pp. 331-2) Aston admitted to the archbishop that he had replied with disrespect, using words both 'offensive to your ears' and foolish in themselves.

doctrine of the eucharist it amounted to denying the validity of the terminology in which the mystery of the sacrament was couched. As Aston's statement of 19 June put it, in answer to the question of the remanence of the bread in the consecrated sacrament: 'I make this protestation that I never put nor taught nor preached that proposition, for I know well that the matter and the speculation thereof passes in height my understanding . . .'[44] It was a disingenuous assertion, designed to draw attention to the falsities of clerical doctrine.

Why did it seem so important to speak of this matter in the vernacular? The use of English in this context was more pointed, and more challenging, than in any other circumstances. The Wycliffite clerks who defied the accepted boundaries of Latin for answering questions on the eucharist were making several points at once: that it was a fraudulent obfuscation to discuss the church's central doctrine in a language alien to lay people; all believers, clerical and lay, shared the same belief; the truths of the faith, as much as the scripture on which they rested, and in whose words they should be expressed, should be open to all alike. To talk sacramental doctrine in English was to make a direct attack on the deception and hypocrisy by which the faith of scripture had been ousted and the people led into error.

In the differences over transubstantiation semantics merged with doctrine. Wycliffe, whose historical razor was here at its sharpest, took the words used by the church as evidence of its error in deviating from scripture. He looked back to the time before Berengar, when the truth had not yet become concealed behind a screen of terms. It seemed clear to him that the new church, not the early church, unfaithfully and without foundation, dreamt up the word 'transubstantiation', which had brought uncertainties and ambiguities into the faith of the eucharist. *Transsubstanciacio*, like *impanatio* and *identificacio* (which existed only in the language of the schools) were all regarded by Wycliffe as 'unfounded novelties', representing doctrine that was recent and without scriptural basis. 'The multitude of these terms', he wrote in *De eucharistia*, 'introduced without authority of scripture, has greatly altered and troubled the church.' To correct doctrine it was necessary to correct errors of speech, which meant returning to the catholic truths of scripture. 'Since the law of scripture has given us sufficient belief concerning the eucharist, it seems presumptuous folly to add novelties to this foundation.' This argument (what Netter called Wycliffe's 'calumny of terms') was of the most direct relevance for lay learning, given the distance of the doctrine of transubstantiation from

---

[44] MS Bodley 647, fo. 70 v (Appendix, p. 71). Compare William Thorpe's reply, below n. 99.

Wycliffe's recommendation that 'we ought openly to tell the people the sentences of scripture necessary to salvation'.[45]

The secrets of sacramental theology (what Wycliffe calls *arcana eucharistie*)[46] were not for lay people. Belief in the sacrament of the altar for those outside the schools entailed accepting the real presence, but not questioning or seeking to understand the miraculous change that took place in the nature of the bread. One received the presence of Christ on the altar as one received the consecrated host, as something given by the clergy. The mystery of the sacrament was veiled. The terminology used by schoolmen in discussing this theology formed part of the veil, as expressions of a world beyond the layman's ken. Words such as *transsubstanciacio, accidens, substancia, subjectare, quidditas*, belonged to quite another sphere of discussion and explication from that of popular preaching. They were alien to vernacular religious instruction up the third quarter of the fourteenth century. Unneeded by laity, they had no English equivalents.

> Lore is ȝouen to cristen men,
> In-to flesch passeþ þe bred;
> As holychirche doþ vs kenne,
> Þe wyn, to blod, þat is so red.
> Þou seest not fleschly þou takest þenne;
> Þy byleve of herte, makeþ þe fast fro ded,
> . . . . . .[47]

---

[45] *De euch.*, pp. 47-9: 'debemus enim loqui palam populo sentencias scripture necessarias ad salutem . . . novella ecclesia ponit transsubstanciacionem panis et vini in corpus Christi et sanguinem; hoc autem non posuit ecclesia primitiva . . . Hic videtur michi quod ecclesia primitiva illud non posuit, sed ecclesia novella, ut quidam infideliter et infundabiliter sompniantes baptizarunt terminum et fantasiarunt multa false ad onus ecclesie . . . Cum enim transsubstanciari sit terminus magistralis, licet fideli trahere eius significacionem ad quemcunque sensum katholicum particularem et sic videtur ambigue et incomplete innuere fidem ecclesie de Euckaristia'; p. 218, ' . . . multitudo talium terminorum introducta sine auctoritate scripture multum alteravit et perturbavit ecclesiam'; p. 229, 'Cum ergo lex scripture tradidit nobis de eukaristia sufficiens ad credendum, videtur quod sit presumptuosa stulticia preter eius fundacionem superaddere novitates'. See also pp. 223, 273, 283, 285-7,293 and 324 for the apology at the end of the book for the scholastic treatment necessary to show the errors of eucharistic doctrine. Cf. *De apos.*, p. 113: 'Et quantum ad materias scolastice practicandas, videtur michi quod standum est in declaracione fidei scripture cum sua logica'. For the phrase *infundabiles novitates* see *Trial.*, p. 350. The sixth of the twenty-four conclusions condemned in 1382 was the pertinacious assertion 'non esse fundatum in evangelio quod Christus missam ordinavit'. Netter, *Doctrinale*, ii, cc. 74-5, col. 447 on, considers Wycliffe's objections to the terms 'accident', 'subject', 'transubstantiation' and *'panis materialis'* as not to be found in scripture. On Berengar of Tour's influence on the development of eucharistic terminology see G. Macy, *The Theologies of the Eucharist in the Early Scholastic Period* (Oxford, 1984), pp. 40, 52-3.

[46] *FZ*, p. 117; *De apos.*, p. 220.

[47] *Twenty-Six Political and Other Poems*, ed. J. Kail (EETS, 124, 1904), pp. 104-5 from 'Of the sacrament of the Altere' in MS Digby 102. The next stanzas include; 'Under dyverce spices [species] only tokenynges, / Though the spices fro hym be went', and 'He dwelleth under ayther spys' which, together with the lines 'In byleve of holychirche, who wyl hym yoken,/ Agen this, non argument may make', seem to reflect the development of vernacular discussion on the eucharist by the early fifteenth century.

Belief of heart called for no quiddities, but for worship and devotion. The sacrament of the altar received by communicants at Easter was 'Christ's own body in likeness of bread'.[48] Their participation was an act of faith, not comprehension.

'In the affairs of the faith', said Netter, 'skilled spiritual men are said to *understand*: the rest of the people only simply to *believe*.' A contemporary of Netter's, a monk with a background of Oxford theology, brought the same point home in a sermon that appears to have been preached in Latin for the benefit of an educated layman. Lay persons ought to believe that by virtue of Christ's words, pronounced by the priest at mass, the body and blood of Christ were present under the species of bread and wine. 'But', continued this preacher, 'the subtlety and circumstances of this point, the manner in which the taste and colour of the bread and wine remain without the substance of bread and wine and other circumstances which ought not to be considered here, are not for you to know, do not appertain to you.'[49]

'Welcome, lord, in form of bread': 'Hail flesch, hail blood'. These were the phrases that marked the perimeters of lay sacramental learning.

> I þe honoure wiþ al my miht
> In fourme of Bred as i þe se,
>
> . . . . . .
>
> Þi flesch, þi blod is swete of siht,
> Þi Sacrament honoured to be,
> Of Bred and Wyn wiþ word i-diht;
> Almihti lord, I leeve in þe.[50]

---

[48] *The Lay Folks Mass Book*, ed. T.F. Simmons (EETS, 71, 1879), p. 118: *Jacob's Well*, i, ed. A. Brandeis (EETS, 115, 1900), pp. 19, 59, 156.

[49] Netter, *Doctrinale*, ii, c. 44, col. 277 (after citing Augustine): 'Vere infra eundem ambitum fidei periti spirituales dicuntur *intelligere*: caeteri populares solum simpliciter *credere*'; R.M. Haines, 'Church, Society and Politics in the Early Fifteenth Century as Viewed from an English Pulpit', *SCH*, 12 (1975), p. 154 n. 78, and on those addressed, pp. 144, 153 n. 75. See also the reproof of lay meddling in eucharistic theology in a sermon written between *c.* 1378 and *c.* 1417 in *Middle English Sermons*, ed. W.O. Ross (EETS, 209, 1940), pp. 127-8 ('the argumentes and the skill that may be of the Sacramente . . . longeth not to the . . . to the that arte a lewd man . . . it is inowyth to the to beleven as holychurche techeth the and lat the clerkes alone with the argumentes'); J. Coleman, *English Literature in History, 1350-1400* (London, 1981), pp. 206-8. Hoccleve's rebuke of Oldcastle on this matter was significantly succinct: 'Thow errest foule eeke in the sacrament / Of the Auter, but how in special / For to declare it needith nat at al; / It knowen is in many a Regioun': *Hoccleve's Works: The Minor Poems*, ed. F.J. Furnivall and I. Gollancz, rev. J. Mitchell and A.I. Doyle (EETS, extra series, 61 and 73, 1970), p. 11. On the limitations of lay understanding of the mass see Manning, *People's Faith*, pp. 4-16 (also p. 69 on difficulties of belief); A. Hudson and H.L. Spencer, 'Old Author, New Work: The Sermons of MS Longleat 4', *Medium Aevum*, 53 (1984), p. 227; also, for the assumptions governing an earlier period, M. Richter, 'A Socio-Linguistic Approach to the Latin Middle Ages', *SCH*, 11 (1975), pp. 69-82.

[50] *The Minor Poems of the Vernon MS*, pt. I ed. C. Horstman (EETS, 98, 1892), pp. 24-5 (from prayers at the elevation): *The Minor Poems of John Lydgate*, ed. H.N. MacCracken (EETS, extra series, 107, 1911), pp. 99, 101; *Twenty-Six Poems*, p. 40; *Lay Folks Mass Book*, pp. 40-1, 130; Kolve, *Corpus Christi*, pp. 71, 81.

'In form of bread': the simple formula was the laconic lay equivalent for transubstantiation in all its complexities.

The use of Latin involved grave dogmatic, as well as linguistic proprieties. The unseemliness of exposing holy mysteries to the raw intelligence and unsophisticated language of the laity was often expressed. 'Many things are to be hidden and not shown to the people, lest being known and familiar they should be cheapened', wrote the author of an early fifteenth-century determination on Bible translation that has been attributed to the Dominican Thomas Palmer. 'The mysteries of the faith', he added, 'are not to be communicated to the simple, nor written' – and Bede was cited in support of this principle. Holy mysteries could be discussed only by those properly equipped to do so, and in the correct language. Latin terms were part of the opacity of eucharistic doctrine. They had no English forms because they needed none. 'Not only is the English language lacking in letters, but also in expressions', wrote Palmer (if it was he), 'since there are no English words and expressions [*nomina neque dictiones*] corresponding to the most well-known and common expressions in Latin'. Though his chief concern was with scriptural translation, some of the examples he cited were particularly relevant to sacramental theology: *ens, substantia, accidens, quantitas, qualitas*.[51]

It is surely one of the more remarkable achievements of the Wycliffites that in the course of a generation they changed all this. Though Palmer and his ilk were obstinate in their refusal to acknowledge the new state of affairs, already by the time these words were written, vernacular terms of the kind claimed to be non-existent were in use. By the end of the fourteenth century the English language had been injected with a range of new words, making it possible to do something that previously was as impossible as it had seemed undesirable: to discuss the doctrine of the eucharist in the vernacular. A number of the words essential for this activity had arrived in English, with their theological meaning, by 1400: for example *subject, substance, accident, transubstantiate, transubstantiation*. Nor was their use restricted to the works of Wycliffites, for they are also to be found in the writings of Chaucer and Trevisa.[52]

[51] M. Deanesley, *The Lollard Bible and Other Medieval Biblical Versions* (Cambridge, 1920), pp. 421, 425, 428, 429; A. Hudson, 'The Debate on Bible Translation, Oxford 1401', *EHR*, 90 (1975), pp. 1, 15-16; Hudson, 'English Heresy?', pp. 273-4. Though the problems of translating the Bible were distinct from those of englishing theology, there was a clear connection in the minds of objectors between the translation of 'holy writ . . . holy doctors, and . . . philosophy', as expressed in Trevisa's *Dialogue between a Lord and a Clerk upon translation*; Fowler, *Bible in Early English Literature*, p. 159.

[52] *MED, accident* 2(a) and (b); *forme* 14b; on *species* ('spices'), see above n. 47. (The *MED* fascicle containing *qualite, quantite* and *quidite,* though published, had unfortunately not crossed the Atlantic when I was writing this essay). The entries under 'subget' so far collected for the *MED* reflect the overwhelmingly Wycliffite context for this theological eucharistic usage. Chaucer, *Canterbury Tales,* The Pardoner's Tale, C 538-9; 'Thise cookes, how they stampe, and streyne, and grynde, / And turnen substaunce into accident'; *On the Properties of Things: John Trevisa's translation of Bartholomaeus Anglicus De proprietatibus rerum* (Oxford, 1975), i, p. 548; 'Cene Day is day of reconciliacioun, of transubstanciacioun, of consecracioun . . . ' For the philosophical

Clearly it was the Wycliffites who were responsible in the first instance for publishing this terminology. Their successful innovation on this score placed the church authorities in an awkward predicament. The usual process of public penance and vernacular recantation could itself perpetuate the offence. A heretic who recanted eucharistic error could scarcely be allowed to publicize the damaging words he repented of; yet failing to gainsay them might seem a defect in penance and refutation, and indirectly to encourage the offence. The greatest care was called for, and we can see signs of the church's anxiety.

An individual case which shows how the church reacted to this problem is the abjuration of William Sawtry at Lynn in the diocese of Norwich on 25 May 1399. Sawtry was given a schedule of the points he had abjured. They were in English and were to be publicly declared to the people. The eighth point concerned the eucharist.

> I sey that I helde it by fals and wrong informacion but now I knowe welle that it is eresye and that brede a none that the word of the sacrament is seyde it is no longer brede materiall but that it is turned in to verry crystes body and that I swere here.[53]

The interesting thing about this is that Sawtry, described as *capellanus pretensus*, allegedly a chaplain, was evidently quite capable in Latin. This became clear at his final examination two years later, when Archbishop Arundel questioned him in some detail on the question of transubstantiation. The eighth article of the Norwich trial, as transcribed in the Canterbury register, records Sawtry's Latin submission.

> Item quantum ad octavum articulum . . . dicit, quod ille panis transubstantiatur in corpus Christi post prolacionem verborum sacramentalium et desinit esse panis eiusdem nature.[54]

terms *fourme accidental, fourme substancyal, accident, qualite, subiecte* and *substaunce* see i, p. 554; ii, pp. 1268, 1355. Cf. the English tract on confession in *English Works of Wyclif*, p. 345; 'And thus power that prestis han standeth not in transubstansinge of the oste, ne in makyng of accidentis for to stonde bi hemsilf'. Coleman, *English Literature in History*, p. 212.

[53] Wilkins, iii, p. 258; Reg Arundel (Lambeth), ii, fo. 182 v. This abjuration, before bishop, clergy and people, was followed the next day by an oath not to preach his conclusions or hear confessions without licence. McFarlane, *John Wycliffe*, p. 151.

[54] Reg. Arundel, ii, fo. 180 v; Wilkins, iii, p. 254 and following, cited at 258. See pp. 354-5 for Oldcastle's trial at which his statement 'that the most worschipfull sacrament of the auter is Cristes body in forme of bred' was insufficient, and he was required to give his opinion on the statement 'that after the sacramental wordes ben sayde by a prest in hys masse the material bred that was bifore is turned in to cristis verray body and the material wyn that was byfore is turned in to cristis verray blode and so ther leeveth in the auter no material brede ne material wyn wych wer ther by fore the seyng of the sacramental wordes'. Reg. Arundel, ii, fo. 144 r.

The seemingly insignificant variations of wording in the two languages reflect the conceptual divide. In the English there is no mention of transubstantiation – officially there *was* no English word for it; this fell outside lay belief. And the vernacular abjuration does not mention the *nature* of the bread, merely states it is no longer material bread. The differences, most conscious and deliberate, were the differences of two worlds.

The bishops could not avoid, to their chagrin, participating in the sacrilege of English theology, but they were strict in censoring out the dangerous vernacular terminology. When Archbishop Courtenay wrote on 12 June 1382 ordering the chancellor of Oxford to see to the publication of the twenty-four condemned conclusions to clergy and people, in English as well as Latin, he specified that this was to be done 'without searching explanation of terms [*absque terminorum curiosa explicatione*]'.[55] Perhaps he thought there had been too much of that already.

Worries about the dangers of popularizing scholastic theology are written across Archbishop Arundel's Oxford Constitutions of 1407. Preachers (and he obviously had vernacular sermons in mind) must suit their words to their audiences. This meant not only restricting the castigation of sins to the persons and classes of those present, but avoiding 'scandalous words' on the topic of the eucharist, or other sacraments. Too little theology might be preferable to too much, and even schoolmasters were warned off instruction on the sacrament of the altar and other theological matters that might prove contentious. Philosophical terminology must be kept where it belonged: 'Since the determinator of all things cannot be confined in philosophical terms, and the blessed Augustine often recalled true conclusions, because they were offensive in the ears of religious . . . ', no one of whatever rank or status was to propound in the course of disputing or communicating any propositions that might sound discordant with the faith, whether inside the schools or outside, 'even if they were capable of supporting such with subtlety of terms' – again that pejorative phrase, *terminorum curiositate*.[56]

---

[55] Wilkins, iii, pp. 159-60; *FZ*, pp. 309-11. However, I would not like to rest too much on this phrase, which also appears in the 1377 papal bulls to Oxford (*sive terminorum curiosa implicatione nitantur defendere; Chronicon Angliae*, p. 175; Dahmus, *Prosecution*, p. 47) and may already have been a stock formula for academic equivocation. Cf. M. Wilks, 'The Early Oxford Wyclif: Papalist or Nominalist?', *SCH*, 5 (1969), p. 87 n. 4 on the pejorative meaning of sophism.

[56] Wilkins, iii, pp. 316-17, constitutions 3, 4, 5 and 8. The need to discriminate between different sorts of hearers (especially the different levels of lay and clerical learning), treated in constitution 3, had long been stressed in ecclesiastical legislation and we can see Wycliffe taking account of it (below pp. 61, 62-3). Haines, 'Education', pp. 161-2, 169. On the blameworthy sense at this period of the words 'curiosity' and 'curious' as implying an inquisitive desire to know things one had no right to learn, see *MED curious* 1(d) and *curiousite* 2(a), 3(a); Hudson and Spencer, 'Old Author, New Work', p. 232, cf. 223. Lollards definitely became associated with curiosity of this kind; see Hoccleve's complaint (*Minor Poems,* p. 13) about those who ask, '"Why stant this word heere?" and "why this word there?"/ "Why spake god thus, and seith thus elles where?"'.

We must now retrace our steps once more, to see if we can elucidate the part that Wycliffe may have played in this vernacular teaching and writing about the sacrament of the altar. There are three types of evidence to consider: what others said; what Wycliffe himself said; and English texts that he might have written.

Statements made near the middle of the fifteenth century may seem too late to carry much weight, but can still throw light on the question. Pecock made some revealing remarks about lay people's attitude to the eucharist, in the course of explaining the Trinity in his *Reule of Crysten Religioun* (1443). Anxious to rebut the idea that he was encouraging dangerous lay arguments on the topic, Pecock retorted: in that case, what about the eucharist? The common people found it hard to credit articles of belief for which there was no evidence. Where the sacrament of the altar was concerned, the church called on them to believe first, that after the sacramental words there was no bodily bread in the priest's hands, but the bread ceased to be; second, that no matter how many portions the eucharistic bread was broken into, and how small each fragment, in each piece would be 'all the full and whole, long and great Christ's body'. If the church thinks it safe to entrust this doctrine to the people, argued Pecock, what I have said about the Trinity can scarcely be called dangerously contentious. Then he added: 'well I know that many of the lay party believe amiss in matter of the eucharist', but there were particular reasons for this.

> þei camen into her erring bi summe clerkis, namelich Johan Wicliffe and hise disciplis, which token bi occasioun of holy writt not wele undirstondyn þe seid errour to þe comoun peple; and what for þe affeccioun whiche þe comoun peple haþ to þe persoonys, and what for þe truste to þe leving of þoo persoonys, and what for þe seemyng of scripture, þei contynuen her erryng . . .[57]

Pecock regarded eucharistic misbelief among the common people as arising from the false teaching of Wycliffe and others, not from an innate disposition to question difficult doctrine.

A generation earlier, less than twenty-five years after Wycliffe's death, a Carthusian translator was more explicit. The short treatise on the sacrament that Nicholas Love appended to his *Myrrour of the Blessed Lyf of Jesu Christ*

See Haines, 'Church, Society and Politics', p. 153 n. 75, on 'isti laici qui nesciunt litteras volunt se smater de profundissima clerimonia', moving high matters and posing the most difficult questions to any clerk; B. Smalley, *Studies in Medieval Thought and Learning* (London, 1981), p. 403.

[57] *Reule*, pp. 71-99, cc. 8-13 of treatise 1, cited at 95-6. The difficulties of the church's eucharistic doctrine were fully treated by Aquinas in the *Summa contra gentiles*, iv, cc. 61-9, see in particular c. 62.

throws interesting light on the development of eucharistic heresy by 1410 – and it is not out of the question that this text received some kind of official encouragement. It was written expressly to refute the heretics who, placing false trust in the power of reason and the evidence of their senses, believed that the bread remained in the sacrament. Eucharistic heresy was the result of misapplying the philosophy of the schools to the doctrine of the church. 'It is great folly and spiritual peril to seek curiously in imagination of reason the marvels of this worthy sacrament.' This 'most marvel of all marvels' belonged to the heights of faith that were removed from the intellect, and the reason why *mychel folk* were deceived was that they chose rather to give credence to what 'a great clerk teaches according to natural reason, than to what holy church teaches hereof only in belief above reason'.

Love, therefore, set about explaining the miraculous nature of the sacrament, and throughout his treatise stressed above all 'the marvels thereof', that were 'above the reason of man'. In the last resort, however, and at the end of his text, he moved just as far into the heretics' territory and terminology as was necessary to complete his refutation, in view of the undoubted fact that the Lollards were misled by the 'great clergy and kunning of philosophy' of their master. Aristotelian philosophy, said Love, was Wycliffe's undoing, for it was Aristotle who had taught him that the accidents of bread and wine, the colour, savour and so on, could not exist without the substance.

> And for as meche as this doctryne of holy chirche is aȝenst the principles of philosophie, that is naturel science, therfore the forseide maister of lollardes reprovede hit and scornede hit: and so he errede hym self and made many othere to erre touchinge the byleve of this holyest sacrament . . .

Love had made the same point in one of the interpolations he added to the *Myrrour*, where also he touched on the miracle of accidents existing without 'their kindly subject'. He there excused his vocabulary. 'These termes I touche here so specially by cause of the lewed lollardes that medlen hem agenst the feith falsely.'[58]

A number of theologians disputed with Wycliffe on the eucharist during his

---

[58] N. Love, *The Mirrour of the Blessed Lyf of Jesu Christ,* ed. L.F. Powell (Oxford, 1908), pp. 205-11, 301-24, quoted at 207-8, 301, 303, 306-7, 319-21. For the presentation of this work to Archbishop Arundel and his inspection and approval of it in 1410 see E. Salter, *Nicholas Love's 'Myrrour of the Blessed Lyf of Jesu Christ', Analecta Cartusiana,* 10 (1974), pp. 1-2; Doyle, 'A Survey', pp. 140-1; idem, 'Reflections on Some Manuscripts of Nicholas Love's *Myrrour of the Blessed Lyf of Jesu Christ', Leeds Studies in English,* new series 14 (1983), pp. 82-93. Doyle suggests that the work may have been circulating some while before it was approved by Arundel, and the fact that the archbishop was in 1400 given fraternity of Mount Grace might indicate his knowledge of or support for the project. (On this see below p. 82 n. 37). By no means all the manuscripts (on which see Salter) include the treatise on the sacrament; a note in one (Salter, p. 14) shows the kind of annoyance Love's harping on the miraculous had for those of Lollard persuasion.

lifetime. They included John Tissington, Thomas Winterton and William Rimington, who belonged respectively to the Franciscan, Augustinian and Cistercian orders. Tissington and Winterton both produced replies to the *Confessio* on the eucharist which Wycliffe (lifting a series of passages from the penultimate chapter of his *De apostasia*) published on 10 May 1381. Their texts, written not long after the appearance of this document, are of interest for what they say of the spread of false teaching. Rimington's work, probably somewhat later, tells more of this aspect of the question and was taken up by Wycliffe in a long reply in the autumn of 1383.[59]

John Tissington, who was one of the twelve masters on Chancellor Barton's commission, called his long reply to Wycliffe's *Confessio* his own *Confessio*. He remarked in it on the scale and nature of popular eucharistic error. Heretics today, he said, are openly teaching that the bread and wine remain in their nature after the consecration, and so far had this gone that it was reported that in many places of the realm people were refusing to communicate at Easter, believing the host to be no more than holy bread. Those 'subtle searchers of scripture' (whose knowledge of holy writ is so vaunted these days, though many think without good cause) might argue about the church's terminology. But where scripture was silent as to form and species, there was a safe and certain tradition for the use of these terms, dating from patristic times. Tissington himself explained the words used by the church for the eucharistic flesh and blood in order to show that many kinds of expression, substantive, verbal and adverbial, were properly applied to the body of Christ. But these terms, relating to how Christ was seen and felt in the sacrament, must be carefully safeguarded when speaking in the vernacular and before lay people,

---

[59] For these and other replies to Wycliffe, see Gynn, *Austin Friars,* pp. 225-7, 260-1; N.R. Ker, *Medieval Manuscripts in British Libraries,* ii, (Oxford 1977), pp. 686-7. Woodford's comprehensive seventy-two *questiones De sacramento altaris* (of 1383-4) referred to doubts about Christ's presence in the divided portions of the host as 'heresis vulgi et simplicium'; Bodley MS 703, fo. 107 r. For the *Confessio* see *FZ,* pp. 115-32; Thomson, *Latin Writings,* pp. 69-71 (note the unusual number of English manuscripts of this text). It seems to have escaped notice and is of some interest (both for the development of this topic and the growing resistance to Wycliffe's views), that the *whole* text of the *Confessio* corresponds, word for word, with large sections of c. xvi of *De apostasia* (see pp. 213/2-16, 219/32-221/13, 222/40-229/37, 230/21-231/9). This may originally have been the concluding chapter of *De apostasia,* for the editor suggests (p. xxxv) that c. xvii, now the last, may have been tacked on as a supplement or appendix (compare the supplement added to the *Trialogus,* which likewise included repetition and vituperation against the friars). *De apostasia* is the middle book of a fairly self-contained trilogy, standing between *De simonia,* of about early 1380, and *De blasphemia,* of mid-1381: it probably dates from late 1380 to early 1381. Both Wycliffe's action in publishing an abstract of this book, and the volley of replies to his so-called *Confessio* – a reaction much more considerable than anything provoked by the long treatments of *De eucharistia* and *De apostasia* – suggests the impact of events that took place during the later months of 1380 and early 1381. We may reasonably postulate that Wycliffe was stung into reformulating or reiterating (a favourite vice!) his view of the eucharist by the judgement of Chancellor Barton's council, perhaps adding another chapter to *De apostasia* at the same time.

keeping strictly to the formula 'in form and kind of bread'. Otherwise the people, prone to idolatry and lacking ability to distinguish what was felt in a thing from what was felt through it, might fall into pagan error.[60]

Thomas Winterton, whose answer to Wycliffe was entitled, peculiarly, *Absolutio*, also dealt with this point. Speaking of the different ways of interpreting scripture, Winterton criticized those who, 'speaking largely and figuratively' said that the eucharistic bread 'is the flesh of Christ', taking the word 'is' for the word 'signifies'. For, Winterton went on, 'these figurative expressions ought not to be spread about as faith necessary to salvation among the lay people, or less lettered, or less learned', since they had no means of knowing how to distinguish between literal and figurative speech, between things done and things signified. It was only learned men who were able to see beyond the direct and obvious meanings of common words. Hence the danger of error and heresy. He quoted Gregory on the fearful nature of mystery, which could seem one thing and be understood as another. It was essential to make clear that what the sacrament of the altar seemed – namely the form of bread – was no other than what was there understood – namely the true body of Christ.[61] ('Welcome, Lord, in form of bread', with no misunderstandings about accident, subject and signification).

Both Tissington and Winterton imply, therefore, that the faith of unlearned laymen was being put at risk through inappropriate eucharistic teaching,

[60] *FZ*, pp. 133-80, at pp. 143-5, 151, 178, 'Dicitur enim quod in multis locis huius regni populus abstinet ab eucharistia in paschate'; cf above p. 294; see also *De euch.*, p. 123, contrasting the consecrated host with holy bread, and *De blas.*, pp. 89-90, where Wycliffe's remarks about Barton's council are related to the Easter sacrament and beliefs about *ille panis consecratus*, p. 173 ('non tamen vulgariter, et coram laicis, conceditur communiter videri aut sentiri [corpus Christi], nisi cum hac determinatione, in forma et specie panis; ne populus pronus ad idolatriam, nesciens distinguere inter sensibile in se, et sensibile in alio, credat speciem panis, aut aliud quod immediate et in se sentitur, esse corpus Christi; et sic ut dictum est, turpieter paganizent'). The *scripture scrutatores* (p. 144) presumably alludes to well-used biblical words; see John 5:39 and Acts 17:11. For Netter, see above n. 45. Tissington's *Confessio* is dated 1381 in MS Bodley 703, fo. 65 v. On Tissington see Emden (O), iii, pp. 1879-80.

[61] *FZ*, pp. 181-238, cited at p. 197 on *predicatio identica* and *predicatio tropologica vel figurativa* ('Ubi pane ponit quod ibi videtur, scilicet formam panis, non esse aliud quod ibi intelligitur, scilicet verum corpus panis'). This central question of the different scriptural forms of speech is discussed by Wycliffe in the eucharistic context in various places (stressing the distinctions between *predicatio ydemptica* and *predicacio tropica*, or between *predicacio formalis, essentialis et habitudinalis*). *De euch.*, pp. 38-41, 200, 225, 230-1, 303-4; De apos., pp. 51, 71-2, 104-6; *Trial.*, pp. 201-2, 266ff; see *English Wycliffite Sermons*, i, p. 347; *Selections*, ed. Hudson, pp. 114, 193-4; Netter, *Doctrinale* ii, c. 20, col. 143 (calling Wycliffe *iste magnus Doctor signorum*), c. 86, col. 515 (referring to this English sermon). On Winterton, see Gwynn, *Austin Friars*, pp. 225-6, 234-5, 260-1, 270 (giving the summer of 1381 as the date the *Absolutio* was published); Emden (O), iii, p. 2062.

teaching that disregarded the common limitations of the vernacular. The exchanges between Wycliffe and Willian Rimington, which lasted several years, also bear on this question.

Rimington, who was prior of the Cistercian house of Sawley in Yorkshire, a doctor of theology and in 1372-3 chancellor of Oxford, became engaged in controversy with Wycliffe as the result of his action in listing twenty-six heretical and erroneous points propounded by Wycliffe, and countering with forty-five conclusions of his own. These conclusions were largely concerned with questions of papal and clerical powers, temporalities and poverty, but three of them were about eucharistic doctrine. Wycliffe, provoked by this charge, replied at length, and finally Rimington, after Wycliffe's death, wrote a defensive riposte in the form of a dialogue between catholic truth and heretical depravity – an onslaught against the doctor of modern error whose 'pestiferous doctrine' persisted among his unknown disciples.[62]

Rimington makes perfectly clear that he is not writing against academic heresy alone. He was concerned with those who (under the cloak of piety, sanctity and perfection) were deceiving and leading into heresy many of the smally lettered, the *simpliciter litterati*, a phrase that appears in both the heading and text of his tracts.[63] He writes of this as a recent phenomenon, and among the examples he gives of the damaging effect of 'this sect' was the 'foul

[62] J. McNulty, 'William of Rymyngton, Prior of Salley Abbey, Chancellor of Oxford, 1372-3, *YAJ*, 30 (1930-1), pp. 231-47; Emden (O), iii, p. 1617; Workman, *John Wyclif*, ii, pp. 122-3; Hudson, *Premature Reformation*, pp. 45-6. These exchanges, of which only Wycliffe's side is in print, are to be found as follows: (i) Rimington's twenty-six errors and forty-five conclusions, MS Bodley 158, fos. 199 r – 217 r; (2) Wycliffe's reply to forty-four conclusions (omitting no. 15), *Opera minora*, pp. 201-57 (the reference p. 230 to preaching *in pugna nuper Flandrensium* dates this to late 1382 or 1383 – bearing in mind that the preaching – see also pp. 206, 245-6 – of the Despenser crusade antedated its inception by some months; M. Aston, 'The Impeachment of Bishop Despenser', *BIHR*, 38 (1965), pp. 127-8, 133-4; cf. Thomson, *Latin Writings*, pp. 233-4, no. 384 (3) Rimington's incomplete Dialogue, MS Bodley 158, fos. 188 r – 197 r, datable to after 31 Dec. 1384 from the reference to the death of Wycliffe, fo. 188 r ('quidam doctor modernorum errorum et heresium . . . mortuus est et eius doctrina pestifera in variis scriptis et in quibusdam ignotis in suis discipulis perseverat . . .). Rimington's twenty-six heresies and errors, though covering the main matters dealt with in the twenty-four conclusions condemned at Blackfriars, are differently worded, less clearly organized, and have both omissions and additions (in particular more points relating to clerical temporalities and lay rights of correction). This raises the possibility that Rimington wrote *before* the council published its condemnation, since on the face of it, it seems unlikely he would have drawn up another parallel list once the twenty-four points were known.

[63] MS Bodley 158, fo. 199 r: 'Iste sunt in summa conclusiones heretice seu erronie que nuper traxerunt in errorem multos simpliciter litteratos'; fo. 200 v, 'Incipit prologus in doctrinam simpliciter litteratorum contra hereses nuper in anglia exortas'; fo. 202 r, 'ad infeccionem simplicium'; fo. 216 v, against those who 'loquendi ecclesie et simpliciter litteratis sunt occasio et causa erroris'.

letter, full of blasphemy, provoking temporal lords and all the people to prosecute the supreme pontiff as a profane apostate and blasphemer'.[64] Rimington listed the events that revealed the working of this poisonous doctrine: first, the resistance which, with the aid of the secular arm, had been offered to the correction of the bishops in London (presumably alluding to Wycliffe's appearances at St Paul's and Lambeth); secondly, the opposition at Oxford to the correction of the chancellor, which threatened the liberties of the university; and thirdly, the rising of the community in London on Corpus Christi Day, itself a reflection of heretical depravity, since the heretics' preaching (including the ability of lay lords to remove temporalities, from which lay people could draw obvious deductions about their power to correct lords and kings) had not been checked, as it should have been, by the ordinaries.[65]

William Rimington, then, was among those contemporaries who saw a connection between the events of 1381 and recent heretical developments. There was nothing unusual about this viewpoint. But, since he seems to have been writing close to these events, we may listen with respect to his observations, even if not accepting his conclusions. Rimington believed that ordinary people had become widely infected by heretical teaching before the 1381 rising, and this spread of heresy included Wycliffe's false view of the eucharist. Though it is not stated in so many words, the direct implication is that the *simpliciter litterati* – those who learnt only through the vernacular – had been imbibing erroneous teaching about the sacramental bread.

Wycliffe's reply opened with an angry retort against this slur on evangelical preachers. Faithful priests upholding the gospel could (he said) rejoice in being called *ydiote* by the ungodly satraps, finding comfort in the words of Acts 4.13 – words which (we may reflect) might be taken as a kind of charter for vernacular evangelizing. For this chapter describes how Peter and John were arrested for their preaching to the people, having converted about five thousand, and when examined caused astonishment in their questioners who; 'when they saw the boldness of Peter and John, and perceived that they were unlearned and

---

[64] MS Bodley 158, fo. 201 r: 'per quamdam epistolam maledictam presumpcionis et blasfemie plenam provocans dominos temporales et populos universos ad prosequendum ipsum summum pontificem tanquam prophanum apostatam et blasphemum': margin, 'nota pro epistola maledicta'. If, as seems possible, this refers to the 'Letter to Pope Urban' (*Opera minora*, pp. 1-2: *FZ*, pp. 341-2) it supports the date of 1378 for this address; McFarlane, *John Wycliffe* p. 89; Workman, *John Wyclif*, i, p. 310, ii, p. 315; Dahmus, *Prosecution*, pp. vi, 141-8; Thomson, *Latin Writings*, pp. 259-61, no. 404. See above, p. 33 for Wycliffe's tone towards the curia in 1378.

[65] MS Bodley 158, fo. 202 r: 'Talis doctrina pestifera verisimiliter fuit iam nuper movens communitatem ad insurgendum contra regem et proceres huius regni quod fatuitatis factum ad finalem destruccionem tam sacerdocii quam milicie in anglia cessisset'. This was the third sign of the effects of the sect, says Rimington, seemingly implying that the royal intervention in Oxford quarrels preceded the 1381 rising. His remarks about this might therefore be set beside the story in *Eulogium historiarum*, iii, pp. 348-9, which linked the chancellor's citation before the council on 22 March 1378/9 with proceedings agingt Wycliffe. Wilkins, iii, p. 137; Dahmus, *Prosecution*, pp. 62-4; Workman, *John Wyclif*, i, pp. 305-6.

ignorant men, they marvelled; and they took knowledge of them'. The Vulgate terms here are worth noticing: *quod homines essent sine litteris et idiotae*.[66] The *simplices sacerdotes* whom Wycliffe defended from Rimington's attack, and the simple who were seen to have been misled, all alike perforce (as *simpliciter litterati*, if not *sine litteris*) communicated in the vernacular.

It seems mistaken to regard Wycliffe's doctrine of the eucharist as 'too academic to be of any practical consequence'.[67] Of course at the heart of his quarrel with current sacramental dogma lay a metaphysical conviction that it was impossible for accidents to exist without subject. But his impassioned concern with the nature of contemporary untruth always had its pastoral element. The presentation of the host as an aggregation of accidents was a matter of common concern. 'The people and a thousand bishops' said Wycliffe, 'understand neither accident nor subject', so why was this novelty, that did not exist in scripture, introduced only to cause difficulty to the faithful?[68] The sacrament of the altar had become a mystery of the wrong kind.

Wycliffe's weighty expositions of the doctrine of the eucharist not only show the important place the laity occupied in his thought, but also contain hints of his vernacular addresses on the subject. It is clear from his prolonged discussions which filled two long books (*De eucharistia* and *De apostasia*), as well as spilling over into many other writings, long and short, that Wycliffe regarded the layman's belief as highly relevant to scholastic interpretation of the sacrament. Thomas Netter was to challenge him posthumously for this approach.[69] The church's departure from the original scriptural eucharist was measured and demonstrated for Wycliffe by its present-day inability to explain its sacramental doctrine to believers. 'God tells the faithful to call the sacrament of the altar bread.' Wycliffe's attack on transubstantiation amounted to an attempt to peel off the accretions of scholastic philosophy and put sacramental doctrine back to where it had stood about the year 1000, using the words not of transubstantiation, but of scripture. 'And as for questions

---

[66] Acts 4.13: 'videntes autem Petri constantiam et Iohannis conperto quod homines essent sine litteris et idiotae admirabantur . . . ', *Biblia sacra iuxta Vulgatam versionem,* ed. R. Weber (Stuttgart, 1969), ii, p. 1703; Hargreaves, 'Marginal Glosses', p. 287. *Opera minora,* p. 201 refers to *sacerdotes fideles* who, as evangelists, did not *scolastice didicerunt,* and see pp. 202, 234-5, 245 for Wycliffe's references to *sacerdotes simplices* – a phrase which was of old usage (for instance in ecclesiastical legislation); Thomson, *Latin Writings,* p. 233 remarks on his here defending sympathizers *extra scholas.*

[67] Leff, *Heresy* ii, p. 545. See also G. Leff, 'Ockham and Wyclif on the Eucharist', *Reading Medieval Studies,* 2 (1976), pp. 1-13. Important here is J.I. Catto, 'Wyclif and the Cult of the Eucharist', in *The Bible in the Medieval World,* ed. K. Walsh and D. Wood, *SCH,* subsidia 4 (Oxford 1985), pp. 269-86.

[68] 'Nam populus et mille episcopi nec intelligunt accidens nec subiectum; quomodo igitur introduceretur preter fidem scripture tam extranea et impossibilis novitas ad difficultandum fideles specialiter? cum illud accidens quod vocant panem sit infinitum imperfeccioris nature quam panis materialis'. *De apos.,* p. 60; see pp. 228-9, 230-1 on accidents without subject and the devotion of the people.

[69] Netter, *Doctrinale,* ii, c. 44, col. 275 et seq.

considered scholastically, it seems to me that one should stand on the decla-ration of the faith of scripture, with its own logic.' Lay people stood closer to true belief concerning the sacramental bread and wine than the Roman church, for, 'notwithstanding the error of glossators, this faith remained continuously in the church among the laity.'[70]

Lay understanding of the eucharist was never very far from Wycliffe's mind, for what the people believed, and the roots of their unbelief, were central both to his argument and his aim. He assumed some kind of relationship between plain speaking[71] – which could include scripture – and the faculty of common sense that controlled the belief of ordinary people. The limitations of belief and the limitations of speech ought both to be recognized, and accommodated.

> We ought to learn from the common experience of our senses, that the priest going to the altar makes [*conficit*] or consecrates from the bread and wine something which remains sensible, which the people understand as the body and blood of Christ.[72]

It was important not to neglect the evidence of the senses – what was felt, what was seen, what was tasted.

> Those who say that the host is falsely called bread and wine . . . are trying to mislead [*sophisticare*] the sense of the people, so that they should not believe what they plainly feel, but be driven to believe an incredible deception.[73]

Belief in the sacrament should not be made difficult beyond limit, as it was by the needless multiplication of arguments and refinements. The law of Christ should be open and accessible, like the form of scripture.[74]

Long before Bishop Pecock pointed out how eucharistic doctrine strained

---

[70] *De apos.,'* p. 121: 'Sicut igitur deus mandat fidelibus quod vocent sacramentum altaris panem vere indubie . . . Sed non erubesco ewangelium vocando hoc sacramentum panem, sicut spiritus sanctus vocat'; p. 113: 'Et quantum ad materias scolastice practicandas, videtur michi quod standum est in declaracione fidei scripture cum sua logica'; p. 223: 'Et, non obstante errore glosancium, ista fides mansit continue in ecclesia apud laycos'. Allusions to error starting in the second millennium are frequent; see pp. 66, 76, 113-14, 127, 128, 130, 147, 148, 160; also *FZ*, p. 114; Netter, *Doctrinale*, ii, c. 18, cols. 127-8; *Rogeri Dymmok Liber contra XII errores et hereses Lollardorum,* ed. H.S. Cronin (Wyclif Society, 1922), p. 93.

[71] For Wycliffe's recommendation of plain style see H. Hargreaves, 'Wyclif's Prose', *Essays and Studies* (1966), p. 3; P. Auksi, 'Wyclif's Sermons and the Plain Style', *ARG,* 66 (1975), pp. 5-23; *Sermones,* i, p. xi and *Praefatio*; iv, sermon 31, pp. 262-75 (p. 266 on the vainglory of the 'subtle theologian' seeking to distinguish his sowing of the word of God from that of the *sacerdos ruralis* . . . *exiliter literatus*; p. 271 on plain speech, *plana locucio*). It was a consistent part of Wycliffe's case that to call the eucharistic host bread would reduce the danger of idolatry; 'per hoc quod nominatur panis foret populus pronior ex naturali ingenio ad cognoscendum quod non est corpus Christi'; *De euch.,* p. 143.

[72] *Trial.,* p. 247.

[73] *De euch.,* p. 188. See also *De apos.,* pp. 149, 152, 160.

[74] *De euch.,* pp. 123-4.

the credulity of believers, Wycliffe had said exactly the same – and drawn different conclusions. Transubstantiation, together with the Trinity and the Incarnation, comprised the most difficult articles of faith, and if all three were rejected by Saracens, it was not surprising the faithful should ask questions. The object, white, round, and hard, that the priest consecrated on the altar, was perceptibly other in nature than Christ's body. And yet, according to the faith, 'the whole body of Christ, blood and spirit, is complete in every point of this sacrament, which among all mysteries of the faith seems the most difficult for a Christian to believe'.[75]

As far as quantity was concerned, no faithful theologian or even layman, said Wycliffe, believed that Christ was seven foot in every part of the host. The seven-foot body of Christ was in heaven, and it was not credible to the faithful that this dimensional body was in the host.[76] And if doubts were raised by common sense, they also arose from the intellect. To accept the creed was one thing: eucharistic belief another.

Wycliffe therefore regarded lay questions about the eucharist as natural, and themselves indicative of the church's falsehood. Suppose a layman of subtle intelligence were to go beyond the expectations of sacramental teaching and ask not 'if . . . ', but 'what . . . ' (*quid est*) of the consecrated host?[77] It could not, it should not, be assumed that questions of quiddity were of interest only to theologians. Understanding the quiddity of the sacrament was an intellectual activity, but that was no reason for deception. Wycliffe regarded it as an admission of error that the 'worshippers of signs' (*cultores signorum*) – as he called the defenders of transubstantiation – were unwilling and unable to explain their position.

> And although the consecrators of the accident know that the people worship the sacrament as the body of Christ, which they say is idolatry, yet they keep silent, fearing they will be asked about the quiddity [*quid sit hoc sacramentum*], so that their lying deception will be perceived.[78]

[75] *Sermones,* iv, pp. 350-1: 'Percipit autem ex fide quod plenum corpus Christi sanguis et anima sit ex integro ad omnem punctum huius sacramenti, quod inter omnia misteria fidei videtur dificillium christiano concipere'. (See above p. 50 on Pecock and p. 27 n. 2 for *De apos.* on the difficulty of sacramental belief). This Easter sermon (no. 42, pp. 343-55), telling the congregation how the sacrament should be recieved, is conjecturally dated 18 April 1378 by Mallard, '*Sermones Quadraginta*', pp. 94-5, 105, who points out that Wycliffe here questions the complete conversion of the substance of the bread.

[76] *De euch.,* pp. 301-2; see also *De apos.,* pp. 100, 109-10, 200, 224; *Selections,* ed. Hudson, p. 17; *Political Poems and Songs,* ed. T. Wright, RS (London 1859-61), i, p. 247.

[77] *De euch.,* p. 119, see also pp. 109-10.

[78] *De Apos.,* p. 163: 'et licet consecratores accidentis cognoscant quod populus adorat hoc sacramentum tanquam corpus Christi, quod dicunt esse ydolatriam, tamen reticent, timendo quod quereretur ab eis quid sit hoc sacramentum, et perciperetur eorum mendax versucia'; pp. 109, 122, 142, 155 for *cultores signorum*; p. 209 'nam cognoscere quiditatem panis est accio intellectus'. Compare *Sermones,* iv, p. 352 (n. 75 above) 'nec est vis nobis quid sit sacramentum, sed est satis

When asked what the sensible sacrament was in its nature, they could only stammer blasphemies about accidents. Their refusal to answer questions made transubstantiation into a conspiracy of silence. They 'unfaithfully conceal the natural quiddity of the sacrament so that people do not understand its distinction from the body of Christ, to the extent that this sect is ashamed to disclose its deception'. They tried to put a stopper on criticism, talking about blasphemy, and saying that such things should not be touched on before the people, and would damage devotion. The line they took towards questions about the sacrament and how it should be understood was that such enquiries were out of order – you should believe as the church believes.[79]

There was a right to know which the church denied at its peril. As Wycliffe saw it, the truth was muffled by ignorance as well as professional secrecy. Part of his indignation arose from the fact that few churchmen – bishops downwards – were capable of understanding, let alone teaching the church's erroneous eucharistic theology. Blindness prevailed to the extent that

in the whole of England you will scarcely find two chapters or prelates who know what the sacrament of the altar is. Their ministers, certainly, know how to question ordinands on the number of the sacraments, and the way in which the sacrament of the altar differs from the others; but since they themselves do not know what this is, it is clear that they have no idea how to distinguish it from the others. And when a secular asks out of native intelligence, whether he ought to believe that this thing, white, round, and otherwise characterized [*accidentatum*] is the body of Christ, they, driven to reply to this question simply say that it is not the body of Christ, but an accident without a subject; because in this way, they argue, any little bit of it would be the same body of Christ, and by consequence any part of the host would be that for anyone; and thus the host would be wholly indivisible, without part. And, the priest having stated that it is not the body of Christ, the clever layman asks, what is it then, substance or accident, flesh or fish?[80]

On the other hand, when it came to the heart of the matter, namely, what happened to the host at the words of consecration, Wycliffe's appeal to the lay worshipper reads differently. Here too, what goes on in the minds of believers is critical. Again and again, Wycliffe remarks that in the mind of the faithful,

nobis noscere quale sit et propter quid'; this passage (pp. 352- 3) is related to what Wycliffe says at the beginning of *De eucharistia*, pp. 11-14, on what should be preached to the laity about the eucharist, including allusion to the objection (p. 13) 'quod ista non sunt dicenda laycis qui nec ipsa concipiunt nec observant . . . '

[79] *De Euch.*, p. 143: 'Adversarii enim infideliter abscondunt naturalem quidditatem sacramenti sic quod populus non cognoscit distinccionem eius a corpore Christi, in tantum quod ista secta verecundatur detegere suam fictitiam'; see also pp. 112, 118; *De Apos.*, pp. 230-1.

[80] *De apos.*, pp. 57-8. See also p. 68; *De euch.*, pp. 108, 119, and below n. 88. Wycliffe's complaints about episcopal and clerical ignorance of this matter reflect the theologians' opposition to canon lawyers (such as Archbishop Courtenay) leading the church. H.A. Oberman, *The Harvest of Medieval Theology* (Grand Rapids, MI, 1967), pp. 372, 376, 378-9, 390; *The History of the University of Oxford,*, i, ed. J.I. Catto (Oxford, 1984), pp. 540-1, 544, 553, 555, 561, 574.

consideration of the nature or quiddity of the host is obliterated or suspended (*sopita* or *suspensa*) at this central moment, when the words of consecration are pronounced. Complete concentration on the person of Christ removed the spiritual understanding from worries about the perceptions of the senses.[81] If Wycliffe seems here nearly to contradict himself, by indicating that understanding is irrelevant at the centre of the sacramental mystery, he also by this means found an escape route that enabled him to avoid denying the miracle of the sacrament.

At this point Wycliffe appears to have been taking his cues from John of Damascus and Grosseteste. In more than one place he refers to the former's analogy of charcoal, whose nature, transformed in fire, could be compared with the sacramental bread.[82] Wycliffe himself, however, turning the transformation back into the mental process of the worshipper, more often adverted to the parallel of an image, such as the crucifix. In contemplating the bread, as in contemplating an image, the believer's whole attention passed from the sign to focus on the signified. The accidents of the host passed from consciousness

> just as someone entering a church does not set his attention on reflecting about the quiddity of the wood of an image or cross, but worships it for what it represents.[83]

Wycliffe applied these words in the *Trialogus* to his interpretation of a gloss of Grosseteste. The same analogy, more graphically expressed, appears not long after in his reply to Rimington, and earlier in *De blasphemia* (giving a cluster of references from 1381-3).

> For just as someone entering a building and seeing an image does not give thought to the nature of the image, whether it is made of oak, box, or willow, but sets his whole attention and devotion on that which it represents, so is it likewise with the sacrament of the eucharist.[84]

---

[81] *De apos.*, pp. 108, 166, 192, 209, 233, 243; *De euch.*, pp. 130, 231.

[82] *De apos.*, pp. 52, 63-4, 65, 120, 143. See St. John of Damascus, *De fide orthodoxa, PG* 94, lib. iv, col. 1150 and compare lib. iii, col. 1002.

[83] *Trial.*, p. 265, 'ut intrans basilicam non infigit sensum suum in consideratione de quidditate ligni imaginis sive crucis, sed ipsum colit quantum suffecerit in signato' – following a reference to Grosseteste on the *De divinis nominibus* of pseudo Dionysius, on which see S.H. Thomson, *The Writings of Robert Grosseteste* (Cambridge, 1940), p. 57.

[84] *De blas.*, p. 24; compare *Opera minora*, p. 212. See *De apos.*, p. 243 for a generalized analogy of an image, and *De euch.*, p. 137 for an analogy from nature – how awareness of the light of the stars disappears in the presence of the sun. See also *FZ*, pp. 107-8, which comments on Wycliffe's use of the analogy of wood transformed into image, and his (frequent) comparison of the worship of crucifix and host; also n. 93 below.

Wycliffe's interpretation of the eucharist swept over a wide horizon, past and present, and challenged a number of conventional boundaries. He gives us reason to suppose that he had himself preached on the sacrament of the altar – teaching doctrine that might have seemed doubtful. A passage in *De eucharistia* described the comfort the faithful could derive from the ability to tell catholic truth freely, providing due regard was paid to the capacities of different audiences. Wycliffe then added:

> And I have chosen to tell the lay people plainly that the sacrament figures the body of Christ, and is consecrated, worshipped and eaten with the intention of remembering and imitating Christ.[85]

Other passages in this same book suggest that vernacular repercussions of the academic controversy had begun already in the early part of 1380.[86] We find Wycliffe sending out distress signals over his championing of Augustine against St. Thomas. He went to considerable lengths to refute the Thomistic argument that it was heresy to posit that the substance of the bread remained in the host. Fully aware of the opposition, he was on the defensive, prickly about heresy in general. Wycliffe accuses his opponents of defaming the university by quite unwarrantably making vernacular charges about scholastic statements. It was an underhand trick, and those responsible ought not to be given any position in Oxford unless they explained this imputation of heresy. Wycliffe, turning the charge of heresy back on his accusers, shored himself up again on the support of St. Augustine. (No wonder the Austin friars stood by him so long!) Evidently he felt sore and threatened. He saw a link between curial machinations and the friars who (he wrote) 'publicly in their sermons incite the people in the vernacular, to destroy as heretics the simple disciples of truth'. Those who had risen in such dudgeon in defence of St. Thomas had really exceeded the bounds of decency – and logic. 'It does not follow; St. Thomas

---

[85] *De euch.*, pp. 304-5: 'nunc loqui uno modo nunc alio secundum capacitatem auditorii, cui loquuntur, ut aliter loquendum est sophistis et aliter piis simplicibus. Ego autem elegi laicis loqui planius quod illud sacramentum figurat corpus Christi et conficitur, colitur et manducatur intencione memorandi et imitandi Christum'. See above nn. 75 and 78.

[86] It does not seem possible to date with any exactitude the moment when Wycliffe went public over his eucharistic theory. One *terminus post quem* (which probably leaves a wide margin) is the *Protestacio* (and related *Libellus*) which, in early 1378, is silent on this issue. In *De euch.*, which was most likely completed and published in mid to late 1380, Wycliffe (p. 183) makes clear that he had published his challenge: 'ideo timendo istam persecucionem severam protestatus sum publice quod volo humiliter corrigi per quoscunque et specialiter per episcopos qui docuerint in ista materia veritatem. Sed volo querere signum, unde doctrine quam asserunt fideliter possum confidere'. Thomson, *Latin Writings*, pp. 67-9, no. 38; pp. 253-5, nos. 399-400; Gwynn, *Austin Friars*, p. 258.

says this, therefore it is to be preached to the people.'[87] The *doctor evangelicus* whose eucharistic teaching set him up as challenger to the *doctor angelicus*, would have us believe that it was not his fault that scholastic sacramental doctrine moved into the vernacular. Others had insidiously started the work. But the step had been taken, and 'prelates of religion . . . in their chapters specially accuse their brethren for preaching in the country [*in patria*] that the sacrament of the altar is not the body and blood of Christ but an efficacious sign.'[88]

Not long after this Wycliffe gives some positive hints about his own vernacular teaching on the eucharist. At the very end of *De apostasia* (i.e. about the end of 1380), as the final words of a concluding chapter which may have been tacked on to the book in response to current controversy, Wycliffe issued a challenge.

> And therefore [he wrote] the people are to be instructed that the sacrament of the altar is according to nature bread and wine, but according to the miracle of the word of God is the body and blood of Christ. And the learned are to be told [*dicendum est scholasticis*] that the sacrament as bread and wine, is the subject of all the accidents that we feel; but as the body of Christ confers grace on all the worthy faithful. This view [*sentencia*] I intend to publish to the people.[89]

---

[87] *De euch.*, pp. 5, 136ff: 'Unde videtur quod illi dogmatisantes qui deficientibus argumentis *defamant universitatem in vulgari* propter dicta scolastica et sanctorum sentencias sint publice puniendi; hoc autem optarem, cum ipsi sint manifeste heretici nisi probaverint quod divulgant aut quod non accipiant dignitatem in Oxonia antequam docuerint heresim quam imponunt' (pp. 155-6); 'sed pseudo Scariotis discipuli agitati a demonio meridiano publice in sermonibus *incitant populum in vulgari*, ut destruant tamquam hereticos simplices discipulos veritatis' (p. 157); 'Non ergo sequitur: Si Thomas hoc asseruit, ergo hoc est *populo predicandum*' (p. 158) – my italics. On the challenge to Aquinas, see pp. 224, 286-7, 294 and *De apos.*, p. 78 where Wycliffe, rejoicing in the views of those who believed 'quod panis et vinum santificata sunt hoc sacramentum', reports that they dared not speak their opinion for fear of impugning St. Thomas and Minorite doctors. For a Dominican defence of St. Thomas in this context see *Rogeri Dymmok Liber*, pp. 92-4, 110-11. See also *De apos.*, pp. 124-6, 168, 189 where Augustine is placed in apposition to Aquinas; the remarks of Manning in *CMH*, vii, pp. 501-2; Wilks, 'Early Oxford Wyclif', pp. 84-5, and above n. 30. For the passage in Aquinas cited by Wycliffe, *De euch.*, pp. 137-8 see *Scriptum super libros sententiarum*, ed. P. Mandonnet (Paris 1929-47), 4, p. 436; 23-6; Lib IV Dist. xi q. 1 art. i.

[88] *De euch.*, p. 183 (preceding the sentence quoted in n. 86) in a passage where Wycliffe is mainly attacking bishops for their ignorance of the quiddity of the host: 'illi prelati religionum qui in suis capitulis accusant precipue fratres suos, quia predicant in patria quod sacramentum altaris nec est corpus Christi nec sanguis, sed efficax eius signum . . . '

[89] *De apos.*, pp. 253-4: 'Sic igitur instruendus est populus quod sacramentum altaris est secundum suam naturam panis et vinum, sed secundum verbi dei miraculum est corpus Christi et sangwis. Et dicendum est scolasticis quod sacramentum, secundum quod panis aut vinum, subiectat naturaliter omnia illa accidencia que sentimus; sed secundum quod corpus Christi, confert graciam fidelibus ipsa dignis. Istam autem sentenciam propono publicare in populo'. See n. 59 above. The section on *Eukaristia* in the Latin *Floretum* (written before 1396) expounds the relationship of accidents and substance at length, with reference to Augustine (BL MS Harley 401, fo. 95 r-v); the English *Rosarium* by contrast, has nothing on this in its greatly abbreviated entry: a deliberate omission. *The Middle English Translation of the Rosarium Theologie*, ed. C. von Nolcken (Heidelberg, 1979), pp. 71-2; 113-14.

The worshippers of signs might do as they wished about publishing their doctrine of an aggregation of accidents. Wycliffe believed that God would see that understanding of the faith kept pace with the publication of the truth. The passage reads unambiguously as a threat, or promise, to tell his eucharistic conclusions to the people in their own language. And we should notice the double address: the people are to be taught one thing; the learned another.

A year to eighteen months later (the duration of time depends on our dating of the two books in question) a passage in the *Trialogus* seems to indicate that Wycliffe had been true to his words, and had gone ahead with this publication. The second chapter of Book IV opens this work's treatment of the eucharist, and Alithia asks Phronesis (the subtle and mature theologian who stands in for Wycliffe) to expound this sacrament, the most venerable and scripturally grounded sacrament, about which 'there is today so much contentious disagreement'. Phronesis naturally obliges, and in so doing refers to his earlier pronouncements.

> But there are many errors on the question of the quiddity of this sensible sacrament, as some say that it is an accident without subject, and others that it is nothing but a collection of many accidents which are not of one kind, against which I have inveighed elsewhere both scholastically and also in the vernacular, because among all the heresies which have ever spread in the church, there was never I think one more craftily introduced by hypocrites, and so many ways deceiving the people.[90]

Here again we find the twofold address: 'invexi alias tam scholastice quam etiam in vulgari'. The errors of the doctrine of accidents had been exposed both scholastically and popularly. This promise could, of course, have been fulfilled by speech as well as writing, but Wycliffe was in the habit of cross-referencing his written works, and it seems clear from other references later on in the *Trialogus* that he had texts in mind here.[91] It seems worthwhile, therefore, to consider the possibility of whether Wycliffe's words might be applied to any of the extant vernacular writings on the topic of the eucharist. And that must send us back, in the first instance, to those vernacular confessions on the eucharist with which I started.

Our main source of these confessions is Knighton's chronicle. The second confession also survives in one other manuscript, the Lollard collection of Bodley 647, which contains in addition the 1382 confessions of Hereford, Repton and Aston I have already described. The Leicester writer, who was open-minded in his vernacular interest, included these confessions too (slightly different in form), and though he jumbled his chronology it is worth noting that he placed the two texts ascribed to Wycliffe respectively before and after the twenty-four Blackfriars conclusions. Knighton's self-evident misreading of these texts does nothing to detract from their potential authenticity –

---

[90] *Trial.*, pp. 247-8. This comes in the part of the text that I would date before May 1382 (see above n. 5).

[91] Below, Chapter 4, p. 117.

perhaps, indeed, it may tell us something about contemporary levels of understanding of the doctrine of transubstantiation. For the chronicler, though regarding Wycliffe as having taken refuge in the vernacular when under threat of prosecution, took the longer, second confession as a complete renunciation, whereas, outspoken in content, belligerent in tone, it was nothing of the sort.[92]

The first question about these texts might well be: why two? One answer to this could be that they originated at different dates. The first short statement, one paragraph of half a dozen or so sentences (all of which could be paralleled in Wycliffe's Latin writings), could be of any date. The second, more than twice the length, must date from after May 1382, since it attacks the decision of the Earthquake Council – 'this council of friars' – as if it were a recent event. Another, perhaps more useful way of viewing the two confessions, is to consider who they may have been intended for, and the differences in their form of address.

It is striking that the first concise statement considers precisely those matters which (as so many passages in his Latin works make clear) Wycliffe thought ought to fill the worshipper's mind at the time of the elevation. And it does so without using any scholastic terms. It was a message to encourage devotion of the right sort for 'God's body in form of bread'. It includes the analogy of the image that we have met elsewhere.

> But as a man leeves for to þenk þe kynde of an ymage, wheþer it be of oke or of asshe, and settys his þouȝt in him of whom is þe ymage, so myche more schuld a man leve to þenk on þe kynde of brede.[93]

The second confession, quite unlike this, takes up the theology of the sacrament in much the same manner and vocabulary as Wycliffe's Latin works. It pursued the polemics of the issue; the long-continued heresy of the church's teaching; the great divide between true believers and those heretics who followed the father of lies; the terrible mistake of Blackfriars. There was an appeal to the king to set the realm to rights. And throughout terms are used that are taken straight from Wycliffite theology: accident without subject, sacramentally God's body; good grounding (i.e. founded in scripture).

---

[92] *Selections*, ed. Hudson, pp. 17-18, 141-4; *Knighton*, pp. 157-62; MS Bodley 647, fos. 63 v – 64 v. The heading to this text in the manuscript has 'Johannes Wycliff', followed by an erasure which seems under ultra violet light to have included 'M . . . ewangel . . . '

[93] *Selections*, p. 17, and above p. 60. Hudson, who (p. 141) aptly describes the two confessions as 'an anthology of phrases that can be paralleled many times', gives as the nearest approximation *De fide sacramentorum*, ed. S.H. Thomson, *JTS*, 33 (1932), pp. 359-65; dated late 1381? by Thomson, *Latin Writings*, p. 71, no. 40. This text, however, does not include the analogy of the wooden image, and although it would be unwise to make too much of this parallel, it is worth noticing, specially as Wycliffe only seems to have begun to use it after writing *De eucharistia*, though the point to which it applies is raised in all his eucharistic discussions.

We may also notice that neither confession includes the phrase 'material bread' which the church regularly employed when questioning suspects, and which Wycliffe (according to Netter) rejected as being unscriptural.[94] So, while the content of the two confessions is not discordant with what we know of Wycliffe's teaching, we might go further and link their differences of presentation with what he said about instructing different sorts of people.

Another English text, whose claims to Wycliffe's authorship are advanced below, also deserves to be considered in this context. The English tract known as *De blasphemia, contra fratres*, whose tripartite treatment of the blasphemies of the friars is related to the text of the *Trialogus* and neatly fits the vernacular discussion alluded to in that book, took antichrist's heretical doctrine of the eucharist as its first blasphemy. Like the second of the two confessions, though at much greater length, this tract attacks the error of those (specially friars) who maintained that 'not of þis bread is makid Gods body, but þat þes accidentis bitoken Gods body'.[95] Here, however, there is no mention of the 1382 council.

The English *De blasphemia* makes free use of the terms familiar in Latin theology: accident and subject, substance, quantity and quality. We also find repeated use of the word *ground* or *grounding* meaning founded or based on scripture, which Anne Hudson has suggested may be specially associated with Lollard usage. For example: 'For it falles to soche men to teche þo bileve by sufficyent foundynge, and eschewe erroures. As, for no mon con grounde accydent wiþouten sugette, no mon schulde aferme þat þis were þo sacrament.'[96] All these examples, as direct transliterations, would have presented no problems of understanding to anyone familiar with the theology whence they derived. Wycliffe's Latin writings often employed the word *fundare* to press home his arguments about returning to the foundation and ground of scripture.

Talking theology in English might call for new words, but some were readily arrived at. Others proved more difficult. *De blasphemia*'s englishing of the Latin verb *subjectare* (meaning to make or be the subject of) by the word *sogetten* or *sugetten* seems to have been an idiosyncratic novelty that did not

---

[94] See above pp. 48-9 and n. 54; Netter, *Doctrinale,* ii, c. 74, col. 448; 'Sic item causatur terminum *transubstantiationem* terminum magistralem, et abjicit terminum *panis materialis* ea de causa . . .'

[95] *Select English Works,* iii, p. 404; below, p. 117.

[96] *Select English Works,* iii, p. 427, also pp. 412-13, 416, 422-3, and 410 ('tho secounde blaspheme grounden thes freris, for thei feynen falsely beggynge in Crist'); cf. *Trial.,* p. 341 (Alithia): 'Videtur enim multis, quod Christus taliter mendicavit, et certum est quod super mendicatione hujusmodi fratrum religio est fundata'; *De off. reg.* p. 165: 'Non enim est credendum vel obediendum homini vel angelo nisi de quanto est fundabile ex scriptura'. A. Hudson, 'A Lollard Sect Vocabulary?', *So Meny People Longages and Tonges,* ed. M. Benskin and M.L. Samuels (Edinburgh, 1981), p. 22, reprinted in idem, *Lollards and their Books* (London and Ronceverte, 1985), pp. 171-2.

catch on. I have not found any other examples of it, useful though it might have been in eucharistic argument.[97] Another rare word in this text (one which sounds Latin enough itself) is *perplex* (confused, obscure). This must also be placed in the category of a new coinage that failed to find circulation, though it does appear in another Wycliffite tract, 'Of Ministers in the Church'.[98] These examples help to show that Wycliffite discussions called for verbal inventiveness, and (as with the Latin neologisms of other periods) some words were short-lived.

At the end of his exposition of fraternal blasphemies, the author of the *De blasphemia* makes some interesting personal observations. Belief, he said, includes many things that have to be taken on trust, not doubted or denied, but rather supposed, guessed, hoped. 'As if a mon asked me wheþer þis bred were Gods body, I wolde nouþer byleve þat, ne dowte hit, ne denye hit, bot suppose þat hit were so, bot if I had contrarye evydence . . . ' Given that God's body was in heaven, it was right to worship the sacrament of the altar, and hearing masses made men more mindful of Christ.

> And so, if prelates opposed me, what were þo sacrament of þo auter in his kynde, I wolde sey þat hit were bred, þo same þat was byfore; ffor þus teches þo gospel þat we shulden bileve. And if þou aske forþer, wheþer hit be substaunse of material bred, nouþer wolde I graunte hit, ne doute hit, ne denye hit, byfore audytorie þat I trowed schulde be harmed þerby, bot sith [? sey] þat I supposid or reputid þat hit is so.[99]

---

[97] *Select English Works*, iii, p. 405; see also p. 427, ' . . . hardnesse and sofftenesse, freelnesse and towghnesse, with soche qualytees, may nowther qualite ne quantite *sogetten*; *Trial.*, p. 259, 'Sed talia accidentia, durities, mollities fragilitas et tenacitas, nec possunt per se nec in aliis accidentibus *subjectari* . . . ' (my italics). No other example of the verb *subjecten* has yet been found by the *MED* editors.

[98] *Select English Works,* iii, p. 406; cf., ii, p. 422, and *MED, perplex* (which only gives one example). For an instance of Latin use see *Polemical Works,* i, p. 362, 'quilibet viator foret dubius vel perplexus'. Of course where the new words remained close to the Latin they could have the advantage of acting as stepping-stones towards it, as pointed out by Rolle in the prologue to his psalter, where he said he sought to use English 'that is most like unto the Latin, so that they that knows not Latin, by the English may come to many Latin words'. Salter, *Nicholas Love's 'Mirrour'*, p. 222.

[99] *Select English Works*, iii, pp. 426-7. (Compare the attacks on episcopal ignorance in *De euch.*, pp. 108, 182-3 and nn. 80, 88 above; on differing audiences above n. 85). For William Thorpe's exact following of this advice in his examination in 1407 see *Fifteenth Century Prose and Verse*, ed. A.W. Pollard (Westminster, 1903), pp. 129-33 – where Thorpe shows himself well versed in Wycliffe's arguments. See p. 130: 'And I said, "Sir, I know of no place in Holy Scripture, where this term, *material bread*, is written: and therefore, Sir, when I speak of this matter, I use not to speak of material bread"'; p. 132: 'But, Sir, for as mickle as your asking passeth mine understanding, I dare neither deny it nor grant it, for it is a School matter, about which I busied me never for to know it: and therefore I commit this term *accidens sine subjecto*, to those Clerks which delight them so in curious and subtle sophistry . . . '

Prelates who insisted on 'wringing out' a categorical 'absolute answer' failed in both divinity and logic, showing themselves incapable of examining for heresy. And, since there were few prelates who knew about accidents and subjects, 'men should beware to bring this in Christian men's belief'.

Once again we are presented with the danger of raising sacramental theology in the wrong company. At this point that tell-tale phrase, 'substance of material bread' appears for the first time in the whole of this text: and the context, be it noted, is that of (hypothetical) official questioning.

'And so, if prelates opposed me . . . ' Was Wycliffe ever confronted by the church authorities over his eucharistic teaching? This had not happened at the time when Thomas Winterton wrote his *Absolutio*, though what he says perhaps suggests that it was in the air. Tearfully contemplating the many errors and heresies in the *Confessio* of May 1381, Winterton still refers to its author as a 'most famous doctor, John Wycliffe'. But he adds, 'heretic I do not call him, since I do not know if he is of a mind to put up a pertinacious defence, or whether he is ready to be corrected, recognizing the truth, and duly submitting himself to ecclesiastical authority'.[100]

Wycliffe was not formally tried, but did he make any kind of submission? He leaves us enough hints to speculate on. He tells us that he had sent the 'satraps' three conclusions about the sacrament, 'with due protestation'.[101] The placing of this remark in the *Trialogus* seems to make it certain that he must have done this well before May 1382. Later on, near the end of the *Trialogus*, in a tantalising parenthesis that comes in an attack on the recent Earthquake Council, Wycliffe mentions how 'I undertook not to use these terms, "substance of material bread and wine" outside the schools'. What does this mean? Thomas Netter had little doubt. Wycliffe, he says, forced by the weight of authority and reason, freely repented of his words.[102] The suggestion is of pressures that, if overwhelming, were informal, rather than formal, and

---

[100] *FZ*, p. 182; Gwynn, *Austin Friars*, p. 261; J.A. Robson, *Wyclif and the Oxford Schools* (Cambridge, 1961), pp. 190-1.

[101] *Trial.*, p. 263: 'Ideo misi alias satrapis in ista materia tres conclusiones, cum protestatione debita', the three points being (1) heretics make the sacrament into accidents; (2) this has spread the most abominable heresy in the church; (3) in gospel faith the sacrament is 'naturaliter verus panis, et sacramentaliter ac veraciter corpus Christi'. No known text seems exactly to fit this bill. Thomson, *Latin Writings*, p. 82 n. 22 suggests the 'Epistola missa archiepiscopo Cantuariensi' in *Opera minora*, pp. 3-6, but this must be dated at earliest to the early summer of 1383: see *FZ*, pp. 125-6 (*De apos.*, 226-7) for the *Confessio's* three points 'in which we differ from the sects of signs': closer, but still not an exact fit.

[102] *Trial.*, p. 375: 'Quamvis autem pepigi extra scholam non usurum istis terminis "substantia panis materialis aut vini", tamen fides necessitat concedere convertibile propositioni terminorum istorum'. See p. 374 for the reference to the Earthquake Council. Netter, *Doctrinale*, ii, c. 74, col. 451 cites these words to show Wycliffe's followers 'quod magister illorum coactus authoritatis et rationis sponte poenituit sic dixisse'; Dahmus, *Prosecution*, pp. 133, 157. Woodford summarized the modern eucharistic heresy of Wycliffites as 'quod manent panis materialis et vinum, et panis sic

Netter, professing surprise that Lollards of his day had not learnt from Wycliffe's example, related this change of heart to the foolishness of insisting on adherence to the words of scripture. Yet, apart from the question of apposition between church formulae and biblical words, we may also be interested in this reference to 'outside the schools', with its implications of what Wycliffe might have been doing in the vernacular.

It sometimes seems possible to detect a more chastened, submissive note in the last writings of one who, for all his fiery contentiousness, regarded himself at the end as *debilis* and *claudus*: debilitated, this is, in scriptural terms.[103] We actually find Wycliffe mentioning Innocent III's role in establishing the doctrine of transubstantiation with a tame, 'that is not for me to discuss'.[104] We find him with uncharacteristic humility submitting all his words, spoken or written, to the correction or discipline of holy mother church.[105] The final word may be left with a sermon in which Wycliffe dealt with several of the points condemned at Blackfriars. He was still outraged by the council's

materialis est corpus Christi et vinum sanguis Christi realiter et sacramentaliter sed non substantialiter et ydemptice'; MS Bodley 703, fo. 107 v. The last known date for Wycliffe's presence in Oxford is 22 October 1381 when he, together with Robert Alington and three others deposited a copy of Gratian's Decretum in the Vaughan and Hussey chest as caution for a loan of £6 3s. 4d.; BL, MS Royal 10 E II, fo. 340 v.

[103] *Polemical Works*, ii, p. 556; see Luke 14:13; J. Lewis, *The History of the Life and Sufferings of . . . John Wiclif, D.D.* (Oxford, 1820), p. 336.

[104] *Trial.*, p. 263, 'non pertinet mihi discutere' (cf. p. 409). This is an astonishing statement in view of the amount Wycliffe found to say elsewhere on the mistakes of Innocent III, in promoting the mendicant orders (see Wilks, 'Early Oxford Wyclif', p. 97 n.2), in altering confession, and – above all – in establishing false eucharistic doctrine. *De eucharistia* and *De apostasia* both contain numerous damaging references to Innocent's role in defining the doctrine of the eucharist at the Fourth Lateran Council of 1215 (in which the word 'transubstantiate' appears officially for the first time), Mansi, 22, cols. 981-2 and for his decretal *Cum Marthe* (*Corpus iuris canonici*, ed. E. Friedberg (Leipzig, 1879-81), ii, cols. 636-9), which Wycliffe saw as having determined that the sacrament was an accident without a subject. In *De blas.* (p. 23) he wrote 'As I've said elsewhere, what is the pretext for saying "If Innocent III says so, it must be true?".' The rare and innocuous mentions of this pope in the *Trialogus* and *Opus evangelicum* seem to demand some other explanation than the fact (which in any case would not normally have restrained Wycliffe) that he had received full treatment elsewhere. It seems more likely that this was one of the topics (or authorities) to which a 'keep off' notice had been attached. Cf. *Opus evan.*, ii, p. 446; 'Ego autem cum sum magis suspectus de heresi, non audeo ita loqui . . . '

[105] *Trial.*, p. 447 (from the *Supplementum Trialogi*): 'Et hinc in omnibus verbis dictis vel scriptis correctioni vel correptioni sanctae matris ecclesiae et cujuscunque membri sui me humiliter subjicio, dum tamen quis loquitur tanquam membrum sanctae matris ecclesiae'. Of course Wycliffe's works are peppered with protestations of his readiness to be corrected, but they usually read rather in the nature of challenges to anyone who could to prove him wrong by scripture. (This one too is qualified, but more discreetly!) Compare *Trial.*, pp. 60, 267; *De euch.*, pp. 127, 183 (above n. 86), 271; *Opera minora*, p. 354.

insanity on the eucharist, but he implies that he had found a *modus vivendi* by renouncing the use of certain words.

> In this matter I asserted for many similar reasons that it is probable that this sacrament is spiritually and really the body and blood of Christ, and questioned further I granted [*et interrogatus ulterius concessi*] that this sacrament is naturally the substance of material bread and wine. Now, however, I keep silence as to these two words 'substance' and 'material' [*nunc autem taceo hec duo nomina substancia et materialis*] not because I believe these terms conflict in their nature with the truth of the matter, but because I do not see why the church should be burdened with them. Therefore I remain with the shorter words expressed in the faith of scripture, conceding that this sacrament is bread which we break, and thus says the apostle . . .

Yet, added Wycliffe still adamant in his scriptural verity

> I always await a declaration from the satraps and specially from the friars in this matter of how and in what manner the bread is the sacrament, or if it ought to be granted that it is bread. But if they all refuse to do this, I myself will hold to my death to the faith of the church revealed by God in his apostle, that this sacrament is bread, and that that bread is truly and really the body of Christ, because the faith of the gospel teaches this, and I consider that the council of those satraps was incomplete and foolish, ostensibly because its members were upset and agitated by the fearful tremor of the earthquake.[106]

In Wycliffe's case the end was not silence. Whatever the immunity he secured for himself, whatever undertaking he may have given about refraining from the public challenging of certain authorities, or certain forms of words, it did not freeze his pen. And both during and after 1382 there were faithful disciples who loyally imitated his example, and echoed and repeated what he said, popularizing the new English vocabulary of sacramental theology. The resonance of Wycliffe's ideas would never have grown as it did without the currency of the vernacular. Surely too it must be granted, as more than hypothesis, that Wycliffe contributed to the vernacular breaching of *arcana eucharistie*. We may remain in doubt as to what precisely he said in English. We can be sure of the importance of his vernacular initiative.

---

[106] *Sermones,* iii, p. 471, from pt. iii, sermon 54, 20 Sunday after Trinity, on Eph. 5:15 ('See then that ye walk circumspectly': for the English sermon for this day see *Select English Works,* ii, pp. 362-5). There are references to the Blackfriars Council, pp. 467-8; on the dating see *Sermones,* i, pp. xxx-xxxi. See also the remark of William Woodford in *De sacramento altaris* on Wycliffe's position after leaving Oxford: 'Iam tarde, postquam recessit de universitate, scribens ad unum militem qui contra eum se posuit, timore ut credo ductus, dixit quod in sacramento est corpus Christi sub forma panis, sed asserit se non explicasse an illa forma sit substancia panis materialis vel accidens sine subiecto sicut, inquit, dicunt heretici'; cited Robson, *Oxford Schools* (from BL, MS Royal 7 B III) p. 192 and comment p. 194.

APPENDIX

Vernacular Confessions on the Eucharist[1]

(1) Nicholas Hereford and Philip Repton

In þo name of God, Amen. Wittynge alle cristen men þat we Nicol Herforth and Philipp Repindon[2] prestis unworthily in prisons[3] of oure gostly fadir þo erchebischop of Canterbirye þo nyntend day of Junii, in þo ȝere of oure Lord a thousande thre hundred foure score and twoo, in þo hous of þo frere pre-choures at London, when we were required to sey what we felde of diverse conclusiouns, we maden þis protestacioun and ȝitte we make þat oure entent was and is to be trewe and meke sones of holy chirche, and if hit happen, as God schilde, þat we erren ageyne þis entent in wordes or werke, we submytten us mekely to þo coreccioun of oure foreseid fadir þo erchebischop, and to alle to whom hit longes to redresse hom þat so erren. And afterward when we were required to sey oure byleve of þo sacrament of þo auter, as to oure underston- dynge to þo puple[4] we knowlechide and ȝitte we knowleche,[5] first þat þo bred þat[6] þo prest takes in his hondes thorw þo virtue of þo sacramental wordes is made and turned vereyly in to Cristis body, þo same þat was taken and borne of þo mayden Marie, and þat suffred deth on þo crosse for monnes kinde and þat laye in þo sepulcre and þat roos fro deth to lyve þo thrid day, and steyed up in to heven and sittes in ioye in þo blis of þo Fadir, and þat schal cum at þo day of dome to deme þo queeke and þo deed. And þo wyne is also turned vereyly in to

---

[1] These texts are from Bodley MS 647, fo. 70 r-v (B). (I have extended abbreviations, modernized *u/v* and introduced modern punctuation). The notes that follow indicate the more significant variants (ignoring minor verbal differences) in the other copies: Knighton's Chronicle, from BL MS Cotton Tiberius C VII, fos. 183 v – 184 v (HK), compared with the copy in BL, MS Cotton Claudius E III fos. 275 v – 276 r (HK2); (in the RS edition *Chronicon Henrici Knighton,* ii, pp. 170-2) and, for the Aston confession, *Fasciculi zizaniorum,* pp. 329-30 (*FZ*). The differences between these versions indicate some editing as well as scribal alterations, and it may be that the Latin version of the second is closer to the original than either English transcript, preserving as it does the (thrice repeated) stress on the teaching of holy scripture. B's switching from *chirche* to *kirke* in (2) does not occur in HK, and though it would doubtless be rash to see here a clue to the language of Aston's original, it is worth noting that MS Bodley 647 seems to belong linguistically to mid-Derbyshire. (I am grateful to Professor Angus McIntosh for his kind help and information on this point).

[2] HK substitutes *and my felowe pristus* for *and Philipp Repindon,* presumably out of loyalty to the reputation of his house.

[3] HK has *unworthy in presence.* This is the only evidence that Hereford and Repton were in custody at this time. See also n. 21 below.

[4] HK *as to ȝoure understondyng outher þe peple.*

[5] and *ȝitte we knowleche* omitted in HK.

[6] ȝo bred ȝat omitted in HK.

his blode;[7] and forthermore we byleve þat þo body[8] of Crist is hool in þo sacrament and hool in everiche part of þo sacrament of þo auter, and also we byleven þat Crist is vereyly in þo same sacrament in his bodily presence to þo salvacioun of hom þat worthily receyven þo same sacrament to hom þat unworthily receyven hit to hor dampnacioun; and þis is oure byleve. And in þis byleve thorw þo grace of God we wil dye for remissioun of oure synnes. And þerfore we praye alle cristen men to whom þis confessioun schal cum to þat ȝe bere us wittenesse of þis byleve at þo day of dome byfore þo hyest iuge Iesu Crist.

And preyes for us per charite   Amen

(2) John Aston

In þo name of god, Amen. I Jon Aston prest unworthy[9] required of my lord þo erchebischopp of Canterbirie þo nyntent day of Junii in þo ȝere of grace a thousande thre hundrid foure score and twoo in þo hous of þo frere prechoures of Lundon to sey what I felde in mater of þo sacrament of þo auter, I have knowlechid and ȝitt I knoweleche þat þo self bred þat þo prest holdes in his hondes is made thorw þo virtue of þo sacramental wordes verely þo self Cristis body þat was borne of þo mayden Marie and taken and suffred deth on þo crosse, and thre dayes lay in þo sepulcre and þo thrid day roos fro deth to lyve and styed up to heven and sittes on þo right honde of God, and at þo day of dome schal cum to deme þo quick and þo deede. And over þis I byleve generaly al þat holy [   ][10] determyns in worde and in understondynge, or what evere holy chirche[11] of God determyns. Off al þis[12] when I was required specialy to sey what I felde of þis proposicioun *Material bred leeves in þo sacrament after þo consecracioun,* I make þis protestacioun þat I nevere putt[13] ne taught ne prechid þat proposicioun, for I wot wil þat þo mater and þo speculacioun þer of passes in heght myne understondinge, and þerfore as mykel as holy kirke[14] telles opunly for to leve in þis mater I byleve. And of þis mater or of any oþer techande[15] þo right byleve of holy kirke þat is [   ][16]

---

[7]   HK adds here *so þat leves aftur þe consecracion of brede and wyne non oþer substance þanþat ilk pat is Cristus flesshe and his blode.*

[8]   HK *þe hole body.*

[9]   *unworthely* in HK.

[10]   word *writte* in HK is omitted in B; *FZ* has *quicquid determinat sacra scriptura.*

[11]   *kyrke* in HK.

[12]   HK unclear at this point but seems to have *determynes of alle þis.* HK2 is (very clearly) the same as B.

[13]   HK *þauȝt; FZ* posui.

[14]   HK omits *as holy kirke; FZ* has *quantum de illa sacra scriptura docet.*

[15]   HK *touchyng; FZ* tangente.

[16]   erasure (? of *nat*) in B; *nouȝt* in HK; *non expressa in sacra scriptura* in *FZ.*

expresse in holy writte I byleve as oure modir holy chirche[17] byleves. And in þis byleve I wil dye.[18] And of þis þing I byseche[19] alle men and alle wymen[20] to whom þis confession comes to here to bere me wittenesse bifore þo hyeste iuge at þo day of dome. And prayes for me pour charite Amen.[21]

---

[17] *kirke* in HK.

[18] This sentence has no equivalent in *FZ*.

[19] *beseke* in HK; *beseche* in HK2.

[20] translated as *christicolas* in *FZ*.

[21] The last sentence is omitted in HK. *FZ* adds (no equivalent in B or HK) 'Hec inquit est confessio pauperis incarcerati, gementis peccata sua et populum obcecatum'.

3

Bishops and Heresy: The Defence of the Faith

Historians, like detectives, often lack evidence, but may know enough to say exactly what it is that they need. Almost every piece of research has holes which, the investigator feels sure, might have been filled had the surviving records only included some critical missing item. Sometimes we can be sure that the precise document we want to establish our hypothesis or to close our dossier must once have existed, though it is no longer extant. That is the kind of absence that is the most annoying and unhelpful to the historian, for whom (unlike Sherlock Holmes) night silence is unlikely to have any positive value.

These reflections were prompted by the thought that Reginald Pecock – who occupies an important place in this essay – might present himself in a different light if we were able to find out more about his episcopal career. If we possessed the register of his nine-year tenure of the see of Chichester (1450-59), we might be better informed about the bishop's personal knowledge of Lollardy, or the preaching that (according to Thomas Gascoigne) Pecock promoted in this diocese.[1] We might – but of course we might not. For even when we do have a bishop's register, it may not tell us all we would like to know, and when it comes to heresy, the record is uneven. There were reasons for that, which should emerge from what follows.

There is, of course, a great deal of material relating to heretical suspects scattered through the bishops' registers from the late fourteenth to the early sixteenth centuries, and Dr. John Thomson's valuable book on *The Later Lollards* drew mainly on this source.[2] But it would be quite wrong to assume that a bishop's register was the first place of record for a heretical examination. Indeed it might well be the case – and here is an unprovable hypothesis – that if we had *all* the records of the late medieval heresy trials that once existed, the

---

[1] 'idem episcopus praedicavit et praedicari fecit in sua diocesi'; *Loci e Libro Veritatum*, ed. J.E.T. Rogers, (Oxford, 1881), p. 35; C.W. Brockwell, *Bishop Reginald Pecock and the Lancastrian Church* (Lewiston, NY, and Queenston, Ontario, 1985), p. 89. Also on Pecock see V.H.H. Green, *Bishop Reginald Pecock* (Cambridge, 1945); J.F. Patrouch, *Reginald Pecock* (New York, 1970); R.M. Haines, 'Reginald Pecock; A Tolerant Man in an Age of Intolerance', *SCH*, 21 (1984), pp. 125-37,

[2] John A.F. Thomson, *The Later Lollards, 1414-1520* (Oxford, 1965).

complete head-count of suspects would derive the greater part of its total from sources other than bishops' registers.[3]

The fullest, most detailed surviving records of heresy proceedings are the judicial records of court processes which were devoted entirely to this issue. The Norwich trials of 1428-31 edited by Dr. Norman Tanner, the Lichfield Court Book of 1511-12 described by Dr. John Fines, and the remains of a court book of Bishop Tunstall of London from the 1520s which John Foxe used (and perhaps abused), all show how detailed such documentation could be.[4] Thanks also to Dr. Fines's investigation of the collections of Archbishop Ussher in the library of Trinity College, Dublin, we know of the survival into the seventeenth century of two other such records that were used extensively by Foxe. For Ussher made notes not only on the Norwich trials, but also on a 'Book of Abjurations' from the episcopate of Richard FitzJames, bishop of London, of 1508-9, and a 'Book of Detections, Confessions and Abjurations' of heretics before Bishop Longland of Lincoln in 1521. All these records (from Norwich, London and Lincoln) were reported by Ussher as being 'in Bibliotheca Lambethana' – where none of them now is.[5]

Apart from specialized court proceedings of this kind, episcopal heresy trials might properly find their place in court books that also dealt with other sorts of cases. The register of Bishop Bubwith at Bath and Wells provides a rather interesting example of this. In 1414, in the aftermath of the Oldcastle fracas, the bishop had proceeded against a group of suspects in Bristol, from where a sizeable contingent of supporters had gone to join the London rising. This action, however, was not recorded in the episcopal register at that time. It was only in 1417 (when Bubwith himself was away at the council of Constance), that the officials he had left in charge of his diocese received a royal writ requesting information about the purgation of these Lollards, who were the subject of a secular indictment. A search was therefore conducted of the registers, and of the 'acts, actions and processes' of the bishop, and the

---

[3] Anne Hudson's *Premature Reformation* (Oxford, 1988), appeared after I wrote this essay, and includes pp. 32-41, 124-5, 447-9, 459-60, some discussion of these matters. However, the chronology of the procedural changes I am pursuing here was not a theme of her book, so it still seems worth clarifying the issue.

[4] *Heresy Trials in the Diocese of Norwich, 1428-31*, ed. N.P. Tanner (CS, 4th ser. 20, 1977); J. Fines, 'Heresy Trials in the Diocese of Coventry and Lichfield, 1511-12', *JEH*, 14 (1963), pp. 160-74 (see p. 161, n. 2, for the pages from Tunstall's Court Book on cases of 1527-8, in BL, Harl. MS 421, used by John Strype in his *Ecclesiastical Memorials* (Oxford, 1822), I, i, chapters vii-viii; I, ii, nos. xvii-xxii. Another section of this manuscript also consists of original documents – of a Marian trial register; P. Collinson, 'Truth and Legend: The Veracity of John Foxe's Book of Marytrs', in *Clio's Mirror: Historiography in Britain and the Netherlands*, ed. A.C. Duke and C.A. Tamse (Zutphen, 1985), p. 42.

[5] J. Fines, 'The Post-Mortem Condemnation for Heresy of Richard Hunne', *EHR*, lxxviii (1963), pp. 528-31; J.A.F. Thomson, 'John Foxe and some Sources for Lollard History: Notes for a Critical Appraisal', *SCH*, ii (1965), pp. 251-7; A.G. Dickens, 'Heresy and the Origins of English Protestantism', lecture of 1962, reprinted in the same author's *Reformation Studies* (London, 1982), pp. 367-9.

information found was entered into Bubwith's register as part of this exchange of letters, when the return was sent to London.[6] Had it not been for this correspondence, which prompted the transcription of the court proceedings into the bishop's register, the Bath and Wells part of this story would now be lost.

The survival rate of court books is lower than that of episcopal registers, but may contribute significantly to our knowledge of heretical suspects. Of the approximately eighty cases Professor Dickens studied in the diocese of York during the Tudor period, only half a dozen or so came from the archiepiscopal registers, almost all the rest from surviving act books of the Court of Audience.[7] Yet there seems to have been no absolute norm in this matter. The records of Archbishop Warham's extensive enquiries into heresy in Kent in 1511 are found entered in his register.[8]

The matter of record (and the loss of records) affects not only *our* knowledge, but also contemporaries' knowledge. One of the questions we have to face in considering the English church's response to the development of heresy, is the manner and stages by which the hierarchy ordered and pooled its experience. When a bishop in the diocese of, say, Winchester or Exeter, found himself faced with the task of examining a person for suspected heretical beliefs, what guidance or help could he derive from the experience of other diocesans? How much sharing of experience was there? At what point did it become obligatory for bishops to send in reports of their heretical proceedings to the archbishop? Is it of any significance (Dr. Fines considered this question), that three of the main sources used by Foxe and consulted by Ussher all fetched up at Lambeth?[9] Were records of heretical abjurations collected and abstracted in some way so that systematic formulae, and questionnaires for suspects, could be drawn up for future proceedings? How much initiative was displayed by the church hierarchy on this issue over the century and a half that heresy, like some kind of venomous ragwort escaping from the 'most beautiful garden' of its Oxford seedbed, kept cropping up all over the 'lovely pasture-land' of England?[10]

---

[6] *Register of Nicholas Bubwith, Bishop of Bath and Wells, 1407-1424*, ed. T.S. Holmes (Somerset Record Society, xxix-xxx, 1914), i. pp. lxix-lxxi, 283-90, 298, nos. 716, 745; Thomson, *Later Lollards*, pp. 22-4. For evidence of Archbishop Courtenay's heresy records being kept separate from his main register see Anne Hudson, *Lollards and their Books* (London, 1985) p. 59, n. 77.

[7] A.G. Dickens, *Lollards and Protestants in the Diocese of York, 1509-1558* (London, 1959); idem, 'Heresy and Origins', in *Reformation Studies*, pp. 366-7.

[8] Reg. Warham (Lambeth), fos. 159r-175v; Thomson, *Later Lollards*, pp. 186-90; Hudson, *Premature Reformation*, p. 134.

[9] Fines, 'Post-Mortem Condemnation', p. 528, suggests that the most likely explanation is that these records were taken to Lambeth 'by an archbishop interested in the history of heresy'.

[10] *Snappe's Formulary*, ed. H.E. Salter (Oxford Historical Society, lxxx, 1924), p. 134. Oxford Ragwort did just this, spreading from the Botanic Gardens in Oxford on to waste ground far and wide across the country. G. Grigson, *The Englishman's Flora* (Paladin edn., St. Albans, 1975), p. 390.

We may think about this reaction as having two fronts: the negative and the positive. The negative (which is where it is necessary to begin) consists of the steps that had to be taken to convert and correct those infected by heretical or erroneous opinions. The positive (which perhaps we do not think about enough) was a more far-reaching and imaginative enterprise of education, intended to meet and defeat Lollards on their own ground by anticipation.

The first part of this programme – if we can call it that – is well known, though looking at it from the specific angle of the hierarchy may give it a different perspective. Between the 1380s and the 1430s a series of new enactments, interweaving cooperation between the ecclesiastical and secular authorities, produced new methods for acting against heretical suspects, designed to overcome weaknesses in the existing judicial procedures.[11] It is worth thinking about this from the bishops' point of view. What did they contribute, and how did these changes affect them?

Even the briefest look at the better known part of this counter-offensive against heresy makes it obvious that the bishops, assembled as court or convocation, played a central role. From May 1382, when William Courtenay ('strong pillar of the church' as a contemporary approvingly described him)[12] called the Blackfriars Council – attended by ten bishops – up to November 1457, when Reginald Pecock made his abjuration before a group of prelates, theologians and others, the hierarchy was closely involved in the hearing of heretical cases and the devising of new procedures against suspects.[13] To be present at the examination of leading Wycliffites was an opportunity for individual bishops to learn about the beliefs, equivocations and evasions of suspects – experience that might prove useful at home in their own dioceses. It was perhaps no accident that the prelates present at the Blackfriars meeting included the bishops of Winchester, Exeter and Salisbury, as well as those of London and Lincoln, whose dioceses may all already have been troubled by unorthodox activities.[14]

In subsequent years a series of heretics were examined in convocation. The assembly of 1401, summoned specially to consider the spread of heresy among laymen as well as clerics, who were meeting in conventicles and secret places and disputing over the sacrament of the altar, heard the cases of William Sawtry and John Purvey. The former had already abjured before the bishop of Norwich in 1399 and had subsequently moved to London where, as a parish

---

[11] H.G. Richardson, 'Heresy and the Lay Power under Richard II', *EHR*, li (1936), pp. 1-28; Hudson, *Lollards and their Books* (London, 1985), pp. 125-39; M. Aston, *Lollards and Reformers* (London, 1984), pp. 38-43, 77-78; Thomson, *Later Lollards*, pp. 220-36.

[12] *Fasciculi zizaniorum*, ed. W.W. Shirley (Rolls Series, London, 1858), p. 272.

[13] The sources (and modern views) differ as to the composition of the group before which Pecock capitulated; Green, *Pecock*, p. 54; E.F. Jacob, 'Reynold Pecock, Bishop of Chichester', *PBA*, xxxvii (1951), pp. 121-53 (at 136-7), reprinted in his *Essays in Later Medieval History* (Manchester, 1968) (pp. 17-18).

[14] *FZ*, p. 286. Bishop Brinton of Rochester (also present) had been caught up in another kind of trouble – the 1381 revolt. See above, p. 32 n. 15.

priest, he had reportedly gone back to preaching heresy.[15] John Purvey had been named (with others) in commissions of the late 1380s into the preaching of heresy in the dioceses of Worcester, Hereford and Salisbury. There is no record of his having been officially charged, but by February 1401 he was behind bars in the archbishop of Canterbury's castle at Saltwood.[16] Both men, therefore, had come under suspicion in more than one diocese and Sawtry, a relapsed offender, was burned soon afterwards at Smithfield – the first to suffer this penalty.

Other trials in which convocation took part after this included those of John Badby (who, after his previous condemnation by the bishop of Worcester was sentenced in the convocation of 1410), Sir John Oldcastle (whose case came up three years later), William Taylor (heard in 1421 and again in 1423 when he was condemned), and Richard Wyche and William White, both of whom were eventually convicted and burned a number of years after their examinations. It seems fairly obvious that none of the leading heretics during the earlier phases of the Lollard movement was finally condemned without at least one hearing before convocation. These were all men of dangerous prominence, whose obdurate error, recidivism, and influence that spread across the boundaries of dioceses secured them a trial of this kind. The cumbersome exchanges involved in coordination between different episcopal jurisdictions made for difficulties (not unlike the experience of some modern police forces), and retarded the pursuit of peripatetic suspects – a fact which may itself have something to do with the establishment of Lollard communities in areas near the unique junction of four dioceses.[17] The church's choice of convocation as the forum for hearing offenders who had crossed so many boundaries was surely a matter of policy.

If it seems right to suppose that church leaders were anxious to do all they could to secure retractions from errant believers, it was also the case that they wanted to be sure that justice was *seen* to be done. At a time when delivery to the death sentence must have been a hard decision to take (whatever contemporary heretics and later Protestants said about this), corporate judgement eased the burden on individual prelates. Also not to be left out of account was the self-evident advantage of giving maximum publicity to the refutation of error. Thus in 1401 Sawtry's condemnation and degradation was preceded by the archbishop's solemn exposition in the vernacular, from the episcopal

---

[15] Wilkins, *Concilia*, iii, pp. 254-60; K.B. McFarlane, *John Wycliffe and the Beginnings of English Nonconformity* (London, 1952), pp. 150-52.

[16] Wilkins, *Concilia*, iii, pp. 260-62; Hudson, *Lollards and their Books*, pp. 86-9.

[17] This must surely have been a relevant factor for the Chiltern Lollards, in addition to their location at one end of the huge diocese of Lincoln, which at its southernmost tip meets the dioceses of Salisbury, Winchester and London. See R.G. Davies, 'Lollardy and Locality', *TRHS*, 6th Series, 1 (1991), pp. 191-212, for a recent appraisal of these communities. The problem caused by heretics' moving from diocese to diocese to evade proceedings by was stated in *De heretico comburendo*; *Statutes of the Realm*, ii, p. 126, 2 Henry IV, c. 15; see also A.K. McHardy, 'The Dissemination of Wyclif's Ideas', *SCH*, Subsidia 5 (1987), *From Ockham to Wyclif*, p. 367.

throne in St. Paul's (where he sat in full pontificals, attended by the bishops of London, Lincoln, Hereford, Exeter, St. Davids and Rochester), before a large crowd of clergy and people, of the entire process against this heretic. Purvey had publicly to renounce his articles at Paul's Cross, likewise in English, before the people gathered there for the Sunday sermon.[18] Combating heresy inevitably involved the publicizing of proscribed opinions, and if this sometimes seemed risky, it also helped to prepare those clerks whose business it was to prevent the proliferation of error.

During the earlier stages of these defensive moves against heresy, it does not seem possible to unravel the links between the localities and the centre, the precise modes of cooperation between bishops, archbishop and convocation. Only with the Oldcastle rebellion and the accession of Archbishop Chichele can we see the obvious signs of concerted action. This was indeed a turning-point, in more than one respect.

Sir John Oldcastle put Archbishop Arundel and his bench in a most embarrassing fix. There was nothing new about courtiers dabbling with doubtful teaching, but for a royal henchman obstinately to defend heresy was unheard of, and the ultimate undesirable. The bishops (with the lower clergy breathing down their necks) had to consider breaking normal conventions, and turning the arm of the law against one of their social equals – a member of the gentry who were supposedly chief defenders of the law. The extreme awkwardness of the situation was reflected in the staged, delicate moves by which Sir John was interviewed and the case against him presented. When convocation met on 6 March 1413 and began to consider the problem, Henry IV was still king. The accession of Henry V two weeks later compounded the dilemma facing the hierarchy, in view of the new king's friendship with their suspect.[19] Could Henry be depended on?

In the land that had 'dronke of the poisoun of heresie', what hope could there be if the king actually supported the heretics? This would be a case of the blind leading the blind into the pits, down 'the dirk [dark] aleye of heresie'. The pressures (of course wrapped up with due tact and adulation) on Henry V during these first months of his reign suggest that the unthinkable was being thought.

[18] Wilkins, *Concilia*, iii, pp. 259, 260. See above p. 48 for the earlier proceedings against Sawtry.

[19] McFarlane, *John Wycliffe*, pp. 162-6; Hudson, *Premature Reformation*, p. 116; Wilkins, *Concilia*, iii, pp. 338, 351-3 (p. 352 for the lower clergy in convocation pressing the prelates for action against Oldcastle). See also P. McNiven, *Heresy and Politics in the Reign of Henry IV* (Woodbridge, 1987), p. 220ff; P.J. Horner, ' "The King Taught us the Lesson": Benedictine Support for Henry V's Suppression of the Lollards', *Mediaeval Studies*, 52 (1990), pp. 190-220.

What mighten folk of good byleeve seye,
  If bent were our kynges affeccioun
To the wrong part, who sholde hem help purveye?
  A kyng set in that wrong opinioun
  Mighte of our feith be the subversioun.[20]

Thomas Hoccleve chose the occasion of Henry's ceremonial reinterment of Richard II's bones in Westminster Abbey to appeal to the king. Maybe he took a cue from the inscription on Richard's monument, an epitaph which claimed defence of the church against heresy among this monarch's achievements. The poet surely spoke for others who, at this juncture, desperately desired an earnest of Henry V as 'Crystes knyght', and true 'Champioun' for holy chirche'.[21]

The same hope (or anxiety) moved those members of Oxford University who in 1414 addressed Henry V with a list of needed church reforms. The extirpation of heresy was among these, and the academics went so far as to suggest that any diocesan found negligent in this duty ought to be deposed from episcopal office. Not that these advisers wished to by-pass convocation. Indeed, by invoking the examples of Constantine and Theodosius they wanted the king as a 'most religious knight of Christ' to call the clergy together in this hour of need. Christian princes who defended Christ's church from such misfortunes deserved the highest praise, and so, it was suggested, Henry V would be taking a wise step were he to give secular officials (such as sheriffs, mayors and bailiffs) the duty of tracking down heretics, as a means of reinforcing the bishops.[22]

It seems likely that one important result of the Lollards' attempted rebellions, most notably that of 1414, was to make the episcopate better informed about the nature of the heresy. Archbishop Arundel had already moved in this direction when in October 1413 he circulated throughout the province of Canterbury the process of the trial and sentence of Sir John Oldcastle. All the bishops were to be sent verbatim copies ('we order it to be copied, word for word, and made known') so that they could publish to the people, in their cathedral cities and parochial churches, the truth concerning these erroneous opinions 'in a loud and intelligible voice, and in the mother tongue'.[23] And recorded it duly was, and is to be found where it was enrolled by the recipients,

---

[20] *Historical Poems of the XIVth and XVth Centuries*, ed. R.H. Robbins (New York, 1959), pp. 107-8; *Hoccleve's Works*, i, *The Minor Poems*, ed. F.J. Furnivall (EETS, ES, lxi, 1892), p. 48, cf. pp. 39-40; *Henry V: The Practice of Kingship*, ed. G.L. Harriss (Oxford, 1985), p. 25.

[21] Hoccleve, in Robbins, p. 107. For the inscription on Richard II's tomb, which includes the line 'Obruit hereticos – et eorum stravit amicos', see E.W. Brayley and J.P. Neale, *The History and Antiquities of the Abbey Church of St. Peter, Westminster* (London, 1818-23), ii, pp. 108-9.

[22] Wilkins, *Concilia*, iii, pp. 360, 365 (no. 43). The Leicester Parliament took this step in 1414; *Rot. Parl.*, iv, p. 15; *SR*, ii, pp. 181-7, 2 Henry V, c. 7.

[23] Wilkins, *Concilia*, iii, pp. 353-7, cited at 357.

for instance in the registers of Bath and Wells, and Lincoln.[24] This long report, which included both Oldcastle's English statement of belief and the vernacular questions that had been put to him, might well have proved useful to those diocesans who, in the months and years after the rising was suppressed and even after Oldcastle himself had been finally caught and executed, found themselves on the trail of his sometime supporters.

As historians of Lollardy have already made plain, one trial record could influence another.[25] The procedure of examining Wycliffite suspects on a set questionnaire is not known to have existed before the 1420s. Before that time each diocesan had, apparently, to stake out his own ground on the basis of existing canon law.[26] The questions a bishop or his officials put to suspects depended on their own knowledge, which might or might not have included some previous experience of Wycliffite tenets, texts and teaching. After the 1414 rising this state of affairs changed and the system of investigation became steadily more centralized and regularized.

In the early summer of 1416, with Henry Chichele installed at Canterbury and Sir John Oldcastle still in hiding, convocation passed a statute that made the counter-measures against heresy altogether less haphazard. Firstly, provision was made for regular enquiries at least twice every year, to check on illicit meetings and the possession of suspect English books in all parishes in the province of Canterbury where heretics were thought to live: secondly, and equally important, all findings of this kind that were made – the processes of those convicted, and specially all abjurations of heresy – were to be certified to the next convocation, and the records handed over for keeping in the registry of the court of Canterbury.[27] The central register of offenders had (in theory) at last been created. Recidivists (such as William White, William Taylor and Richard Wyche) should in future be able to receive the measure of their own words.[28] For, as Chichele's statute put it, anyone who in future needed to

[24] *Reg. Bubwith*, i,, pp. 154-65, no. 455; *Register of Bishop Philip Repingdon, 1405-1419*, ed. M. Archer (Lincoln Record Society, 57-58, 74, 1963, 1982), iii, pp. 10-13, no. 24.

[25] Thomson, *Later Lollards*, pp. 224-6; Hudson, *Lollards and their Books*, pp. 125-40.

[26] Thomson, *Later Lollards*, p. 224. For the bearing of the canon *Excommunicamus* (which threatened papal sanctions against a ruler who did not purge his land of heresy), on the proceedings of 1414, see F.W. Maitland, *Collected Papers*, ed. H.A.L. Fisher (Cambridge, 1911), iii, pp. 154-5.

[27] *Register of Henry Chichele*, ed. E.F. Jacob (Oxford, 1938-47), iii, pp. 18-19; Wilkins, *Concilia*, iii, p. 378. E.F. Jacob, *Archbishop Henry Chichele* (London, 1967), pp. 69-72, relates this measure to Chichele's promotion of university graduates in the fight against Lollardy.

[28] This matter of record was all the more important given the interpretation of relapse in the fifteenth-century English church. William Lyndwood (who gave the legal opinion on which Taylor, having twice abjured, was condemned in 1423), explains that a relapsed heretic was one who had gone back twice on an abjuration; the first failure made a man a *lapsus*; the second a *relapsus*. William Lyndwood, *Provinciale* (Oxford, 1679), comments on 'De haereticis', p. 296, notes l, n and o; p. 305, note c; cf. *Corpus iuris canonici*, ed. E. Friedberg (Leipzig, 1879-81), ii, cols. 1071-2, *Sexti Decretalium*, Lib, V, tit. ii, *De haereticis*, cap. viii; *Reg. Chichele*, i, pp. cxxxiv-v; iii, pp. 168-9.

consult a previous process in implementing proceedings, could have access to it through the official of the court of Canterbury. This new mandate was circulated to the bishops and is to be found, duly on file, in various registers.[29]

What may be regarded as the final stage of this procedural network was reached in 1428. Canterbury Convocation that year was much preoccupied with the question of heresy (both at home and abroad) and the formulation of improved defences against it was high on the agenda of the meeting. It seems certain that Archbishop Chichele was spurred (in every sense of the word) into action by his own personal experience. It is from this time that we have that rare, vivid description of him (in a letter to William Swan), riding about his diocese for several days and nights in hot pursuit of Lollards who were reported to be planning a new rising. It must surely have been an exceptional sense of urgency that caused the archbishop (at the age of about sixty- six) to undertake this strenuous mission. It was seen in terms of a search and destroy mission by the correspondent who described it. And the numerous heretics who, as a result of this campaign, were overcrowding Chichele's prisons that summer, contributed to the crisis convocation was called on to consider.[30] The archbishop, urging his diocesans, just before convocation's summer recess, to make diligent enquiries into heresy, instructed them to return records of their findings with the names of suspects and proceedings taken against them. Once more, it was the pooling of information that he had in mind, and the record of the Norwich proceedings of 1428-31 which Ussher found at Lambeth in the seventeenth century, may have arrived there as the result of Bishop Alnwick's obedience to this order.[31]

The new formulas that were arrived at during this meeting drew an even clearer line of communication between the archbishop at the centre and the bishops in their dioceses, easing still further the task of conducting heresy trials. From now on, the ordinaries had at their disposal both sets of questions to put to suspects, and also a set formula for those abjuring heresy and error.[32] Discretion was still called for, since Lollards were not to be pigeon-holed, and questions needed tailoring for different circles or groups. But mid fifteenth-century bishops could feel themselves on surer ground than their predecessors when confronted by heresy. Bishop Beckington of Bath and Wells had a much easier time, when he set about examining a suspect in 1448,[33] than his

---

[29] Thomson, *Later Lollards*, p. 223, cites examples, and points to the concomitant registration of the statute of the 1414 Leicester Parliament against heresy. See also *Register of Robert Hallum*, ed. J.M. Horn (Canterbury and York Soc., lxxii, 1982), p. 131, no. 920; *Reg. Repingdon*, iii, p. 128, no. 224.

[30] Aston, *Lollards and Reformers*, pp. 77-9.

[31] *Reg. Chichele*, iii, p. 190; *Thomson, Later Lollards*, pp. 223-4.

[32] *Reg. Chichele*, iii, p. 187; Hudson, *Lollards and their Books*, pp. 125-40; Thomson, *Later Lollards*, pp. 227-30.

[33] *Register of Thomas Bekynton, Bishop of Bath and Wells, 1443-1465*, ed. H.C. Maxwell-Lyte and M.C.B. Dawes, i, (Somerset Record Society, xlix, 1934), pp. 120-7, no. 458; A. Judd, *The Life of Thomas Bekynton* (Chichester, 1961), pp. 137-40.

predecessor Bishop Bubwith had had in a similar situation thirty-five years earlier. The effects of these changes on the reported beliefs of suspects, and on historians' knowledge, are another matter.

These provisions, enacted *ad hoc* at moments of need, produced a mesh of support woven between ecclesiastical and secular authorities to contain the spread of heresy. From the church's point of view they were appendages or supplements to existing canon law, which had already long since legislated on this matter. As Maitland pointed out a hundred years ago (in a controversy which itself is now part of history), the provisions of *De haereticis* in the Sext were much more significant to William Lyndwood than the enactments of English parliaments, and the penalty of burning for heresy existed in the Decretals of Gregory IX generations before England added its footnote of *De haeretico comburendo*.[34] The first legislation of the English church specifically dealing with heresy – and the first to feature in Lyndwood's book – was that of Archbishop Arundel. His Constitutions, drawn up in 1407 and promulgated two years later, were annotated fully in the *Provinciale*.[35] They were designed to inhibit heresy at source, by placing controls on the production and reading of Wycliffite texts, and preventing the spread of popular theology.

Archbishop Arundel knew something about the subsoil that nourished popular heresy. He aimed to curb the dangerous growth of speculative vernacular theology, and probably saw that it was necessary not merely to root out dangerous English writings but also to implant alternative reading. In 1410 Arundel officially approved the *Myrrour of the Blessed Lyf of Jesu Christ*, an English version, recently completed by Nicholas Love (prior of the Yorkshire charterhouse at Mount Grace) of the *Meditationes vitae Christi*, a gospel harmony attributed to Bonaventure. The preface expressed the hope and intention that the book would, like other 'bookes and tretees of devought men' reach out 'in english to lewed men and wommen and hem that ben of symple understondynge'.[36] The text explicitly counters Lollardy, and there are enough links between Arundel, Mount Grace and Nicholas Love for it to seem plausible that the archbishop might have sponsored the production of the book.[37] He was also associated with another gospel harmony, Clement of Llanthony's *Unum ex quattuor* (for which one of his chaplains compiled a table

---

[34] F.W. Maitland, *Roman Canon Law in the Church of England* (London, 1898), pp. 79-80, and chapter I on William Lyndwood. On Lyndwood's *Provinciale* see also C.R. Cheney, *Medieval Texts and Studies* (Oxford, 1975), chapter 8. On Maitland's duelling with Malcolm MacColl see G.R. Elton, *F.W. Maitland* (London, 1985), pp. 74-5.

[35] Wilkins, *Concilia*, iii, pp. 314-19; Lyndwood, *Provinciale*, pp. 288-305.

[36] N. Love, *The Mirrour of the Blessed Lyf of Jesu Christ*, ed. L.F. Powell (Oxford, 1908), p. 8. See also above p. 51.

[37] Opinions differ as to the nature of Arundel's connection with the book. A.I. Doyle, 'Reflections on Some Manuscripts of Nicholas Love's *Myrrour of the Blessed Lyf of Jesu Christ*', *Leeds Studies in English*, n.s. 14 (1983), pp. 82-93; Jonathan Hughes, *Pastors and Visionaries: Religion and Secular Life in Late Medieval Yorkshire* (Woodbridge, 1988), pp. 230-34; Hudson, *Premature Reformation*, pp. 437-440.

of contents), which likewise appeared in an English version.[38] Love's *Myrrour* might be regarded as the positive side of the negative agenda of the Constitutions: offering lay men and women a substitute for Wycliffite reading, and presenting devout meditation on the life of Christ in place of provocative questioning of scripture and sacrament.

The extent of any bishop's knowledge of heresy would depend on his reading, as well as his readiness for hot pursuit. As far as I know there was only one bishop who made it his business to delve deeply into the Lollards' vernacular teaching, though he cannot have been alone in this activity, since examining accused heretics necessitated – specially in cases of authors such as William Taylor and William White – some study of their books and tracts.[39] That bishop was, of course, Reginald Pecock, who in the course of a career that included spells in Oxford, St. Asaph and Chichester, familiarized himself with the entire Wycliffite case both by conversing with Lollards and by reading. He knew at first hand the sort of questioning (sometimes seeming so arrogant) that could be expected from the laity – women as well as men.[40] He tells us himself about his talk with heretics.

> I have spoke oft tyme, and bi long leiser, with the wittiest and kunnyngist men of thilk seid soort, contrarie to the chirche, and which han be holde as dukis amonge hem, and which han loved me that that y wolde pacientli heere her evydencis, and her motyves, without exprobacioun. And verili noon of hem couthe make eny motyve for her parti so stronge as y my silf couthe have made thereto.[41]

In addition to such dialogue Pecock also knew the writings of the Lollards. This is something we have to deduce from his surviving works, since the bishop – perhaps understandably – was reticent on this score and, despite all his detailed knowledge of Wycliffite arguments, kept his written sources to himself. His reference to 'the book of Wiclijf' is opaque (though sixty or so

[38] Hudson, *Premature Reformation*, pp. 267-8 discusses the complexion of the English version, *Oon of Foure*, indicating that it is possible 'to see its similarity to Love's *Myrrour*, authorized by Arundel and hence certainly of orthodox origin'. Hughes, *Pastors and Visionaries*, pp. 229-30; B. Smalley, *Studies in Medieval Thought and Learning* (London, 1981), pp. 249-87.

[39] The fifteenth-century hierarchy was certainly not lacking the theological skills needed to counter heresy, though it was professional theologians in religious orders (William Woodford and Thomas Netter) who produced substantial refutations of the Wycliffites. Richard Fleming (mentioned below) reached the episcopal bench with direct knowledge of Wycliffe's Latin works; Stephen Patrington, who became bishop of St. David's in 1415, and died just as he was about to move to Chichester in 1417, was also familiar with heretical writings. J.T. Rosenthal, 'The Training of an Elite Group: English Bishops in the Fifteenth Century', *Transactions of the American Philosophical Society*, new series, 60 (1970), pp. 12-19; Emden, (O), ii, pp. 697-9; iii, pp. 1435-6.

[40] For Pecock's comments on the crude logic and questioning of Lollards see R. Pecock, *The Repressor of Over Much Blaming of the Clergy*, ed. C. Babington (RS, 1860), i, pp. 9, 123; Aston, *Lollards and Reformers*, p. 51; Brockwell, *Bishop Reginald Pecock* (above, n. 1), p. xiii, and for other comments on Lollard curiosity see above p. 49, n. 56.

[41] *Reginald Pecock's Book of Faith: A Fifteenth-Century Theological Treatise*, ed. J.L. Morison (Glasgow, 1909), p. 202 ('dukis' = leaders); cited Green, *Bishop Reginald Pecock*, pp. 21-2.

years later suspects in the diocese of Winchester confessed to reading 'a boke called Wiclif'), but it seems likely he knew some of the Lollard texts we still have, including the *Lantern of Light*, as well as the later version of the Wycliffite Bible.[42]

Lollards themselves had entertained hopes – long before this – that bishops would read their writings. In 1395 the men behind the manifesto of twelve conclusions were very conscious of the audience they wished to reach. They claimed than an exposition of one of their proposals had been read to the king, and by posting this twelve-point address on the doors of St. Paul's as well as Westminster Hall, they made it clear that they were invoking the attention of convocation as well as parliament.[43]

When it came to learning from the Lollards in order to defeat them on their own ground, Bishop Pecock was in a class of his own. There were others – bishops as well as theologians – who gave thought to the sources of error and who had views about combating heresy through education. Most of them, however, confined their attention to the universities and Latin theology. They continued to think in terms of the heresy's academic beginnings and focused their anxiety on preventing a recurrence of events. At the forefront of their concern lay the fear that academic theologians (specially in Oxford) might still be reading Wycliffe and inspired by his works.

By mustering the leaders of the church in Oxford at critical junctures, first Archbishop Courtenay and then Archbishop Arundel hoped to impress the university and those who pursued unorthodox speculations and all who read or (still worse) wrote or edited doubtful texts, with the weight of ecclesiastical authority. The summons of convocation to St. Frideswide's in November 1382 was followed twenty-five years later by the meeting of 1407 which approved Arundel's Constitutions imposing controls on preaching, Bible translation, and the reading of Wycliffite literature. There was plenty of concentration on Oxford after that, including Bishop Repingdon's citation, sent to the chancellor of the university in March 1414, a month after Oldcastle's rising, giving notice of his forthcoming visitation to investigate heresy.[44] This continued anxiety may have been well-founded, if Oxford was indeed central to the continuing production of Wycliffite texts.[45] Cambridge meanwhile, though it

[42] Pecock, *Repressor*, ii, p. 501; Reg. Fox (Winchester), iii, fos. 69v, 71 r; Hudson, *Premature Reformation*, p. 471. On the problematical question of Pecock's sources see Green, *Pecock*, pp. 90, 194-5; Brockwell, *Pecock*, pp. 176-7 (n. 17), 178 (n. 21), 188-9 (nn. 30, 44), 197 (n.118).

[43] *Selections from English Wycliffite Writings*, ed. Anne Hudson (Cambridge, 1978), pp. 24-9, 150-55; see below, pp. 109, 113.

[44] *Snappe's Formulary*, pp. 114-15, 181-6; *Reg. Repingdon*, iii, p. 117, no. 193; Thomson, *Later Lollards* pp. 211-12.

[45] Anne Hudson, 'Wycliffism in Oxford 1381-1411', in *Wyclif in his Times*, ed. A. Kenny (Oxford, 1986), p. 81; *Premature Reformation*, pp. 108-9, 119.

did not escape attention,[46] was able to adopt a holier-than-thou attitude, thanks to its apparently clean slate.

> For which by recorde, all clarks seyne the same,
> Of heresie Cambridge bare never blame.[47]

John Lydgate, thus ending his instructive verses on Cambridge, doubtless reflected local loyalty, but the claim seemed unimpeachable.

Fears of the dread influence of Wycliffe on men of learning continued to haunt educational patrons all through the fifteenth century, which suggests how (in a kind of reds-under-the-bed syndrome) alarms themselves could become institutionalized. Both King's and Queen's Colleges, founded in Cambridge in the 1440s, reflect this anxiety, which seems to have been given a boost by the proceedings against Bishop Pecock. After his condemnation in 1457 a clause was added to the statutes of King's, requiring scholars to take an oath on admission renouncing the opinions, errors and heresies of Wycliffe and Pecock. The same thing seems to have happened at Queens'.[48] Did the renunciation of heresy itself become something of a convention, alongside the expectation that in the best-ordered houses, inmates would not hunt, fish, or keep in college a 'monkey, bear, fox, stag, or hind, or any other unwonted or rarely seen wild beasts or birds' – as specified in the statutes of King's?[49]

Lollards, however, were not particularly rare birds in the 1440s. And the idea that one could positively *educate* heresy out of existence was very much in the wind. The fifteenth century was an age of increasing educational benefaction in which bishops – themselves a well-educated group of men – played a significant part.[50] The modes of this didactic response were various. While some of the bishops concentrated on the training of teachers, and the learned theological armoury, others had in mind the devotional framework of the faith

---

[46] On Arundel's visitation of Cambridge in 1401 (which enquired after Lollard suspects), see I.J. Churchill, *Canterbury Administration* (London, 1933), i, p. 337; ii, p. 152; Reg. Arundel (Lambeth), i, fos. 492v – 493r; cf. T. Fuller, *History of the University of Cambridge*, ed. M. Prickett and T. Wright (Cambridge, 1840), pp. 127-35.

[47] *The Minor Poems of John Lydgate*, ed. H.N. MacCracken, pt. II (EETS, OS 192, 1934), p. 655; D. Pearsall, *John Lydgate* (London, 1970), pp. 218-19,

[48] *Documents relating to the University and Colleges of Cambridge* (HMSO, London, 1852), ii, pp. 623-4; Green, *Reginald Pecock*, pp. 53, 68-9; Thomson, *Later Lollards*, pp. 212-14.

[49] *Documents relating to . . . Cambridge*, ii, pp. 542-3. (It was common form for college statutes to prohibit the keeping of hawks and hounds; cf. Peterhouse, p. 29).

[50] This aspect of the episcopate has recently attracted a lot of attention. Richard G. Davies, 'The Episcopate', in *Profession, Vocation, and Culture in Later Medieval England*, ed. C.H. Clough (Liverpool, 1982), pp. 51-89; Helen Jewell, 'English Bishops as Educational Benefactors in the Later Fifteenth Century', in *The Church, Politics and Patronage in the Fifteenth Century*, ed. R.B. Dobson (Gloucester, 1984), pp. 146-67; Joel T. Rosenthal, 'Lancastrian Bishops and Educational Benefaction', in *The Church in Pre-Reformation Society*, ed. C.M. Barron and C. Harper-Bill (Woodbridge, 1985), pp. 191-211; Virginia Davis, 'William Waynflete and the Educational Revolution of the Fifteenth Century', in *People, Politics and Community in the later Middle Ages*, ed. J. Rosenthal and C. Richmond (Gloucester, 1987), pp. 40-59.

provided through service of the saints whose relics and images were impugned by Lollards, or the vernacular reading that at some levels of society seemed to have been arrogated by the heretics with such damaging results.[51]

The Queens' College in Cambridge, founded 'for the extirpation of heresies and errors, the increase of the faith and the enhancement and support of the clergy' in 1448,[52] followed the intention expressed twenty years earlier by Richard Fleming, bishop of Lincoln. In 1427 Fleming obtained a charter for the foundation of Lincoln College, Oxford, which he planned as a kind of counter-Wycliffite seminary, specifically aimed at the extermination of heresy. Fleming had plenty of inside knowledge both of Oxford and of Wycliffe's writings, since he had been a member of the university committee of twelve which had so laboriously listed 267 heresies and errors in Wycliffe's works, and he had also attended the later sessions of the council of Constance. The founder's words, echoed in those heard by convocation in 1428, reflect his concern about the plague of heretical opinions so dangerously (it seemed) on the increase at that time. His college was to be a bulwark against that threat, a small group (*collegiolum*) of front-line theologians, trained for defence of the faith.[53] Appropriately, among the books Fleming left his college was the most up-to-date work on that subject – the recently completed second part of Thomas Netter's huge *Doctrinale fidei catholicae*.[54] It also seems properly consistent with the founder's aim that fifty years later the statutes of the 'second founder', Thomas Rotherham, provided for the college's theological studies to be put to practical use by the provision of evangelical preaching, English sermons to the people, in the churches of All Saints and St. Michael's several times a year, including at Easter when communicants were preparing themselves to receive the eucharist.[55]

Pecock similarly set out to build educational defences, but the method he lit on was entirely different. Himself a man of learning with an Oxford career which had brought him into contact with Richard Fleming, Pecock would have been the last to deny the academic sources of Wycliffism. But he grasped, more firmly than any other contemporary, the vernacular nettle of Lollardy – and got badly stung. The educational foundation that Pecock regarded as essential was not of the usual kind at all. It was not an institution with solid buildings and

---

[51] On the liturgical and religious foundations (in which bishops were closely involved) as part of this response see Jeremy Catto, 'Religious Change under Henry V', in *Henry V: The Practice of Kingship*, ed. Harriss, pp. 97-115; emphasis on Corpus Christi Day processions (p. 109) could have been important in countering Wycliffite objections to worshipping the host. Drama might also help here; for readings of the Croxton *Play of the Sacrament* see A.E. Nichols, 'The Croxton *Play of the Sacrament*: A Re-Reading', *Comparative Drama*, 22 (1988-89), pp. 117-37. And not to be forgotten is Henry VI's devotion to the cross and the five wounds – personal but also instructive.

[52] *Documents relating to . . . Cambridge*, iii, p. 1.

[53] *Statutes of the Colleges of Oxford* (HMSO, Oxford and London, 1853), i, pp. 7-8, 11, 24. Cf. Fleming's phrase (p. 8) 'haereticorum sectas plus solito invalescere' with *Reg. Chichele*, iii, p. 188. A. Clark, *Lincoln* (College Histories, Oxford: London, 1898), pp. 1-3, 6-7.

[54] Emden (O), ii, p. 698.

[55] *Statutes of . . . Oxford*, i, p. 26; Clark, *Lincoln*, pp. 26-29.

a charter, but a library, and a floating library at that – a kind of library without walls. He devoted enormous labour to the writing of a vernacular *summa theologica*, something that had not previously been attempted and which was attended with tremendous difficulties, both doctrinal and linguistic. He took it on himself (and not surprisingly this brought him into trouble) to restate the essentials of the faith, presenting them under his own new formulae of 'Seven Matters of Religious Knowledge', and 'Four Tables of Moral Virtues'. He even felt sufficient assurance (though this proved costly, in the eventual burning of his books) to indicate deficiencies in the Creed and the Ten Commandments.[56]

There was a sense in which Pecock's work belonged to the tradition that had produced Archbishop Thoresby's catechism a century earlier. But he stepped outside that tradition by taking fully into account the way in which Wycliffites had broken the accepted boundary that had always hitherto divided university theology from popular belief. He believed that the common people, obstinate as some of them were, as he put it, against clerks and prelates, were capable both of logic and learning, provided this came to them in an appropriate form – and in their mother tongue.[57]

Bishop Pecock was nothing if not an educator. Like those who in these years were collecting funds for the new Oxford divinity schools, he saw the defence of the faith as a campaign. The process of reconverting the 'wicked school' of contemporary English Bible-men was comparable to the English conquest of Normandy.[58] Pecock regarded his books as essential weapons for that conversion, extending the pastoral office of teaching and preaching on to the written page, where it could be handled, heard and meditated by the lay party. He envisaged these English writings – texts of sermons, books of theological instruction – being circulated among those men and women whose intellectual curiosity (as well as Bible reading) had made them so disputatious about the faith.

> Certis ofte han men and wommen come to me [reported Pecock], and seid; 'Thus hath a doctour seid in this mater; and thus hath a doctour seid in thilk mater: and thus hath this famose precher prechid: and thus hath thilk famose precher prechid:'[59]

The bishop's readiness to listen and reply, charting paths through these credal sand-dunes, helped to resolve the doubts of those who thus collected and shuffled authorities, ferreting about in the warrens of preachers' words. He proposed to send his written texts on the same mission. In order, he said, that these writing in the lay people's language may take their effect for reforming the people:

---

[56] Green, *Pecock*, p. 23; Brockwell, *Pecock*, pp. 61-2, 126, 138-9. On Pecock's neologisms see above, p. 34, n. 19.

[57] Pecock, *Repressor*, ed. Babington, i, p. 9; cited Green, *Pecock*, pp. 15-16.

[58] Thomson, *Later Lollards*, p. 214; Pecock, *Repressor*, i, pp. 86, 90.

[59] *Repressor*, i, p. 91.

it is not ynough that the seid bokis be writen and made and leid up or rest in the hondis of clerkis, though fame and noise be made greet to the seid lay peple of suche bokis, and that tho bokis schulde opene to hem that thei erren; but tho bokis musten be distributid and delid abrood to manye, where that nede is trowid that thei be delid. . . .

These books were to be written 'in greet multitude', and to be properly corrected, and then sent on their way to be either given or lent at large, wherever they were thought to be most needed.[60] Pecock seems to have learnt something from the Lollards' own book trade.

Pecock, therefore, did not think it good enough for these English books to be available in libraries or held for reference in clerical custody.[61] They must be numerous enough, and accessible enough, to be in the hands of lay men and women at home. If he was here meeting Lollards on their own ground, we ought also to bear in mind that his texts may have been just as various in kind and format as those of the heretics. It would surely be wrong to assume (specially given the tiny fraction of Pecock's works that are extant) that he expected his questioning parishioners to plough through the whole of the *Donet* or the *Book of Faith*. He himself abstracted the *Donet* into the shorter *Poore Mennis Myrrour*, and the letter absolving Pecock which Calixtus III sent to Archbishop Bourchier in 1458 referred to Pecock's having compiled for the people libels and tractates and quinternions.[62] It seems safe to assume that short texts or pamphlets – gatherings of a few pages – including reports of sermons, were among the books Pecock wanted to see in circulation.

Since we only possess half a dozen out of the total of forty to fifty known titles of Pecock's planned oeuvre, it is impossible to assess his achievement properly.[63] Does this poor survival rate (for the books that we do have exist only in single copies) suggest that the circulation of his writings was paltry, and that the authorities acted swiftly enough to forestall implementation of the essential part of his programme – duplication and dissemination? Following the Wycliffite literary initiative as he did, the bishop lacked one essential that had done so much for the other side: a circle of co-workers and followers to copy, correct and circulate his works. That is – so far as we know. Pecock certainly had friends who sympathized with his aspirations, and we know the names of two who suffered on that account.[64] He himself complained in the

---

[60] *Book of Faith*, pp. 116-17; cf. R. Pecock, *The Reule of Crysten Religioun*, ed. W.C. Greet (EETS, OS 171, 1927), pp. 19-20, 99, 392.

[61] For 'the unspoken assumption that books are the common possession of all', lying behind Wycliffite criticism of the works of learning held in friars' libraries, see R.H. and M.A. Rouse, 'The Franciscans and Books: Lollard Accusations and the Franciscan Response', *SCH*, Subsidia 5 (1987), *From Ockham to Wyclif*, pp. 369-84, cited at 380.

[62] Green, *Pecock*, p. 238; *CPL , 1455-64*, pp. 76-78; 'libellos seu tractatus aut quinternos . . .' On the forms of Lollard books see Hudson, *Lollards and their Books*, pp. 183-4; idem, *Premature Reformation*, pp. 200-204.

[63] Brockwell, *Pecock*, pp. x-xii; Green. *Pecock*, pp. 238-45.

[64] See below p. 92, and n. 76.

Donet (much of which was written before 1444), that part of this work and another had been 'runne abrood and copied' against his will, through the discourtesy and indiscretion of the friends to whom he had loaned them.[65] He had not intended these books to go further until they had been properly examined by himself and approved by the authorities. He made much the same claim at his trial in 1457, when it was an obvious and convenient argument.

It was perhaps inevitable, once Pecock had retracted and admitted his error, that his name should be bracketed with those whose misbeliefs he had sought to correct. The authorities rumbled out their accustomed batteries, and pushed the offending bishop into a predictable corner. Pecock's works were publicly burned, three folios and nine sets of quires (? quinternions) going up in the bonfire at Paul's Cross in London at the time of his abjuration on 4 December 1457. The bishops were instructed to follow suit, and to hunt out and destroy copies of the offender's works that were supposedly in the hands of many men and women. As so often before, attention focused on Oxford. A fortnight after the London book-burning another took place in the university, at Carfax. And nearly twenty years later, when in 1476 Edward IV was concerned about the alleged spread of Pecock's writings, the chancellor and heads of Oxford colleges were ordered to search for works of Wycliffe and Pecock.[66]

I have stressed the uniqueness of Pecock's educational strategy for support-ing the faith. But it is right to place this in context, and that in turn may help us to see that despite the disappearance of most of the bishop's *summa*, his vision was not without some positive influence. For there are some rather interesting interconnections in the field of secular theological learning, which we can trace through a group of friends in London.

Between 1431 and 1444 Pecock held a position in London, where he was rector of St. Michael Paternoster Royal and master of Whittington College. The latter was quite a new foundation. It had been established by the will of Richard Whittington, the celebrated mercer who was thrice lord mayor of London, and who when he died in 1423 was buried in his parish church of St. Michael Paternoster Royal, the rebuilding of which he had started in 1409. Whittington certainly patronized learning, and the friends charged with administering his residuary estate saw to it that this munificence was carried further after his death; 'his executors with his goods founded and built

---

[65] R. Pecock, *The Donet*, ed. E.V. Hitchcock (EETS, OS 156, 1921) pp. 6-7; cited Green, *Pecock*, p. 49 n. 2.

[66] E.F. Jacob, *Essays in Later Medieval History* (Manchester, 1968), p. 19; Green, *Pecock*, pp. 58, 61, 67-8. The bishop of Ely (whose diocese included Cambridge) reported that he found no such books.

Whittington College, with alms houses for thirteen poor men, and divinity lectures to be read there for ever', John Stow recorded.[67]

During his lifetime Whittington had also endowed a new library at the Greyfriars, London, of which he laid the foundation stone in 1411.[68] In addition, it was thanks to the terms of his will that the Guildhall Library came into being. This library, described by a recent authority as 'a new kind of institution for the study of theology', opened in 1425.[69] It was a chained library, composed mainly of works of theology, and open to the general public. This institution (naturally of interest to anyone who sought scriptural and theological education) seems to have flourished and gained the support of fresh bequests.

The man who was chiefly instrumental in seeing to the Guildhall Library foundation was John Carpenter, common clerk to the city of London from 1417 to 1438. A man of cultivated tastes and wealth, who died in 1442, Carpenter was for many years adviser to the mayor and aldermen. As Whittington's most trusted (and longest-living) executor, it can be assumed that he took the leading role in seeing that the residuary estate of this city plutocrat was channelled into this bookish bequest.[70]

John Carpenter was a great bibliophile. His own will (dated 8 March 1442) includes an extremely interesting and eclectic list of books, ranging from legal formularies and treatises on letter-writing (a predictable interest, in view of his career) to architecture, works of Aristotle, Seneca and Petrarch and (aptly) Richard de Bury's *Philobiblon*. Theological works loom large, and some of these items reflect the widening interests of the literate gentry of his day. A book in French containing the ten commandments, twelve articles of the faith and seven theological virtues, had belonged to Sir Thomas Pickworth, a man who had a prominent diplomatic career under Henry IV. John Carpenter also owned the long Latin book written by Roger Dymoke in the reign of Richard II against the twelve conclusions published by the Wycliffites in 1395.[71]

Two of the people to whom John Carpenter left bequests were Reginald Pecock and another John Carpenter – Master John, who was probably a

---

[67] *A Survey of London by John Stow*, ed. C.L. Kingsford (Oxford, 1908), i, pp. 243-4; J. Imray, *The Charity of Richard Whittington; A History of the Trust Administered by the Mercers' Company, 1424-1966* (London, 1968), pp. 3, 6-12, and chapter iii, pp. 38-48; C.M. Barron, 'Richard Whittington: The Man behind the Myth', in *Studies in London History*, ed. A.E.J. Hollaender and W. Kellaway (London, 1969), pp. 197-248. For Whittington's will see *Reg. Chichele*, ii, pp. 240-44.

[68] C.L. Kingsford, *The Grey Friars of London* (Aberdeen, 1915), p. 170. Whittington paid the bulk of the cost of the new library – £400 of the total of £456 16s. 8d.

[69] Nicholas Orme, *English Schools in the Middle Ages* (London, 1973), p. 83.

[70] R. Smith, 'The Library at Guildhall in the 15th and 16th Centuries', *Guildhall Miscellany*, 1 (1952), pp. 3-9; 6 (1956), pp. 2-6; E.M. Borrajo, 'The Guildhall Library: Its History and Present Position', *The Library Association Record*, x (1908), pp. 381-95. On John Carpenter (and the date of his death) see Imray, *The Charity of Richard Whittington*, pp. 13, 15, 38; Orme, *English Schools*, pp. 44, 46, 83-4; *Reg. Chichele*, ii, pp. 242-3, and the next note below.

[71] Thomas Brewer, *Memoir of the Life and Times of John Carpenter* (London, 1856), pp. 121-144 for Carpenter's will and the books mentioned in it.

relative and certainly a trusted friend. Pecock received from the older Car-penter the sum of twenty shillings, while Master John was given a book on architecture (a suitable present since later in life, as bishop of Worcester, he was to be an active builder). In addition, Master John Carpenter became executor for his namesake, while Pecock (with another of the testator's friends) was given responsibility for seeing that any outstanding books from the testator's library found their way into the library of the Guildhall. Together, therefore, they had the task of ensuring that any worthwhile texts should be placed in the new library 'for the profit of the students there, and those discoursing to the common people' – as the terms of the will put it.[72]

These two men, who were thus associated in promoting an institution which – as part of its objective – was helping lay people to help themselves to theology, were old friends. They were exact contemporaries (aged fifty or so at this time), and their connection went back to student days at Oxford, when they had both been at Oriel College, and simultaneously held fellowships there for about ten years. They had been ordained together to successive orders by Bishop Fleming of Lincoln, on the same three days in December 1420, February and March 1421. Long after that their lives continued to run parallel, making it possible for this friendship to continue. During the 1430s, when Pecock was master of Whittington College, Carpenter was warden of St Antony's Hospital in the city of London – positions which they still held at the time of the 1442 will. The two men became bishops in the same year, 1444, John Carpenter being promoted to Worcester when Pecock was appointed to St. Asaph.[73]

Carpenter outlived Pecock by some years and died (after an episcopate of over thirty years) as bishop of Worcester in 1476. We know nothing about how he reacted to the deprivation and final seclusion of his old friend. But we do know that in 1464 (after Pecock's death), Bishop Carpenter did something unusual, that harked back to the concerns they had shared a quarter of a century earlier. He founded another public library.

The library started by Bishop Carpenter was in Bristol, attached to the guild of Kalendars in the church of All Saints, as part of his plans for the reform of that guild. There was an interesting theological emphasis in the ordinances which the bishop issued for the guild in 1464. Future priors of the Kalendars were to be theologians, good at preaching as well as instructed in both Old and New Testaments, and the duties of the office included giving a public lecture in the library once a week and preaching whenever possible in the city of Bristol. Another feature of the foundation was the new library, which the bishop had built at his own expense. This was a *public* library, open to all comers every weekday, for two hours in the morning and two in the afternoon. It was

[72] Ibid, pp. 137-8, 143-4 (cited at 143); cf. pp. 52-3, 60-61, on the probable connection between the two Carpenters.

[73] Emden, (O), i, pp. 360-61; iii, pp. 1447-9. For Carpenter see R.M. Haines, 'Aspects of the Episcopate of John Carpenter, Bishop of Worcester 1444-1476', *JEH*, 19 (1968), pp. 11-40.

modelled on the Guildhall foundation which Carpenter knew all about, and like the other city library this was to be an evangelical centre for orthodox study and teaching. Bishop Carpenter also started a foundation of this kind in 1464 in his own cathedral city, in the Carnary Chapel at Worcester.[74]

These three city libraries (in London, Bristol and Worcester), are a kind of family group of a special kind. Dr. Orme suggests that they were intended particularly for the local clergy, the rectors, vicars and chaplains of the city churches who could have used such public collections of books to hone up their preaching ability – and perhaps their scriptural knowledge. It is surely right to put such people first, when thinking of the objectives of the founders. Collections of Latin theology could only appeal to a limited public, though one cannot help thinking that that might not have prevented a layman like Walter Brut, or a lay woman like Margery Kempe (or for that matter one of the housewives who were ready to accost Reginald Pecock), from poking a nose inside the door.

Such a thought might even have occurred to Bishop Carpenter, for Pecock and the Lollards were not far from his mind when he started planning his Bristol library. In 1448 he had made some disturbing discoveries about a Bristol group of heretics, one of whom – a Lollard teacher – had been supplying others with suspect reading.[75] The new educational establishment at All Saints might at least in part have been designed as an orthodox centre to counter such undesirable activities. It is also indicative of the lasting link that bound Carpenter to his wayward and original friend, Reginald Pecock, to find that in 1458 the man appointed to be prior of the Bristol Kalendars was a bachelor of theology called John Harlow. For Harlow was suspect as a supporter of Pecock. He had had to leave Oxford in 1457, being debarred from his doctorate in theology as a result of royal instructions to the university authorities. This was the man chosen by Carpenter to serve his Bristol foundation, and Harlow did so until six years before his death in 1486.[76]

It seems not unreasonable to connect these library foundations with other actions taken by bishops in defence of the faith in the fifteenth century. The hierarchy had learnt through this period that popular heresy was nourished by an underground vernacular literature. Lay reading in theology was a development they had had to come to terms with. If the discovery, prosecution and conversion of individuals who had been theologically misled was their prime concern in combating heresy, it was also self-evident to some that educational initiative of a positive kind was needed to serve lay people's interests. Pecock

[74] N. Orme, 'The Guild of Kalendars, Bristol', *Bristol and Gloucestershire Archaeological Society Transactions*, xcvi (1978), pp. 32-52 (this and the next paragraph owe much to pp. 40-43); idem, *English Schools*, p. 85.

[75] Thomson, *Later Lollards*, pp. 34-5; Hudson, *Premature Reformation*, pp. 131, 208, 272, 458.

[76] Orme, 'The Guild of Kalendars', pp. 41-43; cf. Emden (O), ii, pp. 875-6 (which lacks this interesting connection). Master Thomas Leominster (Lempster) was another of Pecock's adherents, who was deprived of his benefice in Denbighshire in Nov. 1458. *CPR, 1452-61*, p. 465; Green, *Pecock*, pp. 33-4; Emden (O), ii, p. 1125.

and the Carpenters were in some ways poles apart. A library with chained books – however helpful the books themselves might be – was not at all Pecock's ideal. He wanted his works to be taken home to satisfy the call for domestic theology, to be on hand whenever the urge to read or hear arose. But these three individuals did share the same underlying aim: the enlargement of theological learning among the laity by means of open access to literary sources. And that was a need that Lollards had themselves pointed to, when they complained so sorely about good books being inaccessible in the libraries of conventual foundations.

Chained or unchained books: it is a topic with resonances for today, now that the library without walls has become a new possibility. Perhaps day-dreaming about lost bishops' registers might be displaced by day-dreams about the day when, at the press of a button, every bishop's register that *does* survive may be summoned into our studies on the flickering screen. Those who love the smell of books and the feel of parchment may not be too excited at that prospect. But one fifteenth-century bishop would surely have been thrilled by the possibilities of such technology – Reginald Pecock.

Fig. 8 Christ, barefoot, at the head of a well-shod procession of clergy of all ranks – from priests to bishops, cardinals and pope – bearing relics and monstrance containing the eucharistic host, greets a pilgrim. The accompanying text explained that this signified the gracious reception of foreigners into the Christian community. 1491 woodcut by Michael Wolgemut.

4

'Caim's Castles': Poverty, Politics, and Disendowment

> . . . pars sacrilegii est rem pauperum dare non pauperibus . . . [1]

> Isti autem sunt stultificati idiotae . . . nescientes inter paupertatem et mendicationem distinguere . . . [2]

In the early fifteenth century, *Jack Upland's* comprehensive invective against the friars included the following charge. 'These ben cockers in convents and covetous in markets, marrers of matrimony and Caym's castle-makers'. 'Jack', returned Friar Daw (whose reply to the sexual accusation was less than comprehensive),

> Jack, thou sayest that we bilden the castles of Caym,
> It is God's house, old shrew, that we ben about.[3]

These exchanges relate to a piece of Wycliffite typology that by this time was commonplace. The adaptation of Middle English legends of Cain (or Caim, as usage then commonly had it) to help damn the mendicant orders became prominent about 1382, and the extended currency of the term 'Caim's Castles' can be attributed to Wycliffe. I have chosen this phrase as a useful point of entry into an aspect of disendowment politics that seems to be important, though it is not usually put first: namely the bearing on them of the controversy over mendicant poverty, which was still very alive in the fifteenth century.

The attributes of Cain in late medieval literature and art were various – and all bad. Cain was of course the prototype murderer, a fratricide at that. He also stood for possession – false possession – and indeed his name is associated with

---

[1] St. Jerome, Epist. 66, 8; *Corpus scriptorum ecclesiasticorum latinorum,* liv (Vienna and Leipzig, 1910), p. 657.

[2] *Joannis Wiclif Trialogus,* ed. G. Lechler (Oxford, 1869), pp. 348-9.

[3] *Jack Upland, Friar Daw's Reply, and Upland's Rejoinder,* ed. P.L. Heyworth (Oxford, 1968), pp. 57-8, 76. On the development of allegations of friars' seduction (spiritual and physical) see A. Williams, 'Chaucer and the Friars', *Speculum,* xxviii (1953), pp. 511-13; E.D. McShane, *A Critical Appraisal of the Antimendicantism of John Wiclif* (Rome, 1950), p. 32.

the Hebrew word meaning to acquire or get.[4] In addition, by a process of association, Cain came to be thought of as a heretic. Thanks to a fusion accomplished in early exegesis, the passage in Genesis 4 describing the offerings of Cain and Abel became linked with the parable of the sower's wheat and tares in Matthew 13. In fact Genesis tells of Cain offering fruits of the ground while Abel offered the firstlings of his flock, but they came to be seen in terms of true and false offerers of tithe – Abel rendering his best beast, or sometimes pure wheat; Cain giving wheat mixed with tares.[5] 'Caim cum lolio'; these words were placed over Cain's head in a twelfth-century sculpture that clearly depicts the weeds among the wheat. From here it was not a long step to the association of Matthew 13 – the heretical cockle in the clean corn.[6] To call the friars Cainites was therefore to blacken them with a cluster of damning qualities, most useful for some controversialists from the 1380s. Moreover Genesis used a phrase to describe cursed Cain that seemed perfectly fitted to the wandering mendicant. The condemned brother, 'a fugitive and a vagabond in the earth', was identifiable as the vagrant friar.[7]

Wycliffe made use of this typing in several of his works. In *De mandatis divinis* (of the mid 1370s), when discussing different sorts of theft under the

[4] *The Wycliffe Bible Commentary*, ed. C.F. Pfeiffer and E.F. Harrison (London and Edinburgh, 1963), 9. For typical remarks on the cupidity of Cain see FitzRalph's *De pauperie salvatoris*, ed. R.L. Poole (WS, 1890), pp. 328, 369, 399; *EWW*, 374, 'cayme, that is possession . . . ' This tract against clerical property, here citing a sermon of Odo of Cheriton, links Cain's false possession with the poisoning of the church by Constantine (see below note 20), interpreting 'Am I my brother's keeper?' (Gen. 4:9) as 'What charge is to me of the souls, so that I have well ordained for the temporal goods'. Jude 1:11, commonly cited in this context, coupled Cain with Balaam in the avarice/false possession stakes; *The Lanterne of Liʒt*, ed. L.M. Swinburn (EETS, OS 151, 1917), pp. 16, 132; cf. Reginald Pecock, *The Repressor of Over Much Blaming of the Clergy*, ed. C. Babington (RS, 1860), ii, p. 480.

[5] A theme made familiar in plays of Cain; e.g. *The Chester Mystery Cycle*, ed. R.M. Lumiansky and D. Mills (EETS, SS 3, 1974), pp. 33-41; in *The Towneley Plays*, ed. G. England and A.W. Pollard (EETS, ES 71, 1897), pp. 14-17, Abel's 'trussell' which burns so easily is contrasted with Cain's sheaves containing 'thistles and briars' which only smoked.

[6] This paragraph owes much to Pearl F. Braude, '"Cokkel in oure Clene Corn": Some Implications of Cain's Sacrifice', in *No Graven Images: Studies in Art and the Hebrew Bible*, ed. J. Gutmann (New York, 1971), pp. 559-99, reprinted from *Gesta*, vii (1968), pp. 15-28, which shows how both brothers' sacrifices came to be represented by bundles of wheat (adulterated and pure), whereas earlier images more accurately portrayed a sheaf and a lamb. Cf. also O.F. Emerson, 'Legends of Cain, especially in Old and Middle English', *Pubs. of the Modern Language Assn. of America*, xxi (1906), pp. 831-929; *Middle English Dictionary*, ed. H. Kurath and S.M. Kuhn (Ann Arbor, 1954-), *s.v.* 'Caim'.

[7] 'vagus et profugus eris super terram'; Gen. 4:12 (cf. *Chester Mystery Cycle*, 38 'idell and wandringe as an theyfe'): '. . . *Cainitae* deberent vagi et profugi exulare'; Wycliffe, *Trialogus*, p. 437. For this association see P.R. Szittya, 'The antifraternal Tradition in Middle English Literature', *Speculum*, lii (1977), p. 312; idem, *The Antifraternal Tradition in Medieval Literature* (Princeton, 1986).

Fig. 9a, b Cain killing Abel with an ass's jawbone (Genesis 4:8, cf. Judges 15:15), as depicted (above) in a German Bible of 1478–80 and (below) by Hans Sebald Beham in 1533. In the background the sacrifice that caused the quarrel: Cain's sheaf (above) droops beside Abel's.

seventh commandment, he turned to the sin of Cain and his avaricious cheating over tithes. Wycliffe called the 'heresiarch Caym' the initiator of injustice in the Old Testament, while Judas played the same role in the New Testament.

> So, just as the heresiarch Caym was the first plainly unjust in the old law, the beginning of injustice in the secular arm, so Scarioth was by the same avarice the first plainly unjust heresiarch in the time of the law of grace, and the beginning [of injustice] in the name of clerks.[8]

In the section of his *Trialogus* which was written after the so-called Earthquake Council of 1382, where the four orders of friars had played such a prominent part in condemning his heresies, Wycliffe included a discussion of the origin of the different mendicant orders. He accused the friars of the most mendacious claims in their quest for antiquity, the Austins asserting that they were founded by St. Augustine, the Carmelites romancing about their origin on Mount Carmel in the time of Elisha. Such claimants were the true descendants of the father of lies. And there are some, Wycliffe went on, who seeing this tide of lying

> make out that these four orders took their beginning in CAYM, and so the voice of his brother Abel cried to the Lord from the ground to shape the malice of these friars. In witness of which the four letters of this name CAIM give the initials of these four orders, according to the sequence in which the friars pretend they originated . . .

i.e. C. for Carmelites with their bogus Old Testament claim; A. for the Austins – moving on many centuries to the time of Augustine; J. for Jacobites, or Dominicans; and M. for Minorites, looking respectively (and more respectably) to St. Dominic and St. Francis.[9]

This anti-fraternal acrostic may have made its popular appearance in the flow of exchanges that took place after the Blackfriars Council in May 1382. An English poem against the friars, which has been dated to this time (though on inconclusive grounds), versifies the C-A-I-M acronym to illustrate the truth

---

[8]   *Tractatus de mandatis divinis*, ed. J. Loserth and F.D. Matthew (WS, 1922), p. 372. On Judas as the epitome of venality see J.A. Yunck, *The Lineage of Lady Meed* (Notre Dame, IND., 1963), pp. 3, 26, 35, 100-1, 125-6, 136, 243-4, 259, 267.

[9]   *Trialogus*, pp. 361-2. (The historical element in this criticism deserves notice). Cf. p. 306 for Wycliffe's use of the term *'Caymitica institutio'* to describe the wrong (covetous) sort of clerical possession. The term Jacobites for the Dominicans (derived from the Paris convent of Saint-Jacques) was established usage; W.R. Thomson, 'The Image of the Mendicants in the Chronicles of Matthew Paris', *AFH*, lxx (1977), p. 16; A.G. Rigg, 'Two Latin Poems against the Friars', *Mediaeval Studies,* xxx (1968), pp. 111-12.

'that men say of them/in many divers land', that the friars' origin lay with 'that caitiff cursed Caym':

> thus grounded caym these four orders,
> that fillen the world full of errors & of hypocrisy.[10]

Who coined this acrostic? It could have been Wycliffe, though given the long-standing controversies surrounding the mendicant orders he could equally well have borrowed this word-play. I have not been able to trace an earlier usage, and Wycliffe might have been referring to himself when, in a sermon, he alluded to the remarks of a certain 'someone' on this topic. Speaking there of the friars as having lie-stained lips and blood-stained hands, he wrote: 'and thus (as someone says – *ut quidam dicit*) these homicides of the race of Caym are figured in the four-letter name' – C. for Carmelites etc.[11] At any rate and whoever invented the acrostic, the extended use of this Caimite vocabulary in the later fourteenth century certainly owed much to Wycliffe.

---

[10] *Historical Poems of the XIVth and XVth Centuries*, ed. R.H. Robbins (New York, 1959), pp. 160, 333. The ascribed date is based on the Latin poem (cited in note 73 below) that precedes this in the manuscript, and which describes the Earthquake Council. As these are not paired poems the deduction is doubtful. Another poem that uses the acrostic is *Mum and the Sothsegger,* ed. M. Day and R. Steele (EETS, OS 199, 1936), pp. 41-2. This is interesting in that it attributes the acrostic to FitzRalph, and (losing sight of Wycliffe's historical criticism of mendicant foundations) uses the four initials to signify vices (crooked Carmelties, amorous Austins, Judas-like Jacobites, 'monsyd' = cursed-working Minorities). As the editors point out (p. 115), there is no support for the attribution to FitzRalph. For a systematic attack on the four orders of friars which impugns their false foundation claims see *Pierce the Ploughmans Crede,* ed. W.W. Skeat (EETS, OS 30, 1867), pp. 3, 10, 12, 15.

[11] *Sermones*, ed. J. Loserth (WS, 1887-90), ii, p. 84, quoted by McShane, *A Critical Appraisal*, p. 15. For Wycliffe referring to himself as *quidam fidelis* see A. Hudson, 'A Lollard Sect Vocabulary?', in *So Meny People Longages and Tonges: Philological Essays,* ed. M. Benskin and M.L. Samuels (Edinburgh, 1981), p. 17; *Polemical Works,* ed. R. Buddensieg (WS, 1883), ii, p. 692, cf. p. 671 and below note 89. For another allusion to the acrostic see the fiercely antimendicant letter *'De fratribus ad scholares'* in *Opera minora,* ed. J. Loserth (WS, 1913), p. 15 ('nomine Caym quatuor Fratum ordines in se continens . . . '). There are two questions here: who first applied Cain's false possession specifically to the friars, and who devised the acrostic to emphasize this? I have not found FitzRalph doing either, but the origin of this Caimite antimendicant vocabulary is elusive and all that can be said with certainty is that it was after 1382 that it became prominent, and acquired heretical associations. Wycliffe's laboured play on the letters and syllables of c-a-r-d-i-n-a-l-i-s in *De blasphemia,* ed. M.H. Dziewicki (WS, 1893), pp. 65-80, is on the same lines as the c-a-i-m device. Both Thomas Netter (a Carmelite) and William Woodford (a Franciscan) attacked Wycliffe for his fatuous Caim acrostic, pointing out that Ca*i*n not Ca*i*m was the proper ancient form (and, as Netter indicated, the N belonged to the Hebrew word for acquisition). Wycliffe did in fact use both forms (cf. *Supplementum trialogi* in *Trialogus*, pp. 437, 444). See Thomas Netter, *Doctrinale,* ed. B. Blanciotti (Venice, 1757-9), i, cols. 614-16; *Fasciculus rerum expetendarum et fugiendarum,* ed. E. Brown (London, 1690), i, pp. 264-5.

'Caim's Castles' was of the same currency. In the text appended to the *Trialogus* on the endowment of the church, Wycliffe returned to the topic of the friars, their houses and churches. Why should they build themselves such towers and monstrous edifices at the expense of the kingdom? It was the devil working in them the avarice of Cain. 'It would be to the advantage of kingdoms', he wrote, 'were the expenses of which friars despoil kingdoms to be distributed to the poor for the building of humble houses'.[12] There is an implicit contrast here between the tall and sumptuous buildings of the mendicants and the lowly dwellings of the poor. The contrast appears again in one of Wycliffe's last writings (*De fundacione sectarum,* datable to the third quarter of 1383), where he attacks the blasphemous excesses of mendicant convents, all built of thefts from deprived Christians and completely incongruous with any imitation of Christ. Thus, he wrote, they fraudulently despoil the destitute to make their 'Caimitical castles' (*castella caimitica*).[13]

'Caim's castles' proved a useful shorthand for the unacceptable face of mendicant possession. It appears in a number of English Wycliffite texts, where its usage always advertizes a Lollard viewpoint, even if there was not exact consistency of meaning. It is worthwhile spending a moment on this changing usage, since it may tell us something about Lollard development.

In the seven or so Lollard texts in print that use the term 'Caim's castles', most apply it as Wycliffe did to the buildings of the four mendicant orders: 'a Caim's castle of friars'; 'Caim's castles of the new orders'; 'by this spoiling they builden Caim's castles', and so on.[14] Others show the phrase taking on a wider meaning. It parts company from the mendicant acrostic to be used against all unjustifiable non-parochial church buildings. 'What advantage shall a poor man have that he suffers against his will his alms to be borne to caim's castle to feed a flock of antichrists?' The author who asked this question (in the vernacular *De officio pastorali*) had in mind not only friary churches, but also cathedrals and royal chapels and colleges of studies to which parish churches were damagingly appropriated. He warned any member of a religious order

---

[12] 'ad aedificationem domorum humilium pauperibus sint dispersae'; *Supplementum trialogi,* pp. 444-5.

[13] *Polemical Works,* i, pp. 39-40, cf. pp. 194-5. *Castrum caymiticum* and *castra caimitica* also appear in *Opus evangelicum,* ed. J. Loserth (WS, 1895-6), i, p. 349, and *Tractatus de officio pastorali,* ed. G.V. Lechler (Leipzig, 1863), p. 38. Cf. Netter, *Doctrinale,* i, cols. 614-16 on Wycliffe's use of the term, including the objection that Caim built a city (Gen. 4:17), not castles. Wycliffe said as much himself (*Supplementum trialogi,* p. 444). Cf. Augustine, *De civitate dei,* lib. xv, c. 1, and for the Cain-and-Abel prototyping of the two cities passing into the Apocalyptic doctrine of the two churches see R. Bauckham, *Tudor Apocalypse* (Appleford, 1978), pp. 55-62.

[14] *SEW,* iii, pp. 398-9, 241, 348, (cf. p. 353 on friars' foundation claims).

with a cure of souls deputed to a vicar, to be sure to 'live in poverty as baptist did, not in high castles of caim and lustful [of] food as boars in sty'.[15] Another English text, on the papacy, seems also to have been attacking religious foundations in general when it alluded to the alms collected by antichrist to make 'such caim's castles'.

> Truly in the old law was Solomon's temple a figure of the church in the new law, but not that the church should be such, but free and large under the cope of heaven, and stand in virtues of man's soul; but antichrist will close it now in cold stones that must perish.[16]

'Caim's castles' implied the duality of Cain and Abel: the murderer and the murdered. It was not only a question of rich churches being wrong in themselves; they were built out of the proceeds of misappropriated alms. The grandiose edifices of all religious foundations (monasteries and colleges as well as friaries) could be proscribed with this term. It sums up the apposition between the unapostolic display of such 'costly churches' and (as one of these authors put it) 'old parish churches that were ordained by Christ's apostles'.[17]

Given our inability to date English Lollard texts, it is impossible to build a semantic chronology on these few references.[18] But we do have one dated example which seems to show 'Caim's castles' being used with a still wider meaning. In the year 1393 Anne Palmer and six other Northampton Lollards (two of them chaplains) were accused by Bishop Buckingham of holding the following belief.

> Item, that it suffices every Christian to serve God's commandments in his chamber or to worship God secretly in the field, without paying heed to public prayers in a material building, lest conforming to the pharisees he is accounted a hypocrite;

---

[15] *EWW*, pp. 419-20, 425, cf. pp. 448-9. On chapter 9 of this text (where this first quotation appears) cf. Netter, *Doctrinale*, i, col. 614, citing Wycliffe's *'de cura pastorali'*, c. ix. Netter's citation – though the order is different – is much closer to the English text than anything I have found in the Latin *De officio pastorali*.

[16] *EWW*, p. 478 ('De papa'); cf. p. 129 ('Of clerks possessioners'), and p. 211 ('How Satan and his children') for other instances.

[17] Ibid., p. 448 ('De officio pastorali'); p. 14, 'parish churches fall down for default' while false religious 'make new churches as castles without need'; p. 322 ('Tractatus de pseudo- freris') friars' church buildings ('castle of the fiend') 'destroy holier old places'; *SEW*, iii, p. 369, 'great cloisters and costly, as Caim's Castles' (friary churches).

[18] There are some indications that the phrase was used to condemn non-parochial churches before 1380. Lechler thought that *De officio pastorali* was written before then, and the English work of that title says (*EWW*, p. 457) 'the pope dwelleth in Avignon' (which places it before 1378), and the English tract 'De papa' (ibid., p. 461) refers to 'division of these popes that is now late fallen'.

neither is the material church building held among them as holy church, but rather every such materially built house is called by them 'caym' castle.[19]

Caim's castles are here clearly associated with the rejection of material churches, suggestive of sectarian developments among the heretics.

Two other points in the charges listed against this cell of Northampton Lollards indicate that Anne Palmer and her associates may have had some grasp of Wycliffe's case against church temporalities. They were accused of regarding the endowment of the church by Pope Sylvester as poisoning it – a favourite theme of Wycliffe and others long before him, who recited the story of the angelic voice heard saying at the Donation of Constantine, 'today poison is poured into the holy church of God'.[20] The other matter concerned almsgiving to the poor.

> Item, they are reported to say that it is vain to give alms to any beggar except only to the lame and crooked and blind who are weak or lying paralysed, and that all who give such alms are supporting and sustaining such mendicants in their sins, and whoever gives such alms serves the devil.[21]

I will deal later with the question of poverty and alms. For the moment there are two points worth noticing about this accusation. First, that the criterion for almsgiving was the distinction between the able-bodied and the several categories of beggars. Second, and all-important, is the gospel text that lies behind these words. They derived from the parable of the great supper in Luke 14, when the places of the recalcitrant guests were filled by those brought in from the highways and hedges. The *claudis et curvis et cecis que sunt debiles* of Buckingham's bill echo the Vulgate's *voca pauperes, debiles, claudos, et caecos*. This passage became a locus classicus for Lollards, as it had been a gospel focus for Wycliffe; and as it is important to my argument I shall quote the Wycliffite Bible's version of it.

> But whanne thou makist a feeste, clepe pore men, feble men, crokid, and blynde, and thou schalt be blessid; for thei han not, wher of to yelde to thee, forsoth it schal be yeldun to thee in the rising agen of iuste men . . . Go out soone in to grete stretis

---

[19] A.K. McHardy, 'Bishop Buckingham and the Lollards of Lincoln Diocese', *SCH*, ix (1972), p. 143. Cf. the view abjured by John Skilly of Flixton (Suffolk) in 1429; 'that material churches be but of little avail and ought to be but of little reputation, for every man's prayer said in the field is as good as the prayer said in the church': *Heresy Trials in the Diocese of Norwich*, ed. N.P. Tanner (CS, 4th Series, 20, 1977), p. 58, cf. p. 53.

[20] McHardy, 'Bishop Buckingham and the Lollards', pp. 141, 143-4. On the legend of the poisoning of the church (which goes back to the thirteenth century, if not earlier) see W. Farr, *John Wyclif as Legal Reformer* (Leiden, 1974), pp. 48-9; P. Gradon, 'Langland and the Ideology of Dissent', *PBA*, lxvi (1980), p. 185. (The present essay, written before I had read this most valuable lecture, overlaps with its arguments on several points.)

[21] McHardy, 'Bishop Buckingham and the Lollards', pp. 144-5.

and smale streetis of the citee, and brynge in hidur poor men, and feble, and blynde, and crokid.[22]

Lollard attacks on Caim's castles remind us that the heresy was polemical as well as pastoral. But the case against the friars – which was nearly as old as the orders themselves – always remained attached to the serious reconsideration of evangelical life and Christian service. The new-style mendicants' pursuit of 'voluntary poverty and . . . other simple and virtuous living' (as William Thorpe put it)[23] was to place them at odds with old-style professional mendicants, and this perpetuation and revival of the ancient controversy bore closely on the politics of disendowment. Let us now turn to that question.

For roughly a hundred years, from the 1350s to the 1450s (concentrated particularly in the middle of that period), a variety of schemes were floated and ideas sounded for removing some of the temporal possessions of the church. Some were threatening verbal squibs. Others, most notably the Lollard plan of (probably) 1410, were more elaborate programmes. They had different objectives and a variety of results.

Broadly we can see that these ideas surfaced in a period conspicuous for the exigencies of war and war financing, and clearly it is no coincidence that the most daring of these projects appeared in times that produced outstanding new expedients for royal taxation, as well as social unrest and popular heresy. At the same time such proposals, however serviceable they might be (or seem to

[22] Luke 14:13, 21. 'Sed cum facis convivium, voca pauperes, debiles, claudos, et caecos . . . Exi cito in plateas et vicos civitatis, et pauperes ac debiles, et caecos et claudos introduc huc'. *The Holy Bible*, ed. J. Forshall and F. Madden (Oxford, 1850), iv, pp. 196-7. As I show below (pp. 124, 128) the use (or as others thought, abuse) of this passage made and makes it a clue pointing to Lollard sympathies – not necessarily at all the same as heresy. This may be specially clear from the wording – though the biblical allusion has often passed unrecognized by modern editors. For where Luke might seem to indicate *four* classes of poor, feeble, lame, and blind, a frequent (not invariable) Wycliffite reading was *three* different classes of poor: poor feeble, poor lame, and poor blind. 'Christ hath limited in his law who should have such alms, – poor men and blind, poor men and lame, poor men and feeble' (*SEW*, iii, p. 170, cf. pp. 293, 372); 'Christ biddeth men thus to do alms to poor feeble and lame and blind' (*EWW*, p.421, cf. p. 27); cf. *Jack Upland*, pp. 59, 121; *Selections from English Wycliffite Writings,* ed. A. Hudson (Cambridge, 1978), p. 95, line 75. The dominical gospels glossed in York Chapter MS XVI.D.2 include a long commentary on these verses of Luke 14 (second Sunday after Trinity, fos. 141 v-143v) which is moderate in tone and keeps the fourfold division of 'poor men, and feeble and blind and crooked', while making it clear that the rich were excluded and the poor were the chosen. 'God chesith hem, which the world dispiseth . . . for syk men and dispisid in this world bi so myche heren hastiliere the vois of god' (fo. 142v). The 'simple servant' sent to bid men to the supper (with the resurrection implications – 'the supper that is at the end of the world'), is here interpreted as none but 'the order of preachers'. Cf. the three categories in the text for this day in the Wycliffite sermon-cycle: '*and bring into this feast* these three manner of men: *poor feeble men, poor blind men and poor lame men* – these three are God's prisoners that both God and man help with alms'. *English Wycliffite Sermons,* ed. Anne Hudson, i (Oxford, 1983), p. 230. See below n. 105, and n. 91 on FitzRalph's role in the development of this interpretation.
[23] *Selections,* ed. Hudson, p. 31.

be) in the political arena, started out as arguments about religion and spiritual duties. Their idealistic content was not necessarily at risk in unsuccessful brushes with politics.

The bill of 1410 marks the climax of this intermittent sequence, but before considering it we ought to look at its precedents. We must start, therefore, in the later 1350s, at the peak of Archbishop FitzRalph's controversy with the friars. On 26 March of a year we do not know for certain, but quite likely 1358, a letter was addressed to FitzRalph by the chancellor and regent masters of Oxford. The university authorities wanted the archbishop (who was then at the curia) to help them by informing the pope about a recent scandal in the schools. The full horrors of the affair, including the rumpus caused in the faculty of theology, were left to be reported by the bearer of the letter, but the outline was set down in writing. An unnamed scholar (as they wrote)

> at the devil's own prompting publicly determined in the schools against the posses-
> sions of the church, damnably asserting it to be lawful for founders of churches to
> take away goods dedicated to God and the church on account of the abuses of
> clerics, and to transfer and apply them directly to seculars and knights. Also that
> church tithes are due more to mendicant friars than to curates.

For this dreadful offence the disputant was suspended, and was not going to be allowed to resume any scholastic activity until he showed himself duly contrite. The trouble was (FitzRalph was told) that 'we cannot compel him to a public revocation, or to any other punishment, on account of the confidence he has in the magnates of the realm, who, he says, wish to support him in this matter'.[24]

It seems probable that this offender was the 'frater Johannes' who, on Sunday 21 October 1358, had publicly to recant in St. Mary's, Oxford, after the university sermon, the same views as those described in the letter. His offence

[24] 'Hinc est ut dolentes vobis referimus quiddam nuper accidit a fundamentis universitatis hactenus insuetum quod expressam altissimi sapit iniuriam ecclesie preiudicium manifestissime comminatur ac etiam ecclesiastice libertati notabiliter est adversum. Insurrexit enim quidam qui suadente diabolo in scolis puplice determinavit contra possessiones ecclesie dampnabiliter invehendo licere quibuscunque ecclesiarum fundatoribus propter clericorum abusus bona deo et ecclesie dedicata auferre et eadem secularibus et militibus conferre et simpliciter applicare. Secundo quod decime ecclesie magis debentur fratribus mendicantibus quam curatis que quidem ex rumore vulgari et clamore communi scolarium theologie ac etiam ex notorietate clara facti concepimus prout lator presencium vestram reverenciam poterit plenius informare . . . nec possumus eum compellere ad revocacionem publicam, nec ad aliquam aliam penam propter confidenciam quam habet in magnatibus de regno, quos dicit velle se defendere in hac causa . . . ' Sidney Sussex College, Cambridge, MS 64, fo. 126 v. See K. Walsh, *A Fourteenth-Century Scholar and Primate: Richard FitzRalph in Oxford, Avignon and Armagh* (Oxford, 1981), p. 436, to which I owe knowledge of this source. Walsh says the disputant advocated the abolition of tithes, but this seems to be a slip. For the story that the 1409 bull, *Regnans in excelsis,* granted friars the right to tithes see F.X. Martin, 'An Irish Augustinian Disputes at Oxford: Adam Payn, 1402', in *Scientia Augustiniana: Studien über Augustinus, den Augustinismus und den Augustinerorden. Festschrift . . . Adolar Zumkeller,* ed. C.P. Mayer (Würzburg, 1975), p. 306; cf. *SEW,* iii, p. 175; 'friars . . . would that these dimes were given unto them'.

was very serious – witness his punishment and the presence at his revocation of the chancellor and proctors and the superiors of his order (the name of which is unfortunately not known). Friar John had maintained in the schools that tithes belonged to the friars more than to rectors and curates of churches; that the king and temporal lords had the right to deprive evil-living clergy of their possessions, and that the university was a school of heresy. He was fined 100 shillings and was never to lecture again without permission from the chancellor, proctors and regent doctors of theology.[25]

This incident (which so far as we know remained a purely academic affair) sets the stage for later events in several ways. There is the mendicant initiative; there is the alleged interest of secular lords: and there is the linking of tithes with temporal endowments.

The next occasion when disendowment was openly mooted was more public and is better known. This was at the parliament of 1371, when there was urgent need of funds for the French war and the tide was running high against ecclesiastical administrators. It was in the context of parliament's effort to shunt half the burden of this session's taxation on to the clergy that two Austin friars argued the case for sharing ecclesiastical possessions. One of these spokesmen was John Bankin, an Oxford theologian. We do not know the name of the other, though Thomas Ashborne is a possible candidate.[26]

The two friars mustered ecclesiastical law and patristic precedent to demonstrate that the 'common need of the whole realm' overrode all claims to clerical privilege and exemption. Gratian's *Decretum* and the natural law were cited to suggest that all possessions, ecclesiastical and otherwise, were held in common and that, in critical circumstances, individual right must yield to general need.[27] All the temporal possessions of the church (leaving aside first fruits and tithes) had come to it from king and lords for the service of God and relief of

[25] *Munimenta academica*, ed. H. Anstey (RS, 1868), i, pp. 208-11; Walsh, *Richard FitzRalph* pp. 436-7; A.G. Little, *The Grey Friars in Oxford* (Oxford Historical Society, xx, 1891), pp. 81-2. John was said to have propounded these views in his winter lectures this year ('in quadam determinatione sua hyemali'), which presumably means late 1357 or early 1358 and would fit with the March 1358 date for the letter to FitzRalph.

[26] V.H. Galbraith, 'Articles Laid before the Parliament of 1371', *EHR*, xxxiv (1919), pp. 579-82; A. Gwynn, *The English Austin Friars in the Time of Wyclif* (Oxford, 1940), pp. 212-16 (proposing Ashborne as the unnamed friar); K.B. McFarlane, *John Wycliffe and the Beginnings of English Nonconformity* (London, 1952), pp. 45-6, 59-60; J.H. Dahmus, *The Prosecution of John Wyclyf* (New Haven, CT, 1970), pp. 8-9; Gradon, 'Langland and the Ideology of Dissent', pp. 187-9. On Bankin and Ashborne see Emden (0), i, pp. 54, 104.

[27] The well-known passage from St. Ambrose (Galbraith, 'Articles Laid before the Parliament of 1371', p. 581) on selling chalices and church ornaments to redeem prisoners of war was exploited by Wycliffe in the same context; *De civili dominio*, ii, ed. J. Loserth (WS, 1900), pp. 28-9; cf. Gratian's *Decretum*, pt I, dist. 86, c.xviii, in *Corpus iuris canonici*, ed. E. Friedberg (Leipzig, 1879-81), i, col. 302. See B. Tierney, *Medieval Poor Law: A Sketch of Canonical Theory and its Application in England* (Berkeley and Los Angeles, 1959), pp. 32-3, for the influential *Glossa ordinaria* of Joannes Teutonicus explaining the statement 'according to natural law all things are common', by reference to the obligation of charity; 'that is they are to be shared in time of necessity'.

the poor, and in the event of necessity the original donors could properly call on these endowments to help defend the realm. This was an argument calculated to go down well with secular founders, and according to a report of Wycliffe, one lord declared that 'if war is waged against us we must take back from the endowed clergy temporal possessions which belong in common to us and the whole kingdom'.[28] Edging into this case are hints of the idea voiced earlier at Oxford of the conditional nature of church possessions: that clerical endowment was premised on clerical probity as well as the performance of certain services, and in the event of failure expropriation was justifiable. A patristic quotation appended to the friars' articles, which referred to the sacrilege of not giving to the poor the goods of the poor, raised the issue of superfluous clerical possessions.[29] Those who redressed the clergy's charitable lapses by diminishing their wealth, might be blessed by God.

Only two years after this – after Whitsun 1373, if we follow Jeremy Catto's rehabilitation of a story in the continuation of the *Eulogium historiarum* – two friars were once again propounding arguments against temporal dominion in the church. The circumstances were different. The meeting was a great council, not a parliament, and papal, not royal taxation was at issue. But some of the underlying questions were the same, and it is possible that one of the disputants may have been at both meetings, for John Mardisley (Franciscan), the main spokesman against the temporal claims of the pope, was supported by the Austin, Thomas Ashborne.[30]

It was, therefore, specially thanks to the activity of friars that politics and church temporalities got mixed as they did in the early 1370s. That mix was not initially altered by Wycliffe's contribution to the question, though he brought to the topic new prominence, more publicity, and the edge of a fresh

---

[28] *De civili dominio*, ii, p. 7; McFarlane, *John Wycliffe*, p. 46; cf. T.J. Hanrahan, 'John Wyclif's Political Activity', *Mediaeval Studies,* xx (1958), pp. 157-8 (arguing that this remark could equally well be applied to the parliament of Jan. 1377). Cf. *Opera minora*, pp. 424-5 (Wycliffe's reply to William Binham of (?) late 1373) on views of the right to withdraw temporalities which 'olim fuissent in parlamento dominorum Anglie ventilata', and on the arguments used 'in quodam consilio a dominis secularibus'. These remarks (which show Wycliffe in close touch with events at Westminster) might be related either to the parliament of 1371 or the council of 1373.

[29] For the remark about sacrilege and the poor, originally Jerome's, see note 1 above, and below p. 121. This, and other remarks of Jerome incorporated in the *Decretum* on the clergy's duty to be content with food and clothing (1 Tim. 6:8), and that 'whatever the clergy has belongs to the poor' were 'almost proverbial among the canonists'; Tierney, *Medieval Poor Law*, p. 76; *Corpus iuris canonici*, i, cols. 677-8 (*Decretum*, pt. II, causa 12, quest. 1, ccv-vii). Cf. Wycliffe, *De civili dominio,* i, ed. R.L. Poole (WS, 1885), p.353: 'nemo potest donare quidquam ecclesie nisi sub condicione ut serviat Deo in gracia' – a condition that was broken by the abuse of *bona pauperum*.

[30] J.I. Catto, 'An Alleged Great Council of 1374', *EHR*, lxxxii (1967), pp 764-71; *Eulogium historiarum*, ed. F.S. Haydon (RS, 1858-63), iii, pp. 337-9. On Mardisley see Little, *Grey Friars in Oxford*, p. 242; idem, *Studies in English Franciscan History* (Manchester, 1917), pp. 53-4.

theoretical basis.[31] This is not the place to explore Wycliffe's views, but it is clear that what he wrote and said on church ownership had much to do with the winning and losing of his allies, and that in turn reflected back on the politics of disendowment.[32] He presented the pattern of the true church, which had failed its apostolic origin ever since the Donation of Constantine. The secular powers who were called to reform, while not without expected benefits for themselves, were invoked to complete a spiritual task – not merely to resolve a financial crisis. And the failings in temporal possessions afflicted every order of the church, prelates, parish clergy, religious orders, mendicants. Apostolic poverty was always central for Wycliffe, but anti-mendicancy only became a dominant strain during his last years, partly as the direct result of some dramatic changes.

Among the twenty-four heresies and errors in Wycliffe's writings condemned at the Blackfriars Council in May 1382, two consecutive errors dealt with temporalities and tithes.[33] They should be considered together: namely;

That temporal lords may at will take away temporal goods from habitually offending churchmen.[34]

That tithes are pure alms, and parishioners may, on account of the sins of their curates, withhold them and freely confer them on others.[35]

[31] Wycliffe's view that the king and temporal lords could justly remove goods from an offending church was attacked, well before the papal condemnation of 1377, by the two Benedictines Uthred of Boldon and William Binham. These texts do not survive but we have Wycliffe's reply (above note 28) called the 'Determinatio' (*Opera minora*, pp. 405-30). McFarlane, *John Wycliffe*, pp. 62-3 dated this controversy 1372-3; G.A. Holmes, *The Good Parliament* (Oxford, 1975), p. 168, cf. p. 14, puts Wycliffe's reply in the latter part of 1373. For Thomas Brinton referring in a sermon of probably April 1375 to the view that goods of churches and monasteries could be removed see *Sermons of Thomas Brinton,* ed. M.A. Devlin (CS, 3rd series, lxxxv, 1954), p. 48. Cf. also Gwynn, *English Austin Friars*, p. 72; Dahmus, *The Prosecution of John Wyclif*, pp. 22-3; Gradon, 'Langland and the Ideology of Dissent', p. 182; *Fasciculi zizaniorum*, ed. W.W. Shirley (RS, 1858), p. 241.

[32] G. Leff, 'John Wyclif: The Path to dissent', *PBA*, lii (1966), pp. 162-3, 169, 171-3; Cf. M. Wilks, '*Reformatio regni:* Wyclif and Hus as Leaders of Religious Protest Movements', *SCH*, ix (1972), p. 118, on 'Wyclif's obsessive demands for the confiscation of clerical wealth', which have been considered in many other works.

[33] Temporalities were a matter of heresy, as well as error, and these two errors (nos. 17 and 18) follow on the heresy (no. 10) of asserting it to be against scripture for men of the church to have temporal possessions. Clause 17 also includes the secular correlative 'that the people can at will correct offending lords' (on which see Wycliffe's comments in *Trialogus*, p. 377). Thomas Walsingham, *Historia Anglicana*, ed. H.T. Riley (RS, 1863-4), ii, pp. 58-9; *Fasc. Ziz.*, pp. 279-81, 494-6; *Concilia*, iii, pp. 157-8; trans. in Workman, *Wyclif*, ii, pp. 416-17.

[34] For the points concerning temporalities condemned in the 1377 bulls, including no. 6; 'If God is, temporal lords may legitimately and meritoriously remove goods of fortune from an offending church', see *Chronicon Angliae*, ed. E.M. Thompson (RS, 1874), p. 182; and for Wycliffe's defence of them, ibid., pp 186, 188-9; *FZ*, pp. 248-9, 254-6. Clause 6 was taken from Bk. I, c. xxxvii of *De civili dominio*, i, p. 267, cf. ii, p. 5ff.

[35] Cf. ibid., i, pp. 340-1. In this part of Bk. I, cc. xli-xlii, Wycliffe was mainly concerned with the use of excommunication as a sanction for tithes. See *Sermones*, iii, p. 471; *Selections*, ed. Hudson, p. 147; and below, p. 121.

In the list of mendicant doctors who subscribed to this proscription were the two Austins, Thomas Ashborne and John Bankin.[36] Their presence must have been particularly galling to Wycliffe, given their earlier championing of a cause so near his heart. The great doctor was furious. Damning allusions to mendicant idiocy at the council were dashed into the work then on his desk – the *Trialogus*. The friars were as good as making Christ a heretic, let alone trying to make heretics of the king and lords of England, by their denial of the secular right to withdraw temporalities.[37] The point was echoed in English tracts.

> Tell we how friars deceived late our realm at London, in the council; they would deceive our bishops, and also lords and commons that dwell in this realm. They said as belief, that [it] is an heresy to say that [for] men of the church [to] have temporal possessions is against holy writ, whosoever affirms it.[38]

The bitter recriminations against the friars for this miserable volte-face were expressed in Latin and English, prose and verse. And, as contemporaries took note, there was also a new thrust in anti-mendicant arguments, which will be discussed below.

Parliamentary lobbying for disendowment continued for many years after 1382, but it now had to contend with the heretical associations of the case. Also, since the friars were now aligned on the other side, the question of mendicant possessions presented itself more conspicuously. An English tract that marks a stage in this development was addressed to parliament some time after 1382. This text petitioned King Richard, the duke of Lancaster, and 'other great men of the realm, both . . . seculars and men of holy church, that are gathered in the parliament', to support four articles. Two of them concerned clerical possessions. The second defended the legal right of king and lords to remove the temporalities of delinquent clergy – with special reference to offending bishops and abbots. The third article dealt with tithes. If priests sinned and tithes were not used for the purposes for which they were ordained, argued this paper, parishioners could withhold them and divert them to better uses: particularly in question were appropriated churches, from which revenues were siphoned off to pay for luxuries like fat horses, gay saddles and jingling bridles for men who already had overmuch, whereas 'the tithes and offerings should be given to poor needy men'. This case was attached to lengthy pleading against the friars, with specific reference to certain friars of Coventry, who had condemned as heretical the right of secular lords to withdraw temporalities from the church. 'See lords, see and understand, with

---

[36] *FZ*, p. 286.
[37] *Trialogus*, p. 377; for other condemnations of the council see pp. 339, 374-6, 445, 447; cf. *FZ*, pp. 283-5. The fact that these allusions only appear in Bk. IV (and the *Supplementum Trialogi*) helps to indicate the stages of the book's composition.
[38] *SEW*, iii, pp. 233-4; cf. p. 175 (attacking the council's view of tithes), and *Pierce the Ploughmans Crede*, p. 20. Of course eucharistic differences were also critical.

what punishment they deserve to be chastized, who thus unwarily and wrong-fully have damned you for heretics.'[39]

There were several occasions in the last fifteen years of the fourteenth century when disendowment – in one form or another – seems to have come within range of parliament. According to Walsingham (who never failed on spicy stories of threats to his own house), anger about taxation in the parliament of 1385 led to anticlerical moves by the commons. The laity's grant of a fifteenth was made conditional on a clerical grant. Archbishop Courtenay rose in defence of the church and the consent of convocation. Whereupon (relates the chronicler) the enraged knights of the shire, together with some of the lords, furiously threatened the removal of temporalities, asserting that the clergy were too domineering. Such action, they suggested, might improve churchmen's commitment to charity and almsgiving. Walsingham then adds an interesting detail. The proposal was submitted to the king in a short text (*in scriptis brevibus*), which Richard – with proper loyalty to the church – ordered to be destroyed.[40]

Ten years later parliament was again reminded, albeit indirectly, of the role it might play in church reform. The twelve conclusions posted up on the doors of Westminster Hall when parliament was in session in 1395 were presented in the name of 'poor men, treasurers of Christ and his apostles', denouncing to the lords and commons the state of the English church as 'blind and leprous many years by maintenance of the proud prelacy, borne up with flattering of private religion'. Temporal endowment topped the listed articles.

> When the church of England began to dote in temporality after her stepmother the great church of Rome, and churches were slain by appropriation to diverse places; faith, hope and charity began for to flee out of our church . . . [41]

[39] *SEW*, iii, pp. 508-23 (quoted at pp. 508, 519, 515). For the Latin version attributed to Wycliffe see I.H. Stein, 'The Wyclif Manuscript in Florence', *Speculum*, v (1930), p. 97; idem, 'The Latin Text of Wyclif's *Complaint*', *Speculum*, vii (1932), pp. 87-94 (at pp. 88, 91, 93). This text has been linked with the seven *imprecaciones* in *De blasphemia*, pp. 270-1 – heads of reforming proposals which Walsingham set in the parliament of May 1382; *Historia Anglicana*, ii, pp. 51-2; Workman, *Wyclif*, ii, pp. 250-2; *DNB*, *s.n.* Wycliffe. The grounds for connecting these texts are extremely slim, as they overlap on only one point (confiscation of temporalities), and the dating of the four-point address remains conjectural.

[40] *Historia Anglicana*, ii, pp. 139-40; J. Dahmus, *William Courtenay* (University Park and London, 1966), pp. 166-7; Anne Hudson, *The Premature Reformation* (Oxford, 1988), pp. 114-16, 337-42, considers Lollard proposals for disendowment.

[41] *Rogeri Dymmok Liber contra XII errores et hereses Lollardorum*, ed. H.S. Cronin (WS, 1922), pp. 25, 30; *Selections*, ed. Hudson, p. 24. Dymoke's reply to the first conclusion (cf. below. p. 113) says nothing about appropriated churches, which one might read as central to this grievance, given the repeated complaints in Lollard texts about the loss of charity and pastoral care through appropriation. See above pp. 100, 108; *SEW*, iii, pp. 215-16; *EWW*, p. 223; *Selections*, ed. Hudson, pp. 65-6, 172-3; *Remonstrance against Romish Corruptions in the Church*, ed. J. Forshall (London, 1851), pp. 10-12, 93; Workman, *Wyclif*, ii, pp. 95-6, 410. The phrase in the preamble, 'poor men treasurers of Christ', was taken up in the papal letters of Sept. 1395; *CPL*, iv, p. 515. Of the five conclusions singled out for papal condemnation, one was the view that founding prayers for the dead was false alms.

The text that follows, however, does not elucidate this question, though the sixth conclusion dealt with prelates holding secular office and the seventh with special prayers for the dead. Still, we can deduce something about the desired remedies from other sources, as will be seen.

One of Walsingham's most powerful reports of a proposed parliamentary disendowment was assigned by him to the Coventry Parliament of 1404 – the idea being that the king should take over church temporalities for at least one year. There are difficulties about this story, including the fact that Sir John Cheyne, to whom a leading role was attributed, was not (as Walsingham stated in one of his versions of these events) speaker of this parliament. B.P. Wolffe has argued that the chronicler has here telescoped events, and suggests that this incident should be put back five years into the first parliament of Henry IV.[42] We know that Cheyne was elected speaker in that parliament but withdrew, the day after his election, officially for reasons of ill-health. It seems likely that the real reason for his resignation was the suspicion entertained of him as a dangerous critic of the church, who would not be afraid to speak his mind in parliament. According to Walsingham's report of the proceedings of convocation in October 1399, Archbishop Arundel was fearful of moves that might be made in the commons under Cheyne's guidance. In anticipation of this he apparently advised – which is worth noticing – that the commons' anticlericalism might be forestalled by action against pluralism and non-residence.[43] Clearly the archbishop was anxious to take a firm stand at the beginning of the new regime against any Lollard demonstration. But it remains possible, despite some muddled reporting, that clerical disendowment was proposed alongside a resumption of crown lands in 1404.[44]

[42] B.P. Wolffe, *The Royal Demesne in English History* (London, 1971), pp. 76-86, Appendix 'B', pp. 245-7; cf. J.S. Roskell, 'Sir John Cheyne of Beckford', *Trans. Bristol and Gloucs. Arch. Soc.*, lxxv (1956), pp. 58-60, 64-7; idem, *The Commons and their Speakers in English Parliaments, 1376-1523* (Manchester, 1965), pp. 136-7, 354-5; *Rot Parl.*, iii, p. 424b.

[43] *Annales Ricardi Secundi et Henrici Quarti*, ed. H.T. Riley (RS, 1866), pp. 290, 391-4. Cf. (in support of Walsingham's report of this convocation) *Concilia*, iii, p. 242, somewhat misreading Reg. Arundel (Lambeth), i, fo. 53 v; ii, fo. 5 r which reports the clergy's petition against illicit intentions among the laity who, reportedly spurred on by Lollards, 'intendant contra prelatos et alios viros ecclesiasticos in presenti parliamento novas constituciones seu statuta facere, edere, et introducere, contra ecclesie libertatem que non constituciones sed pocius destituciones immo destrucciones merito dici possunt': *Historia Anglicana*, ii, pp. 239ff; 265-7. Relevant to the continuing debate is Richard Ullerston's *Defensorium dotacionis ecclesie*, dated 1401 in the surviving manuscripts, which mentioned the question 'utrum omnes clerici corpore validi ad laborem manuum obligantur': Anne Hudson, 'The Debate on Bible Translation, Oxford 1401', *EHR*, xc (1975), p. 10.

[44] Did the release this year of several Lollard suspects from prison (where Cheyne had also been) have some effect on this stand? Cf. my 'Lollardy and Sedition' in *Lollards and Reformers* (London, 1984), pp. 22-23. While the circumstances of 1399 might have circumscribed any such manoeuvres, a proposed resumption (as some saw it) of clerical temporalities would have arisen naturally in 1404. It should be pointed out, too, that though he made some slips in the *Annales*, it was only in his condensed restrospective account in the *Historia Anglicana* that Walsingham (now omitting the 1399 convocation report), switched his tale of Cheyne's anticlericalism to 1404. It may be that his memory faulted him in thus combining two events because of the similarity of the two

1 A fifteenth-century wall painting of 'Christ of the trades'. The Man of Sorrows, surrounded by an assortment of workmen's tools and with his hands pierced by the bobbins of a loom, holds a huge pair of sheep-shears. Wherever rake, hammer, hatchet or trowel touch Christ's body, blood is drawn. Was this an allegory of Christ's continued suffering for the sins of everyday life, a warning of the wounds inflicted by those who put mundane labour before divine service?

2 Lorenzo Lotto's painting of St. Dominic preaching to a mixed audience in an Italian piazza. A fire warms both the preacher – holding forth from a movable wooden pulpit – and some of his hearers. The women huddled separately at the back listen intently, even if in the cold.

3 Twelfth-century carving of Cain and Abel at Saint-Gilles du Gard. God's hand descends from the cloud to accept Abel's offering of a lamb, while Cain's sheaf is rejected. In the jambs above them are an angel and a devil, the latter signifying Cain's outcast state, as 'of that wicked one' (1 John 3:12).

4 Vermeer's *Woman Holding a Balance* used motifs familiar in depictions of weighing gold (the mirror and the costly pearls), but here the scales are carefully given an exactly central position – and they are empty. The painting of the Last Judgement on the wall behind may associate the scales with those of St. Michael, whose balance believers once supposed could be tipped in favour of souls by the helping hand of the Virgin Mary.

5 Silver-gilt reliquary of St. Eustace (German, *c.* 1300). The wooden head (right) is hollow, and the parcel of relics found in it during restoration in 1956 included fragments of skull.

6 Petrus Christus painted St. Eligius in 1449, probably for the goldsmiths' guild in Bruges, whose chapel dedicated to the saint was consecrated that year. Its moral allusions include the balance (in which the saint weighs a wedding ring for the young couple), which evokes the scales of St. Michael, and the cracked mirror (reflecting two elegant sparks idling in the street with a falcon), which indicates the imperfections of the world.

7 Quentin Matsys, *The Money Changer and his Wife* (1514). The precise assessment of gold is here set beside the contemplation of higher things, from which one may be distracted (like the well-dressed wife, looking away from the illuminated page of the Virgin in her Book of Hours towards the pile of coins), or to which one may give due attention (like the intent reader reflected in the mirror in the foreground).

8 The Golden Calf: print after Maarten van Heemskerck illustrating the first of the ten commandments. Top left Moses receives the Tables of the Law amidst 'the thunderings, and the lightnings, and the noise of the trumpet, and the mountain smoking' (Exodus 20:18).

9 Nicolas Poussin's scene of revelry in *The Adoration of the Golden Calf*. On the left Moses breaks the Tables of the Law (Exodus 32:19). The group of idolatrous dancers also appears (in reverse) in Poussin's *Bacchanal before a Herm* (likewise painted in the 1630s).

10 The miracle of the wounded image in Eton College Chapel. A woman kneels devoutly before a statue of Virgin and Child (barely visible in niche to the right). Behind, a soldier in laced doublet and hose raises his hand to throw a stone and then falls dead.

11 (*Left*) St. George, arrested for denouncing pagan idolatry, is brought before the king (*Hic capitur et ducitur ante regem*). Panel of St. George window, St. Neot, Cornwall.

12 (*Right*) St. Wilgefortis or Uncumber, in Henry VII's Chapel at Westminster, with the long beard that, in the legend, rescued her from marriage, and the cross on which her father had her crucified.

13 A statue of the Virgin and Child miraculously survives a church fire, demonstrating Mary's power to deliver from the eternal fire of hell all those who faithfully serve her. In the story the wooden statue came unscathed through the fire that completely destroyed the church in which it stood, intact and perfectly white.

14 The opening of the seventh seal in Revelation 8, the seven angels with trumpets announcing future calamities: hail and fire burn up trees and grass; a great mountain burning with fire is cast into the sea destroying ships and fish; a burning star falls on the fountains. 'Woe, woe, woe, to the inhabitants of the earth.' Engraving in 1630 Merian Bible.

We come now to the fullest of all these paper plans – the Lollard disendow-ment bill assigned respectively to 1407 or 1410, the latter date seeming the more probable.[45] Kingsford thought that this bill, though composed as a petition of 'all the true commons' to king and lords 'of this present parliament' should be regarded as 'rather a manifesto meant for a popular audience than a serious attempt at legislation'.[46] We have no evidence of any formal parlia-mentary notice, though the silence of the parliament rolls cannot be taken as conclusive.

When we look at the contents of the bill it is clear that it was intended to have much more than popular appeal. The beneficiaries of disendowment were to include king, lords, knights, and squires, as well as the poor and needy, and provision was also made for ordinary priests and clerks and the learned. The detailed arithmetic (which, as has often been pointed out, does not add up) is less interesting than the detailed objectives. The confiscation seems to have been designed to net the revenues of all the English bishops as well as both archbishops,[47] together with seventy-five or so abbeys and religious houses, mainly Benedictine but also some Cistercian, and some of Augustinian Canons. The friaries were not included. Even if (as Anne Hudson has suggested) this is explicable by virtue of mendicant property being vested in the holy see, we still have to square it with a good deal else, including specific proposals by Wycliffe for mulcting the mendicants, parliamentary levies on the exempt religious,[48] and the strong force of Lollard anti-mendicancy. But the case for true mendicants did not go by default in the bill.

The positive proposals were threefold. First was the provision for the new secular endowments of fifteen earls, 1,500 knights, and 6,200 squires, together with enlarged royal revenues. This was linked with the defence of the realm, and places this part of the scheme in line with ideas mooted in 1371 and (probably) 1385 and 1399/1404. The needs of defence (and taxation) were

occasions: i.e. talk of clerical deprivation (not a rare parliamentary occurrence!) possibly occurred in both 1399 and 1404. (There is no evidence of Cheyne being a member of the Coventry Parliament; cf. Roskell, p. 65).

[45] For this text and its various versions see *Selections,* ed. Hudson, pp. 135–7, 203-7; modern-ized in *English Historical Documents,* iv, 1327-1485, ed. A.R. Myers (1969), pp. 668-70. The variants in the different versions, especially the garbled place-names and discrepancies in the arithmetic, indicate that we only have imperfect transcriptions.

[46] *Chronicles of London,* ed. C.L. Kingsford (Oxford, 1905), pp. xxv, 65; *Selections,* ed. Hudson, p. 135. For an attempt to make sense of the arithmetic see Kingsford's notes, pp. 295-6.

[47] If we suppose that the bishop of 'Chestre' means Coventry and Lichfield, all seventeen bishoprics of England are named; the only Welsh one listed is St. Davids. The Latin text in *The St. Albans Chronicle, 1406-1420,* ed. V.H. Galbraith (Oxford, 1937), p. 54, makes it clear that Carlisle, Chichester and Rochester are listed as bishoprics; cf. *Selections,* ed. Hudson, p. 136 and note on lines 77-8.

[48] Ibid., pp. 204-5, 207. Wycliffe's calculation that the friars cost the realm £40,000 (or 60,000 marks) *per annum* appears in several of his works, and in *De quattuor sectis novellis* he proposed an annual levy on them by the king of 1,000 marks or more; *Polemical Works,* i, pp. 255-6, cf. pp. 28, 192-3, 244; *Trialogus,* p. 369. On the taxing of exempt religious see *Jack Upland,* p. 10.

obviously of central interest in the parliamentary context – hence this leading position. Alongside this comes the idea for a hundred new almshouses, which is joined with remarks about worldly clerks and the misuse of funds intended for the poor. These new almshouses seem to have been intended as additions to the existing foundations (estimated by one historian at over 600), and it was stipulated that the income of 100 marks assigned to each for feeding 'needful poor men' was not, as in times past, to be dissipated by proud priests and worldly clerks, but to be administered by good and true secular persons.[49] Thirdly, there was the plan to increase the numbers of universities and secular clerks. The proposed foundation of fifteen new universities is mentioned almost as an aside – though to Kingsford it redeemed the entire scheme 'from any charge of sordid or socialist intention'.[50] Whatever we may think about the sort of institution that was intended, this item of the bill must be seen as having some bearing on the interests of its backers. So also do the 15,000 priests and clerks, sufficiently endowed by 'temporal alms' to fulfil their pastoral office. As glossed in one version, these would be 'good priests and perfect clerks to preach the word of god without flattering or begging or worldly reward to seek therefore'.[51]

Provision for the poor, true curates ('true men', i.e. Lollard sympathizers) and needy beggars, repeats itself in the bill, consorting rather uneasily with the secular endowments sandwiched in between. Priests and prelates were henceforth to live off spiritual revenues, since they had conspicuously failed in their duty to 'help the poor commons with their lordships', and the past lusts and ease of the great had been extorted from 'profits that should come to true men'.[52]

The hundred almshouses constitute an important clue that makes it possible to trace the 1410 scheme back to at least the 1390s. The 'one hundred almshouses for the bedridden [*decumbentibus*]' appeared, with other details of the 1410 plan, in the extracts of John Purvey's heresies listed by Richard Lavenham. This summary cannot be exactly dated, but its allusion to another 'special tract' explaining details of the plans for distributing church possessions, tells of the existence of some document specifically devoted to the

---

[49] Tierney, *Medieval Poor Law*, pp. 86, 155; *Selections*, ed. Hudson, pp. 135, 137, 205; 'and c houses of almesse mo thanne he hath now at this tyme . . . .' Dymoke's estimate of the colleges and hospices which had care of souls and the poor was 'perhaps more than one or two thousand'; *Rogeri Dymmok Liber*, p. 175.

[50] *Chronicles of London*, p. xxxviii. The universities do not feature in Fabian's version, or in that attached (wrongly, according to Anne Hudson) to the 1431 rebellion; *Selections*, p. 204, and cf. 206 on line 68. The *St. Albans Chronicle*, pp. 54-5, mentions only five universities and implies that the 15,000 priests and clerks were to be provided for there (i.e. in study).

[51] *Selections*, ed. Hudson, pp. 136 and 206, note on line 64. However, this comes from a late version and (see previous note) there is an ambiguity about this suggestion, which perhaps belongs with Lollard ideas on schooling preachers.

[52] Ibid., p. 137: Hudson, 'A Lollard Sect Vocabulary?' (note 11 above), pp. 20-21.

disendowment plan.[53] We do not know what this special tract amounted to. But something of the kind seems to have been available by 1395. For the seventh of the twelve conclusions of that year ended with the statement that

> it was proved in a book that the king heard [i.e. it had been read aloud to Richard II] that an hundred of alms houses sufficed to all the realm, and thereof should fall the greatest increase possible to [the] temporal part.[54]

Here, we may notice, it was *only* a hundred almshouses, not a hundred *additional* almshouses, the concern being to reduce the wrong sorts of foundation.

This seventh conclusion of the 'manifesto' concentrated on the point that special prayers for the dead amounted to simony and were the negation of true charity and almsgiving. The merchandise for such prayers for souls, 'made to mendicants and possessioners and other soul priests', was said to be a great burden to the realm. If we set this conclusion beside Purvey's reference to the bedridden, the implication is that prayers for the dead were an impediment to serving the needs of the impotent poor. And Roger Dymoke's reply shows that the needs of the poor (though not mentioned in this seventh clause) were an assumed part of the heretics' case, for he argued that the more colleges and hospitals that were founded, the more people there were to assist the poor.[55]

A careful reading of Dymoke's long book against the 'manifesto' shows how the case for evangelical poverty lay behind the 1395 conclusions. He concentrated his answer to the first point (the church's 'doting' in temporalities) on two matters: first, the necessity of papal government; second, the irrelevance of apostolic poverty to the needs of the church after the period of conversion. Ecclesiastical possessions were necessary for church discipline, 'for the people', said Dymoke (and it reads like a direct dig at the Lollards), 'take no account of the poor and impotent, however just in themselves or in their rule, either to honour or obey them'.[56] Poverty and authority could not be married.

---

[53] *FZ.*, p. 393 (reporting that Purvey invoked king, lords, and commons to implement these proposals). On the problem of dating this source see *Selections,* ed. Hudson, p. 204; A. Hudson, 'John Purvey: A Reconsideration of the Evidence for His Life and Writings', *Viator,* xii (1981), pp. 361-2, 368-9, 379.

[54] *Rogeri Dymmok Liber,* p. 160, cf. p. 306: *Selections,* ed. Hudson, p. 26, cf. p. 29 – which leaves it uncertain whether the book in which the twelve conclusions were 'longly declared' was this or another text. *FZ,* p. 364 has 'in uno libro quem rex *habuit*' for Dymoke's 'quem rex *audivit*' (my italics), presumably from a misreading of 'herd[e]' as 'had'. Could the text the king heard conceivably be that which he had ordered to be destroyed in 1385? (above p.109).

[55] *Rogeri Dymmok, loc. cit.; Selections,* p. 26 and notes, pp. 153 (lines 90-92), p. 205 (line 16ff).

[56] *Rogeri Dymmok Liber,* p. 47; cf. p. 213 on the lack of coercive powers of *prelati pauperes* in the early church. (Of course it has to be remembered that Dymoke's book may be read as a refutation of Wycliffe's writings, as much or more than as a specific redress of the Lollard case. And this does not apply only to the most obvious topic, the eucharist and the *Trialogus* quoted in conclusion 4.)

It is interesting too, that Dymoke's arguments against the recommended hundred almshouses suggest he knew more of this idea than conclusion seven alone. He talks about the dangerous suggestion made to parliament (*parliamento suggerebant*) 'that the English church should be despoiled, and that lands and tenements seized from churchmen could fall into the king's power'. No such statement was made in the twelve conclusions. Dymoke also read into this conclusion a deduction about the endowment of knighthood which, on the face of it, he had no reason to think up for the benefit of his own argument. It would be contrary to the king's coronation oath, he wrote, 'if he were to destroy so many churches and colleges, and distribute their goods among knights, as they [the Lollards] seem to recommend by this assertion'. And again, were the Lollards, he asked, so blinded by avarice that they thought 'to enrich knighthood out of church possessions?'[57] Was this Dymoke's own understanding of the expected gain to the 'temporal part', or did he have some other guide to Lollard plans?

A clause that was attached to the almshouse foundations in the bill of 1410, gives us another pointer that links this proposal with long-standing Lollard interests. It ran;

> and also for to ordain that every town throughout the realm should keep all poor men and beggars which may not travail for their sustenance, after the statute made at Cambridge, and, in case at the foresaid commons might not extend for to sustain them, then the foresaid houses of alms might help them.[58]

The act of the Cambridge Parliament of 1388 here referred to had laid down regulations for the treatment of able-bodied and impotent beggars. The former (in line with the 1349 Ordinance of Labourers) were forbidden alms and to be kept in their place of work, subject to punishment. The impotent, who were allowed to beg, had to remain in their place of residence at the time of the act, or to return to their place of birth.[59] This legislation was of the utmost

---

[57] *Rogeri Dymmok Liber*, pp. 177-8, 175ff. Cf. Dymoke's arguments (pp. 172-3) justifying prayers for founders' souls, whether saved, damned, or in purgatory, and the thirty-first of Wycliffe's thirty-three Conclusions (*Opera minora*, pp. 66-8): 'Whether the defunct progenitors of surviving lords are in heaven, in purgatory, or in hell, it would be expedient in cases where almsdoers abuse their alms for these to be withdrawn and converted to other pious uses.'

[58] *Selections*, ed. Hudson, p. 135; *St Albans Chronicle*, p. 53.

[59] *SR*, ii, p. 58, cf. p. 56; 12 Ric. II, c. vii, cf. c. iii; *SR*, i, p. 308; 23 Ed. III, c. vii. On this legislation see J.A. Tuck, 'The Cambridge Parliament, 1388', *EHR*, lxxxiv (1969), pp. 225-43; Tierney, *Medieval Poor Law*, pp. 128-9; B.H. Putnam, *The Enforcement of the Statute of Labourers* (Columbia, 1908), pp. 71-2, 77-9. Tierney points out that 'the canonists had quite consistently held that able-bodied beggars were to be denied alms in order that they should not be encouraged in idleness', and the prior claims on alms of those suffering from bodily weakness (the old and infirm) were set out in the *Decretum. Corpus iuris canonici*, ed. Friedberg, i, cols. 299, 301 (part 1, dist. 86, cc. vi, xvi, xvii); Tierney, *Medieval Poor Law*, pp. 56-61, 118-19, quoted at p. 130.

interest to Lollards, since it accorded with their continuous insistence on the scriptural duty of almsgiving to the truly poor[60] – who were to be assisted by the hundred almshouses. A great deal was said and written by the heretics on this topic, and they turned to their own use the canon law theory that alms should not be given to the able-bodied. They set the whole question in a new context. To explain will be to recapitulate.

One of the challenging questions put by 'Jack Upland' – with whom we started – concerned the friars' slander that Christ begged other men's goods as they did. 'Friar, since in God's law such clamorous begging is utterly forbidden, on what law do you ground you thus for to beg, and namely of [those] poorer than you are yourself?' Friar Daw, in his answer to this important point (mustering his doctors with the help of the Latin he had picked up as manciple of Merton) cited biblical examples in support of the lawfulness of 'clamorous begging', including the blind beggar who called out to Christ and was healed in Luke 18, and the example of Lazarus (Luke 16; 20-22) who 'cried loud' at the rich man's gate to catch his alms.[61]

This rather peculiar phrase, 'clamorous begging', amounted to a technical term. It was explained in the section on begging (*mendicacio*) in the popular Lollard alphabetical repertory, the *Rosarium theologie,* the full Latin text of which, the *Floretum,* was compiled between 1384 and 1396: the various versions of these compilations were used thereafter well into the fifteenth century. The *Rosarium* classifed begging according to a threefold division: *innuitiva, insinuativa,* and *declamatoria,* innuitive, insinuative, and declamatory, englished alternatively as 'tokening', 'showing', and 'crying' or 'clamorous' begging. These scholastic terms conveyed the differences between legitimate and illegitimate begging. Innuitive begging – that of Christ – was the direct manifestation, through his visible condition, of 'any poor man and needy'. Insinuative begging included verbal asking, as well as showing. 'It is definitively asking by a needy man for bodily alms', but solely in order to relieve his need. Such asking was lawful for those in true need. The third category, 'clamorous begging' (not glossed but implying persistent crying or pleading) was lawful in two conditions: when a man was in extreme necessity, or when a 'strong man' lacked labour or means to support himself. It was

---

[60] Lollards would not have faulted 'lez voegles, lepers, et couchantz sur litz en maladie' as a definition of impotent beggars in the common petition behind the statute, but the act also explicitly excepted the religious from the provisions about the able-bodied poor. *The Westminster Chronicle, 1381-1394,* ed. L.C. Hector and B.F. Harvey (Oxford, 1982), pp. 362-3. (This must surely mean blind and lepers, not 'blind lepers').
[61] *Jack Upland,* pp, 66, 94; cf. *Polemical Works,* i, p. 196.

unlawful when it was done voluntarily and habitually, and by 'strong men' not driven by need. Unlawful begging of this kind was to be avoided at all costs.[62]

These distinctions had formed part of Wycliffe's attack on the friars in the *Trialogus*. In Book IV of that work, Phronesis (the 'subtle and mature theologian' who settles the truth) expounds to the conveniently questioning Alithia (speaking for sound philosophy) the blasphemous heresies of the friars. Phronesis deals with three points: the sacrament of the altar, the mendicancy of Christ, and letters of fraternity. The section on mendicancy explains how the begging of the friars is quite unscriptural and emphatically not that of Christ. Wycliffe drew a clear distinction between the innuitive begging of Christ, 'without petition and vocal insinuation', and the friars' vehement begging from the people, 'clamorously' and 'onerously'. He showed that a major part of these mendicants' offence was their begging as 'strong men', 'strong beggars', not driven by genuine need. The phrase *personis validis, mendicos validos* recurs in this discussion. Moreover, the point was pressed home that the *valide mendicans* was taking alms from the very people who were in need of them, from the poor themselves – from the poor blind, needy and feeble of Luke 14.[63]

The *Trialogus* discussion makes plain that this was not the first exposition of this question. In the course of their dialogue Phronesis three times refers

[62] Gonville and Caius College, Cambridge, MS 354/581, fos. 75 v-76 r; the Latin version of this passage is in Gonville and Caius College, MS 232/118, fos. 205 v-208 r. See *The Middle English Translation of the Rosarium Theologie*, ed. C. von Nolcken (Heidelberg, 1979), for the dating of this work and selections (not including this passage) from the former manuscript. In the fuller section on *Mendicitas* in BL, MS Harl. 401 copy of the *Floretum* (I am grateful to Anne Hudson for sending me a copy of this) the distinctions of begging are pursued at less length and do not form the starting-point of the discussion. The *Rosarium* entry harps on the unlawfulness of begging by 'strong men', and alludes to the prohibition of this in *'Codic. de mendicantibus valid. L. unica'* – a citation of Justinian which could have come from any number of intermediate sources, including Aquinas, William of St. Amour (Williams, 'Chaucer and the Friars', p. 506, n. 28); and cf. John Pecham, *Tractatus tres de paupertate*, ed. C.L. Kingsford, A.G. Little, F. Tocco (British Society of Franciscan Studies, ii, Aberdeen, 1910), pp. 177, 185. The *Rosarium* ends its comment on begging with an allusion to the supper of Christ (in Luke 14) to which there came 'but beggars, feeble men, halting and blind'. See *An Apology for Lollard Doctrines*, ed. J.H. Todd (CS, xx, 1842), pp. 108-13, for an exposition of the thesis that 'it is not lawful to religious to beg', which draws on some of the same sources as the *Rosarium,* and also expounds the 'divers manners' of begging 'by sign or by token or by express voice', as manifesting need 'by word or work or token'. Christ begged by 'showing' his need. But 'wilful [i.e. voluntary] begging of stalwart men' was forbidden to Christians, and 'the alms of the poor shall not be given to them that are sufficient and mighty to travail'.

[63] *Trialogus*, pp. 38, 338ff. at pp. 341-2, 343-4; cf. also Wycliffe's letter 'De fratribus ad scholares' (of about the same date as the *Trialogus*) which attacks the friars as 'validi mendicantes' (*Opera minora*, p. 18); *Polemical Works*, i, p. 312; and for friars begging not 'innuitive vel insinuative . . . sed clamorose ac eciam importune', *Sermones*, iv, p. 13; *Pol. Works*, i, pp. 187-8, 366-7ff. I have not found any helpful discussion of the development of this terminology, as employed by Wycliffe or anyone else. Cf. St. Thomas's distinctions of licit and illicit begging; *Summa theologiae*, II, ii, quaest. clxxxvii, art. V ('utrum religiosis liceat mendicare'), which cites the civil code's punishment of strong beggars, who begged neither for utility (i.e. justifiable causes) nor of necessity; and, on Christ's voluntary poverty, III, quaest. xl, art. iii. It is possible to

Alithia to his vernacular treatment of the blasphemies of the friars. 'Three blasphemies out of many I showed to the people concerning these friars in the vernacular'; and 'I am glad to say about this in Latin what I formerly expressed in English'. At another point he seems to suggest that he is condensing the arguments scored against the friars' defence of mendicancy in his previous work.[64]

As it happens, there survives an English text that exactly fits this description. Thomas Arnold printed in 1871 (from Bodley MS 647, which was the only copy he had found), a vernacular tract that expounds these same three blasphemies of the friars, entitling it (after Bale) *De blasphemia, contra fratres*.[65] The English version does not read like a translation. It uses its sources differently, sometimes changes the order, and introduces fresh illustrative material.[66] But the vernacular tract does make use of the same scriptural passages (with less citation of chapter and verse than the Latin), covers the same ground, and has some close verbal echoes. (For example, the same rather unusual image, 'each knot of a stree' or straw, *nodulum straminis,* is used in either case for comparison with the worshipped host).[67]

trace the radical change in Wycliffe's views on this issue. In the *Trialogus* he turned on their head arguments he had used earlier in defence of the friars; cf. *De civili dominio*, iii, pp. 7-10, where he mentions the threefold kinds of asking in order to support the legitimacy of friars' begging. Cf. *De apostasia*, ed. M.H. Dziewicki (WS, 1889), pp. 31-2, for a condemnation of inordinate begging of friars and reference to 'clamorous begging'.

[64] *Trialogus*, pp. 338, 349; cf. pp. 341-2 ('Dixi alias in lingua multiplici, quomodo mendicatio est satis aequivoca, sicut oratio . . . alias descripsi mendicationem . . . Feci hoc in vulgari multiplices rationes').

[65] *SEW*, iii, pp. 402-29; cf. *Trialogus*, pp. 338-53ff; J. Bale, *Scriptorum illustrium maioris Brytannie catalogus* (Basel, 1557-9), cent. sexta, p. 453. Arnold, (*SEW*, iii, p. 402), followed by Workman (*Wyclif*, i, p. 330), compared this tract with Wycliffe's Latin *De blasphemia*. The only person who seems to have noticed the link between these texts is A.G. Little, *Grey Friars in Oxford*, p. 82, n. 3.

[66] FitzRalph is cited in the English (*SEW*, iii, p. 412), but not the Latin version, on the begging of Christ. FitzRalph's arguments against the voluntary begging of the friars were undoubtedly a valuable precedent, but the case was carried further under Wycliffite impetus. Mendicancy had not been a central topic in FitzRalph's *De pauperie salvatoris,* but came to the fore in 1356-7 and seems to have been at the centre of controversy thereafter: 'Defensio curatorum' in *Trevisa's Dialogus*, ed. A.J. Perry (EETS, OS 167, 1925), p. 80ff; and see K. Walsh, 'The "De Vita Evangelica" of Geoffrey Hardeby, O.E.S.A. (*c.* 1320 – *c.* 1385): A Study in the Mendicant Controversies of the Fourteenth Century', *Analecta Augustiniana*, xxxiii (1970), pp. 151-261; xxxiv (1971), pp. 5-83, especially pt. 1, p. 255 and pt. 2, pp. 21-3, 74ff for some of the lines on which Wycliffe parted company from FitzRalph, and on how the Wycliffite attack concentrated attention on the issue of evangelical poverty. (Cf. also above note 63 and below note 91). I am aware that I have only nibbled at the edges of this large subject.

[67] Some of the passages cited (without specific references in the English) were biblical commonplaces (e.g. the woman of Samaria in John 4:7; cf. the sermon on mendicancy in *Selections*, ed. Hudson, p. 94), but the overall interrelationship of matter seems too extensive to be accounted for by this. There is not room to present this case properly here, since it calls for an analysis of style as well as content. *Trialogus*, iv, cc. 27-30 (pp. 338-53) has the same three divisions as the English, the two central chapters being devoted to mendicancy. There are correspondences between the English text, pp. 415-29, and passages in the *Trialogus* down to c. 38, not at all in the

Could this text possibly be a rarely authenticated English work by Wycliffe? The thin disguise of Phronesis in the dialogue perhaps allowed for some enhanced freedom of speech, and Wycliffe (though not prone to caution) knew how to hedge his words. Extreme hesitancy is always in order before putting a name – or a date – to Wycliffite vernacular tracts. This is probably as near as we can hope to get to an authorial claim by the evangelical doctor himself, and that is not something to pass over, though it needs more detailed assessment than is possible here.[68] Quite apart from the question of authorship, the relationship of the two texts suggests that the English version may have originated before the meeting of the Blackfriars Council,[69] and the priority of an English over a Latin text is noteworthy.

Thomas Netter, who quotes the English tract (in Latin), took it as Wycliffe's and refers to it alongside the *Trialogus*. He used it to rebuke Wycliffe for his attempt to put a wedge between the begging of the friars and the begging of Christ.[70] The vernacular text pursued even more insistently than the Latin, the argument that the friars' begging was not that of Christ because it was clamorous and they were strong beggars. 'To know frauds and falseness of friars, must we know what is begging, and manner of begging.' 'Some beggen of men in word, and some beggen in deed . . . and some cry by word after temporal goods in evil manner, after more than they should have . . . if he wilfully [voluntarily] beg, and has no need, he is a cursed beggar, reproved of

same order. In addition, the English text pp. 403-6 on the eucharist is related to *Trialogus*, iv, cc. ii-v (pp. 247-61). Wycliffe himself (Phronesis) tells us (p. 339) to turn back to this earlier passage, and we find there (p. 248) another reference to a previous vernacular discussion. 'Sunt autem in materia de quidditate hujus sensibilis sacramenti errores multiplices . . . contra quos multipliciter invexi alias tam scholastice quam etiam in vulgari . . . ' The passage about the eucharistic worship and 'iche knotte of a stree', which comes in the summing up in English (*SEW*, iii, p. 428), appears in the middle of *Trial.* iv, c. 27 (p. 339). As an example of the kind of version one would not expect of a straight translator cf. the passage quoted above, p. 95, note 2. 'Isti autem sunt stultificati idiotae, qui nescientes inter paupertatem et mendicationem distinguere, primam, quae perfectionem sonaret, dimittunt, et secundam cupide ut Ischarioth amplectuntur' (*Trial.*, pp. 348-9): 'Bot thes blynde blasphemes con not depart beggynge fro povert, for bothe acorden sumwhat' (*SEW*, iii, p. 415).

[68] For other hints by Wycliffe on this question see *Opera minora*, ii, p. 74; *De veritate sacrae scripturae*, ed. R. Buddensieg (WS, 1905-7), i, pp. 349-50. As Anne Hudson has recently pointed out in 'Lollardy: The English Heresy?', *SCH*, xviii (1982), pp. 264-5, there is small evidence for Wycliffe's interest in the vernacular before the last years of his life, and (270ff) it was some time after the adverse publicity of 1382 before definite repressive steps were taken against the use of the vernacular. But, after May 1382, openly to claim authorship of a vernacular tract expounding points of lately prohibited teaching might well have seemed inadvisable.

[69] The English *De blasphemia*, unlike the corresponding chapters of the *Trialogus*, makes no mention of the Blackfriars Council.

[70] Netter, *Doctrinale*, i, bk. iv, c. iii, col. 829; 'Dixit enim in libello *De blasphemiis*, cap. ii, secundae blasphemiae: et idem habet ubi supra in *Trial.* lib. IV, cap. xxvii'; Netter then gives a Latin version of *SEW*, iii, pp. 412, 11. 3-12, 16-19 (cf. *Trial.* c. 28, pp. 341-2). Netter (using the example of the woman of Samaria in John 4) was here arguing the case that Christ did himself beg vocally, and attacking Wycliffe's 'Judaic' idea of 'nodding' (innuitive) begging. Wycliffe corrected William of St. Amour, who had denied that Christ ever begged, since he recognized that scripture said otherwise, but he also wanted to exclude the friars and so produced the argument that Christ

God.'[71] Christ was poor and needy and a beggar, but he never asked help in words, vocally.

When the friars turned the tables on Wycliffe, he turned the law of the gospel back on them. He took the accepted canonical distinction between true poor and strong beggars, and placed the friars firmly on the wrong side of the gospel law. There are several contemporary (or near-contemporary) notices of this strategy. The author of the continuation of the *Eulogium historiarum*, himself very probably a Franciscan, described Wycliffe's determining at Oxford in 1382 against the religious orders, including the argument that 'the begging of able-bodied friars is unlawful, and they should labour for their sustenance . . .'[72] This year Wycliffe's supporters were preaching on the same lines, including Nicholas Hereford at Oxford and William Swinderby at Leicester.

A summary of Hereford's famous sermon, delivered at St. Frideswide's, Oxford, on Ascension Day 1382, survives in an official notarial record. Even this condemnatory report conveys a sense of his impassioned pleading against the temporal failings of all orders in the church, special attention being directed against the acquisitiveness of the religious orders and mendicants. Hereford was at pains to show how founders' wishes were being contravened by the life style (lordly equipages, high houses and great churches) of the religious, whose excess revenues should be used to help the poor, not spent on the rich and powerful – an abuse of *bona pauperum*. He slated the begging and extortions of the mendicants (particularly those in the university) and the folly

begged, 'sed insinuative, et non clamose cum Fratribus . . . assignat Christo mendicitatem tantum per nutus . . . ' – an idea, Netter indicated (col. 830) specifically Wycliffe's own. While, however, showing Wycliffe's contribution to the antimendicant argument, Netter saw Wycliffites as *Amoraei,* continuing the tradition of William of St. Amour and 'his son' FitzRalph: *Doctrinale*, cols. 842, 846, 850-1, 855, 895 etc.

[71] *SEW*, iii, pp. 410-11.

[72] This year too, he added, Wycliffe's followers withdrew alms from the friars, saying mendicants ought to work and preached only for gain, attacking them and their errors in English tracts: *Eulogium historiarum,* iii, pp. 354-5. This report, though perhaps written (like Knighton's) a good many years later (see Catto, 'An Alleged Great Council', p. 766) is worth notice, not only for its retrospective view of the importance of this year in the attack on the mendicants, but also for what it says about Wycliffe's disciples working at the compilation of sermons, travelling throughout England to preach Wycliffe's doctrine *nobilibus et literatis* as well as to lay people. (See Hudson, 'Lollardy: The English Heresy?', p. 271). For William Woodford on Wycliffe attacking the mendicants after their condemnation of his eucharistic doctrine in 1381 see *Fasc. Ziz.*, pp. 517-18; Workman, *Wyclif*, i, p. 186. The Blackfriars Council perhaps led contemporaries to overemphasize the importance of 1382, and its last two articles condemned the views that friars should get their sustenance by manual labour, not begging, and that almsgivers to friars were excommunicate. But the split between Wycliffe and the friars was in the making from 1378, and from our point of view the question is when the case against mendicants as strong beggars began to be publicized. This remains uncertain, though Nicholas Hereford's preaching (see next note) suggests that this was being done at least by Feb. 1382. McShane, *A Critical Appraisal*, pp. 2-6; E. Doyle. 'William Woodford, O.F.M., and John Wyclif's *De Religione', Speculum,* lii (1977), pp. 329-36.

of giving money for prayers to intercessors who could only invoke the anger of God. Possessioners and mendicants alike threatened the peace of the realm, and they would never be humbled until their possessions and mendicancy were dealt with. The preacher invoked the community to undertake this task with outstretched hands. If the king were to remove the possessions and riches of these orders as he should, he would not need to tax the poor commons. The sermon ended with a lament that the realm lacked justices (*iusticiarii*) to execute this supreme justice, and so it was left to faithful Christians to take up the work – as Hereford trusted they would – and so perform God's will.[73]

We do not know if William Swinderby used such rousing words. In the sermon he delivered on Palm Sunday 1382, in Leicester, he certainly attacked the friars, reportedly maintaining that begging by the able-bodied was forbidden in secular law and nowhere sanctioned in evangelical law, that Christ never ordered anyone to beg, and that nobody should give alms to a person better clothed or housed than himself.[74] From this time on, anti-mendicancy was firmly entrenched in Lollard teaching.[75]

Almsgiving was, of course, linked with tithes, and we cannot leave this topic without considering them. It is clear, from the instances I have cited, how often the case against church endowment was associated with tithes. Temporalities and spiritualities were viewed together. The right of temporal lords to remove lands from offending prelates was paired with the right of parishioners to withhold tithes from offending curates. Reginald Pecock later seized on this double issue when, in the third part of his *Repressor,* he set about justifying, at some length, the church's endowments. Two arguments, Pecock saw, had to be answered together: first, that bishops and other clerks who did not live virtuously 'may justly be unpossessed, (that is to say, may justly be put out of possession of the same goods)'; and secondly, the idea that if any clerk failed to

---

[73] *FZ*, pp. 296, 303, 305; S. Forde, 'Nicholas Hereford's Ascension Day Sermon, 1382', *Mediaeval Studies*, 51 (1989), pp. 205-41; Hudson, *Premature Reformation*, pp. 70-72, 337-8. For arguments used by Hereford before 18 Feb. 1382 representing friars' mendicancy as spoliation of the poor, and for his and Repton's replies to the 24 Conclusions on this question, see *FZ*, pp. 292-5, 305, 324-5. For a defence of mendicancy against these attacks see the Latin verses in *Monumenta Franciscana*, i, ed. J.S. Brewer (RS, 1858), pp. 598-9.

[74] *Chronicon Henrici Knighton*, ed. J.R. Lumby (RS, 1889-95), ii, pp. 174-5; McFarlane, *John Wycliffe*, p. 122; J. Crompton, 'Leicestershire Lollards', *Trans. Leics. Archaeol. and Hist. Soc.*, xliv (1968-9), pp. 20-22. Swinderby also maintained that tithes were pure alms and could be withheld from priests of evil life.

[75] For questions about religious orders, including whether friars ought to labour with their hands rather than beg, in the questionnaire of (probably) 1428, see A. Hudson, 'The Examination of Lollards', *BIHR*, xlvi (1973), pp. 154-5. For Richard Wyche's view of friars' begging as unlawful, *spontanea clamosa*, see *FZ*, pp. 380-1, 502, 504-5; F.D. Matthew, 'The Trial of Richard Wyche', *EHR*, v (1890), p. 531. The case against friars as 'clamorous' able-bodied beggars can be traced in various texts, witnessing to the Wycliffite contribution to antimendicant literature: e.g. *Pierce the Ploughmans Crede*, p. 23 ('Whereto beggen these men and been not so feeble . . . Withouten any travail untruly they liveth./They be not maimed men, nor no meat lacketh'), p. 4 ('With sterne staves and strong they over land straketh'); *Lanterne of Liȝt*, p. 54 (against almsgiving to 'strong staff-beggars and strikers over the land, and groaners without cause').

fulfil his spiritual office, then the people 'may justly withdraw the tithes and offerings' and all other dues.[76] These were the twin remedies Wycliffe had advocated to cure the church of its ills: the king and secular lords should remove temporalities from offending prelates; the people, 'poor subjects', should withdraw offerings and tithes from offending parish clergy.[77] Behind both recommendations lay the idea of the pristine purity of the evangelical church, combined with the belief that divergence from that state had disinherited Christ's true poor.

At some unknown date Wycliffe addressed himself to a series of eight 'difficult questions' about tithes that had been put to him by a 'distinguished friend'. They included: 'In what land and for what reason were tithes given to knights?'; 'Whether before the time of Gregory X Christians were allowed to pay predial and other tithes to the most indigent poor?'; and 'Whether it is a sin to give things of the poor to those who are not poor, since, tithes being the tribute of the poor, it seems sacrilege to pay tithes to offending curates?' Wycliffe fudged his reply to the first question. His answer to the others is more illuminating, and it is worth noting that the last of these three questions is related to the quotation cited by Bankin in 1371 – which goes back to a letter of Jerome. Wycliffe affirmed that tithes are the goods of the poor. Rectors should use them to relieve their people, receiving themselves (the criterion here was 1 Timothy 6:8) sufficient sustenance in food and clothing. But, Wycliffe added, it often happened that poor parishioners thought their curate could live more economically, especially if he laboured like poor laymen and made the most of his temporalities (though that might endanger his pastoral work). There might be a case then, for thinking it 'permissible and meritorious to withdraw tithes from a curate abusing them and to spend them on other pious uses'.[78]

After Wycliffe others were more explicit in saying that tithes could be paid direct to the poor. 'Dymes or tithes are alms or goods of poor men, truly for to

---

[76] Pecock, *Repressor*, ii, pp. 380-1. Cf. *Remonstrance*, ed. Forshall, pp. 14-16; for Purvey's and Swinderby's pairing of these two issues see *FZ*, p. 394, and *Registrum Johannis Trefnant*, ed. W.W. Capes (CYS, xx, 1916), pp. 240, 263-6, and for two defendants who in 1430 renounced the view that tithes and temporalities should be withdrawn for the benefit of the poor see *Norwich Heresy Trials*, ed. Tanner, pp. 141, 147 and below p. 129. Of course tithes were an intrinsic part of the case for disendowment in the supposition that a properly evangelical ministry would subsist on tithes and offerings.

[77] *Opus evangelicum*, ii, p. 363. Cf. *De simonia*, ed. H.-Fränkel and M.H. Dziewicki (WS, 1898), pp. 93-4 for three remedies for dealing with the endowed orders (number one, the miracle that God would enlighten the pope, scarcely counted); *Opera minora*, pp. 45-6 (no. 19 of the 33 Conclusions '*de paupertate Christi*') on how the elemosinary failings of rectors and curates should be corrected by patrons of churches withdrawing endowments, just as the king should correct negligent prelates by removing their temporalities.

[78] *Opera minora*, pp. 12-15 (ending with a passage on why the law of the church/antichrist judged otherwise). On 1 Tim 6:8, frequently cited as the criterion for the acceptable reception of tithe, see *Trialogus*, p. 419; for Wycliffe's view of tithes as *bona pauperum*, and Augustine's 'tithes are the tribute of needy souls', *De blasphemia*, pp. 34-5; *De civili dominio*, pp. 320, 338, 340, 345, 353 etc.; see notes 29, 35, above.

be offered', opened the section on this topic in the *Rosarium theologie,* which ended with a note stating that it was Gregory X who had ordered tithes to be paid to parish churches, instead of being freely disposed of by the payer.[79] There were a number of vernacular texts which made quite clear that the proper destination of tithes was Christ's poor. 'I cannot see by God's law but that tithes may be divided among Christ's poor men, the which Christ tells in the gospel, as poor feeble, and poor lame and poor blind' – categories (those of Luke 14) which should include priests among the foremost.[80] The implication was that the clergy received tithe by virtue of being poor, instead of the poor receiving tithe through the ministry of the clergy. There would seem to have been some justice in bishops accusing Lollards of saying 'that no man is holden to tithe in manner now used of the church, but such tithes and offerings by the law of God should be given to poor needy men'. The prevaricating defence put up against this point argued that if curates were themselves poor and needy, assigning tithes as they should to other poor people, then there would be no harm in rendering such dues to them.[81]

The canon law provision that a proportion of tithes (in England generally accepted as a third, though the initial division was fourfold) should be given to the poor did, of course, provide some genuine basis for these claims. There was, moreover, a body of opinion in early Christian sources which maintained that church property belonged to God and the poor, to be dispensed by churchmen for all those in need. On this theory the clergy's role was that of steward, and there are some early examples of tithes being paid direct to the poor.[82]

There were Lollards who, though not conversant with the whole of the early church precedent, were sure of their ground. Nor were they alone in their

---

[79] *Rosarium theologie,* ed. von Nolcken, pp. 62-3, 109-10. This misapprehension about Gregory X was repeated elsewhere (see below, p. 129) and derived from the *Polychronicon.* It was, as Selden pointed out, wholly mistaken to suppose that the parochial right to tithe started at the council of Lyons in 1274. See *Polychronicon Ranulphi Higden,* viii, ed. J.R. Lumby (RS, 1882), pp. 256-7; J. Selden, *The Historie of Tithes* (London, 1618), p. 147; and for William Thorpe's use of this source, including the argument that Christ taught payment not of tithes, but of alms to 'poor needy men', *Fifteenth Century Prose and Verse,* ed. A.W. Pollard (Westminster, 1903), pp. 143-4.

[80] *EWW,* pp. 431-2; cf. pp. 415, 421 ('De officio pastorali'); p. 132 ('Of clerks possessioners'); *SEW,* iii, p. 175.

[81] *Selections,* ed. Hudson, pp. 19, 21 (no. 3), and notes pp. 146-7; cf. Thorpe, *Fifteenth Century Prose and Verse,* ed. Pollard, p. 145. Cf. also on the right to withhold tithe Swinderby's views in *Reg. Trefnant,* pp. 239-41, 263-4, 280, and the devious logic of *Remonstrance,* ed. Forshall, pp. 12-18, which moved via documented 'corollaries' from the position that Christians should give support to faithful curates, to the proposition that tithes and offerings should be withdrawn from sinful curates.

[82] Gelasius in 494 ruled a quadripartite division of tithes (between bishop, clergy, church fabric, and poor), but this came to be superseded by a threefold one (between clergy, church fabric, and poor). See R.A.R. Hartridge, *A History of Vicarages in the Middle Ages* (Cambridge, 1930), pp. 1-2; G. Constable, *Monastic Tithes from their Origins to the Twelfth Century* (Cambridge, 1964), pp. 11, 21-3, 43, 49-56; Tierney, *Medieval Poor Law,* pp. 21, 40-1, 43, 70, 73-4, 148. Cf. *Mum and the Sothsegger,* pp. 45-7 on the threefold division and the claims of the poor.

persuasion: witness the long-drawn out proceedings against William Russell, warden of the London Greyfriars, who preached publicly in the capital in 1425 'that personal tithes do not fall under the commandment of God's law', and so, 'if custom were not to the contrary, it would be lawful to Christ's people to dispose of them to uses of pity to poor men'.[83]

Poverty was a continuous theme – if not an obsession – in Lollard writings. Naturally it was presented in gospel terms. The poor man is the only true image of Christ, and the 'wrongs and extortions of poor men' are premised,[84] as Piers Plowman's vision was premised, on a passionate concern for biblical justice. But the hurts of contemporary life were not all described in scriptural terms. Some are sharp with the reality of direct experience. 'I see thine image gone in cold and in heat in clothes all to broken with outen shoon and hosen, an hungered and a thirst'; 'poor men wander in storms and sleep with the swine'; 'poor needy men that have naked sides and torn sleeves and their children starve for cold'; 'poor bedridden men that may not go'[85] – to take a sample of quotations from four different texts. It was this world that the poor preachers professed to share and that, as 'poor men, treasurers of Christ and his apostles', they aspired to reform.

The admissions of their opponents, who repeatedly adverted to Matthew 7 ('beware of false prophets') made it plain that the Lollards, or enough of them to be noticeable, really did present an evangelical appearance. The consensus on this, from a variety of hostile witnesses, is fairly impressive. 'They have nothing more', wrote Dymoke, 'than a certain appearance of humility of posture, in lowering of the head, abandonment of clothing, and pretence of fasting, they pretend simplicity in words, affirming themselves to be burning with love of God and neighbour.'[86] A preacher who, not long after 1390, was able to capitalize on a recently recanted Oxford Wycliffite, glossed the usual

---

[83] *Register of Henry Chichele*, ed. E.F. Jacob (CYS, xlii, xlv-xlvii, 1938-47), i, pp. cxxxv-cxxxvi; iii, pp. 118-57, 173-9 (quoted at 152); trans. in *Eng. Hist. Docts.*, iv, ed. Myers, pp. 707-9; *Munimenta academica,* ed. Anstey, ii, pp. 374, 376, cf. i, p. 270, n. 1; C.L. Kingsford, *The Grey Friars of London* (Aberdeen, 1915), pp. 57-8; Little, *Grey Friars in Oxford*, pp. 85-6, 257-9; idem, 'Personal Tithes', *EHR*, lx (1945), p. 67. Emden (O), iii, pp. 1611-12, indicates that Little was wrong to suppose that Russell had studied at Oxford. Cf. ibid., ii, p. 1258, and Little, *Grey Friars in Oxford*, p. 259 for the case of William de Melton, another Franciscan and an Oxford doctor, who in 1427 caused the university to seek the aid of Duke Humphrey and the council against his itinerant preaching against tithes.

[84] *Selections,* ed. Hudson, p. 88.

[85] *The Praier and complaynte of the ploweman unto Christe* (Antwerp, 1531), sign. Cv r; *EWW*, p. 211 (cf. p. 210), p. 14; *SEW*, iii, p. 383.

[86] *Rogeri Dymmok Liber,* p. 307, cf. pp. 6, 314; and on the 'treasurers of Christ' claim, pp. 25, 28, 92, 226, 228, 311. Both friars and Lollards were accused of wearing russet (a coarse cloth, originally grey or brown in color) 'that betokeneth travail upon earth', as a kind of poverty costume. *Pierce the Ploughmans Crede,* p. 27; *Trialogus,* p. 337; *Jack Upland,* pp. 85, 151; *Norwich Heresy Trials,* p. 75; H.L. Cannon, 'The Poor Priests: A Study in the Rise of English Lollardry', *Annual Rept. of the Am. Hist. Assn. for 1899* (Washington, 1900), i, pp. 451-82; G.F. Jones, 'Sartorial Symbols in Mediaeval Literature', *Medium aevum,* xxv (1956), pp. 63-70.

verse of Matthew; take heed, said Christ, 'of false prophets, yea, false Lollards, that come to you in clothing of meekness and holy living, for to teach or preach you'. The fact (he went on) that they go 'to-ragged and to-rent and show outward' was no guide to their true hearts.[87] Even Walsingham, writing about the sorry end of Oldcastle's followers, admitted the ostensible 'modesty, patience, humility, and charity, of speech and appearance' which so belied the inner depravity of such men.[88] The likelihood is that this constant harping on the deceptiveness of externals was necessary because the preachers' poverty really did look convincing – and attractive.

Concern for the poor – the truly evangelical poor, not the pseudo-poor – powered the anti-mendicant case. 'For Christ', wrote Wycliffe, 'instituted that men should bodily help the poor and weak, poor and halt, poor and blind, which these sects withdraw by their false inventions baselessly introduced.'[89] The mendicant friars, who were so overburdened with great houses and valuable possessions, maintained that the alms which belonged to the poor feeble men, poor crooked men, poor blind men and poor bedridden men should be given to these hypocrites. The constant criterion was the passage from Luke 14 which I quoted at the beginning, used not only to define the proper recipients of alms, but also to exclude others, distinguishing true beggars from strong beggars – i.e. friars.[90] Thomas Netter, who devoted a chapter of the *Doctrinale* to this abuse of these verses in Luke's gospel, attacked Wycliffe for the misconstructions he placed on these words. 'Consider O Wycliffe', he wrote, 'how here, no less than elsewhere, you have erred

[87] *Three Middle English Sermons,* ed. D.M. Grisdale (Leeds School of English Language, Texts and Monographs, v, 1939), pp. 65-6. (Of course the 'false prophets' of the sermon on the mount was applied just as often by Wycliffites to the friars: e.g. *English Wycliffite Sermons,* ed. Hudson, i, p. 253 – alluding to the three offences of the *Trialogus*; 'of the sacred host, of begging of Christ, of letters of their brotherhood').

[88] *St. Albans Chronicle,* p. 80; cf. *Historia Anglicana,* ii, pp. 299-300. As it has been treated elsewhere I have not attempted here to consider the effect of Oldcastle's rising on the politics of disendowment. But even in the 1450s the aims of 1414 may not have been entirely dead. In the short-lived rising of John Wilkins in Kent in May 1452 some rebels had ideas of clerical dispossession and looked to Lord Cobham to support their plans. As reported in one charge these sound authentically Lollard: 'that priests throughout England should have no possessions or chattels except a chair and a candlestick for studying their books': R. Virgoe, 'Some Ancient Indictments in the King's Bench referring to Kent, 1450-1452', in *Kent Records,* ed. F.R.H. Du Boulay (Kent Arch. Soc., xviii, 1964), pp. 257-9. Cf. *EWW,* p. 380 against clerical possession on how ' . . . a chair, and a candlestick . . . ben according to a studier or a contemplative man' (= 2 Kings 4: 10). For an apparent echo of the old disendowment scheme in 1464 see Hudson, *Premature Reformation,* p. 340.

[89] *Polemical Works,* i. p. 47. This is one of many instances (see note 22 above) in Wycliffe's and Lollard writings where the allusion to Luke 14 has gone unnoticed. For some other examples of Wycliffe's use of this passage see ibid., i, pp. 308, 311; *Trialogus,* pp. 305, 343-4, 354; *De ecclesia,* ed. J. Loserth (WS. 1886), p. 286; *De officio pastorali,* i, pp. 18-19; *Sermones,* i, p. 230 (expounding four categories), cf. ii, p. 186; iii, p. 500; iv, pp. 19, 105. For Wycliffe referring to himself in 1383/4 as *debilis et claudus,* see *Pol. Works,* ii, pp. 543, 556.

[90] *EWW,* pp. 27, 387, 421.

in the gospel of Jesus Christ, by thus promoting the common poor before the holy poor of Christ, namely friars and monks, in taking alms.'[91]

The worst of it – from the Lollards' point of view – was that in failing to imitate the poverty of Christ, these strong beggars expected the poor to support their expensive faults. To be sure, there was plenty to be said about the gross life-style of monks and bishops. But their misuse of temporal possessions seemed to impinge less directly on the poor and more on the upper ranks of society, the well-to-do lords and gentry. If friars 'increase begging with great cry', the chief sufferers were those who could least afford almsgiving, and if 'poor men are defrauded of livelihood, then the friars are much worse than other religious, and are blasphemers against Christ, and are mankillers of poor men, both in bodies and souls'. Friars were to ordinary people what monks and chantrists and collegiate clergy were to gentry – blasphemous despoilers.

> Certis it seemeth by open reason and works, visibly, that as religious possessioners destroy knights and squires by amortising of secular lordships, so friars destroy the commons by subtle and needless begging.[92]

The attack on church ownership was two-pronged. At one level were the temporal endowments of bishoprics, monasteries and colleges, whose lordly estates could only be remedied by lordly means – centrally, with the help of parliament. On another, local level, humble people, by withholding alms and tithes, could take steps towards reforming the mendicants and parish clergy.

Because the idea of parliamentary disendowment had so little positive effect and left no trace in official records, historians have tended to discount such Lollard political aspirations.[93] This seems mistaken. Opponents, as well as supporters, gave serious (sometimes fearful) consideration to disendowment projects;[94] and we can point to several spheres in which statute law and legislation might have encouraged Lollard hopes of parliamentary action.

---

[91] Netter, *Doctrinale*, i, bk. iv, c. x, col. 861. Cf. col. 860 for Netter's objection that Wycliffe abused the gospel text by taking *pauperes* as an adjectival description of *debiles, caecos, et claudos*, thereby making three categories out of what should be the fourfold *pauperes et debiles, caecos, et claudos*. FitzRalph seems to have given the lead here, arguing (against the begging of friars) that the 'feast of beggars' of Luke 14 excluded poor men who were stalwart and strong, just as much as rich men who were feeble, halt, or blind: 'Defensio curatorum' in *Trevisa's Dialogus*, p. 88. See Wendy Scase, *Piers Plowman and the New Anticlericalism* (Cambridge, 1989), pp. 63, 152, for FitzRalph's role in this reading, and the wider implications of this debate.

[92] *Remonstrance*, ed. Forshall, pp. 95, 97; cf. *SEW*, iii, p. 372.

[93] E.g. May McKisack, *The Fourteenth Century* (Oxford, 1959), p. 291; Cronin in *Rogeri Dymmok Liber*, pp. xxxiff.; W.T. Waugh, 'Sir John Oldcastle', *EHR*, xx (1905), pp. 440-1; Kingsford, above p. 111. Cf. Myers in *Eng. Hist. Docts.*, iv, p. 629.

[94] Dymoke, for instance, talking about the suggestions made to parliament for spoiling the church (above, p. 114) adds that 'as yet, thank God, no lord has agreed with them' ('nullus . . . adhuc assensit'; *Rogeri Dymmok Liber*, p. 178). While doubtless meant as a warning this *adhuc* implies an open-ended situation. Trevisa's *Dialogus inter militem et clericum* (Trevisa's *Dialogus*, pp. 1-38) with its arguments (comparable to those used in 1371) that common need of the realm

The examples of the Templars and the alien priories were not missed by Wycliffe and others who mulled over the idea of secularizing church property. When it came to the theory of the case, the idea that all ecclesiastical endowment was conditional, and ultimately secular in origin, was something laymen were not reluctant to believe, and its application could be both general and particular. The rights of lay founders over their religious foundations could seem to lead in a fairly straight line towards the argument that clerical shortcomings were open to correction by responsible laymen.

Founders' rights were safeguarded in law, to the extent that endowments might be reclaimed from a church that was negligent in performing contracted services. Wycliffe insisted on the legal rights of founders, and pointed to the legislation of Edward I. The second Statute of Westminster (1285) made it possible for founders or their heirs to sue by writ of *cessavit* in the lay courts for recovery of lands held by religious houses, in the event of stipulated services not being carried out.

> But if the land so given for a chantry, light, feeding the poor, or for the support and doing of other alms, be not alienated but such alms be withdrawn for the space of two years, an action shall lie with the donor or his heir to seek the land so given in demesne, as it is ordained in the Statute of Gloucester . . . [95]

An example of such an action is that taken in 1341 by Margaret de Roos, who regained lands granted to the abbey of Creake in Norfolk, because the abbot had failed to provide the services specified in the endowment charter – including singing masses in the chapel of Margaret's foundation and daily liveries of bread to the poor.[96] Another such case was that brought in 1387 against the abbot of St. Osyth in Essex by Robert Hotot, for recovery of sixty acres of land, on the grounds that for two years the abbey had failed to find a chaplain to celebrate commemorative masses in a chapel in Stowmarket, Suffolk. This foundation was already over a century old, having been established by Herlwin Hotot in the time of Henry III, and six generations of Hotots lay between Herlwin and his heir who brought this action in the King's Bench

---

overrode clerical privilege and that restoration was in order when founders' wishes for works of charity were neglected, shows the currency of such ideas. See also A. Hudson, 'A Lollard Quaternion', *Review of English Studies*, NS xxiii (1971), p. 441, and idem, *Selections,* Text 26. For BL Egerton MS 2820, a fine copy of a variant version of *The Clergy may not hold Property* which was evidently made for a well-to-do owner, see *Selections*, pp. 185-6; *English Wycliffite Sermons,* i, p. 194.

[95] *SR*, i, p. 92; 13 Ed. I, c. 41. E. Tatnall, 'John Wyclif and *Ecclesia Anglicana*', *JEH*, xx (1969), p. 30; Farr, *John Wyclif as Legal Reformer*, pp. 104-5; Wycliffe, *De civili dominio*, ii, pp. 39-41, and for statements of the rights of founders and their heirs *Opera minora*, pp. 42-5, 63-4 (nos. 18 and 30 of the 33 Conclusions). For Lollards on the role of founders in correcting endowments see *FZ*, p. 394 (Purvey); *EWW*, p. 392; *Remonstrance,* ed. Forshall, p. 91-2.

[96] Farr, *John Wyclif as Legal Reformer*, pp. 106-7.

under Richard II.[97] Time was no bar to the sense of property in founders' heirs – witness pleas voiced at the Dissolution. And those who were so conscious of their rights over individual religious houses might have been persuaded to think in terms of correcting offending institutions as a class.

Bishops' temporalities (the 'great manors, castles, and . . . great lordships of baronies', as Pecock defined them)[98] clearly presented an easy target for secular resumption. Their post-Reformation history shows the eventual implementation of such a policy. It was advocated long before. The Lollard tacticians who thought of episcopal confiscation in 1410 and (perhaps) 1404, were enlarging on suggestions of Wycliffe, who in several works indicated the advantages of such disendowment. 'The king', he pointed out, 'often took into his hands the temporalities of his clergy.' 'It is not strange for kings to correct clerks.'[99] Not only was the king able to remove temporal possessions, movable and immovable, from clergy who were guilty of treason or other crimes; he was also in a position to retain during pleasure the temporalities of bishops when these came into his hands in the normal course of events. Wycliffe explained more than once that a means to the gradual reconquest of antichrist would be for the king to retain such temporal lordships permanently, thereby preventing them from ever returning to mortmain. The live hand (*manus viva*) could thus eventually cheat the dead hand (*manus mortua*).[100] This, moreover, should be through action in parliament. Among the examples of such contemporary parliamentary forfeiture, one that must have brought special satisfaction to Lollards was the case of Henry Despenser, whose temporalities were taken into the king's hands for two years after the failure of his much vilified crusade.[101]

Another matter on which it was reasonable to seek parliamentary remedy was appropriation. The damage done to parochial almsgiving by the appropriation of benefices, on which Lollard writers harped so insistently, was also a topic of parliamentary concern. Petitions about this were presented on a number of occasions; and one of 1391, alleging the loss of charity, hospitality, and other aid to poor parishioners caused by appropriations, had some effect. It resulted in a statute providing that, when licences were issued in chancery for appropriating parish churches, the diocesan should allocate an annual

[97] *Year Books of Richard II: 11 Richard II, 1387-1388,* ed. I.D. Thornley (1937), pp. xxxi, 72-5. The outcome of this case is not known.

[98] Pecock, *Repressor,* ii, p. 400.

[99] *Polemical Works,* i, p. 283; *Opera minora,* p. 409.

[100] *Polemical Works,* i, pp. 281-3; cf. *Trialogus,* p. 313; *De ecclesia,* pp. 331-2; *Opera minora,* pp. 41-2; *De apostasia,* p. 88; H. Kaminsky, 'Wyclifism as Ideology of Revolution', *Church History,* xxxii (1963), p. 67 and n. 82; Farr, *John Wyclif as Legal Reformer,* p.152, n. 85; Gradon, 'Langland and the Ideology of Dissent, p. 187; Tatnall, 'John Wyclif and *Ecclesia Anglicana,* pp. 31-4. On royal exploitation of episcopal vacancies in the thirteenth century and the question of whether Henry III and Edward I deliberately prolonged vacancies for financial reasons, see M. Howell, *Regalian Right in Medieval England* (1962), p. 167 and chapter V.

[101] *Rot. Parl.,* iii, p. 156b; *Historia Anglicana,* ii, pp. 109, 141, cf. 128; *Westminster Chronicle,* pp. 52-3; Workman, *Wyclif,* ii, p. 69.

proportion of the revenues in aid of 'the poor parishioners of the said churches', as well as making adequate endowment for the vicar.[102] Complaints continued thereafter, but there were clearly grounds for looking hopefully to lords and commons for support over this problem, and this parliamentary record ought to be placed beside the 1395 conclusions and Archbishop Arundel's reported diversionary reforms of 1399.

Concern for the plight of the poor – even in parliamentary legislation – was not motivated only by fears of 'perturbation of the realm'.[103] Alongside the rights of king, patrons, founders, and benefice holders over church endowments, there floated another continent of claimants – not necessarily unrepresented. If it was possible for Lollards to regard the statute of 1388 as constructive legislation for the poor, there were many others whose desire to help the deprived was in no way tangled with heresy.

For those touched by Lollard evangelism, service to Christ's poor was a call that rose above the hostile skirmishings against friars and possessioners. Christ taught, Wycliffe admonished, referring yet again to that well-worked passage in Luke, 'how we ought to give bodily alms to the poor blind, the poor halt, and the poor feeble, and as a result to oblige other strong beggars to work . . . But how can the universal and perpetual endowment of the church consort with this rule of Christ?'[104] The overall endowment of the church may not have been much affected, but we know of a number of almsgivers and payers of tithe who acted on such teaching.

Sir Thomas Latimer (followed by his wife Anne) showed concern in his will for the triple categories of gospel poor, the feeble, blind, and crooked – Wycliffe's 'trinity of the poor', as Netter disparagingly dubbed it.[105] Neither husband nor wife made any bequests to any religious, or requests for prayers for their souls.[106] Two other fifteenth-century knights who were Lollard sympathizers, Sir Thomas Broke of Holditch in Devon and his son, another Thomas, were also mindful of the 'poor, blind or lame man or woman' – likewise to the exclusion of soul masses and gifts to mendicants.[107] Humbler

---

[102] *Rot. Parl.,* iii, pp. 293b-294a; cf. ii, p. 284a, iii, p. 645; *SR*, ii, p. 80, 15 Ric. II, c. vi, cf. p. 136, 4 Hen. IV, c. xii; Hartridge, *History of Vicarages*, pp. 157-8, 198-9; Tierney, *Medieval Poor Law*, pp. 128-9.

[103] *EWW*, p. 27.

[104] *Trialogus*, pp. 305-6; cf. *Polemical Works*, i, pp. 47, 312.

[105] Netter, *Doctrinale*, i, col. 862; cf. col. 859, 'illos tres pauperes'. Cf. Wycliffe in *Trialogus*, p. 305 ('Oportet enim quod in Christi regula sit paupertas in triplici sequenti particula tripliciter intellecta . . . '); *Sermones*, iv, p. 105 ('oportet pauperes in verbis sequentibus triplicare . . . '); *Lanterne of Li3t*, p. 86, ostensibly translating Luke 14, 'bring in to thine house these three manner of people, poor feeble, poor blind, and poor crooked'. See notes 22, 89, 91 above.

[106] *Ancestor*, x (1904), pp. 19-21 ('poor and feeble, poor and blind, poor and crooked', p. 20). Thomas Latimer's will was dated 13 Sept. 1401 and proved 20 April 1402, Anne Latimer's dated 13 July 1402 and proved 27 Oct. 1402. See K.B. McFarlane, *Lancastrian Kings and Lollard Knights* (Oxford, 1972), p. 214; A. Hudson, 'The Debate on Bible Translation, Oxford, 1401', *EHR*, xc (1975), p. 12.

[107] *The Fifty Earliest English Wills*, ed. F.J. Furnivall (EETS, OS 78, 1882), pp. 26-8, 129-30 (1415, proved 1418, and 1439); McFarlane, *Lancastrian Kings*, p. 216. The elder Sir Thomas was

believers in these priorities included Anne Palmer, encountered earlier.[108] And among those who helped to spread the view that tithes might legitimately be transferred from possessioner clergy to indigent poor was William White, in the diocese of Norwich. He admitted in 1428 to having taught that tithes could be withdrawn, providing this was done prudently, since from Christ's passion until Gregory X the people only gave tithes to the poor – which meant proper beggars, since mendicant friars were not then in existence. A certain Thomas Plowman, shipman of Sizewell in Suffolk, seems to have taken this teaching to heart. He confessed in 1430 that he had been giving his tithes to the poor in the belief that this was lawful.[109]

Though the issues and motives for disendowing the church were mixed, the question of the poor was visible throughout. Poverty was a theme that truly transcended the divergence between secular and religious – and for that matter the mutual mistrust between clerical and lay, orthodox and heterodox. It was one of the moving debates of the time. There are periods when poverty is in vogue, and the manner of being poor is also subject to the constraints of fashion. Whereas the eleventh century had seen (as Michel Mollat puts it) a sort of 'exaltation of the dignity of the poor',[110] the late fourteenth and fifteenth centuries witnessed impassioned pleading on behalf of the miseries of the poor. Evangelical poverty was now as much a criterion for redressing social injustice as for imitating Christ, and mendicancy promoted a revaluation of poverty. The contemporary poor were held up as a mirror for would-be imitators of Christ. Poverty was still holy, but far too much of it seemed to be the result of the most unholy misappropriation and neglect.

Revulsion against the temporal possessions of the English church in the fifteenth century existed on many levels, and manifested itself in various ways and places. It reached the political arena by both stealth and direct assault, with largely negative results. The broad appeal of the issue ensured both the continuity of these efforts and, paradoxically, their ultimate failure. The parliamentary approach was pushed off course by the popular one. The call to

M.P. for Somerset in the parliaments of 1395, 1399 and 1410 discussed above. The younger Sir Thomas married Joan Braybrooke, heiress of Oldcastle's wife, Lady Cobham. He took part in the rising of 1414 and was the father of Edward Broke, Lord Cobham, who was looked to by the Kent rebels of 1452 (above note 88). McFarlane, ibid., pp. 207ff, who pointed to the expressions of unworthiness, revulsion towards the flesh, and rejection of funeral pomp as characteristics of Lollard wills, did not analyse this other feature. It likewise (probably more so) reflects an aspect of the evangelical movement that was not in itself unorthodox (ibid., p. 225), though the terminology used – the triple classes of poor – may indicate a link with suspect sources.

[108] Cf. the case of William Mundy of Wokingham (1412) in *The Register of Robert Hallum*, ed. J.M. Horn (CYS, lxxii, 1982), p. 219.

[109] *FZ*, p. 428; *Norwich Heresy Trials*, p. 103, and above note 76.

[110] *Études sur l'histoire de la pauvreté*, ed. M. Mollat (Paris, 1974), i, p. 27. See also idem, *The Poor in the Middle Ages: An Essay in Social History*, trans. A. Goldhammer (New Haven and London, 1986).

disendow – Caim's castles and monastic nests alike – was heard more widely than a mere survey of paper projects and parliamentary gestures might suggest.[111]

Let me end with the planning of a great feast, that pulls some of these different strands together. On 1 August 1424, a great reception was ordered to take place in the hall of the bishop's palace at Lincoln. Four hundred poor people from the area were to be brought in, given meals of varying quality, sums of money of between 20d. and 4d., and a pair of shoes each. Another hundred 'most needy' poor were to be given clothing as well as all the rest. This largesse to the indigent poor of Lincolnshire owed nothing to the reigning bishop, Richard Fleming. Indeed one may wonder how he viewed this projected invasion of his residence. It was ordained as funeral ceremony by the will of Fleming's predecessor, Philip Repingdon, or Repton, the sometime Wycliffite, who four years earlier had taken the extraordinary step of resigning his see.[112]

When he came to make his will, Repton's mind turned back with some remorse to his days of prelatical dignity. He wanted this ceremony at Lincoln to be (as he put it) 'in remission of the sins of worldly vanity committed by me in that place'. Concern for the poor was virtually the sole preoccupation of Repton's will, which contains not a word about masses for his soul after death, gave not a mite to any religious order or foundation. All his worldly goods, down to the last penny, halfpenny and farthing, were allocated to the poor of Lincoln.[113]

---

[111] Did the case against the possessioners have any long-term traceable effects on charitable bequests? This important question (posed by Professor Barrie Dobson) is hard to answer. Undoubtedly people of all classes continued to make bequests to the friars throughout the fifteenth century. Figures (statistically a small sample) cited in Little, *Grey Friars in Oxford*, pp. 101-2ff, suggest a decline in the proportion of wills that included such bequests from the late fourteenth to the early sixteenth century. On Franciscan failure in charitable works (echoing Wycliffe – 'They confounded mendicancy with poverty') and the shift of lay piety to other sorts of foundation, see idem, *Studies in English Franciscan History,* pp. 78, 89-91; J. Moorman, *A History of the Franciscan Order* (Oxford, 1968), p. 364, cf. p. 514. Colin Richmond, *John Hopton* (Cambridge, 1981), pp. 203-4, cites the will of John Tasburgh, who in 1473 left a house and land for poor people to live in, with no provision for prayers for his soul – an informal small secular almshouse. Perhaps further analysis of wills will eventually make it possible to see whether almsgiving in general moved in the direction Lollards had signposted: away from established orders and soul-masses, towards the needy (secular) poor.

[112] *Reg. Chichele*, ii, pp. 285-7; McFarlane, *Lancastrian Kings*, pp. 217-18; *DNB, s.n.* Repington. Repton's will is undated; it was proved 1 August 1424. Richard Fleming at this moment had other things on his mind: R.G. Davies, 'Martin V and the English Episcopate', *EHR*, xcii (1977), pp. 322-4, 326-7. Contrary to his request, Repton was buried in Lincoln Cathedral with an inscribed gravestone.

[113] 'in remissionem peccatorum meorum in seculi vanitate per me miserum peccatorem ibidem commissorum'; *Reg. Chichele*, ii, p. 286. He granted the bare courtesies (sums of 20s. to the clergy and 6s. 8d. to the ringers) to those celebrating his obsequies at St. Margaret's, Lincoln. Margery Kempe's pleased report of Repton's daily charity dispensed to thirteen poor men, shows that he had benefited the poor of Lincoln as bishop: *The Book of Margery Kempe*, ed. S.B. Meech and H.E. Allen (EETS, OS 212, 1940), p. 34. There are other features of Repton's will that suggest

In making this will Repton could have taken as his blue-print a sermon of Wycliffe's on the gospel of the *Missa pro defunctis*, which had explained how burial of the dead was, or could be, one of the seven corporal works of mercy. To be so it should avoid elaborate exequies, sumptuous burial, fulsome sermonizing for the dead, and bequests to friars for soul masses or to religious houses in perpetual alms. Such spending as there was on funeral feasts should be modelled on Christ's words in Luke 14; 'call not thy friends, neither thy brethren, neither thy kinsmen, nor thy rich neighbours . . . but call poor men and feeble and blind and crooked', distributing largesse to the most needy. Could executors, asked Wycliffe, do better than follow the law of God?[114]

Did Repton's executors carry out his wishes? I do not know. Repton himself, committing this funeral feast of the poor to a trusted group of friends, acknowledged that works of charity met with many obstacles and setbacks.[115] The events of his lifetime had proved that, witness all the proposed schemes to redistribute the wealth of Caim's castles. But the fact that they got nowhere should not be allowed to obscure the genuinely idealistic charitable aims that were present, together with materialistic interests, in these proposals. Behind the stream of polemic and discontinuities of politics lay a truly evangelical commitment to the poor. Philip Repton was not alone in showing that there were more ways of championing Christ against Cain than petitioning parliament.

trace-elements of Lollardy: his reiterated anxiety that the bell-ringing at his obsequies should not be loud and clamorous with secular pomp; his request for his body to be committed naked to the earth, *outside* the church, without coffin or tomb (the equivalent of a poor man's burial). Another unusual feature is his thrice stated wish that his funeral service should, if possible, take place while he was still alive. Cf. K.B. McFarlane, 'At the Deathbed of Cardinal Beaufort', *England in the Fifteenth Century,* introd. G.L. Harriss (London, 1981), pp. 118-19 (a reference I owe to a reminder of Dr. J.A.F. Thomson). For other indications that Repton did not lose all sympathy for Lollardy see *Selections*, ed. Hudson, p. 158.

[114] *Sermones,* iv, pp. 17-20 (on John 11:21: cf. pp. 104-7 on feeding the poor and Luke 14). ' . . . omnes tales exequie vel consuetudines quantumcunque sumptuose fuerint non prosunt defunctis . . . Non enim videtur racio quare mundo dives tam sumptuose et sollempniter sepelitur nisi propter mundanam gloriam servandam in genere vel propter solacia in viventibus conservanda'; cf. Repton; 'funeralis mea non pomposa vel sumptuose que magis vivorum solacia vel nugancium spectacula quam subsidia mortuorum . . .': Wycliffe; 'sed melius foret quod . . . magis egentibus forent talia distributa'; Repton; 'centum pauperes ad hoc electi maxime indigentes . . . ' Cf. *Sermones,* ii, pp. 185-6. Of course there was nothing unorthodox in such views. For other examples of the wish to avoid funeral excesses, combined with conventional pieties, see *The Register of Edmund Stafford*, ed. F.C. Hingeston-Randolph (London, 1886), pp. 389-90, 410, 412.

[115] 'opera caritatis multa paciuntur impedimenta et adversa'; *Reg. Chichele,* ii, p. 285. If the executors failed over his burial would they have succeeded better with the *pastus pauperum?*

Fig. 10 The hearse of Abbot Islip of Westminster, a vast temporary structure made for his funeral in 1532, to hold many lights, and with his name along the side. Islip's rebus in stone is still to be seen in the chantry chapel he built in the north ambulatory of the choir in Westminster Abbey.

5

Huizinga's Harvest:
England and *The Waning of the Middle Ages*

Titles, like names, are dangerous. They have a way of coming to exist in their own right to the prejudice, it may seem, of the objects or people who bear them. Study of the relationship of words to things is as old as philosophy itself, but the pursuit of anonymity in literature is relatively recent and no way has yet been found for enabling books, as opposed to authors, to be nameless.[1] Their fortunes may be deeply affected by their titles. Such, I think, has been the fate of Johan Huizinga's most famous book as presented to English readers.

Huizinga's *Herfsttij der Middeleeuwen* was published at Haarlem in 1919 when the author was in his mid-forties. It bore the subtitle of *Studie over levens- en gedachtenvormen der veertiende en vijftiende eeuw in Frankrijk en de Nederlanden*. Literally translated, therefore, the work was entitled 'Autumn of the Middle Ages: A study of the forms of life and thought of the fourteenth and fifteenth centuries in France and the Netherlands'. When *Herfsttij* was reissued in Dutch in 1921 the author himself, in order to meet the challenge of some of his critics, drew emphatic attention to the subtitle as defining the boundaries of the work's scope and sources. First receptions of the book were not auspicious. On his home ground Huizinga was regarded with some suspicion as unscholarly, if not novelistic.[2] But by 1940, five years before his death, *Herfsttij* had come of age in Europe, and the Italian edition published that year was the sixth translated version.[3] The English edition had been issued long before this in 1924, the same year as the German. But whereas the latter,

---

[1] Anonymity (like the title page) is presumably a result of the advent of printing. For play on the possibility of a book with 'no title at all' see Max Beerbohm, *Seven Men* (London, 1919), p. 9. See also Maurice Keen, 'Huizinga, Kilgour and the Decline of Chivalry', *Medievalia et Humanistica*, no. 8 (1977), pp. 1-20.

[2] Kurt Köster, *Johan Huizinga, 1872-1945* (Oberursel, 1947), pp. 99-103, lists the editions and reviews of the book; for contemporary receptions of the various editions see F.W.N. Hugenholtz, 'The Fame of a Masterwork', in *Johan Huizinga, 1872-1972*, eds. W.R.H. Koops, E.H. Kossmann and Gees van der Plaat (The Hague, 1973), pp. 91-103.

[3] The Italian version, preceded by the German, English, Swedish (1927), Spanish (1930), and French (1932), was called *Autumno del medioevo*. Köster, ibid., p. 100.

faithful to the original, was entitled *Herbst des Mittelalters,* the English translation by F. Hopman appeared as we have come to know it, under the name of *The Waning of the Middle Ages: A Study of the Forms of Life, Thought and Art in France and the Netherlands in the Fourteenth and Fifteenth Centuries.* Huizinga himself had cooperated in this edition. It was, as the preface explained, 'not a simple translation of the original Dutch, . . . but the result of a work of adaptation, reduction, and consolidation under the author's directions'.[4] The name, therefore, presumably came with Huizinga's own imprimatur, and so perhaps the introduction of the words 'and art' was intended to stress once again the book's intentions and its limits. It was *not* (we can read with hindsight) offered as a complete survey covering the whole of political and social affairs, but set out to describe the ways in which people lived, thought, and expressed themselves artistically in France and the Netherlands at the end of the medieval period.

It is obvious (and has often been remarked) that the English title represented a change of meaning. Was 'waning' true to the author's intentions? And did this choice of title have any bearing on the influence of the book in English? 'Waning', like 'Autumn', carries implications about the historical process, but there is an ambiguity in one which the other clearly lacks. Autumn is a season of ripeness and harvest as well as of overripeness and fall; it is a time of fruitfulness as well as of mists presaging winter. And implicitly where there is autumn we have in our minds the consciousness of spring – the past spring and the seeded spring to come. We know that these meanings were in Huizinga's mind when he wrote the book. He thought of his autumnal period between two historical springs. The past spring, the spring of the middle ages, was a topic that engaged his attention in the 1930s, when he published several studies on the 'pre-Gothic' twelfth century.[5] The future spring of the Renaissance – or perhaps rather summer, since Huizinga's visualizing mind associated Renaissance with summer sunshine[6] – was a continued presence, as much assumed as acknowledged, hanging over the whole of *Herfsttij.*

---

[4]   *The Waning* (London, 1924), pp. v-vi. I have not attempted to explore this editorial revision, and the remarks which follow are based on this English edition, which had been reprinted eight times (in hardback) by 1967. Karl J. Weintraub, *Visions of Culture* (Chicago and London, 1966), p. 212 n. 13, regards the translation as a 'very inferior, crippled version' of the Dutch original, and it is a pity that the fairly full annotation was omitted in the English version, leaving the reader disconcertingly up in the air.

[5]   Huizinga's essays on Alanus de Insulis, John of Salisbury, and Abelard appeared in 1932, 1933, and 1935, Köster, *Huizinga,* pp. 129, 132, 141; the latter two are translated in *Men and Ideas: Essays by Johan Huizinga,* trans. J.S. Holmes and H. van Marle (New York, 1959). Were these essays conceived as part of a larger work to be called 'The Spring of the Middle Ages'? E.H. Gombrich, 'Huizinga's *Homo ludens*', in *Johan Huizinga, 1872-1972,* p. 142, reads this, though it seems unwarrantably, into a remark of Pieter Geyl, 'Huizinga as Accuser of his Age', *History and Theory,* ii (1962-3), p. 255.

[6]   For such images of sunshine and summer see *Men and Ideas,* pp. 89-90, 179, 252, 260, 305; *Waning,* p. 308.

It is true that in only one place in the book do we find mention of 'the celebrated Swiss historian' Jacob Burckhardt, whose pupil Huizinga in effect was, and whose portrayal of the Renaissance was for him both pattern and counterpattern.[7] But the *Waning* cannot be properly understood without setting it alongside Burckhardt's *Civilization of the Renaissance in Italy*. For not only had Burckhardt set Huizinga a model in the writing of cultural history, but it was also a model which he (like others) regarded as greatly needing modification. 'In many respects cultural history today has the task of breaking away from Burckhardt, without that breaking away at all injuring his greatness or reducing the debt we owe him'.[8] These words appear in the revised version of an address on 'Renaissance and Realism' which Huizinga delivered the year after the publication of *Herfsttij,* in 1920. This, and his well-known essay on 'The Problem of the Renaissance' of the same year, may be read as offshoots from the recently published book and offer invaluable clues as to the place it took in his thinking. They show that we are not wrong to regard *Herfsttij* as one among the various works which gnawed at what Huizinga described as the crumbling edges of Burckhardt's magisterial conception.[9]

We do not have to read far in the *Waning* to see that a main theme of the book is the demonstration that essential features of Burckhardt's southern Renaissance existed earlier in the world of the gothic north. The 'craving for individual glory', the origins of which Burckhardt located in fifteenth-century Italy, was 'essentially the same as the chivalrous ambition of earlier times, and of French origin'.[10] Here, as elsewhere, the Swiss historian had exaggerated, and some of the true roots of Renaissance aspiration – emulation of antiquity, quest for glory, hero worship – sprang from the chivalrous ideals of medieval Europe. If Huizinga's book terminated rather than concluded (as one of his sons later indicated), it came to an end with a chapter on 'The Advent of the New Form' which made the same point. The assumed antithesis between the middle ages and the Renaissance was misconceived, and the contrast between Italy and the north overstated. Classicism 'grew up among the luxuriant vegetation of medieval thought', and 'the characteristic modes of thought of the Middle Ages did not die out till long after the Renaissance'. The last paragraphs of the book harp once more upon the biological metaphor, on renewal, renovation, and the 'inward ripening' of the mind.[11]

[7] *Waning*, pp. 58-9. R.L. Colie, 'Johan Huizinga and the Task of Cultural History', *American Historical Review*, lxix (1964), pp. 608, 611. Huizinga has been described as 'the Dutch Burckhardt', and the latter's influence on the former was lifelong. See H.R. Guggisberg, 'Burckhardt und Huizinga: Zwei Historiker in der Krise ihrer Zeit', in *Johan Huizinga, 1872-1972*, pp. 155, 163, 173.

[8] *Men and Ideas*, p. 289; H. Gerson, 'Huizinga und die Kunstgeschichte', in *Johan Huizinga, 1872-1972*, p. 206.

[9] *Men and Ideas*, p. 289; Werner Kaegi, *Das historische Werk Johan Huizingas* (Leiden, 1947), pp. 16-17.

[10] *Waning*, p. 59.

[11] Ibid., pp. 297, 307. Leonard Huizinga's evaluation is quoted by Hugenholtz, 'The Fame of a Masterwork', pp. 100-101.

One passage in 'The Problem of the Renaissance' reads almost as a summary of this aspect of the *Waning* and may be cited for the light it throws on one side of the book:

> Staring into the violent sunshine of the Italian *quattrocento,* Burckhardt had only been able to see defectively what lay beyond it. The veil he saw spread over the spirit of the Middle Ages was partly caused by a flaw in his own camera. He had seen all too sharp a contrast between late medieval life in Italy and life elsewhere. That beneath the glory of the Renaissance genuinely medieval popular life continued in Italy in the same forms as in France and the Germanic countries had escaped him just as much as that the new life whose advent he hailed in Italy was also emerging in other lands where he could detect nothing but age-old repression and barbarism. He was not well enough aware of the great variety and the luxuriant life of medieval culture outside Italy. As a result he drew all too restricted spatial limits to the emerging Renaissance.[12]

Herfsttij was a demonstration that the 'ripeness and fullness' of Italian Renaissance achievements were a matter of quality, not of essence.[13] The seeds of these fruits existed earlier and outside Italy.

Yet autumn is also fall, withering, and decrease. There is certainly no lack of evidence in the book to justify seeing the period as one of decay and decline. The French edition, which after various vicissitudes eventually appeared in 1932, was called simply *Le déclin du moyen âge* – though Lucien Febvre thought that *crépuscule* (twilight), would have been more appropriate.[14] This seems not unjust when one counts up the number of references to the 'declining,' 'waning', and 'expiring' middle ages, and the talk of the 'decadence of the medieval spirit' with which the book is studded. The very repetition of these phrases is suggestive of the depth to which Huizinga was moved by the spectacle of a culture in decline – whether it was in his own age or in another. Thoughts about America, whose civilization he was considering at the time of composing *Herfsttij,* may well have reflected back onto his views of late medieval culture. 'The mentality of the declining Middle Ages often seems to us to display an incredible superficiality and feebleness',[15] its defects being rooted in the fundamental formalism which Huizinga traced out in its chivalric,

[12] *Men and Ideas*, p. 260; cf. pp. 253-4, 267, 278- 80, 285-6, where the same point is harped on.

[13] Ibid., p. 286; cf. p. 183 for the description of the twelfth-century Renaissance as 'a ripening, a coming of age'.

[14] Hugenholtz, 'The Fame of a Masterwork', p. 101; Lucien Febvre, 'Un Moment avec Huizinga', *Annales*, 6 (1951), p. 493, cited by Colie, 'Johan Huizinga and the Task of Cultural History', p. 626, n. 61. Cf. *Waning*, p. 237 on 'that serene twilight hour of an age', as seen in Jan van Eyck's Arnolfini portrait.

[15] *Waning*, p. 214, cf. pp. 82, 121, 124, 181, 227, 241. See Geyl, 'Huizinga as Accuser', and George Steiner's introduction to the Paladin edition of *Homo Ludens* (London, 1970), p. 13. Cf. Huizinga's remarks in his critique of Spengler, about 'the autumn of our Western culture' (viewing autumn as both maturing and a time of approaching decline), in *Dutch Civilisation in the Seventeenth Century and Other Essays*, sel. Pieter Geyl and F.W.N. Hugenholtz, trans. A.J. Pomerans (London, 1968), pp. 167, 174, 186. For Huizinga's views of cultural imbalance in both his essays on America and in the *Waning* see Weintraub, *Visions of Culture*, pp. 235-6.

religious, and literary manifestations. In all directions he saw discernible features of decline; 'the violent sentimentality, the tendency to see each thing as an independent entity, to get lost in the multiplicity of concepts',[16] were inherent traits of the expiring middle ages which had come to the point of inertia and stagnation, endlessly elaborating upon old formulas instead of continuing to grow and develop anew. The prevailing habit of mind showed itself above all in the accentuation of detail. Things were taken to extremes – 'developing every thought and every image to the end . . . giving concrete form to every concept of the mind'. It was a manifestation of decay. 'The art and literature of the fifteenth century in France and in the Netherlands are almost exclusively concerned with giving a finished and ornate form to a system of ideas which had long since ceased to grow. They are the servants of an expiring mode of thought'.[17]

From this theory the book was conceived. Huizinga himself relates its inspiration, which had 'hit me out of the blue' over ten years before the work was written and published. He was out for one of his regular afternoon walks in the Groningen countryside on a Sunday about 1907, when 'the thought suddenly struck me that the late Middle Ages were not so much a prelude to the future as an epoch of fading and decay. This thought, if indeed it may be called a thought, hinged chiefly on the art of the brothers van Eyck and their contemporaries . . .'[18] The interpretation of the van Eycks, as some reviewers perceived, was central. It nearly gave the book its name and it provided the critical link between the work's main strands of thought. For Huizinga's eventual treatment of the art of the brothers van Eyck was as much concerned to disprove the idea that the realism of their painting could be described as 'Renaissance,' as it was to see reflected in their work the 'twilight hour of an age'. The naturalism of the van Eycks was the core of his dual response to the ideas of both *La Renaissance septentrionale* and *Die Cultur der Renaissance in Italien*.[19]

One might conclude from all this that while the choice of 'waning' was not unjustified, it drew attention to what was in effect only one part of the author's

[16] *Waning*, p. 244.

[17] Ibid., pp. 255-6, 253.

[18] From 'My Path to History', in *Dutch Civilisation*, pp. 272-3, and cf. *Waning*, preface, p. v. (Huizinga's words recall Petrarch's remark about the power of the countryside to promote in him 'great thoughts . . . if indeed a great thought ever does occur to me'.)

[19] *Waning*, pp. 237, 241-4, cf. pp. 262-3, 290-1. See *Men and Ideas*, pp. 244, 265, 289, 297, 303 for further remarks about the van Eycks in the two 1920 essays on the Renaissance. The preface to the Dutch edition which explains this role of the van Eycks and Burgundy as Huizinga's starting point was unfortunately curtailed in the English edition. A.G. Jongkees, 'Une génération d'historiens devant le phénomène bourguignon', in *Johan Huizinga, 1872-1972*, p. 75, points to the probability that at the time when the idea struck him Huizinga had been reading H. Fierens-Gevaert, *Études sur l'art flamand: La Renaissance septentrionale et les premiers maîtres des Flandres* (Brussels, 1905). See also Gerson, 'Huizinga und die kunstgeschichte', pp. 210-12, and E.H. Gombrich, *In Search of Cultural History* (Oxford, 1969), pp. 28-9 (my debts to this invaluable paper are greater than the following notes might indicate).

thesis. The final words of the book summarized its ambivalence. 'A high and strong culture is declining, but at the same time and in the same sphere new things are being born. The tide is turning, the tone of life is about to change'.[20] The ambiguity in the term *Herfsttij* reflected an inherent ambiguity in the book as a whole. But objections could also, of course, be raised to the choice of this original title in Dutch. As Professor Gombrich has pointed out, it implied Hegelian ideas of cultural evolution which Huizinga himself came explicitly to reject, and he later regretted the title he had hesitantly chosen as being too poetical.[21] This is a point to which I shall return in considering the *Waning*'s importance for English history.

The *Waning* was reviewed at some length by C.L. Kingsford in the *English Historical Review* for 1925. He drew attention to the book's underlying principle: that 'we cannot understand the later middle ages unless we appreciate the mental attitude and forms of thought which created the ideals and governed the actions of the men of the time'. It was doubtful however, thought Kingsford, whether 'any study of fifteenth-century England on similar lines could be equally profitable, since England neither in art nor in literature has anything of equivalent value'. Our chroniclers were incomparably thinner; we had no brothers van Eyck. Also, Kingsford implies, the very idea of such a study was somewhat unreal given that 'the political and social evolution . . . was the real moving force of the times'.[22] But was not this completely beside the point? Had not Huizinga specifically defined his objectives and limits? He did not deny (as he thereafter made clearer) that 'the state and its institutions' were 'the most important form of all social life', investigated by historians of the law and the constitution.[23] But cultural history was *not* to be regarded as an amalgamation of other disciplines. It may be hard to define – and harder still to write – but it must be seen to exist in its own right. Kingsford's remarks seem to reflect the stubborn conservatism which has dogged so much of the historical writing on England in the later middle ages.

A glance back over the writings published on English history of the fourteenth and fifteenth centuries during the last fifty years shows the solid predominance of political and constitutional affairs. The conviction that

[20] *Waning*, p. 308. On this dualism in the *Waning* see Paul L. Ward, 'Huizinga's Approach to the Middle Ages', in *Teachers of History: Essays in Honor of Laurence Bradford Packard*, ed. H. Stuart Hughes, et al. (Ithaca, 1954), pp. 168-95, esp. pp. 177-8, 186-9.
[21] Gombrich, *Search*, p. 29; idem, 'Huizinga's *Homo ludens*', p. 140; Jongkees, 'Une génération d'historiens', pp. 78-9. Huizinga had toyed with the titles 'In the Mirror of van Eyck' and 'The Age of Burgundy'; Gerson, 'Huizinga und die Kunstgeschichte', p. 210; see also Huizinga, *Verzamelde Werken* (Haarlem 1948-53), iii, p. 4 for the preface to the 1919 Dutch edition, and iv, p. 450 n. 1 for the regret about the choice of title expressed in the context of criticism of Spengler's metaphysical view of cultural autumn and winter.
[22] *EHR*, xl (1925), pp. 273-5. Professor Hugenholtz, 'The Fame of a Masterwork', p. 98, rather mysteriously finds Kingsford's review 'so confused and incoherent' as to be incomprehensible, though he points to the significance of this remark.
[23] 'The Task of Cultural History' (published 1929, after a 1926 speech), in *Men and Ideas*, p. 64.

history is first and foremost the study of political forms and constitutional developments, to which thoughts about intellectual life, literature, and the arts may be tagged on, almost as afterthoughts, has had a long innings and still rides high to this day. One only has to turn to the relevant volumes of the *Oxford History* to see how historians have gone on sharing Kingsford's view.[24] The idea that history without politics is amorphous, tissue without bones, continues to be expressed and as late as 1968 a leading English historian echoed the strictures of Huizinga's contemporary, S. Muller, the archivist of Utrecht, in criticizing the *Waning* for its 'failure of structure'.[25] The most recently published bibliography on late medieval England reflects these traditional priorities. Constitutional and administrative history, with political history and foreign relations, here have pride of place and between them occupy more than a third of the pages and items. Proceeding via social, economic, agrarian, scientific, and military history we then reach the history of religion (which produces a total exceeding the items of the constitutional and administrative section), and finally, as the last two out of fourteen headings, the history of the fine arts and intellectual history.[26] To arrange is not necessarily to ratify, but even a list can reflect an attitude of mind.

But there have been voices crying in the wilderness, suggesting that politics and the constitution and public life are not all; that the history which looks at 'forms of life and thought' may also be a valid form. As long ago as 1937 K.B. McFarlane delivered a series of lectures on 'English Society in the Fifteenth Century' which in its first planning was subtitled 'Things that get Left Out of Political and Constitutional History'.[27] The same call came to a later generation in the valuable survey published by Professor Margaret Hastings in 1961. 'This generation of historians wants to know about all the levels of past society, not just about rulers and leaders', and 'there is room for a new "high history" of the intellectual and spiritual life of the English people in the later Middle Ages, something to counteract the prejudice which students pick up from the older textbooks which treat this period as a mere interval between the

---

[24] May McKisack, *The Fourteenth Century, 1307-1399* (Oxford, 1959); E.F. Jacob, *The Fifteenth Century, 1399-1485* (Oxford, 1961). Cf. the reviews by Y. Renouard, *EHR*, lxxvii (1962), pp. 525-30, H.G. Richardson, *EHR*, lxxviii (1963), pp. 552-7, and S.B. Chrimes, 'The Fifteenth Century', *History*, xlviii (1963), pp. 18-27.

[25] E.F. Jacob, 'Huizinga and the Autumn of the Middle Ages', in *Essays in Later Medieval History* (Manchester, 1968), p. 150; Hugenholtz, 'The Frame of a Masterwork', p. 97; Geyl, 'Huizingar as Accuser', pp. 244-5. For remarks on the primacy of political history see Herbert Butterfield, *Man on his Past: The Study of the History of Historical Scholarship* (Cambridge, 1955), pp. 41, 84, 116ff.

[26] DeLloyd J. Guth, *Late-Medieval England 1377-1485* (Cambridge, 1976). My calculation of these proportions is based on sections iv to xiv (omitting the first three general headings). Religious History occupies 581 items on 27 pages, compared with 449 items and 21 pages on Constitutional and Administrative History.

[27] K.B. McFarlane, *The Nobility of Later Medieval England* (Oxford, 1973), p. xvi.

thirteenth century and the Renaissance and Reformation'.[28] Historians' failure to meet this challenge meant that old textbooks enjoyed extraordinarily
long lives. The third volume of Stubbs's *Constitutional History* (1878) could be
regarded in 1963 as 'still the indispensable starting point' for study of the
period.[29] Things have however changed. 'Culture and Society' has become a
recognized and respectable topic, not only for renaissance Italy but even for
England's middle ages. And though the search for wider social history is not
the same as the search for cultural history, the replacement of the Hegelian
historical pattern by the Marxist pattern has deeply affected approaches to the
latter.

How are we to explain England's long failure to build on Huizinga's model?
Is it really because, as Kingsford suggested, England (unlike France and the
Netherlands) lacks material for *Kulturgeschichte*? As the author of an admir-
able survey of *English Historical Literature in the Fifteenth Century* published
some years before *Herfsttij*, he might certainly be expected to have known, but
surely, even so, we must reject this judgement. To be without van Eycks does
not mean a lack of painting, sculpture, and architecture; England had no
Chastellain, but we have plenty of other literary sources. Indeed, the very
differences of historical sources may, as Professor Hay has suggested, reflect
and illuminate social and political realities.[30] It was not lack of materials but
traditional thinking that dictated Kingsford's response. The first and most
obvious explanation for this lack must be the perennial slowness of university
studies to adapt themselves to new modes of thought.[31] Inevitably there is
always a time lag between the topics that historians are researching and those
they are obliged to teach or, come to that, between periodical literature and
textbook literature. Probably there is always some gap between what students
want to know and what teachers are ready to teach. Fifty years is a long time to
wait, but perhaps we are now, thanks to a certain amount of cross-fertilization
between disciplines, beginning to shed some of the prejudices that made the
Waning seem academically questionable. Some of the hesitancies that remain

[28] Margaret Hastings, 'High History or Hack History: England in the Later Middle Ages',
Speculum, xxxvi (1961), pp. 228, 251 reprinted in *Changing Views on British History: Essays on
Historical Writing since 1939*, ed. E.C. Furber (Cambridge, MA, and London, 1966), pp. 58-100.

[29] Chrimes, 'The Fifteenth Century', p. 18. Cf. F.R.H. Du Boulay, *An Age of Ambition:
English Society in the Late Middle Ages* (London, 1970), p. 179 where Stubbs heads the
bibliography.

[30] Denys Hay, 'History and Historians in France and England during the Fifteenth Century',
BIHR, xxxv (1962), pp. 111-27. Kingsford's *English Historical Literature in the Fifteenth Century*
(Oxford, 1913; rep. New York, 1963) remains a useful survey, to which have now been added
Antonia Gransden, *Historical Writing in England*, ii, *c 1307 to the Early Sixteenth Century*
(London, 1982); John Taylor, *English Historical Literature in the Fourteenth Century* (Oxford,
1987). In his review of the *Waning* Kingsford had indicated the value that English collections of
private letters could have for revealing 'the practical life of the people'.

[31] For comments on this point see Gombrich, *Search*, p. 45ff; Keith Thomas, 'History and
Anthropology', *Past and Present*, 24 (1963), p. 15ff; R.W. Southern, *The Shape and Substance of
Academic History* (Oxford, 1961).

may be laid at Huizinga's door and accounted for by the concept and form of the book itself.

Apart from its isolation from the norms of academic study, Huizinga's *Waning* is unique in the individuality and originality of its vision. 'The book remains in one's mind as a *tour de force*', wrote an early reviewer, 'a work of learning which can be read easily and which impresses itself on the memory'.[32] It does not lend itself to imitation any more than its author was disposed to found a school of historians.[33] Unlike some other sorts of history that have become famous in our age, such as Lewis Namier's *The Structure of Politics at the Accession of George III* (which has left its mark on English fifteenth-century history), Huizinga did not hand historians a methodological key which they could appropriate and use to open doors in their own periods.[34] Methodology as such was alien to Huizinga. Cultural history as he described it was not a subject with a technique like, say, statistics or physics, which he saw as diametrically opposed to the discipline of history.[35]

There is in fact (as has already been pointed out elsewhere) only one passage in the *Waning* which bears on this question. It occurs near the beginning when the author, illustrating the violent passions of his period from chronicle sources, adds the comment that historians who depended on official documents to the exclusion of contemporary chroniclers would tend to disregard 'the vehement pathos of medieval life'. 'A scientific historian of the Middle Ages, relying first and foremost on official documents, which rarely refer to the passions, except violence and cupidity, occasionally runs the risk of neglecting the difference of tone between the life of the expiring Middle Ages and that of our own days'.[36] This sentence must be read, as Professor Hugenholtz has shown, in the context of Huizinga's profession, with its heightened sense of the potentialities of history as science and its overweening respect for documentary studies. Diplomatic spadework establishing the sources sometimes appeared to have become the very essence of history. Huizinga's remark comes in the nature of an aside and perhaps was only intended as such, but it does I think have some bearing on the long-term reception of the English *Herfsttij*. History in this century suffered overlong from the need to justify itself as a discipline in the face of the claim of science. The search for factual

[32] C.G. Crump, *History*, x (1925-6), p. 164.

[33] On Huizinga's independent spirit and untransferable originality see Colie, 'Johan Huizinga and the Task of Cultural History', pp. 621-2.

[34] John Brooke, 'Namier and Namierism', *History and Theory*, iii (1964), pp. 331-47; Linda Colley, *Lewis Namier* (London, 1989). McFarlane (*Nobility*, pp. xii, xviii, xxxvii, 296-7) was among those who believed in the value of applying prosopography to late medieval studies. The historian to achieve most in this field has been J.S. Roskell with *The Commons in the Parliament of 1422* (Manchester, 1954), *The Commons and their Speakers in the English Parliaments 1376-1523* (Manchester, 1965), and other studies.

[35] See 'The Task of Cultural History', *Men and Ideas*, p. 21.

[36] *Waning*, p. 7; Hugenholtz, 'The Fame of a Masterwork', p. 93ff.

'certainty' took precedence over the pursuit of attitudes and opinions. Charters seemed safer than chronicles, and the discovery of new 'facts' conferred an academic validation to which fresh readings of literary sources were alien.

Taken as a whole, however, the *Waning* constitutes a model – if not a paradigm – of a form of history which, despite its slowness to gain academic status, has won recognition. Huizinga himself defined the nature of this relatively new branch of history in his essay of 1929 on 'The Task of Cultural History'. The cultural historian is a seeker after forms of life, thought, knowledge, art. He is not after rules but the 'striking significance' of phenomena, whose vividness he grasps by a process of near-revelatory intuitive cognition, and which he conveys to his readers not only as ideas, but as images and individual portraits.[37] Vividness was an essential part of the process of historical understanding, and it resided for Huizinga in the visual and in the particularized individual. His own manner of thinking was instinctively visual, so it was natural for him both to stress the importance of this approach to the past and to settle himself happily into study of a period characterized, as he put it, by the 'marked tendency of thought to embody itself in images'.[38]

Changes in the relationship of art and life were bound therefore, on Huizinga's viewing, to affect people's thoughts about the past. To see and study more works of art opened up new vistas on the periods to which they belonged and to ideas about them. As he judged it, pessimistically, the process led to the swamping of intellectual by aesthetic activities. It may rather seem to us, after another half-century's experience of ways of seeing, that the reverse has been demonstrated, in that seeing more has brought an interest in knowing more. Huizinga, born in the period before the opening of the 'Museum without walls', lived long enough to witness its beginnings and to comment on how this altered views of the middle ages.

> Now, our perception of former times, our historical organ, so to say, is more and more becoming visual. Most educated people of today owe their conception of Egypt, Greece, or the Middle Ages, much more to the sight of their monuments, either in the original or by reproductions, than to reading. The change of our ideas

---

[37] *Men and Ideas*, p. 59, cf. pp. 52-55 and for remarks on individuals in history, 'The Aesthetic Element in Historical Thought', in *Dutch Civilisation*, p. 231. Jacob, 'Huizinga and the Autumn', pp. 142-3, comments on Huizinga's moments of illumination.

[38] *Waning*, p. 136; cf. Huizinga's remarks on the visual element in historical understanding in *Dutch Civilisation*, pp. 226, 237, 241, 249, 263, 269. See also Gerson, 'Huizunga und die Kunstgeschichte', pp. 208-9; Weintraub, *Visions of Culture*, pp. 229-30; Gombrich, 'Huizinga's *Homo ludens*', pp. 137-9.

about the Middle Ages is due less to a weakening of the romantic sense than to the substitution of artistic for intellectual appreciation.[39]

The visual, however, was only one part of the formulation of Huizinga's cultural history. This history, though it necessarily embraced politics and the whole of society, came down from the outlines of essential forms to individuals, without whom the reality of the historical process could have no existence. 'He [the cultural historian] not only sketches the contours of the forms he designs, but colours them by means of intuition and illuminates them with visionary suggestion'.[40] These forms and colours – the threads and beads of history – could continue to be valid even when the main construction that they served was no longer acceptable. Thus Burckhardt's *Civilization*, even when its central argument had been pruned, lopped down and modified, was (and is) still read for the penetration of its understanding. As Huizinga put it: 'Burckhardt's general thesis . . . has . . . had its day. But all the individual forms that he hewed and used as building stones, all his chapters about glory, ridicule and wit, domestic life, and the like, still preserve the value of that transcendent masterpiece intact'.[41] And that is surely just as true of our reading of the *Waning*, from which we are separated by exactly the same span of time as Huizinga's contemporaries were separated from Burckhardt's book.

If the 'feeling for forms' lies at the heart of cultural history this seems excessively vague. It was not something that could be taught or prescribed. There appears indeed to have been a certain ambiguity in Huizinga's understanding of these essential 'forms'. On one hand they appear to have been related to the whole 'morphology of the human past' which historians are engaged in constructing: the 'forms and functions of civilization' in its overall development. Such were the creations of Burckhardt, Spengler, and Huizinga himself, as summarized under the names of 'Renaissance', 'Decline of the West', and (for English readers) the 'Waning of the Middle Ages'. Interpretative forms of this kind easily become tendentious – if they do not start that way. Of this Huizinga was himself well aware. He was highly critical of Spengler's 'morphology of world history'.[42] Yet his own *Herfsttij* bore worrying signs of the Hegelian holism in which art, literature, and life are all to be regarded as manifestations of one 'spirit of the age', which was part of an inexorable dialectical process.

[39] *Waning*, pp. 222-3 on the decline of romantic interpretations. In 'My Path to History' Huizinga described his youthful activity in mounting art exhibitions, including an illustrated lecture of 1897 based on travel photographs of Italian art. 'It is hard to imagine today', he wrote in the 1940s, 'how hard it was to get good reproductions of old masterpieces'; *Dutch Civilisation*, p. 259: cf. pp. 9-10, 46, 64-5 and Gerson, 'Huizinga und die Kunstgeschichte', p. 221 for Huizinga's association of intellectual laziness with increased visual material, and on the damage done to art by photographic reproduction, *Homo Ludens* (Paladin ed., 1970), pp. 228-9.

[40] *Men and Ideas*, p. 59.

[41] Ibid. (Burckhardt's *Civilization* was first published in 1860).

[42] Ibid. pp. 60, 65; 'Two Wrestlers with the Angel', in *Dutch Civilisation*, pp. 165-6; Gombrich, *Search*, pp. 29-30, 32, 46; Geyl, 'Huizinga as Accuser', p. 247.

On the other hand, as his remarks about Burckhardt indicate, Huizinga's cultural history consisted of sectional 'building stones'. And these other forms, which might more appropriately be regarded as themes, interpretative *topoi*, did not of themselves necessarily carry or imply qualitative historical judgements. One might suggest here that Huizinga, like Burckhardt, bequeathed us building stones ('the hierarchic conception of society', 'the idea of chivalry', 'the vision of death', 'religious thought crystallizing into images'), which have remained valid and fruitful even when his main interpretation of the period has not. The *Waning* is full of 'forms' of both kinds, but the reason why we go on reading it is surely because we remain stimulated by the specific themes, while we may be critical of the general interpretation. That said, it has to be admitted that Huizinga shows a tendency to confuse the issue by blurring mental habits and forms of thought (whose study remains the legitimate task of cultural history) with woolly observations about 'the spirit of an age' or 'the soul of this epoch'.[43]

Huizinga, as he himself made clear, was not writing about England (not that that prevented criticism on this score!),[44] but both his methodology – if we can call it that – and his morphology have left their mark on the study of English history. Let us take the methodology first. Historians have here been given a lead by followers of another discipline. If Huizinga's idea of cultural history has commended itself more to students of literature than to historians, one reason is obviously the nature of the sources. The study of attitudes and forms of thought must be concerned with what people composed as well as with what officials recorded. There is a sense in which, as Huizinga said (though he also qualified this statement), 'literary history is cultural history'.[45] So it is not really surprising to find that departments of literature have made a larger contribution towards the study of late medieval English culture than have departments of history. As one illustration of this one might set the relevant volumes of the *Oxford History of English Literature* alongside those of the *Oxford History of England*.[46] A good survey of fifteenth-century society, based on the *Paston Letters*, was written by a literary historian.[47] Another famous literary study on this period, C.S. Lewis's *Allegory of Love* (1936), though framed as an enquiry into a 'dominant form' of literature, may seem to

[43] E.g., *Waning*, pp. 47, 206, 217, 237, 307. For criticism of Huizinga's 'specific morphology' (in its narrowest sense) see Geyl, Huizinga as Accuser', p. 255.

[44] It seems a little unfair that Professor Jacob, whose own book on the fifteenth century contained so little on the growth of English dissent (for which he was criticized by H.G. Richardson in the review mentioned above, n. 24), should have charged Huizinga for this omission. 'Huizinga and the Autumn', pp. 148-9.

[45] *Men and Ideas*, p. 85, cf. p. 65.

[46] I.e., comparing the works mentioned in n. 24 above with H.S. Bennett, *Chaucer and the Fifteenth Century* (Oxford, 1947), and (though with less advantage) E.K. Chambers, *English Literature at the Close of the Middle Ages* (Oxford, 1945).

[47] H.S. Bennett, *The Pastons and their England: Studies in an Age of Transition* (Cambridge, 1922; rev. ed. 1932).

constitute a valid exemplification of one of Huizinga's building forms, by enlarging our understanding of one of the dominant strands of contemporary thought.[48] There are more recent examples. It is surely significant that Gervase Mathew's *The Court of Richard II* (1968), one of the best examples we have yet had of cultural history for this period, emerged from 'many years of lecturing for the Oxford English faculty'.[49] In the study of the Lollard movement historians have missed a great mass of evidence by neglecting the literary sources, and we have had to wait for a student of literature to remedy the omission which detracted from the value of part of K.B. McFarlane's *John Wycliffe and the Beginnings of English Nonconformity* (1952) and still more from J.A.F. Thomson's *The Later Lollards, 1414-1520* (1965).[50] Such has been historians' frequent shortsightedness towards the resources of literature that a recent book investigating the influence of the first phase of the Hundred Years' War on 'the thoughts and feelings of Englishmen', voices the very same plea that Huizinga expressed more than half a century ago.

> It is unfortunate that historians' just suspicions of the value of chronicles to the study of certain aspects of political and social history should have led to a more general neglect of the genre. Particularly in the history of social and moral ideas and attitudes the evidence of the chronicles is often invaluable . . . The literature of the fourteenth century is evidently a *terra incognita* for many historians.[51]

The narrowing effects of academic boundaries have made students of literature more in touch with Huizinga's aims than historians themselves have been. If an 'image' in literature is comparable to a 'fact' in history, the realms of elucidating the two may be wholly different. Literary formulas cannot be accounted for without some reference to forms of thought, whereas historians may find it possible to 'explain' past events by the arrangement and manipulation of further 'facts' and events. One has the impression that the discussion of ideas and forms of thought are commoner currency in the study of literature than they are in the study of history, so it does not seem to be coincidence that Huizinga's task has been taken up more readily by specialists in literature and the arts than by historians. It is not simply that Huizinga made predominant use of art and literature to excavate his building stones. It is also because historians have tended to be too economical, not to say one-sided, in their quarrying of materials.

Considerations of Huizinga's morphology brings us back to his title. The implications of 'waning' and 'decline' have both overawed and provoked

---

[48] C.S. Lewis, *The Allegory of Love: A Study in Medieval Tradition* (Oxford, 1936).

[49] G. Mathew, *The Court of Richard II* (London, 1968), foreword. The original suggestion for a book combining 'political history with an analysis of social ideals' was made to the author by F.M. Powicke.

[50] Anne Hudson, *The Premature Reformation: Wycliffite Texts and Lollard History* (Oxford, 1988), marks the culmination of this achievement.

[51] John Barnie, *War in Medieval Society: Social Values and the Hundred Years War, 1337-99* (London, 1974), p. xi.

historians. England was historiographically prejudiced – almost, one might say, from the start – to regard the fourteenth and fifteenth centuries as a period of decline and decay. Tudor justificatory propaganda, which rose to the level of a national myth, exaggerated the scale of fifteenth-century disorder for the benefit of the new dynasty, and Shakespearean assumptions long governed views of the late medieval scene. Under the shadow of the Wars of the Roses and the social and economic dislocation associated with them, the later middle ages were all too readily written off as a time of anarchy and degeneration, in church and state alike. Even when the partisan nature of the 'Tudor myth' came to be recognized, there still remained one seemingly incontrovertible aspect of decline: population decline. Could the considerable reduction in population effected by the Black Death and subsequent plague and disease have resulted in other than an overall recession: retreat from marginal lands, urban shrinkage, diminished total production? Economic recession was linked with general cultural decline. There seemed every reason to endorse Huizinga's thesis, even though he had himself (remarkably) said nothing of plague or economic depression.[52]

'The verdict pronounced by Huizinga in his famous study, *The Waning of the Middle Ages*, that the Middle Ages had dragged out their last years in gloom and decay, was thus endorsed, apparently, by every fresh piece of research that was done.'[53] Rather ironically, then, although his book was in a sense quite marginal to English history, it struck peculiarly sympathetic resonances in England where, thanks to the emphasis conveyed by its title, it contributed to the preexisting negative view of the period. The *Waning* helped to imprint the 'myth of decline'. The terms which seemed most appropriate for fifteenth-century England were 'waning, sterility, abuse, corruption and decline . . . it was seen as an age of exceptional violence and lawlessness . . . an age of cultural barrenness between the time of Chaucer and Langland at one end and the Tudor poets and humanists at the other. Huizinga had done his best for France and Burgundy, but this was not England; his very title, *The Waning of the Middle Ages*, had set an oppressive and negative tone . . . '[54]

Exaggerations, like great errors, may themselves be productive. Dialectic is no more necessary in historiography than it is in history, but its processes may promote study. The very overstatement of decline has led to reactions in the other direction. At every point we have had to revise or modify older views. The old clichés about the Wars of the Roses which helped, as McFarlane put it, to make the later fifteenth century repulsive 'to all but the strongest-

[52] As pointed out by Peter Burke in his account of Huizinga published in *The Listener*, 22 February 1973, p. 242.

[53] A.R. Bridbury, *Economic Growth: England in the Later Middle Ages* (London, 1962; new ed. 1975), p. 20.

[54] From Chapter 1, 'The Myth of Decline', in F.R.H. Du Boulay, *An Age of Ambition* (above n. 29), p. 11.

stomached' have been rebutted.[55] The domestic fighting of the fifteenth century did not decimate the old nobility, nor did it cause great disruption of life. It may now seem like a misnomer to use the term civil war at all for disturbances in which, as Commines pointed out, no buildings were destroyed, and our view of the disorderliness of late medieval society at large must be seen to be owed in part to the very richness of its documentation. As regards fighting overseas, the idea that the Hundred Years' War contributed to the wastage of native resources has been questioned in the light of more know- ledge of the rewards, profits, and investments which came from England's commitments in France. And in the English economy as a whole it has been realized that an overall reduction of population and cultivated land is consis- tent with the increasing prosperity of certain classes. The improved situation of wage earners and leaseholding farmers may have been accompanied by greater output per head, as well as by enlarged per capita wealth or income. A.R. Bridbury's *Economic Growth: England in the Later Middle Ages* (1962) presented a picture the very opposite of decay, of an England 'vivid with promise', including urban and industrial prosperity, in which the later middle ages have become 'a period of tremendous advance not only constitutionally, but also in social and economic affairs'.[56]

Where literature is concerned, Huizinga has been taken to task for the bleak impression he conveyed, which hardly left room for belief 'that England could have produced in this period in Chaucer not only one of her greatest poets but one of the sanest and most humane'.[57] As for spiritual affairs, the phenomenon of dissent seems a symptom of vitality, not of decay. 'The chief characteristic of English religious life in the fourteenth century is the growth of moral fervour among the laity', and the emergence of Lollardy needs to be set in this context, as does the significant figure of Reginald Pecock, whose abortive endeavours point not 'to the spiritual deadness of the age but to the preponderance of the English devotional tradition'.[58] The last sentence of Professor Jacob's *Fif- teenth Century* summarizes this change of interpretation. 'So far from running down in this period, religion, not merely in literary and artistic forms, but in the fervour of corporate devotion and in popular appeal achieves a place in the ordinary life of the country which it has seldom been accorded by historians of pre-Reformation England'.[59] Vigour, vitality, growth, fervour; these are the

[55] K.B. McFarlane, 'The Wars of the Roses', *PBA*, l (1964), p. 87. Also on this revision see McFarlane's *Nobility*, pp. 15, 146-9; S.B. Chrimes, *Lancastrians, Yorkists and Henry VII* (London, 1964), pp. xi-xiv; J.R. Lander, *The Wars of the Roses* (London, 1965); Charles Ross, *The Wars of the Roses: A Concise History* (London, 1976).

[56] Bridbury, *Economic Growth*, pp. 22, 108.

[57] Douglas Gray, *Themes and Images in the Medieval English Religious Lyric* (London and Boston, 1972), p. 30, cf. pp. 27-8.

[58] K.B. McFarlane, *Lancastrian Kings and Lollard Knights* (Oxford, 1972), p. 224; E.F. Jacob, 'Reynold Pecock, Bishop of Chichester', in *Essays in Later Medieval History*, p. 34. Cf. the remarks of V.H.H. Green, *Bishop Reginald Pecock* (Cambridge, 1945), pp. 73, 75, trying to fit Pecock's character into Huizinga's 'waning' model.

[59] Jacob, *Fifteenth Century*, p. 687. (Cf. n. 44 above.)

chosen words in use today. The difference in judgement is reactive, signalized by bows towards Huizinga. Far from being on the wane or in decline, English society in the fifteenth century is represented as vigorous and expanding, thanks to its inner resilience.[60]

Yet at the same time that Huizinga's descriptive title has been discarded, historians (and others) have freely made use – as Huizinga would have wished – of his 'building stones'. Certain ideas and themes of *Herfsttij* have proved fertile in germinating further study, to the extent that the book must be recognized as seminal for the cultural history of the period, in England as well as further afield. Attention has been given to courtly culture and royal pageantry and propaganda. Besides Mathew's book on Richard II's court mentioned above, we have for the very end of the period Sydney Anglo's *Spectacle, Pageantry and Early Tudor Policy* (1969) and John Stevens's *Music and Poetry in the Early Tudor Court* (1961), works that show what remains to be done for the intervening years, which have only been examined piecemeal.[61]

On the theme of chivalry, while the idea and the ideal have continued to be studied as Huizinga viewed them, as elements of social life which held both ethical and aesthetic significance, advances have been made in what might be called the cultural history of the Hundred Years' War. Understanding of the essential framework of the laws of war – laws which themselves embodied chivalric convention and towards which Huizinga had taken some tentative steps – was greatly enlarged by the publication of Maurice Keen's *The Laws of War in the Late Middle Ages* (1965). There have been increasing efforts to place the war in its social context, to examine not only its connection with social change, but also the implications of changing attitudes towards it. 'Mind and Outlook' formed a part of the consideration of war in H.J. Hewitt's *The Organization of War Under Edward III, 1338-62* (1966), and two other books reflect this interest. In *Society at War: The Experience of England and France During the Hundred Years War* (1973), C.T. Allmand explored (through assembled texts), alongside the practices and enticements of the war, late medieval thinking about it and the impact of the conflict on the civilian population. John Barnie's *War in Medieval Society: Social Values and the*

[60] Idem, 'Huizinga and the Autumn', p. 153. For a summary of this overall reinterpretation (also looking back to Huizinga) and the replacement of ideas of decline and decadence by vigour, vitality, and progress, see Bertie Wilkinson, 'The Historian and the Late Middle Ages in England', in *Essays on the Reconstruction of Medieval History*, ed. V. Mudroch and G.S. Couse (Montreal and London, 1974), pp. 133-45.

[61] The two books mentioned here were published at Oxford and London respectively. See Stevens, pp. 153, 188, 235 for acknowledgments to Huizinga, especially his chapters on courtly love. On the fifteenth century there are several articles by J.W. McKenna (Guth, *Late-Medieval England*, nos. 635, 799) including 'Popular Canonization as Political Propaganda: The Cult of Archbishop Scrope', *Speculum*, xlv (1970), pp. 608-623; and P.E. Gill, 'Politics and Propaganda in Fifteenth-Century England: The Polemical Writings of Sir John Fortescue', *Speculum*, xlvi (1971), pp. 333-47.

Hundred Years War pursued the attitudes and ideas of the English as they responded to the first sixty years of war through aristocratic, knightly, and chivalric conventions, in a fresh spirit of patriotism, or debating the pros and cons of war.[62]

Another sphere in which Huizinga's perceptions have been taken further – not specifically in the English context – is 'The Vision of Death'. 'No other epoch has laid so much stress as the expiring Middle Ages on the thought of death', wrote Huizinga.[63] His omission in this context of the impact of contemporary plague and mortality has been remedied by various studies, while the relevance of Huizinga's views for English medieval poetry on 'Death and the Last Things' has been critically assessed by Douglas Gray in his *Themes and Images in the Medieval English Religious Lyric* (1972).[64]

This is not a bibliographical survey, but these fairly random examples show that the influence of Huizinga's *Waning* remains pervasive, even if no longer persuasive. We have continued to work, topically at least, along his outlines, and there are signs that historians are learning greater respect for his ideas of history. Cultural history, despite the remaining hesitancies towards it, is becoming more acceptable in that the study of the past now seems to demand some concern for forms of thought and attitudes and, along with that, an ear for literary sources. Professor F.R.H. Du Boulay's *An Age of Ambition: English Society in the Late Middle Ages* (1970) is an excellent exemplification of this, with its exploration of 'attitudes towards authority' and its full use of such sources as *Piers Plowman*, the *Paston Letters* and the *Plumpton Correspondence*.[65] It is easier now than it was in the early 1960s, at the time of Professor Hastings's article, for students of history to find out about all levels of society and to learn something of contemporary 'forms of life and thought'. We have done a little to rectify the over exclusive concentration which previous generations gave to political history. C.T. Allmand's remarks about the study of the Hundred Years' War are symptomatic of a wider trend.

---

[62] Of these works, Hewitt's was published in Manchester, Allmand's in Edinburgh, the others in London. See Keen, p. 239, for a signal of debt to Huizinga. Despite the contribution of works such as John Harvey's, including his *Gothic England: A Survey of National Culture, 1300-1500* (London, 1947), and V.J. Scattergood's *Politics and Poetry in the Fifteenth Century* (London, 1971), we still have no adequate general assessment of the architectural and literary impact of the war.

[63] *Waning*, p. 124. Among the works that have pursued this theme mention may be made of James M. Clark, *The Dance of Death in the Middle Ages and the Renaissance* (Glasgow, 1950); A. Tenenti, *La vie et la mort à travers l'art du XVe siècle* (Paris, 1952); T.S.R. Boase, *Death in the Middle Ages: Mortality, Judgment and Remembrance* (London, 1972). Cf. also Philippe Ariès, 'Huizinga et les thèmes macabres', in *Johan Huizinga, 1872-1972*, pp. 104-15; idem, *The Hour of Our Death* (Harmondsworth, 1983: first pub. Paris, 1977; K. Cohen, *Metamorphosis of a Death Symbol: The Transi Tomb in the Late Middle Ages and The Renaissance* (Berkeley and London, 1973).

[64] Chapter 10, pp. 176-220, esp. 179ff.

[65] See n. 29 above.

> There is a need to study wars in terms of the societies in which they were fought, to underline the fact that wars not only affected the historic development of societies and social groups, but were often less affected by the principles over which they were fought than by the needs of people who became involved in them . . . Attitudes to war were undergoing a change.[66]

We may have moved towards Huizinga by employing some of his building tools. But have we moved away from him in the architectural plan? If no real equivalent of the *Waning* has been written for late medieval England, perhaps this has to do with the difficulties that have been found in endorsing Huizinga's historical aims. Does rejection of the idea of the 'declining middle ages' imply rejection of any attempt at a cultural survey as gross oversimplification? Is it indicative of historians' approaches to the period that in shying away from 'waning' and 'decline' as descriptive of England in these centuries, they have failed to substitute any convincing alternative? It has seemed easier to plump for the double bill with paradoxical implications. Kingsford's *Prejudice and Promise in XVth Century England* (1925) does not stand alone; there is J.R. Lander's *Conflict and Stability in Fifteenth-Century England* (1969), and A.R. Bridbury's title, *Economic Growth: England in the Later Middle Ages*, straightforward though it may sound to the uninitiated, reads as a challenging paradox to anyone familiar with once prevalent conceptions of the period. Professor Du Boulay's *Age of Ambition* could seemingly just as well have been named 'An Age of Anxiety'.[67] Prejudice, promise; conflict, stability; anxiety, ambition; title, profit; ostentation, retirement; ruthlessness, piety; decay, growth: it is not hard to multiply the conflicting qualities which confront us in the fourteenth and fifteenth centuries. Huizinga's portrayal of the age presented vividly this coexistence of opposites, and historians, albeit perhaps unconsciously, have continued to feel the need for the ambiguity of his 'autumn'. This quality of paradox was something that older historians, surer than we can be of the biological nature of the historical process, could pass off under the name of 'transition', rather as an individual's rebellions and growth pains could be shrugged off as symptoms of adolescence. If this will no longer do, what have we got to put in its place?

The fact that Huizinga's treatment of the period now seems oversimplified and overstated should not be allowed to frighten us away from all attempts at cultural synthesis. Forms of life, thought, and art may not be so unitary in their manifestations as Huizinga depicted them, but we need not therefore deny them all interconnection. To believe that a satisfying interpretation of an age

---

[66] Allmand, *Society at War*, p. 192, cf. p. 13.

[67] Kingsford's book (the Ford Lectures for 1924, published at Oxford) was a collection of essays which describe some of the 'promising' expansive aspects of the period to demonstrate Tudor prejudice. Lander's (published London) is a more general survey, to which may be added the introduction to his reprinted essays, *Crown and Nobility, 1450-1509* (London, 1976), pp. 1-56. Du Boulay, *Age of Ambition*, p. 40 (on Bridbury) and pp. 66-67, 145, 156, 160-62 (on the anxieties of the age).

involves looking at society and culture as a whole need not impose the tyranny of holism. It seems wiser to take the view that 'obviously there is something in the Hegelian intuition that nothing in life is ever isolated, that any event and any creation of a period is connected by a thousand threads with the culture in which it is embedded'.[68] Perhaps as historians we need help in singling out those threads, or an example in boldness to conceive the wider view. If so, we might look towards a discipline to which, in its pioneering days, Huizinga himself felt drawn: that is, social anthropology.[69]

Huizinga made use of anthropological findings in his work, and cultural history as he thought of it may seem to lend itself more readily than do some other kinds of history to anthropological approaches. If, in general, anthropologists tend to be more concerned with analyzing a particular society at a given period of time than with investigating social change and movement, Huizinga had something in common with them. For he was, as Rosalie Colie pointed out, more interested in continuity than in change, concerned with the static rather than with the dynamic aspects of history.[70] Although, as a historian, he was necessarily involved in the discerning of old and new, his book on the fourteenth and fifteenth centuries was a portrayal of the character of an epoch, and as such his task (and the task he envisaged for the cultural historian) was comparable to that of the portrait painter. The sitter is static; what one reads of his past and his future is delineated through this present pose. And if society, like an individual, is never completely at rest, ideas change at different rates from the people who hold them. They may be of interest for that very reason, studied for their static qualities. Indeed, it is arguable that a society's ideas about itself, and its cultural models and images, are always out of step with social realities.[71] 'The conception of society in the Middle Ages is static, not dynamic', wrote Huizinga in the *Waning*.[72] This observation throws light simultaneously on his own approaches, the period he was describing, and the possibilities of applying his insight in other ways.

[68] Gombrich, *Search*, p. 30ff.

[69] For Huizinga's reading in his late teens of E.B. Tylor's *Primitive Culture* (1871) which, he later said, 'opened up perspectives that, in a sense, have inspired me ever since', see *Dutch Civilisation*, p. 250; Gombrich, 'Huizinga's *Homo ludens*', p. 138. Anthropological findings featured conspicuously among the widely ranging material Huizinga drew on for *Homo ludens*. On the pioneering work of Tylor (1832-1917) see Mary Douglas, *Purity and Danger* (London, 1966), p. 13ff.

[70] Colie, 'Johan Huizinga and the Task of Cultural History', p. 623; Ward; 'Huizinga's Approach to the Middle Ages', p. 171. Obviously this is not true of all anthropology; cf. the general remarks on history and anthropology in Thomas, 'History and Anthropology', pp. 4-5, and the Conference Report on 'History, Sociology and Social Anthropology', *Past and Present*, 27 (1964), pp. 102-8.

[71] See for example Professor Duby's remarks about the models of the perfect knight and the perfect clerk in France from the twelfth to the fourteenth centuries. Georges Duby, 'The Diffusion of Cultural Patterns in Feudal Society', *Past and Present*, 39 (1968), pp. 8-10. Cf. also the questions raised about the role of the 'formalized social past' by E.J. Hobsbawn, 'The Social Function of the Past', *Past and Present*, 55 (1972), p. 3ff.

[72] *Waning*, p. 48 (cf. Pelican Edition, p. 58).

If we seek fresh insight into the seeming discrepancies in late medieval England, some integrating method of looking at different forms of life and thought, and in particular (since the most recent surveys have failed in this) of setting religious developments beside others of the time, perhaps the social anthroplogists can help us. It might be helpful, for example, to think about late medieval society in terms of the social relationships called by Mary Douglas 'group' and 'grid': respectively the bounded social unit (family, household, retinue) and the 'rules which relate one person to others on an ego-centred basis', such as, at that time, the hierarchical assumptions of society. There may be stimulus in the suggestion that 'the destruction of categories of any kind is a symbolic act which replicates social life overstructured by grid, the experience which has always driven people to value unstructured personal experiences and to place their faith in a catastrophic event which will sweep away all existing forms of structure'.[73] Was not this par excellence a period of 'unstructured personal experiences', of cataclysmic expectations (a period, in fact, not unlike our own)? It might be illuminating to look at the various destructive activities of the period as a whole. Perhaps there are some common tensions behind the acts of attempted or effected destruction, real, symbolic, or literary, that we encounter in these centuries. The destruction of court rolls and the burning of the Savoy by the rebels of 1381, the breaking of images and the monastic levelling proposed by the Lollards, the tearing up of the pardon in *Piers Plowman*, may all tell us something about contemporary frustrations and the apprehended contrast between restrictive external forms and inner personal realities.

There is no lack of evidence in later medieval England of the stresses in traditional forms, both ecclesiastical and secular. Lordship was under pressure. The advances made through this period towards a money-rent estate economy steadily undermined the social reality of the seigneurial bond, so that though we do not know the degree we cannot but recognize the landlord's 'alienation from those who inhabited and worked the soil of which he was lord', and the resentments felt by tenants towards servile dues.[74] Similar forces (changes of population, wages, and prices, an increasingly mobile labour force, and the undermining of traditional patronage by market pressures) operated in the church to increase the alienation of clerical proletariat from church hierarchy. The hierarchical paternalistic forms remained theoretically intact but were at odds with the way many people lived their lives. There was a weakening of social boundaries of the kind which Professor Douglas has postulated as being associated with 'doctrinal emphasis on internal, emotional states'.[75]

---

[73] Mary Douglas, *Natural Symbols: Explorations in Cosmology* (London, 1970), pp. viii, xvi.

[74] McFarlane, *Nobility*, p. 217; Christopher Dyer, 'A Redistribution of Incomes in Fifteenth-Century England', *Past and Present*, 39 (1968), pp. 11-33.

[75] Douglas, *Natural Symbols*, p. 14, cf. pp. 8, 19.

The fourteenth and fifteenth centuries were one of the great ages of retreat from institutional forms. Does it have to seem crude to look at these developments as a whole? The retreats of religion are only too evident. 'The period was one . . . much given to private devotions, to private chapels in the houses of the laity, the privilege of appointing one's own confessor with a portable altar and no parochial responsibility – and hence independence of episcopal surveillance . . . The contemporary spirit in religion was puritan, biblical, evangelical, anarchic, anti-sacerdotal, hostile to the established order in the Church'. Such support as the Lollards gained from the knightly class represented 'a moral revolt by the laity against the visible Church, a rejection of sacerdotalism in favour of the personal, immediate contact between the believer and his Creator'.[76] The same motivations are evident in the lives of late medieval mystics or near-mystics – Richard Rolle or Margery Kempe – and in the most popular form of contemporary religious foundation, the chantry, which represents an institutionalized form of the services of the personal household chaplain. We might even regard the increasing pursuit of literacy, in certain of its manifestations, as part of this same phenomenon of dissatisfaction with the rituals of existing forms and withdrawal into private spirituality.

Within or alongside traditional hierarchical links there grew up other forms of association that strike us as more personal, collateral, or horizontal. 'Bastard feudalism' was a more personal form of contractual relationship than the tenurial bond which it superseded. The pursuit of profits and security, spiritual or material, often seemed to be achieved most effectively by relationships in which the idea of lordship was set aside in favour of a bond more domestic and familial. Fraternities flourished in this age; brotherhood-in-arms though not new to the period was a valued form of affiliation for legal or illegal ends, sometimes formed of bands of blood brothers, at others through contracts drawn up for services in war or business partnership. One wonders if it is significant of more than the gaudy spirit that the company of escapists who left plague-ridden Florence for the pleasures related in the *Decameron* formed a single youthful age-group. Already too, we can detect the beginnings of another comparable development which was to become more marked in the future, namely the transference of religious aspiration to the domestic household group. The spectacle of Thomas More, turning his Chelsea household into a community which as nearly as possible followed monastic observance, has earlier precedents. There was John Gerson, endorsing the aim of his sisters to pursue a religious life in their family home, or the communities of English Lollards and German Waldensians, whose spiritual calling seems largely to have been followed and transmitted in domestic circles.[77] Spiritual lordship may have become suspect; spiritual fatherhood was another matter.

---

[76] McFarlane, *Lancastrian Kings and Lollard Knights*, p. 225.

[77] My indebtedness here, and perhaps elsewhere, is to John Bossy's stimulating review article 'Holiness and Society', *Past and Present*, 75 (1977), pp. 119-37.

Social history is no more cultural history than is literary history. But we have to start somewhere and Huizinga himself told us that 'the true problems of cultural history are always problems of the form, structure, and function of social phenomena'.[78] It seems clearer than ever now that forms of thought have to be studied in connection with social experience. As a guide Huizinga has done much for us, and we can still learn from him.[79] To assess the influence of his *Waning* is not easy for, as Edmund Wilson said, 'it is hard to judge very brilliant books', and it may be a long while after publication before the resonances of a splendid synthesis begin to be registered.[80] Huizinga's *Waning of the Middle Ages* has undoubtedly made one thing clear to us: naming a period resolves nothing, but may make historians more aware of their own uncertainties. Yet books, like people, have to live with their labels and, since we all suffer from the feeling that to be nameless is to be nonexistent, it also seems that to find a name is – at least to some degree – to find a character.

'Waning' appeared to have done for the late medieval north something of what 'Renaissance' had done for the south: to have made its essence recognizable. Both titles give cause for argument. And whether or not there are more genuine elements of contradiction in northern culture than there are in that of the south, they have certainly come to seem more evident than they did in Huizinga's day. We have rejected 'waning' as a satisfactory descriptive title, but we still value *The Waning* as a book. And neither the name nor the book has yet found its replacement. We may leave the last word with Huizinga. 'We can give it [the quality of an age] a name by means of which we can more or less understand one another, but we cannot determine it. And in this indeterminateness of its supreme object the close connection between historical knowledge and life itself is revealed anew'.[81]

[78] *Men and Ideas*, p. 59.

[79] Cf. the recent plea to medieval historians to take a wider view and study society and culture as a whole, advanced by Norman F. Cantor, 'The Interpretation of Medieval History', in *Essays on the Reconstruction of Medieval History*, pp. 16-17. But I would not go so far as Professor Cantor who calls the *Waning* 'the one book which makes any sense of the bizarre political history of France and England in the late fourteenth and fifteenth centuries'.

[80] Edmund Wilson, *The Bit Between My Teeth* (New York, 1966), p. 137. After forty years, remarked E.F. Jacob ('Huizinga and the Autumn', p. 144), the *Waning* 'seems more significant than it did when it appeared'.

[81] *Men and Ideas*, p. 76 (the end of the essay on 'The Task of Cultural History'). Huizinga had a good deal to say about the effects of naming periods with terms such as 'Renaissance' or 'Baroque'; cf. ibid., pp. 183, 243ff; *Dutch Civilisation*, pp. 11-13, 97-8, 103; *Homo ludens*, pp. 207-8; and see Gerson, 'Huizinga und die kunstgeschichte', pp. 215- 6.

6

The Northern Renaissance

Oh century! Oh letters! It is a joy to be alive!
> Ulrich von Hutten, Letter to Willibald Pirckheimer, 1518.

In heaven's name, what an age will soon be upon us! How I wish I might be young again!
> Erasmus, Letter to Guillaume Budé, 21 February 1517.[1]

How fortunate it is for us, how unfortunate in many ways it was for him, that Erasmus lived nearly twenty years after the writing of these words! Had he died – as he himself, like others at the time, fully expected – in his fifties instead of his late sixties, at the outset of the Lutheran revolt, subsequent historians as well as contemporaries might have enjoyed the doubtful and no doubt endless pleasures of speculating on his position. How would the greatest exponent of northern humanism have acquitted himself in this dividing of ways?

Happily we have been spared that conundrum. Erasmus lived long enough to be appealed to by both sides and to respond with his own pen to Luther's stand. But he was already deeply misunderstood. It reflects both on the ambiguity of his own utterances and on the confusions of the moment that contemporaries were so ready to cast Erasmus for roles entirely alien to him. The heartfelt prayer in which Albrecht Dürer (in the privacy of his diary) apostrophized Erasmus as a 'knight of Christ', the David who could take Luther's place in felling the Romish Goliath,[2] was as misplaced as the hostile efforts of men such as Diego Lopez Zuñiga, who attempted to portray him as the prince of heretics, especially Lutherans. The very range of his utterances ensured such misreadings of Erasmus's position. And these misunderstandings

---

[1] Lewis W. Spitz, *The Religious Renaissance of the German Humanists* (Cambridge, MA, 1963), p. 111; A. Renaudet, *Préréforme et humanisme à Paris pendant les premières guerres d'Italie 1494-1517* (Paris, 1916), p. 688 n. 5; *Opus epistolarum Des. Erasmi Roterodami*, ed. P.S. Allen and H.M. Allen (Oxford, 1906-58), ii, p. 479, no. 534; *The Correspondence of Erasmus*, trans. R.A.B. Mynors and D.F.S. Thomson, annotated by Wallace K. Ferguson, (Toronto, 1974-   ), 4, p. 250.

[2] *The Writings of Albrecht Dürer*, trans. and ed. W.M. Conway (London, 1948), p. 159; *Dürer: Schriftlicher Nachlass*, ed. H. Rupprich (Berlin, 1956-69), i, pp. 171-2.

show how, in the 1520s, the ground was shifting in ways which made Erasmus himself seem shifty. All he had accomplished was in a sense related to these changes, and yet they seemed to be taking the world away from, not towards, the objectives to which he had devoted his life. It is paradoxical that while Erasmus could only deplore the growth of religious dissension, and while the Reformation ended hopes of accomplishing much that he had worked for, knowledge of his writings was enlarged by these widening divisions.

It is natural that any account of what has come to be called, rather unhelpfully if not confusingly, the Northern Renaissance, should centre upon Erasmus. In any period of history it is rare for one man to become the spokesman of a whole generation. Erasmus is the more remarkable in that he was the first European to do so. He demonstrated the very possibility of an individual addressing a continent. He created and, in doing so, assumed what has been called the 'kingship of the pen'.[3] And by making himself into the literary arbiter of Europe, whose views were read and respected by popes, kings, bishops, men of learning and a vast number of ordinary educated contemporaries, Erasmus contributed to and affirmed what by 1520 had become an undeniable fact – the intellectual initiative of the north. To understand how this came about we must consider the influences which shaped the northern humanists.

Greek Studies

The movement which we know as the Renaissance was a matter both of fresh skills and of fresh ways of thinking. Central to both was the revived study of Greek. Throughout this period Latin learning and scholarship continued greatly to predominate, but the vanguard of humanist educators was formed by the minority who possessed knowledge of Greek, the key to those founts of literature of which Cicero was thinking when he wrote about *humanitas*. Behind the excitement of the revived study of classical antiquity lay a passionate belief in the possibility of educating individuals – and societies – to higher levels of achievement. Many northern successors to Vittorino da Feltre and Guarino da Verona eagerly took to heart the teaching of Quintilian and Cicero, who had looked back to Greek models and Greek literature for the ideal of man discovering and shaping his whole self and learning to the full, through a rounded education, the means of expressing it. 'Distinguished men of letters have represented to us', ran letters patent of Francis I appointing a king's printer for Greek in 1539, 'that art, history, morals, philosophy, and

[3] Marcel Bataillon, *Erasme et l'Espagne: recherches sur l'histoire spirituelle du XVIe siècle* (Paris, 1937), p. 80 on Erasmus's accession to the 'royauté de la plume'. Cf. M.A. Screech, *Erasmus: Ecstasy and the Praise of Folly* (Harmondsworth, 1988), p. 2; 'a man whom kings could write to and who could write to kings'.

·ER·ROT·

TERMINVS

Corporis effigiem si quis non uidit Erasmi,
Hanc scite ad uiuum picta tabella dabit.

Fig. 11 'Erasmus im Gehäus': Holbein's last portrait of Erasmus, a
woodcut of 1535, the year before the humanist's death. His hand rests on
a herm of Terminus, the god of boundaries, the emblem of his seal ring.
Terminus concedo nulli was his motto.

almost all other branches of learning, flow from Greek writers, like rivers from their source'.[4]

John Colet, writing to Erasmus in 1516, bemoaned his lack of Greek, 'without some skill in which we can get nowhere'.[5] After Petrarch's abortive efforts to read Homer in the original a great many individuals laboured painfully to acquire this linguistic skill. If the lack of Greek was annihilating, the possession of it might seem everything. Was it not Greek letters and Greek literature which Raphael Hythloday took to and taught in Utopia? Latin, on the other hand, could there be left out of account since to the Utopians 'in Latin there was nothing, apart from history and poetry, which seemed likely to gain their approval'.[6] The achievement of skill in Greek is therefore an obvious way of tracing the spread of humanist learning, and it demonstrates the generation gap – of more than one generation – that existed between the revivals of learning in the north and in Italy.

Enthusiasm for the Greek sources of learning was urgent enough, as Petrarch's example shows, to send men back to school when they had reached a time of life which to them – though not to us – was well past middle age. Alexander Hegius (1433-98), for example, who became headmaster of the chapter school at Deventer when Erasmus was a schoolboy there, was over forty when he learned Greek from Rudolph Agricola at Emmerich. Another man who humbled himself to learn from a younger, more gifted contemporary, was John Fisher (1459-1535), bishop of Rochester. Fisher had already played a large part in introducing both Greek teaching and Erasmus to Cambridge when in the summer of 1516, on his way to Dover, the celebrated humanist found himself acting as schoolmaster to his patron during a ten-day stay at Rochester.[7] Perhaps Erasmus had Fisher in mind when he wrote of the four men of his acquaintance, all famous for their works, none of whom had learned Greek before reaching forty.

It is clear that this enthusiasm, and the means of satisfying it, derived in the first instance from Italy. Early Renaissance patrons in the north – in England, Hungary or France – looked to Italy to satisfy their needs, whether for texts, teachers or designers. So a succession of instructors carried the knowledge of Greek from Italy to other parts of Europe. Gregorio Tifernate of Città di Castello had lived in Greece and taught Greek in several Italian towns before he began eighteen months of lecturing at Paris in 1458. Among the enthusiastic listeners who benefited from his teaching were Robert Gaguin, Guillaume Fichet and Wessel Gansfort. In England the instruction given at Oxford in the

---

[4] A. Tilley, *Studies in the French Renaissance* (Cambridge, 1922), p. 147.

[5] Allen (ed.), ii, p. 257, no. 423; *CWE*, 3, p. 311. On Colet's lack of Greek see John B. Gleason, *John Colet* (Berkeley, Los Angeles and London, 1989), pp. 58-9.

[6] St. Thomas More, *Utopia*, ed. Edward Surtz (New Haven and London, 1964), p. 103, cf. p. 12.

[7] Allen (ed.), ii, pp. 268-9, 317, nos. 432, 452; *CWE*, 3, pp. 324-5; 4, p. 39; H.C. Porter, 'Fisher and Erasmus', in *Humanism, Reform and the Reformation. The Career of Bishop John Fisher*, ed. Brendan Bradshaw and Eamon Duffy (Cambridge, 1989), pp. 81-101, at p. 84.

1460s by Stefano Surigone inspired the interest of William Sellyng, who was to make himself a Greek expert and one of the leading English humanists of the century. Others of his countrymen followed Surigone in both English universities. And Surigone himself, who also taught at Cologne, Strasbourg and Louvain, was one of several Italians to be found in this period teaching rhetoric in German universities, where they may have helped to seed the taste for Greek learning.

Italy provided not only the stimuli, but also the means of learning – such as manuals and grammars from Italian presses, or the scholarship founded at Louvain by Raymond di Marliano to enable a student to pursue his studies in Italy. In some cases, however, Greek was brought north (as it had originally been taken to Italy) by Greeks themselves – some of whom came secondhand, as it were, from Italy. Several Greek refugees found their way to England in the later fifteenth century. The scribe Emanuel of Constantinople, one of several Greeks patronized by George Neville, archbishop of York, stayed some years in England and may have taught Greek to various people (perhaps including William Grocyn) besides his patron, to whom he presented a transcript of Demosthenes in 1468. And in the 1480s John Serbopoulos of Constantinople, who had links with Emanuel, was residing in England and transcribing Greek texts for academic patrons. In Paris, likewise, Greek studies were encouraged by the arrival of Greeks. After Tifernate's short-lived courses there, the teaching of Greek was resumed in 1476 by George Hermonymos of Sparta. He was not a very competent teacher, to judge from the later complaints of his pupils, but some of them were exceptionally able: Budé, Erasmus, Beatus Rhenanus. Reuchlin, at any rate, was satisfied with the opportunities which Hermonymos provided, while Lefèvre became his friend. Meanwhile in Spain in the early sixteenth century, the textual studies at Alcalá owed much to the Cretan Demetrios Doucas, who had had experience of Greek printing in the office of Aldus Manutius in Venice.

Jacques Lefèvre d'Etaples, the greatest French exponent of humanist learning in his day, for whom this linguistic enlightenment was of supreme importance, thought that its inception could be dated. In the preface to his *Commentaries on the Four Gospels* in 1521, he remarked that the increased knowledge of languages in his time, unmatched since the days of Constantine, 'began to return about the time Constantinople was taken by the enemies of Christ, when a few Greeks, notably Bessarion, Theodore of Gaza, George of Trebizond and Emanuel Chrysoloras, took refuge in Italy'.[8] This passage is interesting for two reasons. First, it shows the false premises on which, scarcely

---

[8] *The Catholic Reformation, Savonarola to Ignatius Loyola: Reform in the Church, 1495-1540*, ed. John C. Olin (New York, 1969), p. 114. Theodore of Gaza was in Italy, teaching Greek at Ferrara, in the 1440s; George of Trebizond, who came to Italy in the second decade of the fifteenth century, taught at Vicenza and Mantua in the 1420s and 1430s; Bessarion, having made a great impression as Greek envoy at the Council of Ferrara-Florence, was appointed cardinal in 1439 and thereafter made his mark at the Roman curia.

more than two generations after the event, the enrichment of western Greek learning was attributed to the fall of Constantinople in 1453. All the emigrants Lefèvre named – assuming that the Chrysoloras he referred to was the celebrated Emanuel who taught Greek in Florence at the end of the fourteenth century – were in Italy before 1453. Second, this very misconception tells us something of great significance about contemporary attitudes toward Greek. For while it is undoubtedly true that individual Greeks contributed to the increased knowledge of their language and literature in the west, the erroneous conviction that this was a consequence of the fall of Constantinople was the result of an obsession, and one which (paradoxical as it might seem) was most powerful outside Italy. Faced with the spectacle of advancing Islam, Italy, it is true, produced some outstanding crusading enthusiasts. But from the days of Pierre Dubois and Roger Bacon and Ramon Lull, to Philippe de Mézières and up to Cardinal Ximenes and Guillaume Postel, it was transalpine Europe which germinated much of the most constructive thought on this tormenting issue.

Lefèvre's words draw attention to the intimate relationship between thoughts about Greek studies and the fate of the eastern church. For a great many people at the time, perhaps most, the context in which Greek learning was considered was not ancient but contemporary, not the Greek of Plato and Aristotle but rather that of the schismatic church in the east. This had, as we shall see, a profound effect upon the reception of humanist studies in the north. And it meant that the study of Greek in the fifteenth century (and later) still in part belonged, as it long had, to a missionary sphere. Such provision as was made to keep the study of Greek alive during the middle ages was largely related to hopes for reunion with the Greek church. This, for instance, was what inspired the foundation at Paris in the thirteenth century of a college to teach Oriental languages; and it was the need to be able to debate with Greek theologians and to keep open the lines of communication with Constantinople which accounted for Greek being taught at the papal court at Avignon in the first half of the fourteenth century.

Bearing this in mind, it seems likely that the negotiations between the eastern and western churches which took place at the Council of Ferrara-Florence in 1438-39, and the short-lived agreement which resulted, were of much greater significance in fostering Greek studies in the west than the long-fabled events of 1453. It might be taken as a reflection of the stimulus provided by the council that Piero del Monte, who was then far away in England serving as papal collector, was spurred (despite the unpropitious circumstances) to take up again the study of Greek which he had started in Ferrara;[9] or that the university founded at Catania in Sicily in 1444 included the unusual provision for studies in Greek. Studies undertaken in such a setting might include, or

    [9] R. Weiss, *Humanism in England during the Fifteenth Century*, 2nd edn (Oxford, 1957), pp. 25-6.

lead to, any number of interests, but they were by no means necessarily in any degree humanist.

At the same time that humanist interests beyond the Alps grew, in certain places, with the help of Italians or native-speaking Greeks, many more individuals were finding their way to Italy. The earliest indigenous exponents of humanism in the north were those who – whether or not they had gone there expressly for this purpose – had experienced Italian culture first-hand. The mission which took Guillaume Fichet to Milan in 1469-70 played a part in the beginnings of the first Paris printing press which he and Jean Heynlin, prior at the Sorbonne, established in the college that year. Itself a humanist undertaking – its first book was the model letters of the Italian Gasparino Barzizza and in 1471 appeared Lorenzo Valla's *On the Elegances of the Latin Language* – the press marked the real arrival of humanism in Paris.[10] Among those who rejoiced with Fichet (and urged him on to publish his own *Rhetoric*), was his friend Robert Gaguin – another who had direct experience of Italy.

Veteran students from German universities enlarged their capacities, and sometimes their vision, by pursuing their studies into Italy. Wessel Gansfort (*c.* 1419-89) had studied at Cologne, Heidelberg and Louvain, and had already begun to learn Greek and Hebrew, before his visit to Italy in 1470-71, where he met both Cardinal Bessarion and the future pope Sixtus IV. Gansfort's interest helped to promote linguistic studies, particularly through the stimulus he gave to two younger men, both of whose fame surpassed his: Agricola and Reuchlin.

Rudolph Agricola (1444-1485), a man of widely ranging interests and a versatility reminiscent of Castiglione's courtier (he illuminated manuscripts and built an organ, besides writing a life of Petrarch), was accepted as an equal by the Italians. He lived among them off and on for ten years (1468-79) and it was in Italy that he learned both Greek and Hebrew. Unlike Erasmus, who held him in great respect (treasuring the glimpse he had of him as a schoolboy at Deventer), Agricola was able to talk fluently to the Italians in their own vernacular; also unlike his great successor, he left few literary works. His influence, for all that, was great, partly for the very reason that he had so fully assimilated the best of what was to be learned in Italy, and was able to communicate his enthusiasm to others. Agricola, like Vittorino da Feltre before him and John Colet after him, was one of those gifted men who leave it to their pupils to enlarge the range of their virtues – and *virtù*. Erasmus, who could appreciate this quality (emphatically not one of his own), and who had through Deventer and Alexander Hegius a direct link with Agricola, was happy to commemorate this genealogy of scholars in which he was the third

---

[10] L. Febvre and H.-J. Martin, *The Coming of the Book*, trans. D. Gerard (London, 1976), p. 174; Elizabeth L. Eisenstein, *The Printing Press as an Agent of Change* (Cambridge, 1979), i, p. 399, n. 323.

generation. Agricola, he wrote, forty years after this teacher's death, was 'the first to bring us a breath of more humane learning out of Italy'.[11]

Johannes Reuchlin (1455-1522), whom Erasmus also celebrated in a very different connection, made several visits to Italy after his first journey in 1481 when he studied in Rome. It was in Florence later on that he was able to do most to advance his intellectual interests, thanks to the inspiration of that exceptional polymath, Pico della Mirandola. There Reuchlin became interested in the Hebrew studies to which he made so enormous a contribution, and there he found the teachers who enabled him to make his first strides forward with that language. Florence had a special magnetism during these last years of the fifteenth century, when the fame of Marsilio Ficino's Platonic academy added to the artistic radiance of Medici circles. Three great English humanists whose achievements – Greek as well as Latin – were extolled by Erasmus were all affected by the spell of Florence. Thomas Linacre (1460-1524), chiefly celebrated for his knowledge of medicine (which included translations of Galen) spent twelve years in the city; he was joined there by William Grocyn (*c.* 1446-1519), who took to student life in his forties to attend lectures and study Greek; John Colet (1467-1519) spent three years deepening in Italy his interest in Ficino's Platonism.[12]

Not for nothing did Linacre, on his way home to England at the turn of the fifteenth century, erect an altar at the top of an Alpine pass which he dedicated to Italy as the 'holy mother of studies'.[13] The debts owed to Italy are too numerous to count, and contemporaries were all too aware of them. On both sides of the Alps there was plenty of talk – defensive on one side, proud or arrogant on the other – about Italian superiority and transalpine barbarism. 'The Italians', wrote Erasmus in England in 1509, 'usurp culture and eloquence, and hence they're all happy congratulating themselves on being the only civilized race of men. In this kind of happiness the Romans take the first place, still blissfully dreaming of the past glories of Rome . . .'[14] At about this time Benvenuto Cellini, invited by Pietro Torrigiano to accompany him to London to work as an assistant on the royal tombs at Westminster, haughtily refused, placing an alleged insult to Michelangelo by Pietro above any desire to set eyes on 'those brutes of Englishmen'.[15]

Yet, in fact, by about 1500 the balance of learning was significantly changing. The hope which Agricola had expressed thirty years earlier was already being realized: 'that we shall one day wrest from haughty Italy the reputation

[11] Allen (ed.), i, p. 2, no. 1; *CWE*, 9, p. 294, no. 1341A; J.E. Sandys, *A History of Classical Scholarship* (Cambridge, 1906-8), ii, p. 127; Henry de Vocht, *History of the Foundation and the Rise of the Collegium Trilingue Lovaniense, 1517-1550* (Louvain, 1951-55), i, pp. 148-58.

[12] Gleason, *John Colet*, pp. 42-52 puts the case for Colet having spent a good part of his Italian stay in Florence. See below at n. 58.

[13] Sandys, *A History of Classical Scholarship*, ii, p. 226.

[14] Erasmus, *Praise of Folly and Letter to Martin Dorp*, trans. B. Radice (Harmondsworth, 1971), p. 133.

[15] *The Autobiography of Benvenuto Cellini*, trans. George Bull (London, 1966), pp. 27-8.

for classical expression which it has nearly monopolized . . . and free ourselves from the reproach of ignorance and being called unlearned and inarticulate barbarians'.[16] Jibes about barbarians might long continue, but the need to travel south for the civilizing influence of Italy became progressively less impelling.

When Erasmus first arrived in England, in the summer of 1499, he received a most pleasurable surprise. He found there a group of cultivated men, well acquainted with Italy and with humanist learning, who had reached that degree of intellectual sophistication he had seen and admired in Agricola. Colet, Grocyn, Linacre and More – especially the first and last – recognized Erasmus's qualities and did something important for him: they showed him where he belonged. Many influences, necessarily, went to the making of so complex a personality as Erasmus. Clearly this visit meant much to him, particularly the meeting with Colet in Oxford, but there is no need to suppose that it caused some violent alteration in the course of his intentions for his life. Rather one might see it as a kind of homecoming, as he arrived for the first time (and Erasmus was now at least thirty) in a circle which shared his ideals and had already gone further than he had towards achieving them. Erasmus reached England with the reputation of a poet, but his training, his commitments, and his concerns involved much more than that. When he went back to Paris he was greatly fortified and stimulated by the examples of his new-made friends in England, and was in pursuit of objectives which had long been smouldering in his mind – to perfect his Greek for biblical studies.

Erasmus did not need Italy for his humanist outlook or his humanist training. He had found in England, as he wrote soon after this visit, so much good scholarship, 'profound and learned and truly classical, in both Latin and Greek, that I have little longing left for Italy, except for the sake of visiting it'. And it was in Paris that he learned his Greek. Admittedly the going was not always easy. 'My readings in Greek', he wrote in March 1500 to his friend Jacob Batt, 'all but crush my spirit; but I have no spare time and no means to purchase books or employ the services of a tutor'.[17] Yet despite repeated complaints about such deficiencies he stuck to his purpose, and by the time he at last reached Italy in 1506 it seemed to do little for him. 'I knew more Greek and Latin when I went to Italy than I do now', he wrote with the confidence of retrospect in 1531. 'My literary education owes nothing to Italy – I wish it owed a great deal. There were people there from whom I could have learnt, but so there were in England, in France, in Germany. In Italy there was really no opportunity', since I had gone there simply for the sake of seeing the place'.[18]

---

[16] Spitz, *Religious Renaissance*, p. 25.
[17] Allen (ed.), i, pp. 273, 285, nos. 118, 123; *CWE*, 1, pp. 235, 249-50; M.M. Phillips, 'Erasmus and the Classics', in *Erasmus*, ed. T.A. Dorey (London, 1970), pp. 6-7.
[18] Erasmus, *Apologia adversus rhapsodias calumniosarum querimoniarum Alberti Pii* (Basel, 1531), pp. 57, 60; see M.M. Phillips, *The 'Adages' of Erasmus* (Cambridge, 1964), pp. 65-9, for a summary of Erasmus's controversy with Carpi, including a translation of this passage.

Fig. 12 Hans Burgkmair's memorial engraving – like a Roman epitaph – of the laureate Conrad Celtis, made at his request shortly before he died. His hands are crossed over his books, while Apollo and Mercury mourn above him.

This is not to say, of course, that Erasmus's scholarship, and perhaps his style – as opposed to his education – did not benefit considerably from what Italy had to offer. The greatly enlarged edition of the *Adages* brought out by Aldus in 1508 bears witness to the enrichment provided by manuscripts which the author was able to consult in Venice, while the Platonic influences evident in both the *Praise of Folly* and the *Enchiridion* show how Erasmus followed the studies of Italian humanists. But it remains true that he had found his humanist training and sense of values before he ever went to Italy.

A number of other famous humanists of the north who were contemporaries of Erasmus reflect this diminished dependence on Italy. Sir Thomas More, unlike Colet, Linacre, and Grocyn – all of whose achievements he surpassed – was educated entirely in England, and learned his Greek with Grocyn and Linacre, as well as with William Lily (who had acquired his in Rhodes). Lefèvre d'Etaples, though impressed by his Italian meetings with Pico della Mirandola and Ermolao Barbaro, does not seem to have learned Greek in Italy, but in Paris after his return. Meanwhile in Germany Conrad Celtis (1459-1508) was the first leading humanist of the empire to have received a humanist education at home before setting foot in Italy – and others of his generation distinguished themselves in humanist letters without ever going there at all.

Humanist learning can therefore be said to have arrived in northern Europe by the earlier years of the sixteenth century. If we judge it in this way, taking the continuous availability and fluency of Greek as an important criterion, it seems that the north took almost a century to catch up with Italy. How is one to explain this time-lag? It is not as if the north had not been in close contact with the best of Italian efforts since the days when Petrarch met Richard of Bury in Avignon and there made discoveries which greatly helped his textual restoration of Livy. In the fifteenth century there were individuals who became polished stylists, with claims to genuine humanist distinction, in many parts of Europe. In France, Nicolas de Clémanges (*c.* 1360-1437) explored the resources of monastic libraries and found a complete text of Quintilian twenty years before Poggio Bracciolini, whose discovery of a copy of this work at St. Gallen in 1417 had much greater repercussions. Poggio himself, learning in 1451 of a dean of Utrecht who had collected several manuscripts of Cicero, was astonished to find a man so devoted to eloquence and good letters 'so far from Italy'.[19] Yet currents of humanism flowed – almost underground – in places where the opportunities existed. Paris was one such place, where there seems to have been a trickle of humanist interests among officials of the royal administration: men such as Jean Lebègue (d. 1457), who followed his father in the king's service, and was the owner of a library which included both classical texts and works of Leonardo Bruni. The fashion for antiquity seeped steadily northwards through the fifteenth century, sometimes emerging rather strikingly in the names which aspiring humanists bestowed upon their offspring. It was no accident, surely, that Humphrey, duke of Gloucester, the first significant patron of Italian humanists in England, named his daughter Antigone, or that Willibald Pirckheimer – whose father and grandfather had both studied in Italy – had sisters called Sabrina and Euphemia.

It takes more, however, than the enthusiasm of individuals to change long-established outlooks and institutions. It needs continuity of support – or revolutionary technology. Such promising humanist beginnings as there were in Parisian circles, or in England around Duke Humphrey, did not succeed in creating lasting new patterns of study in the north. To account for this failure it is not sufficient to point to the effects of the Hundred Years' War in France, or the Wars of the Roses in England. There was, after all, plenty of dislocation in the sixteenth century – and yet these studies survived. One obvious contrast between Italy and the rest of Europe in this formative period is the range of available patronage. In the fifteenth century the north could boast nothing to compare with the brilliant rivalry of Italian courtly society in Florence, Milan, Ferrara, Urbino, Rome and Naples. Individuals such as the duke of Gloucester or John Tiptoft, earl of Worcester, or Matthias Corvinus of Hungary were exceptional and isolated, incapable of effecting a permanent change in the course of studies. In the 'gothic' north, patrons themselves needed educating, and for fashions to change many people have to become aware of changes of fashion. From the end of the fifteenth century, royal actions did a great deal – if

[19] De Vocht, *Collegium Trilingue Lovaniense*, i, p. 110.

Fig. 13 Dürer's 1524 engraving of his closest friend and exact contemporary Willibald Pirckheimer, the full-blooded and learned Nuremberg humanist.

largely indirectly – to increase northern awareness of the exuberant world beyond the Alps. Between the Neapolitan venture of Charles VIII of France in 1494 and the sack of Rome by the troops of Charles V in 1527 (which damaged a number of Italian prospects), military affairs brought many different sorts of people into contact with the dazzle of Italy. Some of the plunders contributed directly to northern scholarship. John Lascaris, prised out of Medici Florence, was persuaded to settle in Paris, where he furthered the study of Greek. And the wholesale transfer to France of the Visconti-Sforza library from Milan enormously enriched the resources of the French royal library – which both Lascaris and Budé helped to reorganize when Francis I moved it to Fontainebleau.

When humanist learning finally became established in the north it had the advantage not only of royal patrons like Francis I and Henry VIII, but also of tools which made it possible to bypass or overtake established institutions and traditional modes of study. The arrival of printing made the teaching and learning of humanists – and others – less dependent upon formal institutional methods. What Aldus did for Greek grammar Reuchlin later did for Hebrew, and the strides forward which northerners were able to make in both languages in the early sixteenth century were closely linked with the availability of printed texts. Erasmus, deservedly famous as the first man of letters who earned his living by his pen, and who has left a vivid description of himself working against the clatter of Aldus's press, was only one of the increasing numbers whose living and learning revolved around printers' offices.[20]

Northern and southern scholars shared many of the same desires and objectives. They wanted to recover the ancient world in order to recreate the new. For both, skill in Greek was an indispensable prerequisite. Yet there were age-old differences in the worlds north and south of the Alps, differences of outlook and education, which affected this transference of learning. In the north, where university teaching had always been more clerical than it was in Italy (with its tradition of secular learning), the study of theology held the place of honour which was given to law and rhetoric in the south. Theology, as we shall see, had its place in Italy, but the schools and scholars to which it owed its fame belonged elsewhere. These differences affected the transposition of humanist interests to the world beyond the Alps.

The experiences of Poggio Bracciolini on his disappointing visit to England in 1418-22 might be taken as an indication of what was to happen later on a larger scale. Works of the church Fathers at first seemed to Poggio second-best reading matter when he found himself, lacking materials to pursue his classical interests, taking to the study of St. Augustine, St. Jerome, St. John Chrysostom, but this gave him so great an appreciation of these authors that he regretted (at that time) the labours spent on other studies. Also indicative are the book tastes of Poggio's patron, Duke Humphrey, which reflect the concerns of the handful of other great English book-collectors of the fifteenth century. He pioneered in trying to form as complete a classical library as possible, but the translations which were made for him from the Greek were mainly works of theology or philosophy which would serve scholastic purposes. Not surprisingly, since learning is conditioned by upbringing and previous experience, what English humanists brought home from Italy was often chosen to fit, rather than reconstruct, the architecture of their domestic learning. The Greek manuscripts surviving from the collection of the accomplished humanist Robert Fleming (*c.* 1415-83) are religious works; and William Sellyng (d. 1494), the prior of Christ Church, Canterbury, whose proficiency in Greek was commemorated on his tombstone, turned his Italianate skill to translating a sermon of Chrysostom.[21]

'Time was', wrote Roger Ascham in *The Schoolmaster* (published in 1570, two years after his death), 'when Italy and Rome have been . . . the best breeders and bringers-up of the worthiest men . . . But now that time is gone'.[22] Doubtless many still disagreed with him, including those who, following in the steps of their forebears a century earlier, assumed that the paths of education should lead them to Italy. But however one judged the Italian scene

---

[20] See the passage cited n. 18 above; Eisenstein, *The Printing Press*, i, pp. 180, 223; and on Hebrew studies see G. Lloyd Jones, *The Discovery of Hebrew in Tudor England: A Third Language* (Manchester, 1983), pp. 1-38.

[21] Weiss, *Humanism in England*, is still a useful account of these developments.

[22] Roger Ascham, *The Schoolmaster (1570)*, ed. Lawrence V. Ryan (Ithaca, NY, 1967), p. 60.

in the later sixteenth century, its indispensability for the educational needs of northerners was surely a thing of the past. To recite the glories of the renaissance of letters, as John Leland had some years earlier, seeing how Greek and Latin and Hebrew were being studied and cultivated, meant recalling the achievements of Spain and France, Germany and England, alongside Italy.

Already there were towering figures to prove Leland's point. In Spain there was Elio Antonio de Nebrija (1444-1522), who used his ten years' experience of Italy to work for humanist studies at home, and whose publications included grammars in Greek and Hebrew as well as Latin. In France the work of Guillaume Budé (1468-1540) could be measured against that of Erasmus who was reportedly envious of the Frenchman's *De asse* (1515), a pioneering work on Roman coinage which revealed the author's profound knowledge of antiquity. Budé was deeply concerned with the restoration of Greek. He helped to promote its study in various ways, including the publication in 1529 of his *Commentarii linguae graecae* and a few years later of a work in which – demonstrating the convictions he shared with other northern humanists – he defended Greek learning from the imputation of heresy, arguing its value for Christian studies.

The greatest contribution of all, of course, was that of Erasmus. Some of his most successful works were deliberately composed to fulfil the educational needs of 'barbarous' northerners. The *Colloquies*, with their witty exchanges and pungent dialogue on contemporary affairs and failings, were written as models for schoolboy Latin and, though they provided pleasure for many other sorts of readers in their various editions after 1518, that remained their primary purpose.[23] The same was true of the *Adages* (whose first appearance was in 1500), another work which Erasmus – who saw his books as children it was his duty to bring up and improve – lived with and enlarged through the course of his life. This growing collection of ancient proverbs, repeatedly supplemented by Erasmus's reading and annotative comment, was intended as a storehouse of the learning which the author had found so lacking in his youth. The *Colloquies* and the *Adages* were two of the great books of the Renaissance, and it is significant that they, like so many other influential works of the time – Castiglione's *Courtier*, for example – stemmed from that educational impulse which was the ruling humanist passion of the day. Erasmus, looking back on his work near the end of his life, could feel that he had served this need:

> When I was a boy in my native Germany barbarous ignorance reigned supreme, to touch Greek was to be a heretic. And so for my part, small as it is, I have tried to stimulate the young to struggle out of the mire of ignorance towards purer studies. For I wrote those volumes not for the Italians but for the Dutch, for Brabant and Flanders. Nor have my attempts been entirely unsuccessful. So that learning might

[23] *The Colloquies of Erasmus*, trans. Craig R. Thompson (Chicago and London, 1965), introduction, pp. xxi-xxxiii.

serve piety, I wrote the *Enchiridion Militis Christiani*; I increased the *Adagia*, because I was ashamed of the scantiness of the first edition.[24]

Northern humanists produced works of rhetoric, poetry, history, and epigraphy comparable to those of their Italian predecessors and contemporaries. It was, however, the field of theology which gave northern studies their leading and most significant direction and which produced in the work of Erasmus the peak of their achievement. In him we can see the tools, methods and wisdom of the *studia humanitatis* of the south grafted onto the Christian piety of the north to reach a new growth. It was a change of emphasis, not a break. Italian humanist learning, taken home and transplanted in the north, grew into a rather different tree. Or should one say that northerners cultivated a graft which Italians had tried but failed?

Devotio Moderna

The spiritual, as opposed to the intellectual, beginnings of the movement we are considering must take us back to the late fourteenth century. At this time when, after long years of papal absence from Rome, the contested election of 1378 opened a lengthy period of schism, the voices of northern Christians – admonitory, heretical, quietistic, or simply pious – seemed to take on an independent note of their own, as they called their spiritual leaders to task or sought for other means of religious regeneration. The same critical period that saw St. Catherine of Siena multiplying her appeals for reform, John Wycliffe moving towards a more extreme doctrinal position and John Gerson formulating his views of conciliar authority, produced the beginnings of a movement which drew upon and replenished the springs of piety in northern Europe for many years to come. This is the movement already known in the fifteenth century as the *Devotio Moderna*, the most famous branch of which is the Brothers of the Common Life.

The two starting-points of the *Devotio Moderna* indicate the two directions in which, in the following century, it was to extend its influence. In 1374 Gerard Groote (1340-84), who had abandoned an academic career in Paris to take up a life of evangelical preaching, turned his house in Deventer into a hostel for a group of pious women. According to the constitution he drew up five years later, they were to live a communal life, sharing work and expenses, bound by no obligations of vows, and free to depart as they wished. After Groote's death, his friend and disciple Florence Radewijns (*c*. 1350-1400) brought to completion in 1387 the foundation at Windesheim of a monastery which Groote had inspired and which was, according to his wish, placed under the rule of the Augustinian canons.

[24] Phillips, *The 'Adages'*, p. 74; Allen (ed.), xi, p. 183, no. 3032 (Erasmus to John Choler, *c*. August, 1535).

From these simple but inspiring beginnings flowed two currents of vitalizing influence upon contemporary religion. One, more conventional but answering a widely-felt need of the time, was a response to the problem – which became more urgent as the fifteenth century proceeded – of how existing institutions could be made to answer the ancient Christian call to an ascetic monastic life. Groote and his followers were far from alone in recognizing this need, but the foundation at Windesheim proved particularly capable of meeting it, and grew into a congregation of houses, linked with the first in spiritual observance and a dedicated monastic life. Although there are signs that by the end of the fifteenth century the movement had lost some of the freshness of its first years and was succumbing to some of the less worthy aspects of contemporary monasticism, the Windesheim Congregation was still a regenerating source. In the 1490s, when French reformers were anxious to improve the houses of Château-Landon in the diocese of Sens and Saint-Victor in Paris, it was to Windesheim that they looked for help. A prominent part in these moves was taken by Jean Standonck, whose dietetic stringencies were criticized as well as suffered by some of those (including Erasmus) who experienced the harshness of the reformed regime he had introduced at the Collège de Montaigu in Paris. Standonck was deeply affected by the spirit of the *Devotio Moderna*. It was he who went to Windesheim to seek help for Château-Landon, as the result of which a mission of six men was sent to France. They included Jean Mombaer (*c.* 1460-1501), whose *Rosary of Spiritual Exercises*[25] influenced Ignatius Loyola.

The other, related part of Groote's movement, keeping to the pattern of his first house of sisters and the groups of his immediate followers at Deventer and Zwolle, remained unattached to any existing order. These Brothers and Sisters of the Common Life joined together in pursuit of a common devotional life which participated in the monastic ideal but imitated it without the formalities of vows or religious habits, and without any life commitment to their profession. Like the first women who came together in Groote's house, they were at liberty to return to ordinary secular life. In these ways they were clearly distinguished from the established orders, with whom, however, they were linked through the Windesheim foundation, and to which they contributed members.

The Brothers of the Common Life also concentrated their activities towards specific ends, notably educational ones. Their common labour before the days of printing was, in particular, the copying of books, and they were also – though here their achievement has been exaggerated – closely associated with the great expansion of education which took place in Germany and the Low Countries in the fifteenth century. They became influential, and affected the lives of many devout and perhaps disillusioned people, because they answered a great need of the period. They helped to provide for the growing educational demands – of laymen, as well as those who intended to enter the church – in the

---

[25] See below p. 176 for this work.

greater urban centres. In times of religious uncertainty and ecclesiastical dislocation, they offered methods of spiritual consolation, islands of contemplative security accessible to any reader who would take as his spiritual weapon a book. The aims were not grandiose, but the results were very impressive. The achievement of the *Devotio Moderna* was not that of a network of schools and teachers – as it has sometimes been made to appear – but that of a less easily definable genealogy of spiritual inspiration, which was carried by individuals and books as well as through continuing institutions.[26]

It is necessary to make clear this distinction between the educational and spiritual influence of the Brothers of the Common Life, since their work in the former sphere seems to have been misunderstood. The Brothers were undoubtedly much concerned with the educational needs of their time, but it is a mistake to think of them as having had a revolutionary impact upon contemporary education. The extent of their teaching was less far-reaching, and the methods they employed less innovative, than has often been supposed. The Brothers were not in the first instance, or ever primarily, schoolmasters, and several of the more celebrated schools with which their name has been linked (such as the chapter school at Deventer, or the city school at Zwolle) cannot be said to have belonged to them or been under their direction. These schools existed before the Brothers were founded, and though John Cele (1350-1417), the famous rector of Zwolle, was in close communication with Groote, he was not a member of the Brotherhood. The Brothers' calling was neither scholarship nor teaching, and indeed both these activities might have been felt to conflict with their pious preoccupations.

From the outset, however, members of the movement devoted themselves to the needs, both material and spiritual, of the increasing numbers of boys who came to be schooled in the towns and cities of the Low Countries. The hostels which they founded to board these schoolboys were in some cases able to provide tuition or guidance for individual pupils, as for instance 's Hertogenbosch did for the youthful Erasmus, who by the time he got there had probably completed all the classes of the school at Deventer.[27] In general, however, what the Brothers offered was spiritual guidance rather than teaching; they were always spiritual mentors and confessors more than they were schoolmasters. Only in a relatively few and late cases do they seem themselves to have taken up teaching and founded or assumed the direction of schools. Among such exceptions was the small grammar school at Louvain which, after it came under the control of the Brothers in 1433, was enlarged in 1470 into a regular boarding school which enjoyed a century's existence. And at Liège, where they had given instruction in their hostel, the Brothers started a school at the turn of the fifteenth century in which Greek and rhetoric were taught in the advanced classes. Such cases were exceptional. The work which the

[26] On the 'hazy limits' of the *Devotio moderna*, see R.R. Post, *The Modern Devotion: Confrontation with Reformation and Humanism* (Leiden, 1968), p. 13.
[27] Albert Hyma, *The Youth of Erasmus* (Ann Arbor, MI, 1930), pp. 131-5.

Brothers did in this sphere reflected their concerns as a whole; the objectives were devotional, not pedagogical, and focused upon the cities where pastoral needs were most pressing. 'We have decided', wrote the Brothers in Zwolle in 1415, 'to live in cities, in order that we may be able to give advice and instruction to clerics and other persons who wish to serve the Lord'.[28]

While recognizing this limitation, it would be a mistake to underestimate the influence of the *Devotio Moderna*. As spiritual directors, the Brothers were able to inspire many, not all of whom subsequently adopted a religious vocation, with the intensity of the inner religious life. Among those who respected the values of the movement, without ever formally belonging to it, were Wessel Gansfort and Erasmus's teacher Hegius. Erasmus himself retained throughout his life the impressions of the early years he had spent in school at Deventer, at the Brothers' hostel in 's Hertogenbosch and in the Augustinian house of Steyn where he was professed. He might in retrospect be critical – especially of unfair pressures to get him into a monastic order – but he took to heart and made his own the characteristics of the circles in which he received his education.

We should not, therefore, look to the Brothers of the Common Life for an enthusiasm for classical scholarship or humanist learning. If some of the schools with which they were associated did occasionally provide such teaching, they stand out from the traditional methods perpetuated by the others. Rarely did the Brothers produce, as opposed to influencing, men of learning. Gabriel Biel, who combined a professorship of theology at Tübingen (1484) with the office of prior of the Brothers at Urach, was unique in his double position. Such lack of intellectual leadership can scarcely be surprising given the constant tendency – which stemmed from the movement's founder – to turn aside from academic disputes and deadening scholastic controversy. 'Why should we', asked Groote, 'indulge in those endless disputes, such as are held at the universities, and that about subjects of no moral value whatsoever?'[29] He had himself shown the way by his rejection of the University of Paris. It was a recipe for devotion more than a criticism. The devout exercises which Groote and Radewijns bequeathed to their successors, and which influenced among others Thomas à Kempis, included the advice: 'Resolve to avoid and abhor all public disputations which are but wranglings for success in argument, or the appearance thereof (such as the disputations of graduates in theology at Paris), and take no part therein'.[30]

This outlook, based upon the belief that there were higher truths to which scholastic argument rendered no useful service, was still a vital force in the *Devotio Moderna* in the later fifteenth century. It resembles an important

---

[28] Albert Hyma, *The Christian Renaissance: A History of the 'Devotio Moderna'* (New York and London, 1924), p. 121. See Post, *Modern Devotion*, pp. 244-58, 346-69, 556-69, on the schools at Deventer, Zwolle, Liège and elsewhere.

[29] Hyma, *Christian Renaissance*, p. 23.

[30] Ibid., p. 172.

strain of humanist thought – though Gansfort wrote, having witnessed the achievements of the humanists of Florence, that while the capacities of the Florentines exceeded those of the men of Zwolle, 'Yet I prefer the incapacity of these to the subtlety of those'. He found St. Paul's accomplishments in 'barbarous' Thessaly and Corinth, as compared with learned Athens, to be a weighty argument against universities: 'It goes to show that liberal studies are not very pleasing to God'.[31] Through the *Imitation of Christ*, the mystical ideal of *docta ignorantia*, learned ignorance, about which Nicholas of Cusa had written, became familiar to the devotional exercises of many who were not bothered by the limitations and defects of university methods. 'Of what value are lengthy controversies on deep and obscure matters, when it is not by our knowledge of such things that we shall at length be judged? . . . Truly, "we have eyes and see not": for what concern to us are such things as *genera* and *species*?' Through Christ, 'the teacher of teachers and lord of angels', the lowly mind could 'understand more of the ways of the everlasting truth in a single moment than ten years of study in the schools'.[32] 'Non alta sapere, sed bene agere': right acting rather than high learning, was the theme of the *Imitation*.

The Brothers of the Common Life did not belittle books or studies; they stressed that learning should be of the right sort. The mind of the reader must be devoutly, not inquisitively or acquisitively, directed; learning is the tool and servant of piety; intellectual subtlety has no independent value. From Groote's time onwards, their meditation focused upon the life of Christ and their learning upon the gospel, the scriptures, and the church Fathers. The labour to which they were especially committed was the work of 'holy writing' and, though the 'good books' they copied were by no means limited to scriptural texts, it was the Bible which was the centre of their daily readings and meditation. *Sacra scriptura* was their daily bread in more senses than one: both as the written labours which earned their living and as the day's learning in Holy Writ. The books which were copied for Groote (who was very well-read in the Scriptures, and who himself employed several scribes and added to his collection of books after he had taken up an evangelical career) were mostly gospel commentaries and texts of the Fathers. And, as the four books which we know as the *Imitation of Christ* show, studded as they are with biblical quotations, it was Bible-reading above all which enriched the mind of the Augustinian canon Thomas à Kempis.

The scriptural preoccupation of the *Devotio Moderna* took two directions which were significant as a foreshadowing of later developments. During the later fourteenth century, at a time when the Bible was being translated into

---

[31] Ibid., n. 15, p. 409; E.F. Jacob, 'The Brethren of the Common Life', in *Essays in the Conciliar Epoch* (Manchester, 1963), p. 131. Gansfort was not formally a member of the movement, as either a Brother or an Augustinian canon, but was closely associated with it, having lived in one of the Brothers' hostels, and having close links with Agnietenberg.

[32] Thomas à Kempis, *The Imitation of Christ*, trans. L. Sherley-Price (Harmondsworth, 1952), bk. i, c. 3; bk. iii, c. 43, pp. 30, 149-50.

various vernaculars, the Brothers participated in the effort to give the laity direct knowledge of Holy Writ. Their own biblical studies – which differed markedly from contemporary university practice in approaching the scriptural text without years of preparatory training – were open to laymen. At Zwolle (where an hour each day was devoted to the study of scripture), after services on Sundays and feast days the Brothers held a lecture or instruction intended for schoolboys, but open to interested comers, at which a biblical passage was read in the vernacular and followed by a talk. Gerard Zerbolt (1367-98) defended the right of laymen to read the Bible in their own language, though he admitted that some of its books, such as Revelation, needed explanation. How much better, he thought, for them to read scripture than the frivolous romances that commonly held their interest.

It was a natural outcome of such beliefs for the Brothers to turn to biblical translation. Some of the translations into Dutch which were made in the later fourteenth century can be attributed to Groote himself, including versions of the psalms and other passages in his Dutch *Book of Hours*. This dates from 1383 and was later often printed, as well as being translated into Low German. Another Dutch biblical translation which appeared before the end of the century, and which evidently stems from the same circles, includes more books of both testaments and prefaces arguing the case for vernacular scriptures. It seems clear that the followers of the *Devotio Moderna* acted on their belief that laymen should have biblical texts in languages they understood: when in the last decade of the fourteenth century, two lawyers put up a justificatory case for the Brothers of the Common Life (whose lawfulness had been called in question), they defended such vernacular scriptures, provided the translations were not distorted. One of them, Everard Foec, also argued the usefulness of schools equipped to teach Hebrew, Arabic and Chaldean – a suggestion which was not new, but which had to wait many years to become even remotely practicable.[33]

In another instance the biblical work of the *Devotio Moderna* was likewise suggestive of future directions. This was not a work of translation but of textual scholarship. John Busch, the chronicler of Windesheim, relates how the Brothers 'attempted to reduce all the "original" books of the Old and New Testaments to the text as translated by St. Jerome from Hebrew into Latin, using the best models obtainable'.[34] For this purpose they had to undertake manuscript research, collecting codices from different libraries in order to collate and correct textual variants. Both the objective and the work were remarkable, and to realize their aim of reconstituting Jerome's original text the Brothers gave the highest respect to the oldest texts and corrected a number of Hebrew expressions. They succeeded in producing an improved version of both books of the Vulgate, corrected throughout according to the oldest

---

[33] Post, *Modern Devotion*, pp. 98-107, 165-7; *CHB*, ii, ed. G.W.H. Lampe (Cambridge, 1969), p. 431.

[34] Post, *Modern Devotion*, p. 305; Renaudet, *Préréforme et humanisme*, p. 215, n. 1.

variants to which they had access, carefully punctuated and revised. It might seem that in this work we have a notable anticipation of sixteenth-century scholarship. There were, however, important differences which make it impossible to describe this labour as humanistic. First, although the Brothers had recourse to the oldest available texts, their aim was not to get back, with a fresh and truer grasp, to the textual context. Their concern was uniformity, not understanding. They wanted a single purified text for liturgical reasons, so that the different houses of their observance should not be using conflicting versions; the choir books in all their monasteries were to employ the one corrected Bible. Given the problems of manuscript diffusion, this was a remarkable enough aim. Also, unlike the humanists' textual studies, the Windesheimers' work on the Bible was static and finite; their investigation ended when they had arrived at their corrected version; it was not extended by the discovery and discussion of further variants. Once they had made their corrected Vulgate it was forbidden to make any textual alterations.

Like all reforming movements the *Devotio Moderna* had its limitations, but the inspiration of its first followers continued to feed subsequent spiritual streams. It was never simply or predominantly a spirituality of laymen, but there was a novelty about the way in which it answered the spiritual needs of seculars – men, women, and boys – in the growing urban centres of the later middle ages. It provided help, in ways which were more informal, less rigid, and more adaptable than the institutions of existing orders, for those who lived in the world of affairs while responding to an ancient ascetic summons – the most venerable of all Christian callings – the imitation of Christ. Perhaps the best way of approaching this far-reaching spiritual heritage, which influenced far more people than ever formally became members of the Brothers of the Common Life or the Windesheim Congregation, is through books.

Most celebrated of all the works produced in the circles of the *Devotio Moderna* is the *Imitation of Christ*. More properly described as four treatises joined together under the later title of 'Admonitions useful for the spiritual life. Concerning the Imitation of Christ and the contempt of all the vanities of the world', this small work, long attributed to John Gerson, is now generally ascribed to Thomas Hemerken of Kempen, or à Kempis, who died in 1471 having spent most of his long and uneventful life as an Augustinian canon in the house of St. Agnietenberg near Zwolle, which was a member of the Windesheim chapter. À Kempis went to school at Deventer, and among his various writings left a testimonial of his awed respect for the 'holy man' Florence Radewijns, of whom he wrote a biography. One of the most striking aspects of the enormous influence of the *Imitation* (of which there were many manuscript copies, as well as early translations and editions) is the way in which spiritual admonitions composed within and addressed to monastic circles could be welcomed and taken to heart by individuals of differing faith living in a variety of worldly circumstances. This reflects not only upon the author – and what he took for granted – but also upon that search for a pruned and simplified piety which characterized some of the strongest spirituality of the time. It turned away from outward ceremonial to concentrate upon exploring and strengthening inner spiritual resources through quiet reading and meditation. So the *Imitation*, which addresses its reader as a confessor might advise a penitent or speaks as a soul communing alone with God, says little about church ceremonies or saints, and nothing in recommendation of pilgrimages, images and relics. The emphasis throughout is upon the inner purification of the humble mind. 'Some carry their devotion only in books, pictures, and other visible signs and representations', but they are mistaken, for while 'Nature regards the outward characteristics of a man: grace considers his inner disposition', 'God walks with the simple, reveals himself to the humble'.[35] It was an ancient message, but one of refreshing simplicity amidst the multiplying ceremonies of the late medieval church.

Another book which belongs to this family was the *Rosetum*, or *Rosary of Spiritual Exercises*, by Jean Mombaer. This work, first printed in full in 1494 and republished twice in the early sixteenth century, likewise has a spiritual lineage of readers.[36] Mombaer – who, as we have seen, was sent to France on one of Windesheim's reforming missions and died as abbot of Livry in 1501 – entered St. Agnietenberg about seven years after the death of à Kempis, in 1477-78. His work, like the *Imitation*, was written to aid that inner meditative life which was the preoccupation of the Brothers (whose whole day, ideally, was an unbroken sequence of spiritual exercises). Mombaer offered to this end a veritable labyrinth of meditations covering all the subjects of piety and acts of religious life, purposefully displayed for easy use and learning, accompanied by a series of mnemonic verses. Great attention was paid to the method of presentation and meditative order. The topics were grouped into 'rosaries' of 150 points and into other clusters of seven for the days of the week, ordered in a logical series to concentrate the mind on a determined theme; the *Chiropsalterium*, which utilized the divisions of the hand, is a visual example of these memory devices. Like Wessel Gansfort, part of whose *Scala meditatoria* was incorporated into the *Rosetum*, Mombaer treated meditation as a methodical ladder. Spiritual exercise of this kind could bring the soul into communion with God at any time and place; without it, the reception of the sacraments was of little profit.

Finally, it is not out of place to consider here Erasmus's *Enchiridion militis Christiani*. This small book, written at Saint-Omer in 1501 at the request of a friend, and first published two years later, holds an important place in Erasmus's oeuvre and points the course of his future work. The name *Enchiridion* (already used by St. Augustine) indicates the character of the work: a pocket-book which should be ready to hand as a spiritual dagger.

---

[35] *Imitation*, bk. iii, cc. 4, 31; bk. iv, c. 18, pp. 96, 137, 217.

[36] An earlier partial edition of the *Rosetum exercitiorum spiritualium et sacrarum meditationum* appeared in 1491: editions were also published in 1504 (Basel) and 1510 (Paris). Pierre Debongnie, *Jean Mombaer de Bruxelles* (Louvain and Toulouse, 1927), p. 305ff; Augustin Renaudet, *Humanisme et Renaissance* (Geneva, 1958), p. 139.

Erasmus, unlike Mombaer and à Kempis, was specifically addressing a lay-man, but the two weapons which he recommended for the soldiering Christian knight were not unlike the tools of piety they had offered:

> Who so ever wyl take upon hym to fyght agaynst the hole hoost of vices . . . must provyde hym of two specyall wepons, prayer and knowlege . . . These twayne cleveth so togyder lyke frendes, the one ever requyring the others helpe . . . prayer verily is the more excellent, as she that communeth and talketh famyliarly with almyghty god. Yet for all that is doctryne no lesse necessary.

Erasmus was here concerned with practical piety – the needs of an ordinary layman for ordered procedures of devotion – and the rules he set down reflect some of the emphases of the *Devotio Moderna*. The essential armoury for the layman's mind was the Bible; he should be equipped by 'fervent study or meditacion of holy scripture'. 'And breade is not so naturall meate for thy body as the worde of god is meate for thy soule'. For one fortified with this nourishment, no assaults by inner enemies need be feared. 'Wherefore if thou dedycate thy selfe holly to the study of scripture, and exercise thy mynde day and nyght in the lawe of god, no feare shall trouble the, neyther by day nor night'. Erasmus, true to his own beliefs, also carefully allowed for the role of secular learning, classical poetry and philosophy, and brought Platonic theor-ies of the spiritual ascent of the soul to serve Christian thinking. He laid great stress on the need to put invisible values above attendance to the visible ceremonies of worship. To honour the bones of saints, to pilgrimage to the Holy Sepulchre, or to make offerings before images were ritualistic acts involving many dangers to true worship of Christ. Invisible piety was what was pleasing to God. The truly Christian knight would 'he[a]re the worde of god within'. He had spiritual wings with which to lift himself up, 'as it were by certayne steppes of the ladder of Jacob, from the body to the spiryte, from the visyble worlde unto the invysyble, from the letter to the mystery . . .'[37] Erasmus, with his ample reading and amplifying aims, added several rungs to the spiritual step-ladder of the *Devotio Moderna*.

Patristic and Biblical Studies

The religious works which were written and edited by the northern humanists were only one part of their literary output, but it is this part which gives their work its distinguishing quality. To regard this as the special achievement of the revival of studies in the north does not mean that we need either to revert to the older view of Italian humanism as essentially pagan or to deny that northern scholars found important precedents for their work in Italy. In this field, as in others, there is no clear-cut line to be drawn between what went on

---

[37] Erasmus, *Enchiridion militis Christiani*, ed. Anne M. O'Donnell (EETS, 282, 1981) – this is the 1534 English translation – pp. 38, 42-3, 44, 45-6, 132, 135. See Screech, *Ecstasy*, pp. 12-13, 35, 102-6, 109ff, 113ff on the *Enchiridion*'s relationship to the *Moria* and Erasmus's central concerns.

on either side of the Alps. Northerners can be seen as continuing, in their own way, what had already been begun in Italy.

Since Burckhardt's day it has come to be seen that true paganizing was exceptional in fifteenth-century Italy, even if the intense study of antiquity undeniably introduced 'some intellectual detachment from older religious convictions'.[38] That concern for stylistic improvement which led Pietro Bembo to advise a correspondent against reading St. Paul (lest his style be spoiled) could lead towards biblical studies as well as away from them. Yet the desire to imitate antiquity might do a great deal to obscure a writer's beliefs. Northern humanists, like their southern predecessors, sometimes used in the pursuit of literary elegance (or what seemed elegant), expressions which seem to belie their Christian vocation. The fact that Abbot Wheathampstead of St. Albans (d. 1465) thought fit to lard a letter to his monks with pretentious allusions to pagan deities and to say, 'we are erecting altars of incense to Neptune' should not delude us – any more than it would have worried his recipients – as to the true nature of his beliefs.[39] Conrad Celtis's understanding of ancient learning went much deeper than this veneer of classical allusion but, though he combined Neoplatonic thinking with savage criticism of the church, he continued to revere the Virgin and the saints while referring to God the Father as Jupiter, and Mary as the Mother of the Thunderer. Erasmus himself is an example, apostrophizing the Virgin as 'that true Diana'.[40]

Some important patristic work was done in Italy in the fifteenth century. The writings of the Fathers were part of the heritage of antiquity which humanists wanted to recover and restore, and the Italians managed to regain various previously unknown Greek patristic texts, and to translate into Latin a number of others. By the time that Humphrey duke of Gloucester commissioned his Italian secretary, Antonio Beccaria, to translate from Greek into Latin several treatises of St. Athanasius, various Greek Fathers had been rendered into Latin by Ambrogio Traversari. Appointed general of the Camaldolese order in 1431, Traversari was a skilled Greek scholar who played a large role in formulating the union between the Greek and Latin churches. He died shortly after, in 1439, leaving among the works he had completed in his relatively short life Latin translations of Chrysostom, St. Ephraem, the life and four orations of Gregory of Nazianzus, and treatises by St. Basil. George of Trebizond, whom we have already encountered through Lefèvre, translated, besides Plato

---

[38] Denys Hay, *The Italian Renaissance in its Historical Background* (Cambridge, 1961), p. 176. See also the remarks on the 'mild tincture of paganism' which accompanied the study of antiquity in J.R. Hale, *Renaissance Europe 1480-1520* (London, 1971), pp. 299-300.

[39] E.F. Jacob, 'Verborum florida venustas', in *Essays in the Conciliar Epoch*, pp. 185-206, at p. 190.

[40] This phrase appears in Erasmus's *Paean Virgini Matri dicendus*, a prayer written probably early in 1499; Eugene F. Rice Jr., 'Erasmus and the Religious Tradition, 1495-1499', *Renaissance Essays from the Journal of the History of Ideas*, ed. P.O. Kristeller and P.P. Wiener (New York, 1968), p. 168 n. 28.

and Aristotle, a number of patristic works from the Greek. Especially significant, in the light of later developments in the north, was the work done in this
field by Giannozzo Manetti (1396-1459) and Lorenzo Valla (1407-57) – though
only the latter had a direct influence on subsequent work. Both these men were
associated with Pope Nicholas V (who did much to encourage translators), and
both found protection at the court of Naples, where Valla wrote his critical
work on the Donation of Constantine and where Manetti took refuge when his
work was attacked.

Manetti's studies are particularly interesting for the way in which they
anticipated later undertakings. As a humanist layman, whose ambition was to
strengthen the foundations of theology by making a fresh translation of the
Bible from the original sources, and who learned both Greek and Hebrew to
carry out this work, it is remarkable that he was able to accomplish as much as
he did. By taking into his service two Greeks, a Syrian and a Jew, Manetti
gained the necessary linguistic proficiency; he collected manuscripts and with
the help of his teacher-servants read the entire biblical text through twice. He
had therefore thoroughly prepared himself by the time he embarked on his
translation, of which only the New Testament and psalter survive. The latter is
outstanding in that it set out in three parallel columns the Septuagint, the
Vulgate text, and Manetti's own text – apparently the first use of this method.
Manetti – like Valla, whose work on the Donation was completed slightly
earlier – was fully aware of the problems and possibilities of applying humanist
linguistic skills to the sources of the faith. He was not afraid to direct his critical
methods upon the most used portions of the Bible, and to rewrite the text
revered by long tradition – that of the Vulgate. In this he was a true precursor
of Erasmus. And, like Erasmus, he encountered harsh criticism, though the
opposition to Manetti was made even fiercer by the fact that he was a layman.
The critics in both cases upheld the same point – the sanctity of the Vulgate
text.

Valla's work has gained fuller recognition than Manetti's because it received
the *imprimatur* of Erasmus. The *Annotations on the New Testament* which
Valla wrote in the 1440s were found by Erasmus in the Premonstratensian
library of Parc near Louvain in 1504 and published by him the following year.
Valla's application of humanist criticism to the Vulgate text, his unflinching
readiness to point out the weakness of this version, and his scorn for the errors
of translators and scribes and for those who stood by them in ignorance of
Greek, are all abundantly clear. He used between three and seven Greek texts
and three Latin translations to make his notes, and defended (in reply later to
the charges of Poggio Bracciolini) alterations in Jerome's hallowed text. 'If I
correct something', he said, 'I am not correcting Holy Scripture but its
translation . . . In that work I was not speaking of the truth of the Gospels but
of the elegance of the Latin language'. He was not reprehending Jerome, but
the textual degeneration of a thousand years. What, indeed, he asked, was

Holy Scripture if not a faithful text?[41] Valla, in fact, true humanist that he was, could contemplate scriptural emendations on grounds of stylistic felicity as well as accuracy. Others might be shocked, but Erasmus had found an ally.

Erasmus's publication of Valla's *Annotations* is perhaps the best-known example of the kind of fertilization which could take place through the conjunction of two worlds. It was not alone. One may regard it rather as the most dramatic example of a gradual process of germination, in which earlier work of Italian scholars was put to use and published by northern humanists. Manuscripts of a number of the Italian translations of Greek Fathers mentioned above had already found their way northwards in the fifteenth century. Several of Traversari's owe their presence in Oxford libraries to the interest of two leading English humanist book-collectors, William Grey (bishop of Ely from 1454 to 1478) and Robert Fleming. Another Oxford man – unlike them no humanist – who owned Traversari's Chrysostom was the crusty chancellor of the university, Thomas Gascoigne.[42] Some of these texts reached more readers after northern presses had put them into print. Thus Traversari's Latin version of the sermons of St. Ephraem appeared in a French translation in Paris about 1500, while the 1480 Bruges edition of his translation of the *Hierarchies* of Dionysius apparently served Colet as well as Lefèvre (who republished this work). The same fortunes attended George of Trebizond, whose Latin text of Cyril of Alexandria was printed by Josse Clichtove. The list could be extended. It seems that northern humanists did much to give their Italian predecessors the benefit of publication. Yet perhaps such editions tell more about associated chains of thought than they do about direct lines of influence. As with Protestant reformers' editions of earlier Hussite or Wycliffite writings, such publications may reflect the confirmation of existing or growing ideas, rather than the prompting of new ones: the discovery and brandishing of allies, rather than the advertisement of actual ancestry. Luther's remark about those who were Hussites without knowing it has its parallel on the humanist plane. A humanist, by definition, knew that he was one, but it was not until long after the invention of printing that he could meet and recognize all the thoughts and works of other humanists. And so, while Erasmus and Hutten were confirmed in views they already held by discovering such support in Lorenzo Valla, various other northern humanists found their work assisted by what had already been done in Italy.

---

[41] 'Ubi quid dicas tu esse sacram scripturam? certe nullam, nisi veram interpretationem . . . Itaque, ne multus sim, si quid emendo, non scripturam sacram emendo, sed illius interpretationem: neque in eam contumeliosus sum, sed pius potius . . . Ego autem in illo opere non de sententia Evangeliorum aiebam, sed de elegantia linguae latinae'. *Laurentii Vallae Opera* (Basel, 1540), pp. 268-9; cf. Raymond Marcel, 'Les perspectives de l' "apologétique", de Lorenzo Valla à Savonarole', *Courants religieux et humanisme à la fin du XVe et au début du XVIe siècle*, Colloque de Strasbourg, 1957 (Paris, 1959), p. 86.

[42] Weiss, *Humanism in England*, pp. 93, 103-4, 132; H.O. Coxe, *Catalogus codicum MSS, qui in colleqiis aulisque Oxoniensibus hodie adservantur* (Oxford, 1852), pt. I, pp. 22, 28, 31-33, 48.

It is surely significant, though, how much had to be done over again. The great achievements in patristic and biblical scholarship in this period were, despite the Italian researches we have noted, mainly the outcome of indigenous northern inspiration, and represented fresh approaches and new beginnings. As at all times when great intellectual changes are in the air, the sources of interaction and influence become too diffuse and vague to be properly traceable. Ideas become part of an individual's way of thinking without his necessarily knowing exactly how he has come by them. Intellectual paternity must always be partly putative. There were, however, some distinctive qualities about the northern ambience onto which humanist concerns were grafted, and these helped to determine the direction of new studies. Northern humanism grew upon and out of the long traditions of transalpine piety and theology.

The study of the Bible should be considered in this setting. As has been seen in the work of the *Devotio Moderna*, it existed on two different levels – as it always had. On the one hand, there was the application of the highest learning to the scriptural text. On the other, there was popular knowledge and the processes by which ordinary unlettered or unlearned persons gained biblical knowledge. In the developing schools of the north in the twelfth and thirteenth centuries, the Bible had been very intensively studied and commented upon, and its central role in the earlier part of that period is indicated by the very name *sacra pagina*, the sacred page, given to the subject in early faculties of theology. 'Theology', however – and the name itself in our sense of the word only arrived in the twelfth century – became distinguished from Bible study as the term for those dialectical methods of exposition and organization which came into use at that time. Such techniques of study (we need perhaps to remind ourselves, after all the invective that has been heaped upon them) were refined tools in their day, extremely useful for reaching systematic formulations of Christian faith and for use in biblical studies.

It seems clear, though, that in the later middle ages a considerable part of such studies – and therefore of the work of theologians – had become dissociated from the direct study of the biblical text. To some extent the study of theology became clogged by the sheer mass of work achieved; in combination with the perennial inertia of great educational establishments, this meant that very strong motivation was needed to make new beginnings. As Erasmus remarked, 'a Faculty never dies',[43] and its failure to do so may come to have a deadening effect. By the fifteenth century the direct study of the Bible had a relatively small place in university theology; many years of preliminary study of other texts, notably Peter Lombard's *Sentences* (*c*.1155-58), were required before the scripture itself was reached. Many students (unlike, for instance, John Wycliffe, with his decades of study at Oxford) did not persevere long enough to reach this point. If we do not yet know enough about biblical scholarship to draw a clear picture of the century and a half after 1350, it seems

---

[43] M.M. Phillips, *Erasmus and the Northern Renaissance* (London, 1949, new edn, revised and illustrated, Woodbridge, 1981), p. 151.

evident enough that 'the fifteenth century must have forgotten or disowned its ancestry: the dossier as a whole gives an impression of stunted growth. Biblical scholarship never achieved the standing of a separate discipline within the framework of sacred science. Students of theology got no preliminary training in language'.[44]

Naturally enough, dissatisfaction at this state of affairs was expressed. Various efforts were also made to regenerate the study of the Bible. In Italy at the foundation of the Collegium Gregorianum at Perugia in 1362, Nicolas Capocci, cardinal bishop of Tusculum, provided that six of the forty scholars were to study theology. He explained this arrangement on the grounds that 'in these days few clerical scholars are to be found who are learned in Holy Scripture [*sacra pagina*] and who know how to expound the word of God to the people'.[45] John Gerson, regent in theology and chancellor of Paris, objected to the sterilities of formal theology and voiced the need to return from its subtleties to Scripture. The reforming movements associated with John Wycliffe in England and John Hus in Bohemia in the late fourteenth and early fifteenth centuries, which originated in the theology faculties of Oxford and Prague, both centred upon a return to biblical sources. And both had the effect of turning attention towards fresh scriptural translation.

To cast even a cursory glance over the vernacular Bibles of this period is to gain some sense of the isolation of academic theology from lay piety. The later middle ages were extremely prolific in the production of vernacular scriptures. By the end of the fourteenth century, the Bible had been translated into French, English, German, Czech and Italian. The number of incunabula editions of these texts measures the extent of contemporary demand. In the year 1471, two complete Italian Bibles were printed in Venice; the first German Bible to be printed, the Mentel Bible of 1466, was reissued in eleven new editions before 1500; before 1501, there had appeared more than thirty editions in six vernaculars.

The Brothers of the Common Life, whose movement, as we have seen, combined a rejection of academic disputes with a simpler scriptural piety, represented one effort to bridge the gap between Christian learning and Christian piety. The northern humanists were making another attempt to draw together these diverging strands – though their work was still maturing when it was overtaken by a fresh tide, in which the popular tended to outweigh the learned. At the heart of their studies lay the application of improved linguistic skills and critical methods to the scriptures and to the Fathers – themselves revered as models for what the humanists were trying to do. This work was humanist not only in the sense that classical languages and classical learning were essential to it, but also in the continuous awareness of the wide purposes

---

[44] Beryl Smalley, 'The Bible in the Medieval Schools', *CHB*, ii, p. 219.

[45] Hastings Rashdall, *The Universities of Europe in the Middle Ages*, ed. F.M. Powicke and A.B. Emden (Oxford, 1936), ii, p. 41, n. 5.

which textual studies served. They were to be the means of spiritual regeneration for individuals and for the whole of Christendom.

Having outlined the general setting, we may turn to the work of individual humanists. In France, Spain, England and the Low Countries many assumptions were shared by Lefèvre, Ximenes, Colet and Erasmus, but one may be as struck by their differences. All were concerned with biblical renovation, but their methods embraced a wide range of criticism. All strove to renew the church; yet it was Erasmus, the only one of the four not to pursue this objective through an administrative office in the church (and who refused a cardinalate), who had far and away the greatest influence on the future – ecclesiastical and secular.

Jacques Lefèvre d'Etaples (*c*. 1455-1536), described by Pomponazzi as 'second to none in learning in this age', might seem in some ways to stand closer to the work of Italian humanists than Erasmus, yet in the end one may judge him to be less truly humanist. Sharing with Erasmus the desire 'to join wisdom and piety with cloquence',[46] to find harmony and enlightenment through a deeper knowledge of classical and Christian antiquity, he too devoted himself to years of textual labours. But in Lefèvre's case it is possible to discern more of a progression, from Aristotelian philosophy to mystical contemplation, while his evangelical piety threatened him more seriously with suspicions of sympathy with Protestant Reform. Whereas Erasmus removed himself from Basel after the outbreak of iconoclastic frenzy in 1529, Lefèvre, charged with Lutheran views in 1525, took refuge in Strasbourg, where the city authorities, steadily moving towards a full Reformation, had lately been removing ecclesiastical images.

Lefèvre made several visits to Italy, but he was a late beginner. His first journey took place in 1491-92, at which time he had published nothing, and his Greek learning (helped by the presence of George Hermonymos in Paris) was also taken up late. Direct knowledge of Italy impressed Lefèvre, like Colet, with Florentine Neoplatonism, but it was the pursuit of Aristotle, rather than Plato, which inspired his Greek learning. Insisting that a proper understanding of Aristotelian philosophy was indispensable to the study of the gospel, he embarked upon thirty years' labour of editing and commenting on almost the entire corpus of Aristotle's works. Between 1494 and 1515 he produced editions of the *Physics, Nicomachean Ethics, Organon, Politics* and *Metaphysics*, and also wrote paraphrases of most of Aristotle's works. Lefèvre's wide reading in the works of ancient historians, orators and poets gave him a familiarity with the world of antiquity which enabled him to move about in it with the ease which distinguished the work of the best humanists. This intimacy and proximity, his union of learning with imaginative comprehension, make it possible to compare pages of his writings with those of Erasmus

---

[46] Eugene F. Rice Jr., 'Humanist Aristotelianism in France: Jacques Lefèvre d'Etaples and his Circle', *Humanism in France at the End of the Middle Ages and in the Early Renaissance*, ed. A.H.T. Levi (Manchester and New York, 1970), pp. 139, 143.

and Montaigne. Yet the comparison has to be made with reservations, for Lefèvre always wanted to penetrate through and beyond antiquity to mystical perceptions alien to these other essayists. Lefèvre, convinced that 'the theology of the Aristotelians agrees and unites with Christian wisdom in a great harmony and concord', was thoroughly humanistic in his rejection of scholastic method and commentary, but Aristotle for him remained more of a 'pious philosopher', moral and orthodox, than he was for secular Italian Aristotelians. Lefèvre's Aristotle was to be seen in the guise of priest and theologian, whose metaphysics and philosophy shone with the 'immense light' of divine illumination, even though God had not yet appeared visibly in the world.[47]

It is understandable that, with this outlook, Lefèvre was attracted by the work of Nicholas of Cusa, as well as Pico della Mirandola's cabalistic learning and Ficino's Platonism. These sympathies bore fruit in various editions, including the hermetic books attributed to Hermes Trismegistus and the *Celestial Hierarchy* of Dionysius the pseudo-Areopagite. Such works reveal the way in which Lefèvre's humanism was irradiated, transcended, and limited by his mysticism. His life reflects both the tension of conflicting traditions and the effort to fuse them. Drawn towards but rejecting the vocation of a monastic life, in a way reminiscent of Thomas More, he responded to the call of active reform by serving in the 1520s as vicar-general to Bishop Briçonnet in the diocese of Meaux. And Lefèvre's religious commitment got the better of his reasoning when he refused to accept such critical arguments as Grocyn put forward for doubting the Dionysian writings as authentic evidence of the early church.

The third and most important part of Lefèvre's work – his scriptural editions and commentaries – was truly evangelical. His search for illumination and Christian regeneration caused him to concentrate increasingly upon the study of biblical texts and made him the most distinguished exponent of Christian humanism in France. He shared – with different emphases – the double concern expressed by Erasmus for purifying the sources of Christian doctrine and making them more widely available. Though unlike Erasmus in his critical inhibitions as well as his style (Lucian was as alien to Lefèvre as he was congenial to Erasmus), Lefèvre showed himself as a critic in his own right. The *Quincuplex Psalter*, which he brought out in 1509, was from this point of view a decisive achievement. It set out in parallel columns the different versions of Jerome's text which Lefèvre had discovered, interpolated with his own resumé and commentary. A contemporary called it a new form of exegesis, and though, as we have seen, Lefèvre was not the first to devise this method – nor

---

[47] Ibid., p. 141; Renaudet, *Préréforme et Humanisme,* p. 155, n. 1; Eugene F. Rice Jr., 'The Humanist Idea of Christian Antiquity: Lefèvre d'Etaples and his Circle', *Studies in the Renaissance*, ix (1962), pp. 126-41; reprinted in *French Humanism, 1470-1600*, ed. Werner L. Gundersheimer (New York, 1969), pp. 163-80.

indeed the first to put such an effort into print[48] – his book marked an important step forward in biblical scholarship. While remaining conservative in his elaborate allegorizing of the Psalms, Lefèvre ventured, despite the limitations of his Hebrew learning, timidly to suggest some textual corrections. Three years later came the Epistles of St. Paul, complete with grammatical notes and commentary. This also broke new ground. Beside the Vulgate text was printed (in modestly small type) a version which Lefèvre had made himself from the Greek, showing his concern to get back, behind the Vulgate if necessary, to the exact thought of the apostle. That Lefèvre's grammatical corrections were often not very felicitous is less important than his readiness to make them – which he himself found it necessary to excuse on the grounds that the Vulgate could not be attributed to Jerome. Within his limits then, Lefèvre was prepared to reject ecclesiastical tradition in the cause of apostolic truth. This was demonstrated still more clearly in the *Discussion of Mary Magdalene* (1518), which argued, contrary to accepted views, that Mary the sister of Martha and Lazarus, Mary Magdalene who was delivered of seven devils, and the penitent who anointed Christ's feet were three different persons, not one. This work occasioned a considerable controversy, in which John Fisher defended the traditional interpretation while Josse Clichtove came to the support of Lefèvre.[49]

For Lefèvre the power of the Gospel was transcendent. 'The Word of God suffices. This alone is enough to effect life everlasting'. He prefaced his *Commentaries on the Four Gospels* (1521) with a call to bishops and kings to devote themselves to intensifying true worship through the Word of God: ' . . . and may this be the only striving, comfort and desire of all, to know the gospel, to follow the gospel, everywhere to advance the gospel'.[50] In the diocese of Meaux, Lefèvre had a bishop to answer this call, and there he was able to work for the cause of evangelical reform, especially through the publication of vernacular scriptures and liturgical translations.

Despite the conclusions of some of his contemporaries, Lefèvre was neither another Erasmus nor another Luther. He stood somewhere in between, sharing views with both, but in the end divided from both, distinct above all perhaps in the quality of mystical illumination without which he believed all humanist labours must leave the mind in some degree of darkness. But such distinctions did not inhibit the alarmist orthodox who were so distrustful of the activities of *humanistae theologizantes*, theologizing humanists. And Lefèvre, whose edition of St. Paul had been criticized for correcting the Vulgate, was in

[48] For the first polyglot Bible text to be printed, a psalter with the Greek and Latin in parallel columns, published by Johannes Crastonus at Milan in 1481, see W. Schwarz, *Principles and Problems of Biblical Translation: Some Reformation Controversies and their Background* (Cambridge, 1955), p. 106.

[49] A. Hufstader, 'Lefèvre d'Etaples and the Magdalen', *Studies in the Renaissance*, xvi (1969), pp. 31-60; Richard Rex, 'The Polemical Theologian', in *John Fisher*, ed. Bradshaw and Duffy (above n. 7), pp. 109-30.

[50] *Catholic Reformation*, ed. Olin (above n. 8), pp. 111-12.

1526 labelled, together with Erasmus, with this disparaging term by Noël Bédier, theologian of the Sorbonne. The grounds of this attack are interesting. Bédier found both Lefèvre's commentaries and Erasmus's *Paraphrases* of the New Testament objectionable in their claim to 'drink from rivers which flow from the very source of divine wisdom, and not from distant rivulets which have degenerated through their great distance from that source; that is to say, they always have in their hands the writings of Origen, Tertullian, Cyprian, Basil, Hilary, Chrysostom, Ambrose, Jerome and others like them, instead of the scholastics, such as Peter Lombard, Alexander Hales, Thomas, Bonaventure, Richard, Ockham and writers of this kind' – and for this they proclaimed themselves humanists.[51]

In the history of Spanish humanism a dominant position is held by Cardinal Ximenes (or Jiménez) de Cisneros (1436-1517), whose Polyglot Bible was the outstanding humanist achievement of the peninsula in these years. Like most men of distinction in his time, Ximenes had his years of Italian experience – in his case six, spent practising canon law in Rome. Later, he turned his exceptional influence and interests towards the concern common to contemporary Christian humanists: ecclesiastical reform, promoted by a programme of studies. Ximenes was an Observant Fransciscan, an order he joined, significantly, years after having entered the priesthood and having occupied a diocesan office. In the 1490s, as confessor to Queen Isabella and archbishop of Toledo, he used his powerful position to direct various reforms, including (simultaneous with Standonck's work in France) the improvement of monastic observance. The two achievements for which he is deservedly famous are those which link him most closely with the ideas of the leading humanists of the north, whom he admired and tried to attract to his country. The foundation of Alcalá University, and the Complutensian Polyglot Bible produced there (*Complutum* being the Latin for Alcalá), belonged, however, to a rather different world from that of Erasmus. Behind the similarities of methods and intentions lay a closer attachment to ecclesiastical horizons, as is attested by Ximenes's ten-year tenure of the rank of cardinal, which Erasmus refused.

The foundation at Alcalá, which finally opened, after years of preparation and building, in 1508, functioned within the context of ecclesiastical teaching and training. Ximenes was anxious to train an elite of educated clerics to serve his church, and theology – to which other arts and sciences were regarded as handmaidens – was to be the queen of his university. Hoping to renew theological studies by an infusion of the *via moderna* from the north, Ximenes made Alcalá innovative in the place it gave to nominalist teaching. The new school was, however, modernistic in other ways as well – and in ways more in tune with humanism. The cardinal was concerned with purifying the sources of learning, with the direct study of the Bible as the central task of theology. He

---

[51] D.P. Walker, 'Origène en France au début du XVIe siècle', in *Courants religieux et humanisme* (above n. 41), pp. 110-111.

also had a grandiose plan (only partially realized) for publishing the whole of Aristotle in both Greek and a new Latin translation.

Greek was for Ximenes the key to true theology, and the greatest novelty of his new university was the study of the Bible through the original languages of both testaments. Already in 1502 he seems to have begun to collect around him what has been described as a small biblical academy of men – Jewish converts and hellenists – whose linguistic accomplishments could further his textual studies. Some of the specialists he attracted to his circle served both in the university and on the great biblical edition. The converted Jew, Alfonso de Zamora, who inaugurated the teaching of Hebrew at Alcalá in 1512, and the Cretan Demetrios Doucas, who held the chair of Greek from 1513 to 1518, both played an important role in the preparation of the Polyglot Bible. Alcalá, like the later foundation of Louvain in which Erasmus played a large part, was a centre for multilingual studies, though the different languages did not have an exact parity. Forty chairs were planned, including one (abortively) for Arabic, but it was those in Greek, Hebrew and Aramaic in the trilingual college of St. Jerome whose achievements became famous. It is to be noted that Ximenes himself accorded precedence to Greek, the chair in which (unlike those in Hebrew and Arabic) was to continue to be filled providing anyone at all was present to benefit from its instruction.[52]

If Ximenes's biblical plans went back to 1502, it was from about 1510 that they began to take definite shape, as he intensified his search for manuscripts. Although he did not live to enjoy the success of the monumental work he had inspired, directed and paid for, the bulk of it was completed by the time of his death. The New Testament was printed in 1514 and, three years later in the summer of 1517, the Old Testament was finished, four months before the cardinal died. In the meantime was concluded an associated work, a triple lexicon for Greek, Hebrew and Aramaic. The whole, finally presented to the world about 1522, represented an immense achievement of printing as well as learning, a genuine landmark in the history of biblical scholarship. Yet one should not jump to the conclusion that Ximenes's aims were those of Manetti or Erasmus. Indeed, we learn something about the context of his work from the way in which he referred to the Vulgate of the Latin church, flanked by the Hebrew and Greek of the synagogue and the eastern church, as resembling Christ between the two thieves. It was essentially a matter of textual restoration, rather than the linguistic emendation dear to the minds of humanists. In some ways there is a closer parallel with the biblical correction of the Windesheimers than with Erasmus's work. Cardinal Ximenes concentrated his batteries of scholarly skills not so much for comparative linguistic studies as to

---

[52] Basil Hall, *Humanists and Protestants, 1500-1900* (Edinburgh, 1990), chapter 1, pp. 1-51, 'Cardinal Jiménez de Cisneros and the Complutensian Bible'; cf. idem, 'The Trilingual College of San Ildefonso and the Making of the Complutensian Polyglot Bible', in *SCH*, v (1969), pp. 114-46; P.S. Allen, 'The Trilingual Colleges of the Early Sixteenth Century', in *Erasmus: Lectures and Wayfaring Sketches* (Oxford, 1934), pp. 138-63.

establish, through textual analysis of Latin, Greek and Hebrew manuscripts, the correct words of tradition for the benefit of the western church. The main objective of the undertaking was to end the multiplication of erroneous versions – multiplying through print even more seriously than they had in manuscript – by reconstructing through laborious comparison of texts the correct Vulgate. The whole operation was attended by a respect for authority alien to mature humanist thinking. To establish from variant manuscript sources the best and most ancient form of the text was a task of considerable magnitude, but the refusal to make corrections beyond the sanctions of such sources was also a considerable limitation. As his own words testify, Ximenes gave the place of honour to the Vulgate, to which the Greek and Hebrew were ancillary.

It would be wrong to disparage Ximenes's work for these reasons. The vital aim of his great labours was spiritual renewal. The verve of the edition lay in the urge to reach the inner pulse of the sacred text, to uncover the 'hidden mysteries' of the divine spirit which lay beneath the shadow of the literal form. This itself can be related to humanistic intentions, and the cardinal expressed hopes of reviving the 'hitherto moribund' study of scripture.[53] Yet the reactions of one of the humanist collaborators on the Polyglot reflect dissatisfaction with its methods. Elio Antonio de Nebrija entered the cardinal's service in 1513, and his Hebrew learning enabled him to do valuable work on the revision of the Bible in its final stages. He was as passionately concerned as was Ximenes for the restoration of the scriptural text, but was prepared to go much further than Ximenes in using linguistic knowledge to improve it. Nebrija would have liked a more rigorous comparative use of the triple linguistic sources; discrepancies in the Vulgate New Testament should be resolved by having recourse to the Greek; to understand differences in the Latin or Greek texts of the Old Testament it was necessary to ask questions about the Hebrew. The logical outcome would have been what Erasmus did, which was far from Ximenes's intention: to correct the Vulgate to the extent of making a new Latin translation. Nebrija himself claimed that his object was to reconstruct the original Vulgate, but he certainly conceived of this task differently from Cardinal Ximenes.

To turn to England and John Colet may seem, after Lefèvre and Alcalá, like moving into a sidestream – if not a backwater – of the humanist world. England in these years produced no great works of patristic or biblical scholarship comparable to those of the continent. Leading English humanists long continued to look abroad for the publication, as well as the purchase, of texts. More's *Utopia* was first published at Louvain in 1516, and the first Greek book was not

---

[53] 'quorum ab aeterno praevisa impositio incredibilem opem affert ad propalandos spirituales abstrusosque sensus et detegenda arcana mysteria: quae sub ipso litteralis textus umbraculo spiritus sanctus velavit': '. . . ut incipiant divinarum litterarum studia hactenus intermortua nunc tandem reviviscere'. Polyglot Bible (1515-17), part i, *Vetus testamentum multiplici lingua nunc primo impressum*, from the prologue addressed by Cisneros to Pope Leo X.

printed in England until 1543. Yet if this tells us something about the narrowness of the book market in England, as well as about the internationalism of contemporary humanist pursuits, it leaves out of account those currents of personal influence which could count for so much. Colet held a respected place among the northern humanists, although he wrote little, and has to be judged by report as well as by his work.

'When I listen to Colet it seems to me that I am listening to Plato himself', wrote Erasmus.[54] Thanks to the commendations of Colet's friends, it is still possible to apprehend something of this outspoken, impetuous, self-denying man, who was able to kindle the spirit of Erasmus and rebuke Henry VIII in public without provoking his ire. As the only surviving child of a family of twenty-two, he devoted much of the inheritance which came to him from his father, a mayor of London, to the refoundation of the school of St. Paul's, where he was appointed dean in 1504. He shared and exemplified the twin dissatisfactions of the best contemporary humanists: with the aridities of traditional modes of learning, and the shortcomings of the institutions of the church. What he learned at Oxford of scholastic Aristotelianism seems merely to have made him aware of what his education lacked. According to Erasmus

> Scotists, who are thought by ordinary men to have minds which are somehow specially acute, seemed to him, he [Colet] used to say, dull and slow-witted, and anything rather than gifted. To argue all the time about other men's opinions and language, gnawing away first at one point and then at another, and cutting everything up into fragments, was the mark of a barren and ill-furnished mind.[55]

Had his search – which he also confided to Erasmus – for a spiritual community 'truly sworn to live the life of the Gospel' been more successful, Colet might have made into the vocation of his maturity the life of retreat which he prepared among the Carthusians for his old age. In those days it was easier to find retreats for the mind than for the spirit. Yet the journey which Colet made to Italy in the 1490s might be seen as a spiritual as well as an intellectual pilgrimage – he went, as Erasmus put it, 'like a keen businessman in search of valuable goods'.[56]

What Colet had vainly sought in England, he found in Italy in the teaching of the Florentine Platonists. Marsilio Ficino (whom Colet corresponded with, but apparently never met) and Pico della Mirandola both profoundly influenced him. The different uses to which Colet and Erasmus put their Italian-Greek experience might be taken as an indication of their differences of upbringing

[54] Erasmus to Robert Fisher, 5 December 1499; Allen (ed.), i, p. 273, no. 118; *CWE*, i, p. 235. See Gleason, *Colet* (above n. 5) for an important reassessment of Colet, which shows how the long-accepted portrait of Frederic Seebohm was based on misinterpretation of Erasmus. This flattery needs to be treated with caution (pp. 111-12 in Chapter 5, 'Erasmus and Colet: First Encounters').

[55] Allen (ed.), iv, p. 520, no. 1211; *CWE*, 8, p. 238; Gleason, *Colet*, pp. 141-4.

[56] Allen (ed.), iv, pp. 515, 521, no. 1211; *CWE*, 8, pp. 233, 239; E.W. Hunt, *Dean Colet and his Theology* (London, 1956), pp. 44-5.

and background, as well as temperament. Whereas Colet went to Italy in his late twenties and returned after four years inspired by humanist teaching and his increased knowledge of Italian Neoplatonism, he was nearly fifty before he became fully alive to the need for profound Greek learning. His continental learning was turned primarily not to literary or scholarly objectives, but to the evangelical work of preaching and lecturing on the text of the Bible. Erasmus, on the other hand, who was not far off forty before he set foot in Italy was by then, as we have seen, master of Greek; and for him the study and restoration of antiquity were the united and preeminent tasks of reform. Whereas Colet took as his forum the traditional organs of pulpit and school, that of Erasmus, more modern and dynamic, was the scholar's study, opened to the world through the printer's office. Colet, though almost exactly the same age as Erasmus, belonged to a different generation. Perhaps this helps to explain the respect which Erasmus had for him, and the friendship that helped bring Colet wider renown.

Colet's concerns, which took fruit in his new school and in his preaching, were essentially biblical. Erasmus, referring to Colet's work at St. Paul's, describes how he adopted the unusual practice of preaching himself at every great feast in his cathedral. 'Moreover, in his own church he did not choose a text at random from the Gospels or the apostolic Epistles, but put forward some one subject, which he pursued in several sermons until he finished it, for example the Gospel of St. Matthew, the Creed, the Lord's Prayer'.[57] The extent to which Colet had absorbed humanist learning became evident soon after his return from Italy in 1496, when he began to deliver a sequence of public lectures in Oxford (possibly to satisfy the requirements for the degree of B.D.) on the Epistles of St. Paul. Colet's form of exposition – either at this time, or later in his life – may not (despite what used to be thought) have been very far removed from traditional homiletic methods, but in his desire to reach and expound the spiritual wisdom of St. Paul he drew on what he had learned from Ficino. He explicitly referred to Ficino 'touching the excellency of love', and in his allegorical exposition of Genesis made use of Pico's commentary, the *Heptaplus*.[58] Colet also showed he was in tune with some of the changing thought of his time in making one complete text the topic for continuous public commentary.

The statutes of St. Paul's school reflect the characteristic ingredients of Colet's humanist piety. His pupils were to unite pure style with pure doctrine. Schooled in the faith through vernacular learning of the catechism, creed and Ten Commandments, the children in his classes were expected to obey the

[57] Allen (ed.), iv, p. 516, no. 1211; *CWE*, 8, p. 235.
[58] John Colet, *An Exposition of St. Paul's Epistle to the Romans*, ed. J.H. Lupton (London, 1873), p. 32; Sears Jayne, *John Colet and Marsilio Ficino* (Oxford, 1963), p. 21ff; J.B. Trapp, 'An English Late Medieval Cleric and Italian Thought: The Case of John Colet, Dean of St. Paul's (1467-1519)', in *Medieval English Religious and Ethical Literature*, ed. G. Kratzmann and J. Simpson (Cambridge, 1986), pp. 233-50; Gleason, *Colet*, pp. 167-84 on 'Colet's Exegesis in Practice', and his essentially homiletic interests.

rules of Latin prosody just as they were to kneel at the sound of the sacring bell. The authors they were to study were all such 'as have the veray Romayne eliquence joyned withe wisdome specially Cristyn' – those who wrote with 'clene and chast laten'. The Fathers appeared as models alongside Sallust and Cicero.

> All barbary, all corrupcion, all laten adulterate, which ignorant blynde folis brought into this worlde, and with the same hath distayned and poysenyd the olde laten spech and the varay Romayne tong which in the tyme of Tully and Salust and Virgill and Terence was usid; whiche also seint Jerome and seint Ambrose and seint Austen and many hooly doctors lernyd in theyr tymes, – I say that fylthynesse and all such abusyon which the later blynde worlde brought in, which more ratheyr may be callid blotterature thenne litterature, I utterly abbanysh and exclude oute of this scole.[59]

Colet, with his desire for double purity, was not quite at home with humanist Christian precepts. He was too conscious of the possible conflict between style and doctrine; his selection of authors safe for youthful study (Lactantius, Prudentius, Sedulius, St. Augustine, St. Jerome, and Baptista Mantuanus and Erasmus) left outside the curriculum some of the best Latin literature. Humanist studies in England certainly owed a debt to Colet, but what he rejected was as much a part of his heritage as what he embraced.

So, once again, we are brought back to Erasmus. It is always hard to do justice to Erasmus, and never more so than in discussion of his biblical and patristic writings, the centre of his life's work. It takes greatness to appreciate the great, especially among contemporaries. It is a measure of Erasmus's uniqueness that he obtained recognition of a previously unparalleled kind among his contemporaries throughout Europe. When he arrived in England he was already known; when he left Basel he was given a ceremonial farewell. He received offers and invitations from Rome and Zürich, from the kings of France and England, from pope and emperor, and made more friends and enemies with his pen than anyone had ever done in the course of a lifetime. Had he chosen to, he could have enjoyed any number of secure positions, secular or ecclesiastical, instead of leading a roving uncomfortable existence which culminated in the horrors of becoming a householder in the antiquity of his sixties. Yet he preferred to remain as independent and unattached as possible, free to speak and write according to his own convictions. There was one overriding reason why he did so; he wished to be free to devote himself to his chosen work – the freeing of captive theology.

Having proceeded this far, it should now be easier for us to see this dedication in its proper setting. Erasmus's achievement was unique in its scale, its scope and its quality, but it also belonged to a context, and among the influences which helped to forge it the *Devotio Moderna* and Colet's England

---

[59] J.H. Lupton, *A Life of John Colet, D.D.* (London, 1909), pp. 169, 279-80; Trapp, 'An English Late Medieval Cleric', pp. 249-50; Maria Dowling, *Humanism in the Age of Henry VIII* (London, 1986), pp. 113-17.

must always be set alongside the critical *Annotations* and Greek studies of Valla's Italy. Erasmus's mind was cosmopolitan, unpledged to loyalties of nation or race; he took the whole of Europe for his library, study, audience – and home. Yet it was as Erasmus of Rotterdam that he made himself famous, as a Dutchman that he wrote, and in his own country that he would have liked to die as a last Dutch prayer escaped from his lips. 'My dear Holland', whose fertility and manners he warmly defended, was 'a country I must always praise and venerate, since to her I owe my life's beginning'.[60] His lifelong devotion to biblical studies, and the belief that good learning and good life were intrinsically associated and had their deepest sources in the Christian gospel, went back to those Dutch beginnings and the nurturing influences of the Brothers of the Common Life.

England, too, through the perceptive Colet and the happy genius of Thomas More, helped to give Erasmus that assurance which is needed to undertake a vast work. What happened to Edward Gibbon on the Capitol on 15 October 1764 happened to Erasmus through various encounters over the years with the living and the dead. While Gibbon was inspired by ruins to write about decline and decay, Erasmus was inspired both by living decay and the examples of others, present and past, to undertake a work of rebirth, to renew the study of the Bible by restoring its text and the whole setting of scriptural knowledge. It was an aim which may have gained something from Colet's example. We do not have to suppose that Colet gave Erasmus anything which was not already present – perhaps more latent than active – in the latter's mind. Their meeting at Oxford in 1499 should be seen not as a dramatic turning-point, but rather in the light of one of the Proverbs of Solomon which Erasmus quoted in his *Adages*, 'Iron sharpeneth iron; so a man sharpeneth the countenance of his friend'.[61] Erasmus was sharpened into delaying no further the inauguration of his *opus*. And the first step towards the fulfilment of that purpose was the acquisition of Greek.

Colet came too late to the realization that Greek was essential for the study of Scripture. He had still not seen this when in 1504 Erasmus wrote to him in a tone of apology (or perhaps irritation) that lingering in Greek gardens was a means of 'gathering by the way many flowers that will be useful for the future, even in sacred studies'.[62] Erasmsus never lost his sense of purpose – even if others could not always see it. By March 1516, however, the world could be in no doubt. The appearance of Erasmus's New Testament was a historic moment for the world at large and for himself. It marked the achievement of an objective he had long been straining towards: the publication of the central document of the faith in its original apostolic language. At this point Colet became aware of the gulf between himself and the New Testament. Erasmus's

---

[60] Philips, *Adages*, p. 210.
[61] Ibid, p. 27.
[62] Allen (ed.), i, p. 406, no. 181; *CWE*, 2, p. 88 (letter of *c*. December, 1504, Paris).

book spurred the forty-nine-year-old dean to school himself in Greek, but he died three years later without achieving this.

There were, therefore, long years of resolute preparation and arduous study behind the achievement of 1516. Another milestone, already noted above, completes the triad of the most formative influences upon Erasmus. Erasmus's 1505 edition of Valla's *Annotations on the New Testament* was the outcome of a delighted recognition. In discovering this work (described by a recent authority as 'probably the most crucial book he ever read')[63] Erasmus discovered his community of interest with one whom he already greatly admired as a master of Latinity. It became clear how humanist philological tools could be used for the highest religious purposes. Perhaps, in taking Valla so much to heart, Erasmus attributed to him some of his own features. But if he transformed what he gained, he was in no doubt as to the value of his debt, and the publication of the *Annotations* was almost like an advertisement for what was to follow. During the decade which intervened between its appearance and that of the *Novum instrumentum*, Erasmus was furiously at work with his Greek, and with writings which prepared the way for his edition. In 1501 he had written four volumes (which no longer survive) on the Epistle to the Romans.[64] And when he left England in 1506 after his second visit, he left behind a manuscript containing a Latin translation of the New Testament which shows how far his project was already taking shape.

Erasmus's New Testament, containing the Greek text together with his Latin translation (first printed in full in 1519), received immediate recognition: applause and opposition. The delight of friends was matched by the criticism of opponents. This might seem surprising in view of the amount of biblical studies and criticism already in progress. What was it that peculiarly distinguished the work of Erasmus? To answer that it was the fullness of his humanist learning is not entirely to beg the question; he had shown himself ready to go further than any of his contemporaries in applying the convictions of his scholarship to the scriptural text – even where it meant rejecting venerable, revered tradition. To his enemies this was nowhere more apparent than in the brazen daring of the title and the impudence of the new Latin translation, which did not merely correct the Vulgate but actually replaced it. To his friends, on the other hand,

---

[63] Louis Bouyer, 'Erasmus in Relation to the Medieval Biblical Tradition', *Cambridge History of the Bible*, ii, p. 494.

[64] Erasmus was long preoccupied by this work and keenly aware of the Greek learning it called for. He stressed the value of St. Paul's Epistles in the first draft of the *Enchiridion*, and in 1514 was again telling a correspondent about the commentaries he had undertaken on the Epistles. Though the four volumes Erasmus referred to have not survived, the title of his paraphrase of Romans indicates that this could be seen as a commentary: *In Epistolam Pauli ad Romanos paraphrasis, quae commentarii vice possit esse* (Basel, 1518). Allen, i, pp. 374-5 (no. 164), 404 (no. 181), 570 (no. 296); *CWE*, 2, pp. 52-3, 86-7, 300; Schwarz, *Principles and Problems*, p. 131; *Erasmus and Cambridge*, ed. D.F.S. Thomson and H.C. Porter (Toronto, 1963), p. 46; B. Hall, 'Erasmus: Biblical Scholar and Catholic Reformer', in *Humanists and Protestants*, pp. 52-85, originally in *Erasmus*, ed. Dorey, pp. 81-113.

Fig. 14 Unfinished charcoal drawing of Erasmus made by Dürer in 1520 on his visit to the Netherlands. The sitting was interrupted by some courtly visitors.

the greatness of the achievement lay in its very freshness: here they had the Gospel readily available for the first time in its original tongue; here they could read (whether Greek scholars or not) the words of the New Testament with a directness and immediacy which endowed them with new life. They might feel they were reading it for the first time. Erasmus did for the New Testament, in his various editions, something comparable to what Aldus Manutius did for the Greek classics; he published the Greek text for the first time in readily accessible form, and in editions much larger, less cumbersome and more 'popular' than the Polyglot of Alcalá.

The alarm aroused by Erasmus's book was expressed to him before its appearance by the Louvain theologian Martin van Dorp. He wrote in terms which were friendly but highly critical. Having referred to the damages done by the *Praise of Folly*, he continued:

> I understand that you have also revised the New Testament and written notes on over 1,000 passages, to the great profit of theologians. This raises another point on which I should like in the friendliest possible spirit to issue a warning. In the first place I say nothing of the efforts of Lorenzo Valla and Jacques Lefèvre in the same field, for I do not doubt that you will surpass them in every respect. But what sort of an operation this is, to correct the Scriptures, and in particular to correct the Latin copies by means of the Greek, requires careful thought. If I can show that the Latin version contains no admixture of falsehood or mistake, will not you have to confess that the labours of all those who try to correct it are superfluous, except for pointing

out now and again places where the translator might have given the sense more fully? Now I differ from you on this question of truth and integrity, and claim that these are qualities of the Vulgate edition that we have in common use. For it is not reasonable that the whole church, which has always used this edition and still both approves and uses it, should for all these centuries have been wrong. Nor is it probable that all those holy Fathers should have been deceived, and all those saintly men who relied on this version when deciding the most difficult questions in general councils, defending and expounding the faith, and publishing canons to which even kings submitted their civil power.[65]

Dorp expressed the horror felt by many theologians at the mere thought of correcting so hallowed a text as the Vulgate, venerated through the church's long usage. And here was Erasmus not merely making corrections and alterations, but offering an entire new Latin version, changing even the very title. This fundamental departure from tradition in the name of improved learning was indeed the crux, and the shock of conservatives was not to be dispelled by Erasmus's claim that his text was intended for private reading, not for formal ecclesiastical use. It is clear that Erasmus had taken a position very different from that of Ximenes, whose corrections were tempered with scrupulous reverence for the Vulgate text. This was carried even to the length of providing a Greek translation of the troublesome *Comma Johanneum* (the spurious addition on the Trinity in 1 John 5:7,8) which Erasmus – also characteristically – omitted, though he restored it, after virulent opposition, in his third edition of 1522. Understandably, it was not Erasmus's New Testament, dedicated to Leo X in the confident hope of its welcome, which received the pope's licence in 1520, but the Polyglot of Cardinal Ximenes. But Erasmus, though his critical methods were very far from perfect, had done something unique for biblical scholarship, and the scandal, as well as the praise, gives the measure of his achievement.

Closely linked with this biblical work was the long series of patristic editions which occupied Erasmus through many years of his working life. Between 1516 and 1530 he brought out (in some cases supplementing his first edition with a later expanded version) editions of Jerome, Cyprian, Hilary, Irenacus, Chrysostom, Ambrose, Athanasius, Augustine and Basil. When he died he was working on Origen. It was a prodigious undertaking, enough in itself to make a lifetime's study for any ordinary man. Given Erasmus's other publications, it is an amazing accomplishment, even allowing for the assistants who helped him with the work. To the editor, these publications were indispensable to the task he had set himself. The Greek and Latin Fathers, classical authors of Christian antiquity, were essential to the true understanding of Christ and the Apostles, and must be read in their right shape. The words which Erasmus put into the mouth of a character in one of his *Colloquies* might well have been spoken by their author:

[65] Allen (ed.), ii, p. 14, no. 304; *CWE*, 3, pp. 20-21. On this letter and Erasmus's 1516 text (nearly 550 pages of the New Testament itself, followed by 450 pages of annotations) see *Erasmus and Cambridge*, p. 43; Phillips, *Erasmus* (above, n. 43), pp. 87-8.

You see this book of the Gospels? In it one talks with me who long ago, as an eloquent companion of the two disciples on the road to Emmaus, caused them to forget the hardship of their journey but made their hearts burn most fervently in their wonder at his enchanting speech. In this book Paul speaks to me, in this Isaiah and the rest of the prophets. Here the honey-tongued Chrysostom converses with me, here Basil, here Augustine, here Jerome, here Cyprian, and other teachers as learned as they are eloquent. Do you know any other talkers so delightful that you would compare them with these? Or in such company, which never fails me, do you suppose solitude can become tedious?[66]

One is reminded of Machiavelli's description of himself on his farm outside Florence, taking off his dirty workaday clothes to attire himself with courtly propriety for an evening's delightful converse with his favourites among the ancients. Erasmus's spokesman was certainly a very Erasmian sort of Carthusian – the kind which More or Colet or Lefèvre might have made – in defending the garb and calling of his order by appeal to such literary pursuits. And the diet of his learning was the Bible and the Fathers, teachers in whom true wisdom and true eloquence were combined.

Erasmus's patristic editions thus formed part of his whole majestic programme. The church Fathers, essential models for scriptural exegesis and for the eloquence of true philosophy, had to be restored to their correct form. As it was, they were hopelessly corrupt. 'Jerome's works', wrote Erasmus, 'especially those on the Bible, have been so corrupted that if Jerome himself were to come alive again he would neither know nor understand his own books'.[67] It was a fate with which their editor could heartily sympathize. Were not some of his own works issued during his lifetime in translations distorted by Protestant enthusiasm? One might, too, see a certain progression in the editions of these works corresponding to changes in Erasmus himself. He came to value the Greek Fathers above the Latin and to give the highest esteem of all to Origen, yet he remained faithful to the end to his early love for Jerome, whose letters he copied with his own hand near the beginning of his career. These two Fathers had a special significance in Erasmus's thought.[68] Jerome, who had been entrusted by Pope Damasus I with the task of revising the Latin text of the gospels, who struggled despairingly with Hebrew, as Erasmus struggled with Greek, and who was accused, like Erasmus, of having dared to tamper with the accepted gospel text, was a fitting patron for the work which the great humanist assigned himself. Origen, to whose works Erasmus devoted the last year of his life, was likewise appropriate company for the stress of those later times. Having been among the Greek Fathers who attracted the

---

[66] *Colloquies*, trans. Thompson, p. 130, from 'The Soldier and the Carthusian'.

[67] Robert Peters, 'Erasmus and the Fathers: Their Practical Value', *Church History*, xxxvi (1967), p. 256.

[68] The importance of Origen (with all his hazards, necessitating reticence and obliqueness) for Erasmus is brought home by Screech, *Ecstasy*, pp. 21-2, 39, 61, 102, 106, 110, 116, 162-3, 171, 176-9, 185-91, 199, 230; on Jerome see Hall, 'Erasmus: Biblical Scholar'.

Fig. 15 Dürer's engraved portrait of Erasmus at work in his study, a less good likeness than that of Quentin Matsys, on which it leant. The Greek inscription says his writings will portray him better.

attention of Nicholas V (under whose auspices a translation was made of one of his writings, printed at Rome in 1481), Origen's works were published more than once in the early sixteenth century. His views upon free will gave him particular interest for Luther's contemporaries, and Erasmus (who respected Origen to the point of saying that one of his pages was worth ten of Augustine's) had recourse to the Greek Father in his dispute with Luther over this issue. But Origen presented a problem, the very problem of authority which lay behind the contest and arguments of the contestants. His works had been condemned at the council of Alexandria in 400. And so Luther chose to reject the authority so valued by Erasmus.

Philosophia Christi

If Erasmus stands at the very centre of the movement we choose to call the Northern Renaissance, the kernel of Erasmus's thought is summed up in what he called *philosophia Christi*. It is a term both straightforward and complex. To see it as an expression of avowed simplicity, carrying subtle undertones, is hardly unjust to the mind of its exponent. Erasmus did not invent the phrase. He was apparently making deliberate use of an archaism taken over – an adoption significant in itself – from the Greek Fathers. And before Erasmus, Rudolph Agricola had referred to the philosophy of Christ in a letter of 1484 which, discussing educational reform and the harmonizing of ancient wisdom and Christian faith, looks forward to Erasmus's meaning.[69]

Philosophia Christi stood for everything that Erasmus loved best. It summarized that blending of ancient wisdom and Christian piety, the alliance of humanist learning and evangelical devotion, to which his writings gave the highest expression. This philosophy represents that world (to which a converted Utopia would have belonged) in which it was possible to exclaim, like a character in one of the *Colloquies*, 'St. Socrates, pray for us!'[70] The two realms of reason and faith, antiquity and Christianity, so long conjoined and so long unsettled in their relationship, were to be fused into a new regenerative being. The writings of antiquity, published at last in their own proper eloquence, were to be the means of reaching contemporary Christian truth. The recovery of what was old would purify and renew. 'For what else is the philosophy of Christ, which he himself calls being born again, than the repairing of human nature, the foundations of which have been well laid?'[71]

In Erasmus's usage the phrase *philosophia Christi* brings together those two diverging strands of biblical learning whose fortunes have been outlined above. If the 'philosophy of Christ' summarized a programme, it was a programme with two united fronts: studies and evangelism. Yet it is unjust to make the distinction sound so categorical, when in its essence it never was. There is in fact no paradox in the circumstance that Erasmus, whose whole life belonged to the international world of those who were literate in Latin, who never published a word in any vernacular and preferred to avoid the bother of speaking one, should be found addressing himself to the interests of ploughmen and weavers. There is a sense in which, as his most heartfelt utterances reveal, they were never out of his mind, and for him it was one of the unspeakable tragedies of Luther's actions that he abused those evangelical obligations which, in their widest and deepest application, Erasmus had always respected. 'And yet the good life is everybody's business, and Christ wished the way to it to be accessible to all men, not beset with impenetrable labyrinths of argument but open to sincere faith . . . we must take thought all the time for the unlettered multitude, for whom Christ died'.[72] In his *Enchiridion*, which was among the books Erasmus could claim he had written 'as a plain man to plain men',[73] appeared (without the name) a definition of Christ's philosophy. But to find the fullest explanations we have to wait for one of the new *Adages*

---

[69] Spitz, *Religious Renaissance* (above, n. 1) pp. 26-7; Screech, *Ecstasy*, pp. 82-3.

[70] *Colloquies*, trans. Thompson, p. 68, from 'The Godly Feast' – always a popular colloquy.

[71] 'Quid aliud est Christi philosophia, quam ipse renascentiam vocat, quam instauratio bene conditae naturae?', from the Paraclesis of 1516, cited Renaudet, *Préreforme*, p. 676, n. 2; Screech, *Ecstasy*, p. 79; *Christian Humanism and the Reformation; Desiderius Erasmus, Selected Writings*, ed. J.C. Olin (New York, 1965), p. 100.

[72] From the letter to Paul Volz of 14 August 1518, prefacing the 1518 edition of the *Enchiridion*; Allen (ed.), iii, p. 363, no. 858; *CWE*, 6, pp. 74-5.

[73] *Luther and Erasmus: Free Will and Salvation*, ed. E.G. Rupp, A.N. Marlow, et al. (Library of Christian Classics, xvii, Philadelphia, 1969), p. 54.

published in 1515, the more famous *Paraclesis* prefacing the New Testament of 1516, and the fuller and more systematic *Ratio seu compendium verae theologiae* which was set before the second New Testament edition of 1519, 'to kindle men's spirits to the study of theology'.[74]

In his *Sileni Alcibiadis*, which appeared in the *Adagiorum chiliades* of 1515, Erasmus had a convenient topic for discoursing on a familiar theme: the contrast between contemptible outward appearances and inner spiritual wisdom. It may be read as an essay on the imitation of Christ. In his humble origins, his poverty, the trials of his life, and the mockery of his death, Christ was 'the most extraordinary Silenus of all'. He could have ruled the earth. 'But this was the only pattern that pleased him, and which he set before the eyes of his disciples and friends – that is to say, Christians. He chose that philosophy in particular, which is utterly different from the rules of the philosophers and from the doctrine of the world; that philosophy which alone of all others really does bring what everyone is trying to get, in some way or another – happiness'. The scriptures exemplified the same theme, the surprising veils concealing hidden truths. 'The parables of the Gospel, if you take them at face value – who would not think that they came from a simple ignorant man? And yet if you crack the nut, you find inside that profound wisdom, truly divine, a touch of something which is clearly like Christ himself'. The Apostles too were such Sileni, unschooled, unlettered, ridiculed, despised. Yet 'what Aristotle would not seem stupid, ignorant, trivial, compared to them, who draw from the very spring that heavenly wisdom beside which all human wisdom is mere stupidity?' The world was stuffed with false appearances; most men were 'like Sileni inside out', not least the men of the world of reputed learning.

> In fact you may often find more true authentic wisdom in one obscure individual, generally thought simple-minded and half-crazy, whose mind has not been taught by a Scotus (the subtle as they say) but by the heavenly spirit of Christ, than in many strutting characters acting the theologian, three or four times Doctor So-and-so, blown up with their Aristotle and stuffed full of learned definitions, conclusions, and propositions.[75]

The philosophy of Christ, it is clear, had very little to do with theological schools. In the *Paraclesis*, Erasmus contrasted the labours spent in pursuit of other philosophies – Platonic, Pythagorean, Stoic, Aristotelian – with those of Christ's. How easy, how simple, how attainable, in comparison, is the teaching of Christ, to be found in so few books, for which so little learning is necessary. Christ's philosophy was as open as the salvation that he preached. It was not limited to scholars learnedly annotating in their studies, or to professors with

---

[74] 'Magnum quidem, ad theologiae studium animos hominum inflammare'; *Novum testamentum omne* (Basel, 1519), p. 13; The *Ratio . . . verae theologiae* dates from January 1518.

[75] Phillips, *The 'Adages'*, pp. 271-4, 276. Screech, *Ecstasy*, illuminating the entire concept of Christian Folly in and beyond the *Moria*, adds to our understanding of the *Sileni*.

years of training in scholastic subtleties; it was the song and solace of ordinary working people. Only a few could be learned; but 'all can be Christian, all can be devout, and – I shall boldly add – all can be theologians'.

> Be only desyrous to be instructe and confirmable to this meake doctrine, and thou hast moch profited. Thy master and instructor (that is the sprete of god) will not from the be absent, which is never more gladly present with eny then with simple and playne hartes. . . . this delectable doctrine doth applye hersilf equallye to all men submittinge her silf unto us while we are childer, temperinge her tune after our capacyte . . . To the childer, she is lowe and playne, and to the greatter she seameth above all capacite. She refuseth no age, no kinde, no fortune, no state and condition. In so moch that the sonne is not more comen and indifferent to all men then this doctrine of Christe.[76]

It is not wrong to hear reverberations in these phrases of the *Imitation of Christ*, for Erasmus's thought belonged to that school. And, given such views, it was only logical to wish that the scriptures should be available in the vernacular. One passage in which Erasmus urges this has deservedly become famous, not only because it linked him with so many of his contemporaries – Protestant and Catholic – but also because these words are among the most urgent that he wrote:

> I would desire that all women shuld reade the gospell and Paules epistles, and I wold to god they were translated in to the tonges of all men, so that they might not only be read and knowne of the scotes and yryshmen, but also of the Turkes and sarracenes . . . I wold to god the plowman wold singe a texte of the scripture at his plowbeme, and that the wever at his lowme with this wold drive away the tediousnes of tyme. I wold the wayfaringe man with this pastyme wold expresse the werynes of his iorney.[77]

What *philosophia Christi* amounted to, then, was a new theology. It stands contrasted, implicitly and explicitly (witness the passages quoted above), with those long corridors of medieval learning which, in the name of theology, led determined students through years of study towards the biblical text. Erasmus's philosophy was not the philosophy of the schools. It embraced, as he was at pains to make plain, the concordant teachings of the best ancient philosophy; but it was centred upon direct religious experience through the scriptures, which was denied by the theology of scholastic argumentation.

The task which Erasmus had assigned himself in common with other northern humanists, but more magnificently – was a work of renovation. He wanted to release theology from the chains which had fettered it since it began to neglect its original sources. The same fate had overtaken these as had befallen classical sources (to which he also attended through his editorial life); the originals had been abandoned and lost because summaries had been

---

[76] *An exhortation to the diligent studye of scripture* ([Antwerp], 1529), *STC* 10493, sigs. [5 r], A i r; *Phillips*, Erasmus, p. 60; *Christian Humanism*, ed. Olin, pp. 96, 100.

[77] *Exhortation*, sigs. [5 v-6 r]; Phillips, *Erasmus*, pp. 60-61; *Christian Humanism*, p. 97.

allowed to replace them. What Justinian had done for Roman Law, Peter Lombard had done for theology. To give the Fathers a freshly prominent position, therefore, was to make room for 'guests of old days returning to claim their right of citizenship'. Those who objected to this work as 'new' had got things upside down, for they were calling '"new" the things that are the oldest of all, and they call "old" what is really new'. It was ridiculous to call innovative the attempt to recover an earlier, more desirable, state of affairs. For, Erasmus continued, 'among the doctors of the early church the knowledge of the Scriptures was combined with skill in languages and in secular literature'. What was new, on the contrary, was what was taught in the schools in the name of theology.

> It is something new, when boys have to learn grammar, to stuff them with *modus significandi*, and read them crazy lists of words which teach nothing but to speak faultily. It is something new to accept a youth as a student in philosophy, law, medicine or theology, who can understand nothing in the ancient authors owing to his ignorance of the language they speak. It is something new, to exclude from the Holy of Holies of theology anyone who has not sweated for years over Averroes and Aristotle. It is something new to stuff young men, who are reading for a degree in philosophy, with sophistical nonsense and fabricated problems, mere brain-teasers. It is something new in the public teaching of the Schools, for the answers to differ according to the methods of Thomists or Scotists, Nominalists or Realists. It is something new to exclude any arguments which are brought from the sources of Holy Scripture, and only accept those which are taken from Aristotle, from the Decretals, from the determinations of the Schoolmen, from the glosses of the professors of papal law, or from precedents (inane for the most part) distorted from Roman law. If we are to be offended by what is new, these are the really new things. If we approve of what is old, the oldest things of all are what are being brought forward now. Unless, maybe, 'new' means coming from the century of Origen, and 'old' means what started up 300 years ago and has gone from bad to worse ever since.[78]

The depth of Erasmus's concern spills out in the headlong rush of his examples: they read almost like a manifesto for humanist studies. One could fill more than a single book with the torrents of invective which flowed in the sixteenth-century tide of indignation against the scholastics. The story certainly does not begin with Erasmus. But he may be allowed to introduce us to an important phase of its development. It is clear from this passage that Erasmus thought learning had degenerated from the development of scholasticism through the 300 years after 1200. This amounted to a rejection of medieval theology as such, from the time when the application of dialectical methods brought the study of *theologia* to overshadow *sacra pagina*. Erasmus's words also illustrate the humanists' objection to scholasticism on the double grounds of style and content – or its lack of both. Those who pursued 'concepts, formalities, quiddities, ecceities' were building vacuous wordy

---

[78] Phillips, *The 'Adages'*, pp. 376-8.

structures destructive to good Latin.[79] Worse still, this empty methodology was allowed to become an end in itself, so that abstruse cobwebs of syllogistic argument were spun endlessly around questions quite divorced from the true sources of Christian knowledge.

Such strictures were, of course, only the negative side of very positive theories, which had particularly clear results in the linguistic studies of the north. Transalpine humanists eagerly cultivated Italian skills in Greek and built onto them, in a more systematic way than was done in Italy, plans for associated skills in Hebrew. There was certainly borrowing here too, for Hebrew studies belong to the history of the Italian, as well as the northern, Renaissance. After Manetti and Traversari (both of whom studied Hebrew), Pico della Mirandola made himself one of the most accomplished Hebraists of the day, and it was under his aegis, as we have seen, that Reuchlin took up Hebrew. In Italy, too, an important start was made in the publication of Hebrew works. A commentary on the Pentateuch by the eleventh-century Rabbi Rashi was printed at Reggio in 1475, and this was probably not the first Hebrew to come from an Italian press. A Hebrew press in Bologna produced the Psalter in 1477 and the Pentateuch in 1482, and the entire Old Testament was issued six years later by the Soncino office near Mantua. This last publication, reissued in two parts in 1492 and 1494 after the Soncino press had transferred to Brescia, was used by Luther for his German translation of the Old Testament. Meanwhile Aldus Manutius led the way in Hebrew, as he did in Greek, by publishing a primer; later a distinguished Italian Hebraist, Santes Pagninus, or Pagnini (1470-1541), wrote a Hebrew lexicon as well as making an influential Latin translation of the Hebrew Old Testament.

The fortunes of Pagnini – influenced as they were by politics and patronage – reflect the nature of the transfer of Hebrew skills from Italy. Leo X, a patron of biblical learning who established a Hebrew printing press in Rome, appointed this scholar to teach Oriental languages, but after the pope's death in 1521 Pagnini moved to France, where he spent the last part of his life; it was at Lyons that his various works were printed. As Hebrew studies migrated north, they gained powerful momentum from the motives of northern humanists. This was evident not only in publications, but also in institutional foundations. The scriptural context in which humanists of the north took the study of ancient languages to heart is evident in the various educational foundations which, like the college of St. Jerome at Alcalá, were trilingual. Admittedly there was some variation in the interpretations given to this term. Bishop Fisher's lecturers in Latin, Greek and Hebrew at St. John's College, Cambridge, corresponded to Ximenes's concern for Greek, Hebrew, and Aramaic, whereas the Belgian humanist Nicolas Clenardus (or Cleynaerts) spoke of his own trilingual studies in Hebrew, Chaldean and Arabic. There can be no doubt, however, that the linguistic triad, whichever form it took, was fundamentally attached to theology, and the promotion of Christian scholarship through philological studies

---

[79] Erasmus, *Praise of Folly*, trans. Radice, p. 155.

of scriptural languages was central to the purpose of these foundations. The most common and successful linguistic combination was that which was most directly biblical: the Christ and thieves of the Complutensian Polyglot. These were the languages patronised by Francis I, whose royal readerships for Greek and Hebrew were planned in 1517, though not until 1530 – thanks to the insistence of Guillaume Budé – did the foundation later known as the Collège de France come into being. In the early years of the sixteenth century, Vienna, Louvain and Oxford likewise acquired colleges for studies in Latin, Greek and Hebrew.[80]

The words and deeds of Erasmus (whose knowledge of Hebrew remained limited) leave no doubt that trilingual learning was integral to the advancement of *philosophia Christi*. To attempt the study of theology without such linguistic preparation was to Erasmus as reckless as it was impious. He used as an example of rash enterprises

> an attempt to interpret Divine Scripture . . . by one who was unschooled and ignorant of Greek, Latin and Hebrew, and of the whole of antiquity – things without which it is not only stupid, but impious, to take on oneself to treat the mysteries of Theology. And yet – terrible to relate – this is done everywhere by numbers of people, who have learnt some trivial syllogisms and childish sophistries and then, heavens above, what will they not dare? What will they not teach?[81]

At Louvain, Erasmus was able to participate directly in the creation of a trilingual foundation like that envisaged on a domestic level in his colloquy 'The Godly Feast', in which the house of Eusebius greeted arriving guests with inscriptions in Latin, Greek and Hebrew, while St. Peter was depicted on the door. From the beginning, Erasmus was the chief prop and adviser of the founder, Jerome Busleiden, and helped to shape his friend's design for the new college at Louvain for the highest educational purposes. After Busleiden's death in 1517, Erasmus did a great deal to help the executors overcome various difficulties, and to set the college on its feet, so that the first classes could be held in 1518. The *Ratio verae theologiae*, which appeared at this time, giving a full account of Erasmus's views upon biblical studies and the need for linguistic preparation in the three languages, amounted almost to a programme for the incipient college. Louvain, 'where men of vast learning will give free public instruction in the three languages' for the honour of studies and glory of Christ, of which Erasmus wrote so glowingly, stood for the highest of his hopes.[82] The future might well have seemed full of promise in 1517 – however later perspectives altered the significance of that year.

---

[80] Basil Hall, 'Biblical Scholarship: Editions and Commentaries', in *Cambridge History of the Bible*, 3, ed. S.L. Greenslade (Cambridge, 1963), pp. 38-93; F. Rosenthal, 'The Study of the Hebrew Bible in Sixteenth-Century Italy', *Studies in the Renaissance*, i (1954), pp. 81-91; Lloyd Jones, *Discovery of Hebrew* (above, n. 20).

[81] Phillips, *The 'Adages'*, pp. 266-7.

[82] *Colloquies*, trans. Thompson, p. 227 from 'The Epithalamium of Peter Gilles' (first printed in 1524 but written ten years earlier) in which Erasmus celebrated the name of Busleiden.

Fig. 16 St. Jerome in his study, with books open at Genesis 1 in Hebrew, Greek and Latin. This early wodcut of Dürer's first appeared in the 1492 edition of Jerome's letters, and was used in the 1520s to illustrate French and Latin Bibles.

Trilingual studies must not, however, be considered only in a humanist setting. They derived also from an earlier ecclesiastical programme, formulated at a time before learning in ancient languages had gained fifteenth-century humanist overtones. At the council of Vienne in 1312, Clement V had issued a decree providing that two teachers respectively in Hebrew, Chaldean (Aramaic), Arabic and Greek should be appointed at the papal curia, Paris, Oxford, Bologna and Salamanca. This comprehensive plan for linguistic education does not seem to have had much success at the time, though funds at least were collected to pay teachers at Oxford and Paris, and some linguistic instruction was given at the papal court. But the scheme was not forgotten. The council of Basel renewed the enactments of Vienne in 1434, and the Clementines which contained the decree (and became part of the *Corpus iuris canonici*) were printed several times in the fifteenth century. The men whose enthusiasm for trilingual studies took such definite shape in the sixteenth century were well aware of this precedent. They could regard themselves as fulfilling a long-planned project of the church – and they claimed to be doing so. Cardinal Ximenes's foundation at Alcalá and Bishop Fox's at Corpus Christi College, Oxford, were both officially based upon the Vienne decree; and Nebrija, Erasmus and More all referred themselves to its authority. One might almost suppose, from the letter of educational advice which Pantagruel received from his father Gargantua, that the programme of Vienne formed part of the utopian ideal of early sixteenth-century education: ' . . . learn the languages perfectly; first of all, the Greek, as Quintilian will have it; secondly, the Latin; and then the Hebrew, for the Holy Scripture-sake; and then the Chaldee and Arabic likewise . . . '[83] Different individuals might choose different linguistic combinations, but all harked back to Vienne.

As soon as one starts to look into this ostensible continuity, however, there appear important differences of emphasis. The programme of Vienne had an essentially missionary aim, in which biblical learning and exegesis were entirely subordinate to conversion of the infidel. This missionary objective of the 1312 decree, which owed much to the ideas and actions of Ramon Lull (who himself learned Arabic for the missionary activities in which he died, and campaigned for language studies to help conversion), stands contrasted with the linguistic aims of sixteenth-century humanists. But it still profoundly moved some of Erasmus's contemporaries. Nicolas Cleynaerts, who added studies in Hebrew, Arabic and Aramaic to his knowledge of Latin and Greek, shared ideas with Lull, some of whose works Lefèvre was inspired to edit. Another who came under Lull's influence was Guillaume Postel (1510-81), an eccentric genius with grandiose missionary ideas who bears some resemblance to Pico della Mirandola in his extraordinary eclecticism and linguistic facility.[84]

---

[83] François Rabelais, *Gargantua and Pantagruel*, ii, c. viii (Everyman edn., introd. D.B. Wyndham Lewis, 1954), i, pp. 163-4. (Gargantua's letter is dated 'From Utopia').

[84] W.J. Bouwsma, *Concordia Mundi: The Career and Thought of Guillaume Postel, 1510-1581*, (Cambridge, 1957).

Yet much of the linguistic study of northern humanists was undertaken with aims unlike those of Lull and Vienne. Differences of this kind seem discernible in the work of Erasmus and Ximenes. The latter, more closely attached to older ideals, entertained plans for a league to attack Islam and reconquer Jerusalem – a scheme which failed, though he did undertake a successful expedition to Oran in 1509. *Philosophia Christi* stood for a rather different world. For Erasmus, and others who shared his views, language teaching and textual studies were indispensable for the improvement not of unbelievers, but of the faithful. Other tasks were far more urgent than extending the bounds of Christendom. The first need was the renewal of Christianity itself. It was a work of conversion, but it looked inwards, not outwards: to the regeneration of individual belief and Christian institutions, the transformation of the Christian, rather than the non-Christian, world.

The campaign to make Greek and Hebrew an integral part of the study of theology, though it found defenders in existing institutions, as well as leading to the foundation of new ones, was accompanied by bitter attacks upon diehard conservatives of the old school who rigidly stuck to scholastic methods and rejected language studies. Erasmus and his allies constantly poked fun at their inveterate ignorance – and their defences of ignorance. 'Anything they don't understand they call Hebrew', remarked Ogygius in the famous colloquy, 'A Pilgrimage for Religion's Sake'. Long after the 'barbarous ignorance' of Erasmus's youth had been dispelled, he continued to lambaste those whose advice to the young was 'Beware of the Greeks, you'll turn into a heretic! Keep away from Hebrew, you might get like the Jews!'[85] Deep differences of outlook in the world of learning issued in several conflicts that show the ways in which the world was dividing before Luther began to make himself famous.

Two of these disputes involved the place of Greek study, and in both of them Thomas More came to its defence. He wrote answers both to Martin van Dorp's objections to Erasmus's New Testament and to the obstreperous opposition raised at about the same time by the 'Trojans' at Oxford against the Corpus Christi College Greeks. These defences are illuminating. In answer to the critics of the new learning at Oxford, More contended that a humanistic training in Greek and Latin, including the classical poetry, oratory and history which were condemned as secular, did 'train the soul in virtue' and lead towards theology, and that without such a foundation in the wisdom of the humanities no theologian could hope really to speak 'to the people'. Moreover, even were it granted that only theology should be studied, it was impossible to do so 'without some skill in languages, whether Hebrew or Greek or Latin'. Theology meant the study of scripture and the Fathers, Greek and Latin, and 'anyone who boasts that he can understand the works of the Fathers without an uncommon knowledge of the languages of each and all of them will in his ignorance boast for a long time before the learned trust his

---

[85] *Colloquies*, trans. Thompson, p. 300; Phillips, *The 'Adages'*, pp. 74, 378.

judgement'.[86] That More himself (so unlike Erasmus) was to spend much of the spiritual and intellectual energy of his later years in prolonged vernacular controversy with William Tyndale, may be taken both as his personal literary tragedy and as an indication of how the Protestant division cut into existing tensions in the northern humanist world.

More spoke as a convinced Christian humanist. Such beliefs are also embedded in his description of the non-Christian world of *Utopia*, a society based upon the ancient cardinal virtues, which accorded a paramount place to education, and which More contrasted implicitly and explicitly with the ills of contemporary Europe. Thomas More exemplified, in fact – in some ways even more than Erasmus, with whom he enjoyed so long and close a friendship – the breadth and diversity of interests which compounded northern humanism. Together they participated in the effort to regenerate Christian society through the restoration of good letters; they were drawn to each other by their common sense of humour and appreciation of satirical wit; the plea for peace which More included in *Utopia* was argued urgently by Erasmus in various writings, notably in his *Querela pacis*. Yet More's later years and death show how their paths diverged, in ways indicative of their differing humanist allegiances as well as of the divisive effects of the Protestant revolt. Unlike Erasmus, More allowed himself to be drawn away from humanist Latin letters, to write his English controversial works. Also unlike his less committed friend, More's humanist sense of duty withdrew him from a Carthusian retreat to dedicated public service, which brought him, under Henry VIII, face-to-face with a terrible conflict of loyalties more acute than any which shook Erasmus.[87]

The long defence which More wrote on behalf of Erasmus against Dorp shows how, in the controversies of this time, the humanists drew together to form a common front. His argument for the return to biblical and patristic studies was accompanied by hard criticism, though he was careful to say that he did not attack all theologians or all their *quaestiones* for, kept in their place, these methods were good for sharpening wits. But they should not be lifelong studies, nor did the church's salvation depend on them. One of More's stories is worth quoting, since it illustrates so vividly what the humanists felt they were battling against. At a dinner party given by a rich and cultivated Italian merchant, there was present a theologian who had recently arrived in England and who hoped to increase his fame for disputation. In the course of dinner this monk repeatedly made a point of refuting whatever was said on any topic with

[86] *The Correspondence of Sir Thomas More*, ed. E.F. Rogers (Princeton, 1947), pp. 115-16; Myron P. Gilmore, *The World of Humanism, 1453-1517* (New York, 1952), p. 214. This letter was written to the authorities in Oxford in March 1518. On Greek studies in Oxford and Cambridge see Dowling, *Humanism in the Age of Henry VIII* (above n. 59), pp. 23-33.

[87] Not to mention differences of character; for a psychological study of Erasmus see N.H. Minnich and W.W. Meissner, 'The Character of Erasmus', *American Historical Review*, 83 (1978), pp. 598-624: recent works on More: Alistair Fox, *Thomas More: History and Providence* (Oxford, 1982); Richard Marius, *Thomas More* (New York, 1984).

a syllogism, and his contrariness continued when the merchant gradually steered the conversation to theology:

> And as it began to leak out that the theologian was not as experienced in Scripture as he was in those subtle questionings [*questiunculi*], he [the host] began to play him up, and to make his argument turn on appeals to authority. He invented on the spur of the moment certain quotations, which seemed to support his case, and which no one had ever heard of before – so freely had he made them up – yet he carefully gave to each an exact citation, attributing one to some epistle of St. Peter, another to St. Paul, another still he placed in the gospel, never omitting to state the chapter – making a point, if the book had only sixteen chapters, to quote from the twentieth. And what did the good theologian do?

He fought back hard, but he had to resort to some acrobatics:

> For he had absolutely no idea of the contents of Holy Writ and never doubted that these quotations were to be found there; being under the obligation of yielding to the authority of Scripture, and at the same time not wanting to be shamed by giving way, he found himself in a tight corner from which he could only escape by Protean manoeuvres. As soon as any non-existent passage from Scripture was cited against him, he said 'well quoted, sir, but I understand the text in this way', and then he would interpret it in two ways,one of which supported his opponent, the other of which provided his own means of escape. And if the merchant pressed the point more closely, and objected that the theologian's was not the true meaning, then this man swore so solemnly that anyone might have believed him, that Nicholas of Lyra interpreted it in this way.[88]

This account illustrates three aspects of contemporary theology which the humanists found objectionable: the delight in disputation, which set ability in the technicalities of debate above regard for the truth; the total, but concealed, ignorance of scripture; and (as a concomitant of both characteristics) the exaltation of scholastic commentary over the Bible itself. It is also interesting that More's playful contestant, whose biblical learning was so profound, was a layman – a man such as Manetti or Dürer's friend Pirckheimer, who combined a life of public affairs in Nuremberg with editing some of the Greek Fathers.

The most outstanding controversy concerned not Greek but Hebrew. It centred upon the leading Hebraist of the time, Johannes Reuchlin. This confrontation is highly significant in that it shows, perhaps more clearly than any other event of the time, the position which had been reached by the northern humanists, presented as they were with a challenge to the very principles of their teaching. Reuchlin, who was born at Pforzheim in Germany in 1455, can be called the first northern humanist whose linguistic crown was really triple, thereby excelling Erasmus, who praised him after his death as

---

[88] *Correspondence of More*, ed Rogers, p. 47; W.E. Campbell, *Erasmus, Tyndale and More* (London, 1949), p. 72; H.A. Mason, *Humanism and Poetry in the Early Tudor Period* (London, 1959), p. 94. More's letter was dated 21 October 1515, and answered Dorp's second letter to Erasmus about the *Moriae encomium*.

'that famous phoenix of learning'.[89] By 1494 Reuchlin's knowledge of Hebrew was sufficiently advanced for him to bring out a work on the cabala, but the book in which he did most for Hebrew studies was the *De rudimentis linguae Hebraicae* of 1506, a Hebrew grammar which was a considerable improvement on all its predecessors, including that of Conrad Pellican produced three years earlier. The alphabet, dictionary and grammar in Reuchlin's book greatly helped the advancement of Hebrew learning; so did the pupils whom he taught and the patrons he persuaded to sponsor the study of the language. He could justifiably regard himself as opening new doors, and remarked of the dictionary in his grammar that, 'before me among the Latins no one appears to have done this'.[90]

Most of the publicity which Reuchlin received for his achievement derived from his opposition. His career and the cause of Hebrew studies became a *cause célèbre*, thanks to the officious actions of a converted Jew called Johannes Pfefferkorn, who sparked an extremely acrimonious dispute. In 1509 Pfefferkorn, whose new-found zeal had already caused him to write at length against Jewish practices, succeeded in getting a warrant from the Emperor Maximilian for the destruction of all Hebrew books except the Old Testament. Among those who objected, Reuchlin, the leading expert, took a reasonable line, suggesting that while obviously blasphemous works should be destroyed, others should be allowed, since understanding of them would be beneficial to Christians. These differences issued in literary polemics; attacked by Pfefferkorn, Reuchlin fired back, including among his targets the theological faculty of Cologne, which from the outset had supported his opponent. Various exchanges took place, culminating in Reuchlin's being cited for heresy before the Cologne inquisition by the inquisitor-general, Jacob von Hochstraten. The proceedings went on for years as the case was appealed to Rome and referred back to a papal commission. By the time Reuchlin's name was cleared in March 1514, the whole affair had become notorious throughout Europe. Not that this was the end of it. Hochstraten appealed against the judgement and in 1520 – by which time the case had become damagingly linked with Luther's – it went against Reuchlin, who submitted.

The book which made this controversy peculiarly celebrated was the *Epistolae obscurorum virorum*, published in 1515 or 1516. Appearing as an anonymous sequel to Reuchlin's own *Epistolae clarorum virorum*, and purporting to be an epistolary collection of Hochstraten, Ortwin Gratius and others associated with Reuchlin's opponents, the letters mercilessly lampooned the Cologne theologians and all obstinate obscurantists who were giving universities a bad name. The authors of this successful satirical work were Ulrich von Hutten

---

[89] *Colloquies*, trans. Thompson, p. 81; 'That famous phoenix of learning, triple-tongued John Reuchlin, is dead', from 'The Apotheosis of that incomparable Worthy, John Reuchlin' (first printed in 1522). At the same time as he celebrated Reuchlin in this way, Erasmus was careful to keep his distance from the controversies surrounding the Hebraist.

[90] *CHB*, 3, p. 44.

and Crotus Rubeanus, both of whom had direct experience (at Cologne and elsewhere) of the academic world they ridiculed so wittily. The *Epistolae obscurorum virorum*, spiced with malice and a caustic sense of fun, open another window onto that polarizing world we have seen through the eyes of More and Erasmus.

Traditional theologians, disparaged as 'theologers', are shown up as ridiculous in their defence of scholastics and scholastic methods, and in their absurd insistence on being addressed as '*magister noster*'. They are represented as resolutely opposed to new learning in any form: to Greek and Hebrew, as tongues with no relevance to theology; to those who talked the 'new-fangled Latin'; to 'new-fangled theologians like Erasmus of Rotterdam' with his corrections of Jerome and the New Testament; to 'Virgil and Pliny and the rest of the new-fangled authors'; and to poets at large – 'the bane of the universities' – as unnecessary, dangerous and threatening the faculties' existence because they lure away students. Old studies and new studies are made to seem irrevocably opposed, with the supporters of the former, fearful of being ousted by the latter, stubbornly maintaining that 'it matters not much with which side [of a given question] a man holdeth, so long as he followeth the ancient ways'.[91]

Obviously the *Letters of Obscure Men* cannot be taken as a fair picture of the German university world. One has only to think of Conrad Celtis, the crowned laureate of Frederick III, taking up his lectureship in poetry at Vienna in 1497, or of Reuchlin himself, who, after all this controversy, ended his life as professor of Greek and Hebrew at Tübingen. The 'new learning' and the universities were by no means as diametrically opposed as the *Letters* make them appear. Yet, greatly exaggerated though it was in this satire, a tension did exist between the old learning and the new – especially in theology – and there were genuine reasons why old arts faculty members might be afraid. Much humanist learning did have an extra-curricular character. It could be pursued outside institutional walls in newer ways: through printed books, by associations formed in printers' workshops, and in learned societies or literary sodalities like those in which Conrad Celtis brought together many German humanists of his day.[92] Erasmus, who had made the whole of Europe his academy, did more than anyone else to open new academic doors. And whatever the winds which Luther set blowing through them, they were not to be shut.

Pfefferkorn's original challenge to Hebrew literature, and the ensuing opposition to Reuchlin, called into question the fundamentals of humanist study: the desire to revive good letters and Christian piety through a fuller understanding of the ancient past, using improved linguistic knowledge to this

---

[91] *On the Eve of the Reformation: 'Letters of Obscure Men'*, trans. F.G. Stokes, introd. Hajo Holborn (New York, 1964, first pub. London, 1909), pp. 27, 36-7, 100, 150, 174, 191, 194-7, 205-6, 233.

[92] Lewis W. Spitz, *Conrad Celtis: The German Arch-Humanist* (Cambridge, MA, 1957).

end. The controversy which resulted made explicit, in ways which were significant for the future, tendencies which had long formed part of humanists' thinking, but which had not before received such loud and clear expression. The revolt against scholasticism varied in time, place, depth and motivation. While it may be seen as a feature of the work of earlier Italian humanists (and the most obvious way of distinguishing the attitudes of fifteenth-century humanists from those of the twelfth or any previous period of classical revival), it was the northern humanists of the sixteenth century who set the seal, as it were, upon this development. Once the opposition between 'old' and 'new' had gained the indelible force of polemical print, the rejection of scholastic methods became virtually a new orthodoxy. Like other forms of repression, it entailed loss rather than gain – a loss of understanding, as well as actual destruction of texts. But the recognition of conflicting orthodoxies had its place in the evolution of thought, scientific as well as literary and theological. 'There are found', Bacon remarked in the *Novum organum*, 'some minds given to an extreme admiration of antiquity, others to an extreme love and appetite for novelty; but few so duly tempered that they can hold the mean, neither carping at what has been well laid down by the ancients, nor despising what is well introduced by the moderns'. Reuchlin and his contestants were far removed from a world in which truth seemed to belong to 'nature and experience' rather than the 'felicity of any age'.[93] Yet their words made a contribution to that dichotomy, itself venerable, between the wisdom of ancients and moderns.

Dividing Ways

Despite all the changes that had taken place, humanists and humanist patrons of the north in 1600, as in 1500, still looked to Italy for models of culture and civilization. In the days of Palladio, as in the days of Alberti and Brunelleschi, Italy provided patterns which the rest of Europe followed. From there Francis I fetched artists to embellish his palace at Fontainebleau, as Henry VIII seems to have employed Italians to decorate his extraordinary palace of Nonsuch. At the end of the century, when John Florio, the English translator of Montaigne, was helping his countrymen (including James I's queen) to gain mastery of Italian at home, many of Shakespeare's contemporaries were still, despite religious impediments, journeying to Italy to improve themselves linguistically and otherwise. There were still ways in which Italy led the world. And if humanist principles prevented Italian from becoming the *lingua franca* of Europe, Italian humanists did much to make Italian the second language of cultivated men for several generations.

---

[93] *The Works of Francis Bacon*, ed. J. Spedding, R.L. Ellis and D.D. Heath (London, 1857-8), i, p. 170; iv, p. 60; *Novum organum*, bk. i, lvi. For remarks about the effect of humanist anti-scholasticism on science see Marie Boas, *The Scientific Renaissance, 1450-1630* (Fontana edn., 1970), pp. 22-3.

The success of the humanists (if one regards it as such) can be measured in the widespread acceptance of their linguistic views. The profound conviction that the best education is to be found in classical letters, that true eloquence and true wisdom must grow together, was fully taken to heart by northern Europe. Its results can be seen in the grinding round of 'Tully' and Terence imposed on boys in school, and in the huge amount of contemporary writing which poured from the presses in Latin. There were individuals who saw the case from the other side, such as Cornelius Aurelius (d. 1523), who wrote a history of the Low Countries in Dutch; Jean Lemaire de Belges (*c.* 1473 – *c.* 1515), who reconciled the rival claims of French and Italian in his *Concorde des deux langages* (published in 1513); and Juan Luis Vives (1493-1540), who pointed out that the practice of ancient diction could never reach the same plane as that of contemporary usage and argued in favour of writing in the vernacular languages. But in general, so intent were the humanists upon the classicism of their formulas for eloquence and elegance, and so remote did the vernaculars seem from these ideals, that it was long before the stylistic criteria of Latin came to be applied to the vernaculars. The theories of the Pléiade and of Joachim du Bellay's *Deffence et illustration de la langue françoyse* (1549) took longer to reach England. Not until near the end of the sixteenth century was a studied effort made to apply to English the rhetorical rules and figures of speech (as opposed to the aureate neologisms) of Latin. And so northern humanists who wished to emulate the Italians (sometimes in a spirit of nationalistic rivalry) did so not in the vernacular but in the Ciceronian Latin they so earnestly cultivated. Robert Gaguin's history of France, Conrad Celtis's *Norimberga* – the prelude to his planned *Germania illustrata* – and Polydore Vergil's *Anglica historia* were all, in their differing ways, written to demonstrate the liveliness of the ancient heritage belonging to these nations.

Should it be taken to indicate the humanists' false sense of direction that the Latin to which they devoted themselves was eventually overtaken by the despised vernaculars, failing to prove permanently viable as the international language of the world of letters? Or that the works for which we value them are sometimes those of which they themselves made light? Both the *Praise of Folly* and *Utopia* were in the nature of holiday works for their authors, yet they are read by those who will never turn to the *Enchiridion* or the *History of Richard III*, let alone the theological writings of Erasmus and More. Undoubtedly there was a large amount of Latin literature written and printed in the Renaissance which remains unread and which, one may think, the world would not have been very different without. Yet that is only the negative side of the question. If More's contemporaries were juster to his intentions than we have been, in valuing his translations of Lucian above his *Utopia*, it cannot be left out of account that Lucian contributed to the making of *Gargantua* and *Pantagruel*, as well as to both *Utopia* and the *Praise of Folly*. It is surely no accident that those writers who speak to us most directly are those who succeeded most fully in steeping themselves in the literature and spirit of antiquity. Erasmus, as a perceptive friend told him in 1516, lived and wrote in a way that made him seem present 'everywhere in Christendom', and part of the secret of his literary skill was his readiness to give himself away. 'You are all generosity, you open yourself to everybody . . . '[94] It was a generosity that Montaigne, essaying himself as the central topic of his study, sifting truth as 'I roll about in myself', carried a whole philosophy further – but Montaigne had benefited from his reading of Erasmus.[95] In both cases profound intimacy with the classics shaped a style which could mirror, as Erasmus felt it should, the writer's soul. 'What pleases the reader best', he wrote, 'is to feel as if he knows the feelings, character, intellect and outlook of the writer as well as if he had spent several years in his company'.[96] We have to wait to see the maturing vernaculars coming into their own, but it seems perverse to deny the enrichment which resulted from this period of fresh immersion in the classical past.

The whole 'renaissance' process involved loss as well as gain. The humanist vision had its accompanying blindness. Whether or not one agrees that there was a 'fatal flaw in humanism which draws a veil over Greek literature in the very act of discovering it' – fatal to the kindling of the poetic imagination[97] – it is undeniably true that the understanding of Greek remained smaller than that of Latin, and that even in the pursuit of Latin excellence there were hampering limitations. Most damaging was that tendency, already encountered in the case of Colet, to cultivate the style of antiquity at the expense of its content – a disjunction between Christian and humanist objectives which has its own ancient history. 'We shall not let the earliest studies be infected with heathen errors', wrote Vives in his *De tradendis disciplinis* (1531). 'Let the scholar begin the reading of the heathen, as though entering upon poisonous fields, armed with an antidote . . . he is to take from them only what is useful, and to throw aside the rest'. Latin and Greek were the best languages, and those which dealt with the subjects most desirable for study. Yet to use them as they ought to be used, care was necessary, and this involved some of the best humanist educators in a kind of censorship. Colet's anxiety to guard his pupils from damaging thoughts determined his selection of authors at St. Paul's. Vives, declaring that 'I have . . . sought to free the sciences from impious doubts, and to bring them out from their heathen darkness into the light of our faith',[98] thought poetry should be expurgated for youthful study. The belief that it was possible to imitate the style of antiquity while avoiding the contaminating influence of some of its best thought contributed to the aridity of certain sixteenth-century studies. Yet the work of the northern humanists, at its best,

---

[94] Allen, (ed.), ii, p. 315, no. 450; *EWE*, 4, p. 36; cited Phillips, *Erasmus*, p. 68.

[95] *The Complete Essays of Montaigne*, trans. Donald M. Frame (Stanford, 1958), p. 499; D.M. Frame, *Montaigne: A Biography* (New York, 1965), p. 184.

[96] M.M. Phillips, 'Erasmus and the Classics', in *Erasmus*, ed. Dorey, p. 25, quoting from the *Ciceronianus* (1528).

[97] C.S. Lewis, *English Literature in the Sixteenth Century excluding Drama* (Oxford, 1954), p. 132; cf. p. 69.

[98] *Vives: On Education. A Translation of the De tradendis disciplinis*, ed. Foster Watson (Cambridge, 1913), p. 7; cf. pp. 48-52, 124-30.

Fig. 17 Erhard Schoen's 'Complaint of the poor persecuted idols', a Nuremberg broadsheet illustrating the fate of church imagery about 1530, reflects the violent aspect of reform which led Erasmus to leave Basel in 1529.

through the animating spirit of *philosophia Christi*, did much to ease the tensions between Christian and pagan values. Erasmus, whose avowed purpose had always been 'to promote studies of good letters [*bonae literae*] and to bring these studies into harmony with theology', declared that 'whatever is devout and contributes to good morals should not be called profane'.[99] This was a view which opened books rather than closed them.

Transalpine humanists did a great deal more than simply continue the work of fifteenth-century Italy. They inherited linguistic skills and the hopes that went with them, but both were extended and transformed in their hands. The idea that the world should be renewed through the study of Latin, Greek and Hebrew was an outgrowth of the sense of renovation which inspired the humanists of Italy and which, asserted with such triumphant affirmation, has done so much to colour our views of the period. But there was a difference. The humanists of the north, with their evangelical dedication, gave a fresh direction to these aims, and applied their critical labours more concentratedly toward the regeneration of Christian society. By about 1516-18 much had been done, in books published or prepared and institutions planned or founded. It might well have seemed that the longed for period of renewal was beginning.

The age which did arrive, however, appeared otherwise. In a sense, it is impossible to assess the achievement of the Northern Renaissance because it was overtaken at a critical moment by another more impetuous movement. The Protestants were also humanists, but they were humanists with a difference. Their sense of priorities, more urgent and decisive, pushed them forward in ways which more deliberate thinkers regretted. The delicate, easily altered balance between the scholarly and the evangelical was pushed down hard on the evangelical side. 'Luther', said Erasmus, who found much to lament in the

---

[99] Allen, (ed.), vi, p. 90, no. 1581 (Erasmus to Noel Beda, 15 June 1525); cf. *Colloquies*, trans. Thompson, p. 65.

spiritual impulsiveness of his younger contemporary, 'attributes very little importance to scholarship, and most of all to the spirit'. The whole Lutheran affair appeared to him a tragedy which had sprung from 'hatred of liberal studies' and threatened the ruin of such work.[100]

Of course there was Protestant humanist work in abundance. Tyndale edited Isocrates, as Calvin did Seneca early in his career. Melanchthon edited many of the classics, and had already published Terence by the time he brought out his Greek grammar in 1518; he was a worthy successor to his great-uncle Reuchlin in triple linguistic accomplishments. Between Wittenberg and Strasbourg and Cambridge there were plenty of educational foundations which demonstrate the application of humanist procedures in Protestant education. But as Erasmus already recognized when, in the summer of 1523, he reluctantly and regretfully took up his pen to write his *Essay on Free Will*, which appeared the following year, Luther's challenge was a threat to his whole world. It seemed to him (and, as Luther himself admitted, Erasmus had put his finger on the heart of the matter) that Luther's view of free will and grace undermined the entire humanist position. It was as if dry land had become water on the map of spiritual certainties open to human reasoning. What to Luther felt like a boundless release of spiritual hope seemed to Erasmus a hopeless plunge into human negation. 'One may object', he wrote against Luther, 'to what does free choice avail if it accomplishes nothing? I reply, to what does the whole man avail if God so works in him as a potter with clay and just as he could act on a pebble?' Their difference was a difference over human dignity, as well as over the means of divine salvation. Luther replied, 'When God is not present and at work in us everything we do is evil and we necessarily do what is of no avail for salvation. For if it is not we, but only God, who works salvation in us, then before he works we can do nothing of saving significance, whether we wish to or not'. Erasmus differed in his more hesitant manner and less categorical viewpoint: 'to those who maintain that man can do nothing without the help of the grace of God, and conclude that therefore no works of men are good – to these we shall oppose a thesis to me much more probable; that there is nothing that man cannot do with the help of the grace of God, and that therefore all the works of man can be good'.[101]

The gulf between them was a matter of method as well as of ultimate spiritual conviction. To set divine grace and the promptings of the spirit so far above human reason seemed to Erasmus to unleash not only irrational spiritual assertiveness, but also uncontrollable conflict. 'Now every Tom, Dick and Harry claims credence who testifies that he has the spirit of the Gospel', which was hardly surprising if the deepest divine mysteries were prostituted before 'common ears'. The new generation seemed to have banished that spiritual liberty which might have served true piety, and to serve instead an

---

[100] *Luther and Erasmus: Free Will and Salvation* (above n. 73), p. 37; Allen, (ed.), iv, p. 340, no. 1141; *CWE*, 8, p. 45; Phillips, *Erasmus*, p. 125.

[101] *Luther and Erasmus: Free Will and Salvation*, pp. 85, 96, 139.

unrestrained liberty of the flesh. Luther, less patient and temperamentally prepared for battle, was ready to justify both the assertiveness and the dissension. 'Take away assertions and you take away Christianity'; 'To wish to stop these tumults . . . is nothing else but to wish to suppress and prohibit the Word of God'. Luther brushed aside as irrelevant and misconceived those hesitations which stemmed from Erasmus's basic differences of character and philosophy. To the man who lived by a revelation, intellectual reservations might seem to be 'slippery writings'; the adherence to slow striving after human improvement makes 'your thoughts about God . . . all too human'. And no man could, in the end, be educated into spiritual vision – it was the learned who were often blind.[102] The new evangelicals certainly built on the work of their predecessors, but they built so urgently that some things had to be left behind. Religious needs could not wait upon stylists and grammarians: where the fate of souls was at stake, Utopias had to be set aside.

Yet it would be wrong to end on such a negative note. The Reformation's release of spiritual energy certainly unleashed considerable forces of destruction, giving grounds for some of the deep pessimism and dire fears of contemporary men of learning. It seemed as if the voices of reason and persuasion, the hopes of reform through peaceful educative processes and the enhancement of Christian piety, were being drowned in the clamour of aggressive disputation. Erasmus, Erasmianism and the religious humanists appeared to have lost the day.

A great deal, however, remained of the movement which we have been considering. Although it flowed into different channels and was transmuted in the process, the development of events in some ways enlarged rather than damped its influence. The impact of the 'Northern Renaissance', as we have traced it, was inherently intellectual, scholarly and artistic, and therefore confined to the limited though influential numbers of those who formed the most highly literate and cultivated circles of the day. The Christian humanists had indeed addressed themselves to the problems of society at large, and wanted to serve the interests of more than a cultured elite. But it was thanks in great part to their successors, often more Protestant than humanist, that essentials of humanist thinking passed into wider and more popular currency through the labours of school-founders and teachers, and a variety of translators and printers. Erasmus himself, as well as the classical authors on whom he had worked, came within the horizons of considerable numbers of vernacular readers.

The influence of the greatest northern humanist long outlived him. Although an 'Erasmian' position became increasingly difficult to maintain during the polarization of thought which resulted from Luther's stand, Erasmus's ideas and works were not only attacked and condemned by Catholics and Protestants alike; they were also used and read by both sides. The essentials of Erasmus's thought, pushed aside from the realm of practical politics, long remained discernible among those individuals who valued toleration and reason as much as they disliked war and militancy, and who appreciated satire and irony as a way of drawing attention to contemporary ills. The range and force of his ideas can be traced in directions which diverge as sharply as Trent and the Jesuits from the Calvinists and Geneva. Like all great teachers, Erasmus taught far beyond the limit of his conscious intentions. From what he thought and wrote, from his marvellous ability to talk from his own peak in an individual, down-to-earth voice, there stemmed many misunderstandings, but also many trains of thought. Erasmus, belonging to two worlds while effectively fashioning a third, amply repaid his debt to man as well as God. He has had many posthumous debtors.

Fig. 18 The Virgin wearing 'a blak cote and abowte hyr a gyrdyll and a bende in hyr hede and bare fote', as she appeared to the disappointed pilgrim in a story that featured in the *Myracles of our blessyd Lady*, published by Wynkyn de Worde in 1514.

7

Gold and Images

In a letter of December 1523 describing his troubles with Julius II in the previous decade, Michelangelo related how the Pope had commissioned him to paint the twelve Apostles in the lunettes of the Sistine Chapel. Soon after starting his design the artist became convinced that the project was off to a bad start. 'I told the pope that if the Apostles alone were put there it seemed to me that it would turn out a poor affair. He asked me why. I said, "because they themselves were poor".'[1]

Vasari reports the Pope's disappointment at the lack of gold and bright colour in Michelangelo's ceiling. The grandiosity of its decor was of a kind that would have amazed Abbot Suger who, four centuries earlier, had lavished gold over the walls and ornaments of Saint-Denis, and who was 'unfaltering' in his justification of this enthusiasm. If St. Sophia in Constantinople seemed to lack in comparison with the gold glistening on doors, walls, altar, crucifix and chalice in Suger's church, the abbot was less abashed by any want of precedent than proud of his lustrous achievement. It might be necessary to safeguard such a treasure-house from the avarice of thieves, but behind this vast expenditure lay a supreme confidence in its power 'to transfer that which is material to things immaterial'. Marvellous workmanship in gold lifted minds to contemplate divine splendour and celestial light. The purest of all metals, the incorruptible substance that was tried by fire, was to transport others, as it transported Suger, so that they might travel (as he put it) through the brilliant lights of his gilded doors to the true light of Christ.[2]

Behind the apparent innuendoes of Michelangelo's retort to Pope Julius there lay a confluence of changing opinions. The use of gold in the service of God was always problematical, and in the fifteenth and sixteenth centuries

---

[1] *The Letters of Michelangelo*, ed. and tr. E.H. Ramsden (London, 1963) i, pp. 148-9. According to Vasari Michelangelo himself had intended, but for a final rush, to add some gold and ultramarine to enrich the draperies, and when the pope afterwards complained about this lack told him that such holy men would have 'despised riches and ornament'. G. Vasari, *Lives of the Most Eminent Painters, Sculptors and Architects*, ed. J.P. Richter (London, 1850-85), 5, p. 258.

[2] *Abbot Suger on the Abbey Church of St.-Denis and its Art Treasures*, ed. and tr. E. Panofsky, 2nd edn. by G. Panofsky-Soergel (Princeton, 1979), pp. 46-9, 62-7, 193.

some of the latent ambiguities came into the open and affected the subsequent employment of this metal in the ecclesiastical arts.

There could of course have been purely artistic reasons for the lack of gold in the Sistine ceiling. Painters who strove to imitate nature more closely came to realize that light (even heavenly light) could be represented and controlled more exactly by other methods than the application of gold. Using gold could seem a hindrance to truthful depiction. Alberti had expressed this view in his treatise *On Painting*. 'There are some', he wrote, 'who use much gold in their narratives. They think it gives majesty. I do not praise it.' Even in depicting a subject made of gold, 'I should not wish gold to be used, for there is more admiration and praise for the painter who imitates the rays of gold with colours'.[3] Though painters' contracts continued to stipulate how altars and other religious commissions were to be embellished with gold,[4] by the time of Michelangelo's Sistine commission there were many examples of work that exemplified Alberti's objective. But the avoidance of gold in delineating the Apostles (and other religious subjects) might have been dictated by a desire for scriptural rather than artistic truth.

The uniqueness of gold – its enduring, untarnishing lustre – made it from early times a paradigm as well as a form of currency. If more proverbial saws have always been attached to gold than to silver the reason is not hard to find. Gold is precious for its metallic properties as well as the scarcity of the mined ore. The magical visual sheen of the worked metal had a power to impress that was enhanced by the associations of its rarity and value.

But the attributes of gold were ambiguous. On the one hand it was a symbol of pure spirituality – the supreme light, the splendour of the divine world (and so used to represent the sky, the aureoles of saints). On the other hand it stood for avarice, the lure that bound sinners to the weight of worldly desires.[5] Also, of course, there was a divide in the use of gold between its aesthetic and practical uses; between art and currency. Its malleability, which facilitated the making of gold plate and the development of gilding, enabled the rarest and richest of metals to be put to a great variety of artistic purposes. But such works of art, being so valuable for their matter, whatever the quality of their craftsmanship, were always at risk and in danger of being melted down and returned to the market-place.

While ambivalence attached to the metal, the church from its beginnings found itself pulled in two directions in making use of gold. In a passage that entered the canon law and was often cited, St. Ambrose drew attention to the

---

[3]   L.B. Alberti, *On Painting*, tr. J.R. Spencer (London, 1956), p. 85. But Alberti was not against putting paintings in settings ornamented with gold and gems.

[4]   *L'or au temps de la renaissance du mythe à l'économie*, ed. M.T. Jones-Davies (Paris, 1978), p. 27; for an example of 1495 see *A Documentary History of Art*, ed. E.G. Holt (Princeton, 1947 [Anchor Books edn, 1957-8]) i, pp. 268-70.

[5]   *L'or au moyen âge* (Publications du CUER University of Provence, 1983), p. 9; *L'or au temps de la renaissance*, pp. 1-2, 27-30, 86. On avarice see A. Murray, *Reason and Society in the Middle Ages* (Oxford, 1985), pp. 59-80.

need to strike a proper balance between the splendour due to the divine cult and liberality in works of mercy. The latter might sometimes override the former, so that 'we may break mystical vessels, in order to redeem captives'.[6] There were times when the holy must go back to the world. Gold, even gold consecrated to the highest of divine services – the vessels used on the altar – should be turned into secular currency in order to help the needy. In the last resort the needs of Christians came before the ornaments of the temple.

Costly church plate certainly was treated in this way. Abbot Suger remarked in passing that the large chalice (it weighed 140 ounces and was apparently of solid gold) which he had made for the main altar of Saint-Denis was a substitute 'for another one which had been lost as a pawn in the time of our predecessor'.[7] It is perhaps a mistake to think of church goods as inalienably consecrated to the service of God when their owners were so ready to convert them into cash. One captive who was redeemed in the manner sanctioned by St. Ambrose was Abbot Mayeul of Cluny, whose monks melted down church ornaments to pay his ransom after he was captured by the Arabs in 972. There are other examples of abbeys stripping their reliquaries and crucifixes of gold to meet royal demands, and of bishops selling vessels to feed the hungry.[8]

Throughout the middle ages the eyes and minds of countless believers were captivated by the rapture of gold. Pilgrims were hugely attracted – if not hypnotized – by the lustre of precious metal and rare gems. The glimmer and glitter of the most famous shrines received ample comment, and we can enter some way into the minds of devout pilgrims when we learn how they visualized the saints whose powers they hoped to tap. Holy persons appeared to suppliants in the guise of known images. Accordingly they were often resplendent in gold and finery. A peasant whose sight was cured by St. Foy of Conques had a vision of the saint which corresponded with the gilded statue reliquary that still survives today. St. Cuthbert made a visionary appearance to a youth of Northumbria clad in shining gold and gems, and Christina of Markyate, ill in bed at Christmas, saw Christ supremely beautiful, wearing 'a golden crown thickly encrusted with precious stones', topped with a cross of gold, sparkling like dewdrops.[9] Some of the extraordinary power of the saints was associated in popular thought with the wholly out of the ordinary richness of their seen presences. The experiences reported by a child during three days of blindness

[6] Gratian, I *Dist.* 86, c. 18 (cols. 301-2); compare *PL* 16, col. 133 for Ambrose, *De officiis ministrorum libri tres*, lib. ii, c. 21, nos. 110-11.

[7] *Abbot Suger on St.-Denis*, pp. 76-7, 217; Murray, *Reason and Society*, p. 71.

[8] J. Sumption, *Pilgrimage: An Image of Mediaeval Religion* (London, 1975), p. 156; *Stow's Survey of London*, ed. H.B. Wheatley (Everyman edn., 1956), pp. 82-3, cites examples of bishops selling plate in times of famine, including Walter Suffield, bishop of Norwich (d. 1257), whose action is recorded by Matthew Paris.

[9] Sumption, *Pilgrimage*, pp. 52, 156, and plate I; *Liber miraculorum Sancte Fidis*, ed. A. Bouillet (Paris, 1897), pp. 9-10; *The Life of Christina of Markyate*, ed. C.H. Talbot (Oxford, 1959), pp. 186-7; *Reginaldi monachi Dunelmensis libellus de admirandis beati Cuthberti virtutibus*, (Surtees Society, 1835), p. 140.

and dumbness, that had been cured by Christopher of Cahors (d. 1272), were of being in a magnificent place in company with the holy man who was dressed in golden clothes.[10] Paradise with its inhabitants was a kingdom of gold.

Expectations of saints were closely linked with expectations of their images. This could result in disappointment, as well as amazement. One of the miracles of the Virgin turns on anticipation of this kind, in a clerk whose love of Our Lady had taken him to Rome in order to see the image of her reputedly painted by St. Luke. Unfortunately 'when he had seen that image him thought it was not so fair as he trowed, wherefore his love and his devotion was not so great as it was before he saw that image'. The disillusioned clerk fell ill, but the Virgin stood by him. She appeared in a vision and told him that despite this lessening of devotion the punishment of his sickness would not last. Interestingly, the clerk who had been so dissatisfied by the lacklustre Roman painting saw the Virgin in a very spartan attire. She was 'clad in a black coat and about her a girdle', with a simple band on her head and bare feet (Fig. 18).[11]

Such simplicity would have pleased the barefoot brigade of church critics. As church interiors (specially rich pilgrimage centres) became more and more encrusted with precious metals and jewels, questions continued to be asked, albeit by a minority. Such critics tended to be won over by the overwhelming weight of traditional practice, or to fall back on a kind of double standard – to the view that the abnegation of the few was not applicable to the many. Bernard of Angers, who was initially so shocked when he saw on the church altar at Aurillac a statue with the features of St. Gerald, made of the finest gold, later became a defender of such images.[12] Even St. Bernard of Clairvaux, who did not mince words when he attacked the 'vanity of vanities' of all this 'gold in the sanctuary', granted that the church's cartwheels of jewelled lights, golden relics and shining walls, while wholly inappropriate for monks, had their uses for simple and devout lay people.[13]

Critics of church gold tended to reiterate the same arguments. Neglect of charity came first: lavishing funds on walls deprived the poor. 'The church is resplendent in her walls, beggarly in her poor; she clothes her stones in gold, and leaves her sons naked; the rich man's eye is fed at the expense of the indigent. The curious find their delight here, yet the needy find no relief'. This case was not lost sight of. St. Bernard's plea was later voiced by Lollards, and

[10] *La religion populaire en Languedoc du XIIIe siècle à la moitié de XIVe siècle*, ed. E. Privat (Toulouse, 1976), p. 234.

[11] *An Illustrated Yorkshire Carthusian Religious Miscellany*, ed. J. Hogg, *Analecta Cartusiana*, 95 (1981), 3, p. 34; BL, Add. MS 37049, fo. 27 r. I am grateful to Milla Riggio for this reference.

[12] *Liber miraculorum Sancte Fidis*, pp. 46-7. On this statue and Bernard's reactions see J. and M.-C. Hubert, 'Piété chrétienne ou paganisme? Les statues-reliquaires de l'Europe carolingienne', *Settimane di Studio del Centro Italiano di Studi sull'Alto Medioevo*, 28 (1982), i, pp. 235-75 (for which reference I thank Judith Herrin). See above p. 12.

[13] *PL* 182, cols. 914-15 from Bernard's *Apologia* to William, Abbot of Saint-Thierry; cited *Documentary History*, ed. Holt, i, pp. 19-20.

Erasmus, who larded the account of his visit to the treasure-house at Canterbury with reminders of St. Thomas Becket's generosity to the poor, pointed to the praiseworthy record of bishops who had sold sacred vessels for poor relief.[14]

Connected with this view, that donors should look after needy people, instead of enriching buildings, was a deeply ingrained fear of gold. To seek and display it – even to serve God and increase devotion – was to risk the sins of covetousness and vanity. Here too Bernard stated a case that others repeated. Ostentation in imagery and churches was designed to attract donors. Gold talked. Believers journeyed and contributed to centres where they saw the best displays. 'Their eyes are feasted with relics cased in gold, and their purse-strings are loosed'.[15] The church, on this view, was engaged in the practice that Aristotle abhorred: making barren money breed.

However, the most important criticism was that which related to popular practice, and here the argument gained in substance as time went on. As the volume of church imagery grew ever bigger, the literate reflected on the different effects of different kinds of saints' depictions. Some commentators came to see that a plain carved statue of a holy person might serve devotion better than a richly painted and gilded one. Gold was a certain lure, but its magnetism was dangerous. It might promote envy rather than respect. Would the riches of Canterbury and Walsingham move a man to love God's commandments and to desire God, or more likely 'make his poor heart sigh, because he hath no such at home, and to wish part of it in another place'?[16] Tyndale's question of 1530 was a challenge, but by this time even some quite moderate critics were ready to admit that costly gilding could hinder charity and enhance vainglory. Even where this did not happen, the simple-minded were misled by dazzling saints. They took the image for the reality and made idols of figures of gold. As Eustache Deschamps put it, many people were convinced by the beauty of the shining gold that these figures were gods. English contemporaries, such as the poet John Gower, were pointing to the same danger, while Wycliffe suggested that the statues of the Virgin so dear to English women were no better than Diana of the Ephesians.[17]

[14] Ibid.; M. Aston, *England's Iconoclasts*, i (Oxford, 1988), p. 113; *The Colloquies of Erasmus*, ed. C.R. Thompson (Chicago, 1965), pp. 306-7. Such charity might go astray (in the eyes of strict reformers). Compare C.A. Pater, *Karlstadt as the Father of the Baptist Movements: The Emergence of Lay Protestantism* (Toronto, 1984) for Melchior Hoffmann's public humiliation of two women who had given the value of a golden chalice to the poor, but had the vessel made into gold chains for themselves.

[15] *PL* 182, col. 915; *Documentary History*, ed. Holt, i, p. 20.

[16] *The Work of William Tyndale*, ed. G.E. Duffield (Appleford, 1964), p. 74, from the prologue to the Book of Numbers.

[17] *Oeuvres complètes de Eustache Deschamps*, ed. le Marquis de Queux de Saint-Hilaire and G. Reynaud (Paris, 1878-1903), 8, pp. 201-3; *Complete Works of John Gower*, ed. G.C. Macaulay (Oxford, 1899-1902), 4, p. 99; G.A. Benrath, *Wyclifs Bibelkommentar* (Berlin, 1966), pp. 35-6, 338; Aston, *England's Iconoclasts*, i, p. 107.

In various quarters it came to be recognized that the quality of an image could have a bearing on its use – and usefulness. The most splendid statues were given the most respect. Gabriel Biel pointed out that those who attributed healing powers to images were apt, in their simplicity, 'to worship beautiful images more reverently than ugly ones, new more than old, those decorated with the special lustre of gold and regal clothes more than naked ones, believing them holier in being more precious'.[18]

This observation began to carry new weight when attached to biblical learning. If representations of saints were – on the church's own theory – the books of lay people, they should themselves be true to the book. Applying the canon of Scripture (as the Lollards did) to church imagery opened up a whole new strategy for critics of church art. It could be argued that images should be as poor as the persons they depicted; that gold and all kinds of sumptuous finery must go, as being untruthful statements. So, there was no place for a Christ 'nailed on the cross with much gold and silver and precious clothes, as a loincloth decorated with precious stones, and shoes of silver and a crown fretted full of precious jewels'; or a John the Baptist 'clothed with a mantle of gold and golden hair'.[19]

It was for the best of reasons that, when images came under reformist attack, golden images received a major share of the invective. For Old Testament proscriptions of idols specifically condemned those of gold and silver. Sixteenth-century reformers who concentrated fresh attention on the biblical prohibitions of images had to face the question whether molten images were specially dangerous. Those who knew Hebrew realized that there were linguistic difficulties in understanding precisely what sort of objects were indicated by key Old Testament texts. In the *Harmony of the Pentateuch*, which he only finished a year before his death, Calvin placed beside the *sculptile* of the Second Commandment in Exodus and Deuteronomy another key passage from Exodus; 'Thou shalt make thee no molten gods'. There was no doubt in Calvin's mind that God comprehended 'all kinds of images, when he forbids the making of molten gods', since he abhorred idols, whatever they were made of. 'But', Calvin went on, 'inasmuch as the insane zeal of superstition is the more inflamed by the value of the material or the beauty of the workmanship, Moses especially condemned molten gods'.[20]

A verse in chapter 20 of Exodus – following the Ten Commandments – made plain the same message. 'Ye shall not make with me gods of silver, neither shall ye make unto you gods of gold'. The most costly images seemed to inspire the

---

[18] *Gabrielis Biel Canonis Missa expositio*, ed. H.A. Oberman and W.J. Courtenay (Wiesbaden, 1963-76), 2, pp. 267- 8.

[19] *Selections from English Wycliffite Writings*, ed. A. Hudson (Cambridge, 1978), p. 84.

[20] John Calvin, *Commentaries on the Last Four Books of Moses, arranged in the Form of a Harmony*, ed. C.W. Bingham (Edinburgh, 1853), 2, p. 116; *Mosis Libri V, cum Iohannis Calvini Commentariis* (Geneva, 1563), p. 208 (on Exodus 34:17, in the exposition of the Second Commandment). By contrast with the Old Testament, there are only twenty-one references to gold/golden in the New.

worst idolatry: 'Idolaters', as Calvin put it, 'indulge themselves more fully in their worship of very precious metals, by the external splendour of which all their senses are ravished'. And images of this kind received prominent attention in the moves against idols. Zwingli, who pointed first to the 'silver gods' of Exodus when putting together the case against images in November 1523, submitted a memorandum to the Zurich Great Council the following month in which he recommended that 'the silver, gold, and other ornamental images shall not be carried again, either on festival or on other days, but the greatest treasure of the Word of God shall be carried in the hearts of men, not the idols before their faces'.[21] Steps had already been taken in Zurich to restrict the use of gilded processional reliquaries, and the following year saw a complete and orderly clearance of all the imagery in the city's churches.

If the Pentateuch directed iconoclasts against idols of gold, a book of the Apocrypha reinforced this drive. The sixth and last chapter of Baruch was the 'Epistle of Jeremiah', which was a sustained onslaught on the Babylonian gods of silver and gold: those unmoving objects carved out of wood, plated with silver and gold, to which sacrifice and worship were given. Baruch 6 was cited by both Wycliffe and Lollards in their condemnations of image-worship,[22] and this chapter received special attention as soon as the attack on idols became a priority of sixteenth-century reformers. A pamphlet called *Vanden Propheet Baruch*, published in the Low Countries in the 1520s and reprinted in 1558, took the form of a commentary on the sixth chapter, intense and passionate in attacking papal idols.[23] In England an edition of the *Epistle of the prophete Hieremie*, 'dissuading the people from idolatry, that is to say, worshipping of images', was printed by Robert Redman before 1540. The translator remained anonymous, but in addressing his text to a friend with whom he had recently been discussing the topic of imagery, he made clear his own rejection of the supernatural powers attributed to images.[24]

Baruch 6 also helped to fortify England's rejection of idols. The Homily against peril of idolatry, which probably did more than any other text to impress the sins of idolatry on English believers, pressed home the ancient concept that idolatry was spiritual adultery:

> They [church images] be trimly decked in gold, silver, and stone, as well the images of men as of women, like wanton wenches, (saith the prophet Baruch,) that love paramours, and therefore can they not teach us, nor our wives and daughters, any soberness, modesty, and chastity.

---

[21] Calvin, *Commentaries*; *Huldreich Zwinglis Sämtliche Werke*, ed. E. Egli et al. (Corpus Reformatorum, 1905-), 2, pp. 654, 814; C. Garside, *Zwingli and the Arts* (New Haven and London, 1966), pp. 146-60.

[22] Aston, *England's Iconoclasts*, i, p. 127, n. 6; *An Apology for Lollard Doctrines*, ed. J.H. Todd (CS, 20, 1842), pp. 85-6.

[23] K.P.F. Moxey, *Pieter Aertsen, Joachim Beuckelaer, and the Rise of Secular Painting in the Context of the Reformation* (New York and London, 1977), pp. 144-6.

[24] *An epistle of the prophete Hieremie* (Southwark, John Redman for Robert Redman [1539?]), *STC* 2792, colophon and prefatory address.

To enrich images was to encourage spiritual fornication, and the idolatrous church no better than a prostitute, painting herself and dressing up in gold, pearls, and jewels. Churches were full of such monstrous objects:

> . . . great puppets, wondrously decked and adorned; garlands and coronets be set on their heads, precious pearls hanging about their necks, their fingers shine with rings, set with precious stones; their dead and stiff bodies are clothed with garments stiff with gold. You would believe that the images of our men-saints were some princes of Persia . . . and the idols of our women-saints were nice and well trimmed harlots . . . [25]

The sometime virtues of donors were now odious incitements to vice. The kings and princes, archbishops and bishops once lauded by Suger for bestowing their finger-rings to make his golden altar frontal, had been as good as Gentiles. Joan Tule, who in 1407 had bequeathed her wedding-ring to the statue of the virgin on the high altar of Salisbury Cathedral, became the accomplice of spiritual fornicators. Maybe Thomas Bilney was paraphrasing some verses of Baruch as well as castigating his contemporaries when in 1527 he alleged that priests gave their mistresses to wear on loan necklaces that had been given to images.[26]

'Put away your golden gods, your silver gods, your stony gods'. Bilney's words, addressed to the parishioners of Willesden (who had their own precious Virgin) in 1527, followed by another attack on idols at the church of St. Magnus in London, where a new rood was about to be gilded, led directly to his arrest.[27] But within a decade Henry VIII had himself decided to take up the case against golden idols, and set England on the path of Zurich's reform.

As the campaign against idolatry gathered momentum in the different centres of northern reform, distinctions between different kinds of idols tended to be lost sight of. Imagery of all kinds went down under the iconoclasts' hammers. Yet there was a time when some pruning of church images, on something like Erasmian lines, was in the air. The idea that images were permissible providing they were not over-rich was being mooted by both critics

---

[25] *Certain Sermons or Homilies appointed to be read in Churches* (Oxford, 1844), pp. 165, 234-5. 'Great puppets' derives from Lactantius, citing Seneca (*grandes pupas*); compare Persius, *Satire* ii, 70.

[26] *Abbot Suger on St.-Denis*, p. 55; *The Register of John Chandler Dean of Salisbury*, ed. T.C.B. Timmins, Wilts. Rec. Soc., 39 (1984), p. 151; *The Acts and Monuments of John Foxe*, 4th edn rev. J. Pratt (London, 1977), 4, p. 648 and appendix VI (Reg. Tunstall fo. 134). Compare Baruch 6:10-11. At Seville in Holy Week women still lend necklaces and jewellery to adorn the Virgins of the *pasos* that are paraded round the city. Dr. Eamon Duffy remembers women giving rings to make a crown for a new statue of the Virgin, made for the Marian year of 1954 at Dundalk. Reformers might have linked such actions with one of their prototype idols, the golden calf, made out of earrings given by the people: Exodus 32:2-4, annotated in the Geneva Bible, 'Such is the rage of Idolaters, that they spare no cost to satisfy their wicked desires'.

[27] Foxe, *A. & M.*, 4, pp. 620-1, 627, 648; compare p. 582 for a critical reaction to newly gilded images *c.* 1520, and 5, appendix VI (Reg. Tunstall fos. 137-8) for Thomas Garrett (Garrard)'s condemnation of gilding images.

and defenders in the 1520s. A German pamphlet printed in Basel about the time of Luther's stand at Worms advocated proscribing all metal and carved imagery in church, while retaining plain pictures of saints mentioned in the Bible.[28] Soon after this a work written by Hieronymus Emser, defending images against Karlstadt's iconoclasm, argued that it was better for church art to be crude than impressive. 'The more beautiful the images are, the more they detain the viewer in the contemplation of art', so it would save money and improve devotion to have really bad images (*ganz schlechte Bilder*).[29]

It seems that in Germany some steps were taken towards forging church art that was poor – in material, if not in workmanship. In the early 1490s Tilman Riemenschneider carved a limewood altarpiece for the town church of Mün-nerstadt that was given a new, cheap finish of monochrome, without any of the customary polychrome and gilding. The figures grouped round the table for the Last Supper in the *Altar of the Holy Blood*, which Riemenschneider made ten years later for St. Jacobskirche in Rothenburg, may have manipulated the tonal qualities of light, but lacked all the emotional manipulation of precious metals.[30] These were plain wooden Apostles – poor in the way Michelangelo indicated. Erasmus was on the track of this chastened fashion when he wrote in 1526 about the altered state of St. James of Compostela. 'And thus so great an apostle, accustomed to shine from head to foot in gold and jewels, now stands a wooden figure with hardly a tallow candle to his name'.[31]

From the sixteenth century on, painters of northern canvases had no need of warnings like those of Alberti against the application of gold. But as it dropped out as an artistic medium, gold enjoyed some favour as a message. Gold itself became a topic in ways that seem to invite reflection on its dangers.

The weighing of gold became quite a popular subject. It lent itself to moralizing. The wife of the money-changer busy with his scales in a painting by Quentin Matsys is turning the pages of a book of hours. The portrayal of all the opulence of worldly goods associated with gold could point a finger at the vanity of possessions, as for instance in Petrus Christus's picture of a young couple buying a ring from St. Eligius (the patron saint of metal- workers), or in Pieter de Hooch's *Woman Weighing Coins* of about 1664. Concentration on the precise assessment of this most precious of earthly substances invited

---

[28] S.E. Ozment, *The Reformation in the Cities* (New Haven and London, 1975), p. 102 (that is, keeping close to the prohibition of graven images).

[29] Moxey, *Pieter Aertsen*, pp. 198-9; see also pp. 218-19 for the concern for simple unostenta-tious sculpture and paintings of the Virgin and saints expressed by the Catholic François Richardot in a sermon of 1567. For Emser's text see *A Reformation Debate*, trans. B.D. Mangrum and G. Scavizzi (Toronto, 1991).

[30] M. Baxandall, *The Limewood Sculptors of Renaissance Germany* (New Haven and London, 1980), pp. 18, 42, 48, 62, 172- 80, 186-90, 261-2. The Münnerstadt altarpiece was painted and gilded ten years later, perhaps suggestive of some contemporaries' dislike of the new style. See also Bernhard Decker, 'Reform within the Cult Image: The German Winged Altarpiece before the Reformation', in *The Altarpiece in the Renaissance*, ed. P. Humfrey and M. Kemp (Cam-bridge, 1990), pp. 90-105.

[31] *Colloquies of Erasmus*, pp. 288-9, from *Peregrinatio religionis ergo* (1526).

Fig. 19a, b Woodcuts of Moses receiving the Tables of the Law and the Worship of the Golden Calf in Cranmer's 1548 Catechism. The latter prefaces a long sermon on the commandment against idolatry; 'thou shalt not worship images, that is to say, thou shalt not gild them . . .'

viewers to make their own assessment of the ultimate value of the world's luxuries. The scales, with their reminder of the weighing of souls, promoted thought of last things. This association is made explicit in the most powerful of these depictions, Vermeer's *Woman Holding a Balance* – once known as *A Woman Weighing Gold*. Immediately behind the head of the pregnant woman in this picture is a painting of the Last Judgement, intimately linking the empty scales in her hand with the fate of the unborn child she carries. Weighing gold and pearls here served allusively the same spiritual purpose as the grand gold doors at Saint-Denis.[32]

Another topic that came to the fore in sixteenth-century painting was directly linked to contemporary criticism of religious art. The worship of the Golden Calf (as described in Exodus 32) was a scene commonly annexed to the Commandments which gained new prominence from reforming attacks on idolatry. In England a small woodcut showing worshippers dancing round the Calf was included in Cranmer's *Catechism* of 1548 (which included a long sermon against idolatry). Abroad, years later, a much more grandiose print, after Maarten van Heemskerck's depiction, showed an unbridled scene of revelry and worship round the Golden Calf. Paintings of this subject, such as Lucas van Leyden's and (in the following century) those of Nicolas Poussin and Jan Steen, developed the theme of sensual excess.[33] The worship of gold – the

[32] *L'or au temps de la renaissance*, pp. 28, 30; L.J. Slatkes, *Vermeer and his Contemporaries* (New York, 1981), pp. 55-6; L. Gowing, *Vermeer* (London, 1952), pp. 135-6; *Masters of Seventeenth-Century Dutch Genre Painting* (Exhibition Catalogue, Philadelphia Museum of Art, 1984), pp. 342-3.

[33] *A Catechism set forth by Thomas Cranmer*, ed. D.G. Selwyn (Appleford, 1978), text, p. 7; F.W.H. Hollstein, *Dutch and Flemish Etchings, Engravings and Woodcuts, c. 1450-1700* (Amsterdam, 1949-) 8, p. 246 (for the Heemskerck print, also illustrating the decalogue); B.D. Kirschenbaum, *The Religious and Historical Paintings of Jan Steen* (Oxford, 1977), pp. 71- 3, 216; L. Réau, *Iconographie de l'art chrétien* (Paris, 1955-9), 2, pp. 205-6.

golden idol – became linked with the worst excesses of sensuality. The vanity of gold outweighed its splendour.

The exchange between Michelangelo and Julius II took place at a moment of critical bifurcation in church art. Differences of opinion about the uses of gold played a role in the division of opinion that thereafter made the churches of northern and southern Europe so dissimilar in appearance. The church of Rome shared the preferences of Pope Julius and acted accordingly. Catholic reformers censored indecorousness in art – not gold. They brushed aside objections that too much splendour, like too much beauty, might block devotion. Loving images was part of loving God, and gilding the church part of the vision of the New Jerusalem.

Fig. 20 Engraving of a silver-gilt chalice (hallmarked 1525), belonging to the church of St Mary, Wylye, Wiltshire.

8

Iconoclasm at Rickmansworth, 1522: Troubles of Churchwardens*

One night in the early 1520s, probably in the first half of 1522, the church of St. Mary's, Rickmansworth, was badly damaged by arson. Iconoclasts deliberately set fire to all the images, to the reserved sacrament on the high altar, to the ornaments and jewels in the vestry, and to the rood and organs in the rood loft. The incendiaries made sure of their blaze by wrapping tow around the rood and pushing tow and banner staves through the bars of the chancel to act as fire-lighters. Their conflagration was also assisted by the large amount (280 pounds) of candle wax in the rood loft. At the same time, the offenders broke open the font and scattered the holy water. As a result of these actions, the chancel and vestry of the church were either severely damaged or destroyed.

The details of this scandalous affair are recorded in the indulgence that was subsequently issued by Cardinal Wolsey and Bishop Longland, promising pardons to all who contributed towards the restoration of Rickmansworth church after its shocking desecration by 'wretched and cursed people'.[1] Rickmansworth lay within the diocese of Lincoln, but as an exempt parish of the liberty of St. Albans, the first responsibility rested with Wolsey – abbot of St. Albans since 1521 – rather than with his friend John Longland. This indulgence (of which only one copy has survived) can from internal evidence be dated only to between the years 1521 and 1530 and is accordingly assigned

---

* This investigation would not have started without Colin Richmond, nor have continued as it has, without Derek Plumb. The former showed me the indulgence printed below and generously proposed this presentation; the latter lit on the chancery proceedings relating to it, and pointed out the usefulness of the lay subsidy of 1524-5. I am grateful to them both, and also thank Peter Gwyn and Katharine Pantzer for so kindly answering questions and sending information.

[1] BL C.18.e.2 (96); *STC*, 14077 c. 68. This indulgence, with its remarkable recitation of the iconoclasts' actions, has received curiously little attention from historians, though it was noticed in the VCH, *Hertfordshire*, ii, p. 385, after being cited by J. E. Cussans, *History of Hertfordshire*, 3 vols. (London, 1870-81), iii, pt. 2, p. 149, Hundred of Cashio. Cussans reports that the indulgence was found pasted inside the cover of a book bought by the BM at Dr. Cotton's sale in January 1868. It is printed in facsimile by K. W. Cameron, *The Pardoner and his Pardons: Indulgences Circulating in England on the Eve of the Reformation* (Hartford, CT, [1965]), p.49.

231

to *c.* 1525 in the *Short-Title Catalogue*.[2] However, other evidence makes it possible to define the incident more closely, and this shows that the repercussions continued for some years and caused considerable trouble for the churchwardens of Rickmansworth.

As a result of the severe damage to their church, the parishioners of Rickmansworth obtained a licence to collect alms for rebuilding and restoration. This ran into difficulties which led to a suit in chancery; and though the outcome of the case is not known it provides some additional information about the iconoclasts' impact.[3]

At the time of the incident the three churchwardens of the parish were Henry Wedon, Henry Evelyn and Richard Foderley (or Fotherley) – all of them, as might be expected, men of some substance in the village. According to their subsequent petition in chancery, they took action after the felonious and malicious robbing and despoiling of Rickmansworth church, 'grete part therof' having been 'distroyed and brent with fyre in the nyghte tyme,[4] wherby the vestementes bokes and ornamentes were petuosly consumed and brent with fyre'. Licence was given by letters patent for the churchwardens or their deputies to collect 'suche benyvolence and charytable almes' as they could from the king's subjects, to rebuild the church and refurnish it with ornaments. Accordingly (they claimed), they had, with the assent of the whole parish, appointed Thomas Carter, Jerome (Gereham or Jerram) Richardson *alias* Uprichard and John Wryght to undertake this collection in the dioceses of Salisbury, Winchester, Chichester, Bath and Wells, Exeter and all the dioceses of Wales, for three years ending on All Saints' Day (1 November) 1525. On this date the collectors were to pay the churchwardens the sum of £10 13s. 4d. and to return a full written account of the sums they had collected. Carter and his associates, however, although they had duly promised to render this account, never paid over the money and refused to provide any record of their collection.

In reply, the defendants, while granting it was true 'that the seyd chyrche of Rykmersworthe was robbed, spoyled, fyred and brent', claimed that the bill against them was insufficient. They raised the question of the negotiations for obtaining Wolsey's indulgence to benefactors of Rickmansworth church. According to the collectors, the churchwardens had agreed to obtain the cardinal's grant of pardon 'under hys gret seale for the seyd colleccioun in the

---

[2] Wolsey's death provides the *terminus ante quem*. The date 1521 is derived from the evidence of the type, since the indulgence was printed by John Skot, whose dates of activity are 1521-37. The absence of a proper 'sh' ligature made Miss Pantzer incline to a date between 1521 and 1525 for the indulgence, which has now been borne out by other evidence. On the productions of Skot ('a slovenly printer') see F. Isaac, *English and Scottish Printing Types* (Bibliographical Society Facsimiles and Illustrations, ii, 1930), nos. 50-2; idem, *English Printers' Types of the Sixteenth Century* (Oxford, 1936), p.11.

[3] PRO, C 1/593/49-50: this action can be dated between 1 Nov. 1525 and 18 Oct. 1529 (from internal evidence and the period of Wolsey's chancellorship).

[4] See below, chapter 9.

¶ Be it knowen to all cryste people which iopeth in theyr hartes of ye power of god shewed by his owne preepous body i fourme of bre= de in ye chyrche of Rykmerswoethe where wretched ⁊ cursed people cruelly ⁊ wylfully set fyre vpon all ye ymages ⁊on the canape ye the blessyd sacramēt was in⁊ tomake ye fyre moce cruell they put towe wt baner staues bytwene ye sparres⁊ braces of ye chaūsell thrughe ye whiche fyre ye sayd chaūsell was brent ⁊ ye pyx was moltē ⁊ ye bles= syd body of our loede Jhū cryst in foeme of brede was foūde vpō the hyghe awter ⁊ nothynge peryshed. Also they brake itenyr veheye put fyre amonge all ye oenamētes ⁊ Jewelles ⁊ brent ye sayd vestry ⁊ all ye was therin. Also in ye rode lofte they wrapped towe aboute ye blessyd rode ⁊ about a payre of oegans ⁊ melted all ye were in ye sayd lofte cōtepnynge in weyght.xiiii.scoe poūde where as ye flabynge fyre was in ye sayd lofte about ye blessyd ymage of Jhū cryst nother ye sayd ymage noe ye towe about it was nothynge hurte thrughe ye myght ⁊ power of our sauyour Jhū cryst. Also tomaynteyue theyr cruell oppynyons they wēte vnto ye fonte ⁊ brake it ope ⁊ dyspoyled ye water ye was halowed therin ⁊ cast it abrode in ye chyrche floe in dyspyte of ye sacramēt of baptyme. And foe as moche as ye substancy all mē of ye sayd parysshe hath inuewed ye kynges grace how honoe rably god was serued in ye sayd chyrche in tyme past, ⁊ also that it pleased hym to shewe his grete myght and power.

¶ Wherfoe my loede Cardynall and legate delatere hath graūted days of pardon releasynge of theyr penaūce in putg   to all the ye   we ony pte of theyr goodes to ye restoeyge of ye

¶   y loede of Lyncolne hath graunted .xl. days

Fig. 21 The indulgence for Rickmansworth church, issued by Cardinal Wolsey and John Long-land, bishop of Lincoln.

seyd dyoceis', meeting the necessary costs and charges. Only after this, they maintained, and the making and sealing of an indenture recording this contract, were they bound to pay the agreed sum of £10 13s. 4d. for the three-year collection. But the wardens had neither secured the pardon nor made the indenture – despite the collectors' own readiness – so they were under no obligation to hand over the money.

The response of Wedon, Evelyn and Foderley to these claims took up the question of the cardinal's pardon. They agreed that they had promised to petition Wolsey to make this grant, with the licence to the collectors, but countered firmly that the costs were to be met by the collectors themselves. The wardens had completed their part of the agreement, having 'moved' the lord cardinal so that Master Tonys,[5] who was then 'servaunt and attendaunt' to Wolsey, had been commanded to make the said pardon and licence, though the three collectors had failed to meet the costs and charges to which they were obliged. Notwithstanding which – according to the churchwardens – Carter, Richardson and Wryght had gone ahead and raised a lot of money. But, though they did not deny the fact of this collection, the collectors had failed to pay up, or to render any account.

The dispute arose from the failure to record in writing the agreement reached orally between the parties. The crux of the matter was the arrangement made for the payment of Cardinal Wolsey's pardon. The collectors maintained that the churchwardens were to meet these costs; the wardens claimed that this obligation rested on the collectors. The wardens also refused to accept that the indenture which the parties had failed to draw up was to have contained the alleged clause recording their obligation to obtain the pardon. The collectors, meanwhile, based their recalcitrance on this lack of the indenture – though they said they had paid over £3, even so. Doubtless they felt themselves to be in a strong position, given this lack of documentary evidence, especially since they could, presumably, flourish the royal letters patent as their authority to collect.

It seems clear that a collection of some kind *was* made, though it is impossible to judge between the rival claims as to its success. Against the assertion of the collectors that £3 'ys more then they have levyed or gathered', after deducting their expenses, we have to set the statement of the wardens that Carter, Richardson and Wryght had 'made ther colleccioun and receyvid the charitable almes and benevolence of the kynges subiettes in the diosises and places in the saide bill specified to a grete summe'.

---

[5]   Robert Toneys or Tones (d. 1526), canon of York, keeper of the hanaper from 8 June 1521 and clerk of the court of chancery, was a leading agent and councillor of Wolsey's in the 1520s. He had entered Wolsey's service by 1515 and was his registrar in the prerogative court set up in 1522-23 for Wolsey's and Warham's joint jurisdictions: through his friend William Burbank, Wolsey's secretary, Toneys received praise in letters of Erasmus; *Opus epistolarum Des. Erasmi Roterodami*, ed. P.S. Allen and H.M. Allen (Oxford 1906-58), iv, pp. 333-4, no. 1138: v, p. 541, no. 1492; Peter Gwyn, *The King's Cardinal: The Rise and Fall of Thomas Wolsey* (London, 1990), pp. 279, 301; A.F. Pollard, *Wolsey* (London 1953), pp. 196, 240-1; PRO, C66/637, m. 22.

The three churchwardens were striving through this action in chancery, to recover the sum of £10 13s. 4d. (or sixteen marks), with which they were in effect alleging that the collectors had absconded. The collectors did not, apparently, deny that they had made their tour and gathered the charitable alms. There seems to be no trace of their activities in the southern dioceses named in these proceedings, though that is perhaps not surprising if they were flaunting legatine authority, and they would scarcely have sought an episcopal licence if their own papers were in bad order.[6]

Although some aspects of this affair (including the identity of the arsonists) remain hopelessly obscure, it is possible to put some flesh onto some of the characters involved, and both wills and court records indicate that repercussions of the iconoclasm continued in the parish for some years. Isabel Hamond of Rickmansworth, who died in November 1522, made her will on 18 September and left 6s. 8d. 'to the reparacion of the . . . church of Rikmersworth'.[7] Her executors were her daughter and son-in-law, Joan and Richard Belch, and the witnesses to the will included the vicar, Mr. Thomas Cotton, who had been at Rickmansworth for forty years,[8] and George Belch – both of whom will reappear shortly. About two years after this, the church repair fund gained 3s. 4d. from one of the parish's more affluent inhabitants, William Dolte, who died in the summer of 1524, leaving his body to be buried (as relatively few were) inside the parish church.[9] There is no means of knowing how the restoration work progressed, but the will of the yeoman blacksmith, John a Dene, who died (aged about fifty-nine) in May 1529, suggests that by this time it was well advanced, for evidently the organ, destroyed in the iconoclasts' fire, had been replaced. 'Item, I bequethe to the reysyng of the organs within the said church of Rykmersworth 6s. 8d'.[10] And by 1536, when Henry Wedon died leaving half a mark each to the church and 'to the gyldyng of the Rood', the structural repairs may have been completed.[11]

---

[6] I have found no mention of the collectors in the printed register of Bishop Clerk of Bath and Wells, or in the unprinted registers of Bishops Audley, Fox and Sherborne, of Salisbury, Winchester and Chichester respectively.

[7] HRO, ASA 2 AR, fo. 183 r. Bequests of this kind were common well before this date so it would be unwise to relate Isabel's bequest to the arson damage. She had been a widow for many years, her husband Thomas Hamond having died in 1499, ibid., fo. 96 r.

[8] Thomas Cotton (Coton), whose career is considered below, was already to be found at Rickmansworth in 1479, before he became vicar.

[9] HRO, ASA 2AR, fo. 190 r. 'Item to the reparacions of the paroch church of Rikmersworth 3s. 4d'. William Dolte was a man of estate (disposing of rights in a house and land called Canons), listed in the subsidy of Jan. 1524 with £8-worth of goods and three servants, PRO, E 179/120/114, m. 5 r.

[10] HRO, ASA 2 AR, fo. 209 v. John a Dene, yeoman (whose will, like Dolte's, was witnessed by Thomas Cotton), was the father of Thomas a Dene – mentioned below – to whom he left his shop with all the implements belonging to it. He gave his age as twenty-five in Aug. 1495, ASA 2 AR, fo. 80 v. With goods assessed at £10 in the subsidies of 1524 and 1525, he was among the wealthiest top twenty of the parish of Rickmansworth; PRO, E 179/ 120/ 114, m. 4 r; E 179/120/ 134, m. 5 r.

[11] HRO, ASA 2 AR, fo. 238 r.

All three of the wardens of 1522 lived long enough to see the iconoclasm that had afflicted their parish turning into official policy, endorsed by the highest authorities in the land. They outlived the old vicar, Thomas Cotton, who was still active in May 1529 (when he witnessed a Dene's will), but by February 1535 had been replaced by William Man.[12] Henry Evelyn, like Henry Wedon, died in 1536, Richard Foderley seven years later, in 1543. Probably the three men were all lifelong inhabitants of the parish. Henry Wedon was a husbandman, who, with his son Thomas, lived in the hamlet of West Hyde on the River Colne, two miles downstream from the centre of Rickmansworth. Henry's goods were estimated at £20 in the subsidy of 1524-5; his son's at 40 shillings; and listed with them was a servant, John Fisher, whose yearly wage was 20 shillings.[13] Henry Evelyn, whose will was proved in September 1536, was of sufficient standing to envisage being buried 'in the parish church or churchyard'. He also lived at West Hyde, in 1524 with both his sons (William and John), and the following year with William and two servants. With goods of £22 Evelyn owed 2 shillings more on the subsidy than Henry Wedon, and he left extensive bequests of money, stock and land to his two sons and four married daughters, some of this land being in the nearby parish of Chalfont. Evelyn's only executor was John Wood, the parish clerk, and besides the sums he left to the church and parish guild of Rickmansworth, his old – almost proprietorial – responsibility towards it was reflected in his bequest of 20 shillings for mending 'the hygh way where moost neid is betwixt my house and my parish church'.[14] Richard Foderley was less propertied than the other two. He lived just outside Rickmansworth, across the river at Batchworth, with his daughter Margery and John Foderley (perhaps his brother), and the income from his lands was put at £3 6s. 8d. at the time of the subsidy. He made his will two years before he died, 'beyng feble yn body and hole yn mynd', and left his

[12] John a Dene's will seems to be the last in the sequence that Thomas Cotton witnessed from 1488 on. William Man was vicar of Rickmansworth, witnessing the will of John Holting the elder, on 1 Feb. 1534/5, HRO, ASA 2 AR, fo. 231 v. The vicar might well have resigned because of old age. There was a Thomas Cotton, M.A., who became rector of Greenford, Middlesex (about eleven miles from Rickmansworth) in Aug. 1518, who resigned in 1528, at which date the Rickmansworth vicar would have been sixty-three; Reg. FitzJames, Guildhall Library, London, M5 9531/9, fo. 77 v (1xxv); G. Hennessy, *Novum repertorium ecclesiasticum parochiale Londinense* (London 1898), p. 175.

[13] PRO, E179/120/114, m. 4 v, E179/120/134, m. 5r; HRO, ASA 2 AR, fo. 238 r. The only relatives mentioned in Wedon's will were his wife Alice and son Thomas. John Knight was one of the witnesses and probably also an overseer. See below n. 62 on the Wedons, or a Wedons.

[14] PRO, E 179/120/114. m. 4 v, E 179/120/134, m. 5 r; HRO, ASA 2 AR, fos. 237 v-8 r. William Evelyn was estimated in the 1525 subsidy at £3; in 1540-1 at £20, E179/120/143. The will does not specify which of the Chalfont parishes he had land in.

soul simply and unconventionally 'unto allmyghte god my maker and Redemer'.[15]

In the meantime, what sort of people were the collectors, and what became of them? There is no one by the name of Carter, Richardson (Uprichard) or Wryght listed in the 1524-5 Subsidy Rolls as holding property in Rickmansworth or any of its neighbouring hamlets. But in the Fishpool ward of St. Albans, eleven miles away, three men are listed whom it seems safe to identify as the three collectors. Thomas Carter and John Wryght (whose names are adjacent in the 1525 return) were both recorded with a servant apiece, the latter's wage increasing from 30 to 40 shillings between 1524 and 1525, while the rating on his master's goods dropped from £5 to £3. Carter remained assessed at £4, his servant receiving £2 wages. Further down the list for the same ward appears the name of Jerome ('Geram') ap Richard, assessed in both years at the lowest rating of 20 shillings, and accompanied in the second assessment by John ap Richard.[16] It seems on the face of it unlikely that the churchwardens would have delegated, or subcontracted, the collection of the parish subsidy to complete outsiders or strangers – and indeed, had they done so, the possibility of subsequently taking the culprits to court would have been severely diminished. Certainly, there were links enough between Rickmansworth and its 'mother church' of St. Albans for it to be possible for Carter, Wryght and Uprichard, if they were living in Fishpool ward in 1521- 2, to have been known and commissioned by Wedon, Evelyn and Foderley on the recommendation of 'divers honeste persones'. Equally, given what happened, and the odium that would have descended on the three men in the narrow world of parish politics if they were recruited from among Rickmansworth's parishioners, they might well have found life there difficult by 1524-5.

Carter, admittedly, is a common name, but it seems very possible that the Thomas Carter who was living at Abbots Langley (about halfway between Rickmansworth and St. Albans) when he made his will on 10 July 1537 was the man of that name who had been appointed one of the Rickmansworth collectors fifteen years or so earlier. At the time of his death – and his will was proved on the same day that he made it – Carter undoubtedly had links with Rickmansworth. For, in addition to the house and land he held in Abbots Langley, Carter also had a house and land in Rickmansworth, which Ellen his wife was to hold until his son Nicholas came of age. Also, besides the sums he

[15] PRO, E179/120/114, m. 5 r, E179/120/134, m. 5 v; HRO, ASA, 5 AR, fo. 37 v (the vicar, William Man, was one of the witnesses to this will, which mentions the testator's brother John). This preamble contrasts with the conventional phrase used by testators like John a Dene or Henry Wedon, who committed their souls 'unto almighty God and to our blessed lady saint Mary and to all the holy company of heaven'. The will of William Spone (1 Oct. 1538), written by the vicar's deputy John Rolff, and witnessed by Foderley, which opened in the traditional way, left the testator's body 'to be buryed in the parisshe churche of Rykmersworthe before the Roode' – suggesting he might have been a believer in the miracle claimed by Wolsey's indulgence. Spone had an official connection with the More, HRO, ASA 3 AR, fo. 15 v, 4 AR fo. 26 v.

[16] PRO, E179/120/114, m. 3 v, E179/120/134, m. 3 v, 4 r.

left to the church of St. Laurence in Abbots Langley, and the 8 pence bequeathed to the shrine of St. Alban, he gave money to the church of Rickmansworth.[17]

The Rickmansworth wills during these years – surviving in some numbers in the registers of the archdeacons of St. Albans – show that the parish had a fraternity or brotherhood of the Virgin and St. Katherine which attracted donations from many testators. The receipts of this guild, together with other parish collections, were treated as taxable in the 1524 subsidy, which collected 5 shillings from the £10 'in the box of our lady fraternyte'. This sum was well ahead of the amounts (between 20 and 30 shillings) contained in the boxes of the Trinity, St. Katherine and St. Anthony.[18] It seems likely that the chapel dedicated to Our Lady of the Island, which stood in the churchyard of St. Mary's, was the home of this fraternity, and, judging by the sums bequeathed to it, this building was constantly in need of repair. It may have been a recent structure, if it can be identified with the 'new chapel' to whose fabric testators left money in 1484 and 1485.[19]

In 1525-6, when the parish still had hopes of clawing back the money collected to repair the damages of the iconoclasts' fire, the two wardens of this guild were George Belch and John Haydon. Six years or so after their term of office had ended, in the autumn of 1532, the parishioners brought a suit against one of these wardens in the archdeaconry court of St. Albans for insufficient accounting. George Belch, whose co-warden had died the previous year, was cited on 30 September 1532 to reply to the charge that he had not rendered proper account for the period of his wardenship of the fraternity of St. Mary of Rickmansworth. The case continued for several court terms until Belch was discharged on 17 May 1533.[20] Though the recent troubles over the collection of the benevolence were not mentioned in this suit, it seems altogether likely that their unfortunate experience in this affair contributed to parishioners' vigilance over the keeping of their funds.

---

[17] HRO, ASA 3 AR, fo. 2 r. Carter also had an interest in woodland in the parish of Watford, which is on the main road between Rickmansworth and St. Albans. Besides leaving sums to their 'mother church' of St. Albans, quite a few testators in the archdeaconry of St. Albans were still making bequests in the 1530s to the shrine of St. Alban.

[18] PRO, E179/120/114, m. 5 r (4d was payable on each of these funds).

[19] HRO, ASA 2 AR, fos 45 r, 47 r. These donations could alternatively have related to the chapel of St. Katherine (referred to below) in Rickmansworth church. Various wills included bequests for repairs to the chapel of 'Our Lady of Ilond', and testators of 1519 and 1526 requested burial in this chapel 'standing in the churchyard of Rickmansworth'. Rickmansworth church was rebuilt twice in the nineteenth century and only the west tower remains from earlier structures.

[20] HRO, ASA 7/2, fos 74 r-5 r, 76 r-7 r, 78, and for the depositions cited below ASA 8/1, fos 54 r-6 r. In this case ('Belcher in causa compoti') Belch was cited as warden of the fraternity on articles concerning 'anime sue salutem'; 'parochiani obiicerunt quod non reddidit compotum pro tempore administracionis sue'. The first three witnesses (Robert Rolle, John Mylward and Thomas Spenser) seem to have been examined on 29 Nov. 1532; William Creke's and Henry Gonner's evidence was heard on 18 Jan. 1533, when Thomas a Dene was cited.

The depositions of the six witnesses who gave evidence in this case indicate that the annual receipts of the Rickmansworth fraternity may have been about £12 or more, derived from several sources. Quarterages produced £4 6s. 8d. a year, the offerings received from women's purifications a further 5 marks (i.e. £3 6s. 8d.), and another sizeable sum was usually raised by the wardens' annual dinner. The main outlay was the stipend of the guild chaplain (£6 13s. 4d.). George Belch and John Haydon stood accused of having received £15 and loose change ('odd money') from the previous wardens – John Hayward and Richard Martyn – when they came into office, and of having had only £9 to hand over to their successors – Henry Gonner and William Hutchinson (Hochynson). Quite a venerable team of village worthies was called on to put the record straight. They included some of the richest, and probably also some of the oldest, inhabitants of the parish – such 'substancyall men' as Wolsey's indulgence alluded to.

The innkeeper Robert Rolle, who had moved to St. Albans in 1528, had before that time lived in Rickmansworth for more than thirty years. John Mylward, yeoman, had also been in the parish for over a generation, while the baker Thomas Spenser, whose bequests in the long will that he made in August 1539[21] included half a mark to the guild of Sts. Mary and Katherine, had by the time of his death likewise lived in the place for thirty-four years. In the subsidy returns of 1524-5, these three men were among Rickmansworth's most affluent inhabitants, being listed as having goods to the value of 10 marks, £20, and 20 marks (£13 6s. 8d.) respectively.[22] Two of the other three witnesses (all described as *litterati*)[23] were younger and had gone up in the world since the time of the subsidy, which had placed them all in the same economic bracket. William Creke, a somewhat garrulous sixty-year old, had spent his whole life at Rickmansworth, but, though of gentle birth (*generosus*), his movable goods in 1524-5 were estimated at only 40 shillings. Henry Gonner, husbandman, aged twenty-eight, and Thomas a Dene, smith, aged thirty, had both benefited substantially from the deaths of their fathers, which brought the latter (son of the benefactor of the organ) his workshop in 1529 and the former the management of a sizeable landed inheritance in the year of the court action.[24]

The testimony given by some of the witnesses suggests that feelings in the parish were running high. Several people remembered the day (it was either a Sunday or a holy day) when Belch and Haydon had come to give their reckoning. Those present on this occasion were said to have included besides

---

[21] See note n. 55 below.

[22] PRO, E179/120/144, m. 4 r, E179/120/134, m. 5 r.

[23] Although the term *litteratus* is only used of Creke, a Dene and Gonner, it seems likely that the first three (older) witnesses also had some degree of literacy (see below on Spenser); possibly these differences of description derived from the different dates of their examinations.

[24] PRO, E179/120/114, m. 4; E179/120/134, m. 5 r. Henry Gonner and Thomas a Dene (the former working for his father, the latter already independent and employing a servant) were listed with goods of £3 and £2 respectively. See nn. 10 and 25 for the wills of John a Dene and Roger Gonner.

Rolle, Mylward, Spenser, Creke, Gonner and a Dene, Richard Foderley (the churchwarden of 1522), Roger Gonner (Henry's father, the most propertied man – in goods – in the parish, who held the lease of Rickmansworth parsonage and died early in 1532) and Thomas Castleman (a churchwarden in 1527).[25] The assembled party gathered in the church house round a table on which the wardens placed their money box and key, a book (presumably their account book) and various paper bills. The box was opened and the money counted, after Henry Gonner 'did cast the bille and tryed the bylle what shuld remayne in the box'. The box apparently contained only £9. Trouble then began. Robert Rolle launched into a furious attack on Belch for having made such a mess of the accounts, and 'with open mouth fowly rebuked the said George Belch and said the same Belch had not doon well'. Belch replied that 'he cowde doo no better than the parissh wold yeve'. His paper bill was deemed insufficient by the parish (according to Thomas Spenser), and he was told to take it away and make a proper account. The money was returned to the box, which was given, together with the book, to the keeping of Henry Gonner, one of the new wardens. The paper bill remained with Roger Gonner and Robert Rolle, since the other new warden, William Hutchinson, was not present and so that Henry Gonner 'shuld not be hold suspect havyng alle in his own handes'. Thomas a Dene, who arrived on the scene between high mass and evensong in the midst of the proceedings (and who seems to have made a quick getaway), heard Robert Rolle declare that the outgoing wardens had lost £6.

Belch himself was vague about his receipts from purifications and quarterages but estimated his total at 17 nobles. He admitted having lost about £5 on the dinner but claimed he had delivered all the rest of his takings in the box, 'and so ther remayne not a peny in his handes'.

The two wardens, George Belch and John Haydon, were both men of substance, neighbours and also friends. Belch (with other members of this family) lived in the hamlet of Chorleywood, about two miles from the centre of Rickmansworth. Haydon's home was a mile or so away, across the valley of the River Chess, at Micklefield Green. Their assessed goods in 1524-5 were equivalent (£12 and 20 marks respectively), though Belch, unlike Haydon, did not have a waged servant.[26] When John Haydon drew up his short will at the end of March 1531, two months before his death, his witnesses were Henry Gonner, George Belch and John Knight (to be encountered again below).

[25] HRO, ASA 7/1, fo. 45 v. In 1524 and 1525 Roger Gonner's goods were assessed at 40 marks (£26 13s. 4d.), and he had three waged servants. His will (dated 31 Aug. 1528, proved 21 Feb. 1532, ASA 2 AR, fo. 219r), in which he expected burial in Rickmansworth church, refers to lands in Isleworth, Middlesex, as well as in Rickmansworth, and some of the land his son Henry was to inherit after the death of his wife Joan, descended from his brother-in-law, John Kyng. A Joan Gonner was living at the time of her death in 1558, ASA 6 AR, fo. 129, in the Rickmansworth parsonage with her son Roger.

[26] PRO, E 179/120/114, m. 4 v, E 179/120/134, m. 5. Other Belches assessed for subsidy in Chorleywood were George's brother Richard, who died in 1528 (£4 goods), and William – a husbandman who died in 1526 – (20s. from land).

Belch – if he can be identified with the man of that name who made his will just before Christmas in 1558, and died about eight weeks later – may have lived to a much riper age. One of the young godsons to whom he left 4d. was George Haydon. A large beneficiary, who both witnessed the will and also was appointed its overseer, was Richard Alexander, gentleman.[27] Both he and John Knight seem – as will appear – to have had an interest in Bible-reading.

Local differences of various kinds may have contributed to the acrimony of this case. The Belches, who constituted quite a local clan in the parish of Rickmansworth, were involved during these years in more than one other suit in the archdeacon's consistory. In the summer of 1528 the case was being heard of *John Kyng* v. *Agnes Belcher*, in which the plaintiff alleged that Agnes was 'in the service and power of Roger Gonner and Joan his wife', so that Agnes, out of fear and coercion, did not dare to confess her contract of matrimony with him. No doubt there may have been more to this than meets the eye (given that Mrs. Gonner was the plaintiff's sister), but Kyng's plea was sufficiently persuasive for Agnes to be removed from the house of this village magnate and sent off to lodge ('sequestered' was the legal term) while the suit was pending, with John Bernard at St. Albans.[28]

In the years that followed the nocturnal firing of its church Rickmansworth may have been an unusually divided parish. But what of the time before that event? Were there any special circumstances that might explain why the iconoclasts chose this place, at this time, for their exceptional attack?

Rickmansworth was no ordinary country parish. As one of the Hertford-shire manors of the abbey of St. Albans (acquired before the Conquest and subsequently appropriated to the sacrist), the vicarage of Rickmansworth was in the gift of the abbot.[29] From the end of 1521 until February 1530 the abbot was Cardinal Wolsey who, when he joined with Bishop Longland to issue the indulgence, was certainly familiar with the place. For, in addition to this link in his chain of church patronage, Rickmansworth was the site of a great house (or palace) which brought Wolsey into frequent residence during the decade in which he held the abbey *in commendam*.[30] Moor Park, or the More, had

[27] HRO, ASA 2 AR, fo. 216 v; 6 AR, fos. 175 v-6 v. Haydon left stock and grain to his two sons and two daughters and was to be buried in the churchyard, whereas Belch, a much more propertied man at the time of his death, expected burial inside Rickmansworth church. Belch's will (below n. 61) was taken up with providing for the maintenance of his household and estate by his three sons and for the upbringing of 'all my yong children'.

[28] HRO, ASA 7/2, fos. 48 r-9v. The family of Belch or Belche, Belcher (see n. 27) is found at Rickmansworth from the fifteenth to the eighteenth century.

[29] R. Newcourt, *Repertorium ecclesiasticum parochiale Londinense* (London 1708-10), i, pp. 862-3. Being only about eleven miles away, Rickmansworth was an easy ride from St. Albans. Documents relating to the vicarage and the abbey's Rickmansworth lands are to be found in BL, MSS Harl. 433 fo. 153 r, and Arundel 34 (a St. Albans register) fos. 37 v-45 v. See also A. E. Levett *Studies in Manorial History* (Oxford 1938), pp. 98, 113-14.

[30] Already before this Wolsey was to be found at the More, for instance, in the spring of 1521, when an informer communicated material relating to the duke of Buckingham, *LP*, iii, pt. 1, p. 490, no. 1283.

belonged in the fifteenth century to George Neville, archbishop of York, who had built there 'ryghte comodiusly and plesauntly'.[31] At his arrest in 1472 the estate was seized by the Crown, in whose hands it remained until the 1520s. Henry VIII then granted the More to Wolsey, who made it one of his chief residences. He enlarged and improved both house and park at considerable expense. Between 1524 and 1529 Wolsey often dated letters and entertained the king and court at this his favourite house,[32] the most grandiose of these occasions being the gathering of French and English notables who met to conclude the Treaty of the More in the summer of 1525. This peace between France and England was signed at the More on 30 August and proclaimed there a week later.[33]

Among those present at the signing of the treaty was Archbishop Warham. Wolsey had invited him to stay, but the archbishop (whose relationship with the cardinal was not exactly cordial) refused. The effusiveness of the note he sent back to the More from Otford on 26 August 1525, in response to the cardinal's 'very loving offer of a lodging for me' in this 'moost goodly and delectable maner', betrays a sense of embarrassment. 'Albeit, your grace not displeased, I wold bee well contented to bee with my folk at my old host the vicar of Rigmansworth, your gracis chapellaine, being in myne opinion a very honest and loving man'.[34] The incumbent with whom Warham was proposing to lodge his party was Mr. Thomas Cotton, whose character the archbishop seems here to have been defending, rather peculiarly one might think, particularly in view of the fact that Cotton was (we learn) Wolsey's own chaplain.

In 1525 Thomas Cotton was somewhat over sixty – about ten years younger than the archbishop.[35] He had been associated with Rickmansworth for at least forty-five years and may well have served as assistant parish clerk before gaining charge of the living. In November 1479, when Mr. John Wynton was vicar, Cotton was remembered in the will of a local testator, and a few years

---

[31] *A Chronicle of . . . King Edward the Fourth, by John Warkworth*, ed. J.O. Halliwell (Camden Society, 1839), pp. 25, 70.

[32] Cussans, *History*, iii, pt.2, p. 149; VCH, *Herts.*, ii, p. 376. Pollard, *Wolsey*, p. 325, cites du Bellay thinking the More more splendid than Hampton Court. The cardinal's sumptuous building works included galleries 'all gilted above'; *LP Addenda*, 1, i, pp. 156-7, no. 467. The king seems to have taken over the property when Wolsey became *persona non grata* by the end of March 1530, and Catherine of Aragon was relegated to the More from August 1531 to the summer of 1532. On Wolsey's building at the More see *Cardinal Wolsey: Church, State and Art*, ed. S.J. Gunn and P.G. Lindley (Cambridge, 1991), pp. 35-6, 91-3; Heather Falvey, 'The More: Archbishop George Neville's Palace in Rickmansworth, Hertfordshire', *The Ricardian*. ix (1992), pp. 290-302.

[33] T. Rymer, *Foedera* (London 1739-45), vi, pt. 2, pp. 21-32; *LP*, iv, pt. 1, pp. 717-18, nos. 1600-3.

[34] PRO, SP1/35, fo. 264 r; *LP*, iv, pt. 1, p. 715, no. 1591. Reg. Warham (Lambeth), ii, fo. 385 v, records Warham at Lambeth on 26 Aug. 1525.

[35] Cotton gave evidence in the summer of 1495 on the validity of a Rickmansworth will, and then stated that he was aged thirty and more, HRO, ASA 2 AR, fo. 80 v.

later he was celebrating a trental for another parishioner.[36] When Wynton died, after a ministry of nearly a generation, in November 1480, the vicarage passed to an Austin friar, Thomas Hemingford, who, as incumbent of the neighbouring Sarratt, already had a hand in Rickmansworth affairs. But Thomas Cotton was in the line of succession, for Abbot Wheathampstead granted the nomination to the vicarage to George Daniel, esquire, and John Ashby (both inhabitants of Rickmansworth), who put him forward – an annual pension of 10 marks being reserved. This was in January 1481, when Cotton was described as chaplain, not yet master. The following year, now with the title of *Magister*, Cotton became vicar of Chesham, a few miles away in Buckinghamshire. He resigned this living after six years, towards the end of 1488, and presumably succeeded to the Rickmansworth vicarage at this time. Meanwhile Thomas Hemingford, who held several Hertfordshire livings, was deprived of Sarratt on the grounds of apostasy in May 1485, but continued to frequent Rickmansworth after that.[37]

The personality of this long-lived vicar seems impenetrable, for his occasional appearances in the records offer no clues. There is no reason to suppose that Thomas Cotton was particularly litigious, though he appears in several lawsuits during his incumbency. He brought two cases in the court of the archdeaconry of Buckingham in 1496, both in pursuit of dues owing, and both of which were settled in his favour. William Hide of Denham was cited for withholding a mortuary and William Rede of Amersham for failure to pay tithe – the latter offence clearly being of some proportions since two local vicars were among the four men who supported the award under a penalty of £5.[38] Years later Cotton appeared as a defendant in a suit in chancery relating to the descent of some property in Rickmansworth, which hung fire because of the inaccessibility of the deeds relating to it. The case of 1519 stemmed from a

---

[36] HRO, ASA 2 AR, fos. 35 r, 42 v, wills of John Gardyner (16 Nov. 1479) and John Rydale (24 Nov. 1482).

[37] *Registrum Abbatiae Johannis Whethamstede*, ed. H.T. Riley (RS, London, 1872-3), ii, pp. 118-19, 124, 189-90, 199, 227, 236-7, 273; Newcourt *Repertorium*, i, pp. 862-3; A. Hamilton Thompson, *The Abbey of St. Mary in the Meadows, Leicester* (Leicester, 1949), p. 116; P. Heath, *English Parish Clergy on the Eve of the Reformation* (London, 1969), pp. 55, 177; Cussans, *History*, iii, pt. 2, pp. 117, 161. (George Daniel, esquire died in 1491/2, HRO, ASA 2 AR, fo. 62 r. On John Ashby see below.) Cussans (followed by the VCH, *Herts.*, ii, p. 385) interpreted Hemingford's apostasy as probably 'nothing more than a leaning towards Lollardism'. As vicar of Sarratt, Hemingford was left 10 marks by Eudo Stokker in June 1473 to celebrate masses at Rickmansworth and other Rickmansworth testators left him money in the following years. He was still vicar of Rickmansworth in Aug. 1483 (when he witnessed the will of John Wynkborn, esquire) and was supervisor of a will in July 1484; in Oct. 1491 Cotton is mentioned as vicar, HRO, ASA 2 AR, fos. 14 r, 24 r, 25 r, 35 r, 36 v, 41 v, 45 r, 60 r,. See Emden (C), p. 163, for the Thomas Cotton who was scholar of Eton and King's Colleges, holding a fellowship at the latter from 1479 till *c.* 1485.

[38] *The Courts of the Archdeaconry of Buckingham, 1483-1523*, ed. E.M. Elvey (Buckinghamshire Record Society, xix, 1975), p. 170, no. 241; p. 175, no.247

will made over twenty years earlier, in which the testator had surrendered his copyhold into the hands of the vicar and John a Dene.[39]

Thomas Cotton may have been unadventurous in his ecclesiastical career, but life at Rickmansworth was certainly not uneventful. His parish, with its highway leading to London,[40] and the palatially royal scale of the More, was near the centre – sometimes itself became the centre – of national events. And his parishioners, if they were a mixed and sometimes contentious bunch, included many who were loyal and generous to St. Mary's Church. They regularly (richer and poorer testators alike) left money for church lights and forgotten tithes in their wills. Some of them also, under Thomas Cotton's guiding hand, sought to improve the furnishings of the parish church and saw to the building of a new vestry.

John a Dene's mother, Margaret a Dene, was one in a line of Rickmansworth widows whose minds turned, at their time of will-making, to the needs of St. Mary's. Her choice in 1496 was of vestments, and, in addition to altar cloths, she wished her executors to buy as soon as possible a cope and two tunicles of purple violet, to match the vestment that had been given to the church by Roger and Joan Belch. Others, such as Thomas Gray, who died six years later, preferred the glint of metal; like Mrs. a Dene he gave her son responsibility as executor for seeing that the 8 marks he left for this purpose were spent on buying a chalice. John a Dene was in demand in these matters, in 1504 finding himself charged with purchasing an antiphoner, 'as good as can be conveniently bought' on behalf of William Sebyn (who died that April, aged forty-eight). If such bequests displayed ample goodwill towards the testators' place of worship, it is also surely no coincidence that the vicar was so often on hand to witness their final dispositions and, presumably, ready to prompt with suggestions about lacks in his church's inventory. Two wills of 1502-3 reflect this influence. Richard Tredway wanted his executors to buy 'a good and an honest surples for the vicar of Rikmersworth to doo god service in to the honour of the parissh', while John Stokker requested the purchase of 'a sufficient masse boke well written and well notyd aftir the discretion of the vicar of Rikmersworth and other such as can skill of such thynges', the book to remain in the parish 'for ever'.[41]

Whatever his pastoral qualities, Thomas Cotton evidently knew how to look after the material prosperity of his church. Possibly it was as a result of this spate of donations that, some years after he became vicar, the parish embarked

---

[39] PRO, C1/595/13, C1/596/21; HRO, ASA 2 AR, fo. 91 r. Cotton's co-defendant in this suit was John Fazakerley, nephew of William Seward. In 1498 Thomas Seward [Sywarde] had wished John Fazakerley to have first refusal of the purchase of his house; it was the custody of the deeds relating to a messuage and garden that was at issue in the subsequent suit.

[40] Several testators left sums for the repair of the *via regia*, called 'ridgeway lane', leading from Rickmansworth towards London, HRO, ASA 2 AR, fos. 15 v, 33 r, 41 v.

[41] HRO, ASA 2 AR, fos. 80 v, 83 r, 106 r, 111 r, 113 r, 117 v. Roger Belch died in 1476; ibid., fo. 24 r. John Stokker wished to be buried in the churchyard of Rickmansworth 'besyde my frendes that are partid to the mercy of god'. His wife thought better of this.

on building a new vestry. In the summer of 1506 John Frere bequeathed 7 shillings 'toward the makyng of a new vestyary' in Rickmansworth, and the following year Edward Metcalfe left half a mark in his will for the church's 'new storehouse'. Work was still in progress in 1509 and 1511, when further sums for the new building were received from John Gibbs and John Durrant,[42] but by January 1513 the structure was nearing completion. In January that year Jane Stokker, the rich widow of John Stokker, made her will and gave 6s. 8d. 'to the fynysshyng of the newe work in the chyrch of Rykmersworth'.

Jane Stokker did not do things by halves, and she thought about the contents of the new vestry, as well as her own memorial in the church. Her executors (John Head, her son-in-law, and Richard Carter), together with 'the sadde of the parissh', were given the task of purchasing a silver cross to the value of 20 marks, which was 'to remayne to the parissh of Rikmersworth for ever'. They were also (again with the advice of 'the discrete of the parissh') to see that the new window that was still unglazed in the chapel of St. Katherine was glazed as soon as possible. This charge was reinforced by Jane's provision that she should herself be buried in St. Katherine's chapel, where her husband John – contrary to his own expressed wishes – had already been interred. She wanted the executors to buy a marble stone 'to be leyde on my husbond John Stokker and me with a knowlage on the same who they are that are buryed there under', and a discreet priest was to be hired at a stipend of 9 marks a year, to sing for two years at the altar of St. Katherine for the Stokkers' and all Christian souls.[43]

Towards the end of the following year, in October 1514, another well-heeled widow followed Jane Stokker's example. Anne Ashby, who died at the end of February 1515, wished to be buried 'within the parissh chirch of Rykmersworth afore the ymage of saint Kateryn in the new Ile of the said chirch'. Anne's husband, John Ashby, had died nearly sixteen years earlier in the summer of 1499, leaving a long and unusual will (which was proved in the prerogative court of Canterbury). He, too, wished to be buried in the new aisle at Rickmansworth, 'bitwixt John Rolfe and thentre into the saide chapell', and his final dispositions gave the briefest mention to his worldly estate, being almost entirely concerned with thoughts of the hereafter and his funeral arrangements, specifying how five priests 'and no mo' were to celebrate and how loaves representing the five wounds and other devotions were to be

---

[42] HRO, ASA 2 AR, fos. 129 r, 132 v, 142. Metcalfe requested burial 'within the parissh chirch of Rikmersworth before the Image of Saint Christofer'. Gibbs left 3s. 4d. 'fabrico novi vestiarii', and Durrant 6s. 8d. 'edificacioni dicte ecclesie in hoc anno fiend'.

[43] Ibid., fo. 151 v. The executors and discreet of the parish were to hire 'an honest preest which can syng in the quere and also can doo such thynges as are convenient to a discrete preest to doo', his stipend to be 9 marks. The supervisors of this will were Thomas Cotton and Thomas Creke esquire. Stocker's farm lies across the River Colne, a little way downstream from Rickmansworth; J.E.B. Gover et al., *The Place-Names of Hertfordshire* (Cambridge, 1938), p. 83.

distributed to poor men and women.[44] John's widow, who was more concerned than him with the solid goods of this world, endowed her church with some expensive plate, directing George Ashby, her son and sole executor, to spend £5 on a pyx of silver and gilt and £2 on a pair of silver cruets, all of which were 'to remayne to the chirch of Rykmersworth'. One of the witnesses of this will was the vicar, Thomas Cotton, who wrote the document with his own hand. He was also a beneficiary, being left Anne Ashby's beads of 'white ambre gawdid with silver and gylt and corall'.[45]

There was nothing exceptional about these bequests, nor was Rickmansworth unique in the piety which caused it to enlarge its church in this last bout of pre-Reformation ecclesiastical building. But in this parish, Tudor asset-stripping was anticipated by destruction of another kind, and the church fire was a real slap in the face for the relatives of all those recent testators whose donations we have encountered. The fact that the vestry which was burnt in 1522 was a new building, and that many of its valuables had been lately acquired (was the pyx that melted in the fire Anne Ashby's?), certainly gives food for thought. If Thomas Cotton shared with his great master of the More a taste for the ostentatious externals of worship, he might have aroused not only the generosity of some of his parishioners but also the consciences of others, whose beliefs centred on different religious priorities.

Perhaps some individuals felt a call to vindicate the honest poverty of the church of God. 'Alle holi seyntis acorden in this, that oure chirche material that is ordeyned for parischynes . . . schal be made with vertuouse meenes, and in an honest mesure. But on alwise it must be fled, that in this chirche ther schewe no pride, neither outtrage [excess] passingli, over the boundis of povert' – whether in stonework, timber or lead, or 'in chalise, booke or vestment'.[46] The message written a century earlier in *The Lanterne of Liȝt* had not been forgotten. Bishop Smith of Lincoln (who died at the beginning of 1514) is reported to have had thirty men of Amersham branded on their cheeks

---

[44] PRO, PROB 11/11; HRO, ASA 2 AR fo. 95 r. Ashby's will, which opens with expressions of his own unworthiness and biblical-sounding thoughts on the transitoriness of human life ('. . . noo permanent citie of dwellyngplace butt as a floure muste vanishe and passe hens . . .'), went on to express his 'stedfaste assurance in thynfynite and precellyng mercy of god . . . and through the merites of his glorious passioun I undoubtedly truste to be partyner of that eternall reward perpetuall felicite and pardurable joie which is ordened and prepared unto his synguler lovers . . .' This trust was committed to the intercession of the glorious Virgin. Apart from 3s. 4d. to the high altar of Rickmansworth, or whatever church he was buried in, Ashby left nothing to any church fabric, and he stipulated 'that for the pompe of the worlde noo dyner be made' at his month's mind except for the priests and clerks and those invited by his wife and executors.

[45] HRO, ASA 2 AR, fo. 159 r (will dated 21 Oct. 1514, proved 1 Mar. 1515, and stated to be 'written with the hand of the said vicar of Ryk'). Anne Ashby's will is so very different from her husband's that one wonders whether they held opposing views on church pomp and ceremony, or whether it was by agreement that he left his widow to make these provisions. Is it significant that she seems so much closer than him to Thomas Cotton?

[46] *The Lanterne of Liȝt*, ed. L.M. Swinburn (EETS, os cli, 1917), p. 41; M. Aston, *Lollards and Reformers* (London, 1984), p. 150.

because 'they could not abide idolatry and superstition' and were always talking against it.[47] One of the suspects who came to Bishop Longland's attention was accused of maintaining that all the world was as well hallowed as the church or churchyard; and it was as good to be buried in the field as in church or churchyard.[48] Such believers would have had little enough sympathy for the last wishes of Jane Stokker or Anne Ashby.

Personal loyalties were undoubtedly involved in the parish's response to the Rickmansworth scandal, for some of the men who became caught up in the troubles over the wardens' accounts were among the 'discreet' who, years earlier, had been active in seeing to the erection of the new vestry. John a Dene, Roger Gonner, Robert Rolle, Richard Foderley and John Mylward – all of whom we have encountered above – were among the witnesses of Jane Stokker's will, and some of them were also on hand when the earlier testators mentioned above made provision for the vestry building.[49] John a Dene in particular was prominent, no doubt because he was at this time the abbot of St. Albans' bailiff at Rickmansworth. Knowing this adds poignancy to a Dene's bequest to the new church organ, shortly before his death in 1529.[50]

Although it does not seem possible to discover the names of any of the iconoclasts, there is a *prima facie* case for suspecting Lollard involvement. Rickmansworth was close to one of the main centres of known Lollard influence. Amersham lay only ten miles away to the west, and there were villagers who had lands or family links with Watford to the east and Chalfont St. Peter to the west. There is also some specific evidence pointing to the possible spread of Lollard opinion in Rickmansworth itself. The very detailed evidence which John Foxe extracted from a (now lost) register of Bishop Longland's heretical proceedings in the diocese of Lincoln in 1521 includes abstracts of two depositions which mention our parish. The first was made by Thomas Holmes, who detected (among a large group) 'Andrew Randal and his wife of Rickmansworth: because they received into their house Thomas Man flying for persecution, and for reading Wickliff's wicket. Also the father of Andrew Randal'.[51] The second set of names came from one John Groser.

John Grosar, being put to his oath, detected Thomas Tykill, Thomas Spencer, and his wife; and John Knight. This John Grosar was examined whether he had a book of the Gospels in English; who confessed that he received such a book of Thomas Tykill, morrow-mass priest in Milk-street, and afterwards lent the same book to Thomas Spencer, which Thomas Spencer with his wife used to read upon the same. And that it was lent to John Knight, who at length delivered the book to the vicar of Rickmansworth.[52]

[47] John Foxe, *The Acts and Monuments* (hereinafter cited as A & M), ed. J. Pratt (London, 1877), iv, p. 124; J.A.F. Thomson, *The Later Lollards, 1414-1520* (Oxford, 1965), p. 87.
[48] Foxe, *A & M*, iv, p. 235.
[49] HRO, ASA 2 AR, fos. 129 r, 132 r, 142 r.
[50] Ibid., fos. 130 r, 151 v, refer to a Dene holding this office in 1506 and 1513.
[51] Foxe, *A & M*, iv, p. 226.
[52] Ibid., p. 233.

We can discover a little more about some of these people. Several of them were living in Rickmansworth at the time we are concerned with, and some of their wills are extant.

Thomas Spenser, John Knight, William and John Grosar, and several members of the Randal family, are all listed in the Rickmansworth assessments of the 1524-5 subsidy.[53] The estimates of their goods ranged between £13 6s. 8d. and £2, which meant that, while Thomas Spenser was on a par with the village's chief landholder (George Wyngborne),[54] and John Knight (£4) was well above the average, John Groser's and Andrew Randal's 40 shillings apiece placed them among the majority of Rickmansworth's inhabitants whose worth in goods or wages for the purposes of tax were put at between 20 and 40 shillings.

We have already encountered the baker, Thomas Spenser. He was evidently a village worthy. His name appears during the 1520s and 1530s as witness or executor to various individuals in Rickmansworth (including John a Dene), and, as we have seen, he was called to give evidence in the suit about George Belch's account. Spenser's long will, drawn up in August 1539 and proved the following October, is mainly concerned with the very substantial legacies (including considerable quantities of silver) left to his five sons and four daughters, but is also suggestive of intellectual interests. It was witnessed by 'Mr. doctor Norbury', and in it he requested Mr. Shaw of Queen's College, Oxford, to sing for his soul.[55] This was presumably Lancelot Shaw, a much younger man than Spenser, who had become fellow of Queen's five years earlier in 1534, and was to be provost of the college during Elizabeth's reign.[56] One would like to know what linked him with the baker of Rickmansworth.

John Groser, Grocer or Grosser of Rickmansworth died in February 1528. He had made his will a fortnight before Christmas. It was a very brief document – so curt as to seem unusual. All it said was: 'First I bequeth my soule to god, my body to be buried in the churchyard of Rykmersworth. Also to the high awter 4d. to Saint Albans shryne 2d. The residiw of my goodes I geve to denys my wyff.' Noticeable are the omissions of the clauses that are almost invariable in the wills of other testators; the bequests of sums (usually

[53] PRO, E 179/120/114 m. 4 r, E 179/120/134, m. 5 r include Thomas Spenser, 20 marks in goods, John Knight, £4 in goods, and William and John Groser, 40s. in goods each. William Groser was still alive in 1543 (see below) when he was appointed overseer by Knight.

[54] George Wyngborne, or Wynkborn, gentleman, whose income from lands (those lying in Watford, as well as at Croxley in the parish of Rickmansworth, where he heads the tax return) was put at £10 in the subsidy, died in Nov. 1526, HRO, ASA 2 AR, fos. 197 v-8 r.

[55] There are two copies of Spenser's will: HRO, ASA 3 AR, fos. 15 v-16 v, 4AR, fos. 27 r-8 r, of which the latter seems better. Shaw was left 33s. 4d. to sing for three months for Spenser's and all Christian souls and, if unable to do this himself, to 'commytte hit to som of his brethern'. Besides his Rickmansworth property (which he left, with his bakehouse, to his wife Anne), Thomas Spenser held land in Middlesex and Buckinghamshire. Henry Gonner was one of the overseers of this will, and William Groser one of its witnesses. (The vicar is not mentioned.)

[56] Was this Robert Norbury, the Benedictine who was admitted B. Th. at Oxford in 1523? Shaw was a doctor of theology by 1549 and died in 1596; Emden (O), *1501-1540*, pp. 417, 512.

2d. from poor parishioners) to every light maintained in St. Mary's church; the list of witnesses; and the introductory clause in which the soul was customarily willed 'to almighty God and to our Lady Saint Mary and to all the holy company of heaven'.[57] On their own these omissions might not amount to much, but read in conjunction with Foxe's report, they are interesting, if not incriminating.

Compared with the Grosers, whom they seem to have outclassed, the Randals were quite thick on the ground at Rickmansworth. The senior Randal at the time of the church-burning was probably Stephen, who apparently had more than one house and who held land in the hamlet of West Hyde, where his goods in 1524-5 were estimated at over £7. At this time Stephen and his wife Joan had three sons living in the parish: Robert, the youngest, was a wage earner (quite likely working for his father); John was already well set up with possessions to at least half the value of his father's; Andrew was settled in the hamlet of Croxley, in the manner of an older son. By the time Stephen died, in the spring of 1531, things had changed. Possibly John had died, for Stephen's will only mentions Andrew, his eldest, and Robert, his youngest sons.[58] Andrew appears to have lived on until 1572, having made his will at a time of sickness ten years earlier. His grandson Robert was made heir to his lands in Rickmansworth and Chesham, with the coffers, tables, cooking pots, six silver spoons, and the mill, cart and plough that made up so much of the husband-man's inheritance. Andrew, in his patriarchal old age, did not lack substance. He was able to leave one of his relations £6 13s. 4d; his wife Elizabeth had the occupancy of half his house, and the inventory of his goods totalled over £40.[59] Fifty years earlier, when he was charged with having harboured the Lollard missionary, Thomas Man, Andrew Randal can only have been a very young man.

Less can be said of John Knight, the borrower of the book of English Gospels which came to Rickmansworth from London and was read by the Spensers. He appears on various occasions, acting as witness or executor, alongside other familiar village notables such as George and Richard Belch, John Haydon and Henry Wedon, as well the vicar, William Man, and parish clerk, John Wood. This unexceptionable activity shows him associated, among

[57] HRO, ASA 2 AR, fo. 202 v. John Groser witnessed the wills of John Stokker and Edward Metcalfe (above nn. 41-2) in 1502 and 1507. Did he have a change of heart thereafter?

[58] PRO, E 179/120/114, m. 4, E 179/120/134, m. 5. The Subsidy Rolls include, besides Stephen Randal (£7) with his sons Robert (20s. in wages) and John (goods £4) in the hamlet of West Hyde: Andrew Randal (40s. goods) in Croxley hamlet; and a John Randoll (goods of £10 and a servant) in Rickmansworth itself. The variously spelt Randal, Randolf and Randalff seem all to be the same family. Stephen left half his Rickmansworth land and his 'nether house' to his youngest son Robert. This will was witnessed by John Butterfield, Roger Fuller and John Man (all surnames that featured in Longland's proceedings, Foxe, *A & M*, iv, pp. 230, 238; HRO, ASA 2 AR, fos. 195 r, 216 r.

[59] HRO, ASA 6 AR, fo. 24 v; A 15/713. Obviously, there must be some doubt about this identification.

others, with Thomas Spenser and Andrew Randal. Knight's will, made in November 1543 and proved early the following year, shows that he – like Thomas Spenser, though much less propertied – was a baker, and their common trade clearly brought them together. He held a house on lease from William Evelyn, which was to be shared after his death by his mother and his widow Joan. John Knight seems to have been childless, and the overseers of his will were his brother William and William Groser.[60]

None of this amounts to anything remarkable, but Knight's appearances with the two wardens of the parish guild, John Haydon and George Belch, seem indicative of a group of friends. Though the deaths of the three men spanned as many decades, their wills shared some common features. Knight in the early 1540s, like Haydon in the early 1530s, bequeathed his soul simply 'to almighty God'. George Belch, in a different climate after the accession of Elizabeth, commended his soul in a grander preamble to the persons of the Holy Trinity.[61] All three omitted any mention of the Virgin. All three also refrained from making any bequest to the fabric of Rickmansworth or any other church. Perhaps, dining rights apart, they might have shared reservations about some of Rickmansworth's services to St. Mary, in parish church and guild.

In the close-knit world of village relationships, the subtle gradations of local standing are crudely reflected in the figures of the subsidy return and seem still opaque when viewed through the more detailed, but yet formalised, words of wills. Rickmansworth shows the problem of delving below the surface of Foxe's reporting.[62] Like any other heresy charge (in this case more doubtfully, since we lack the original court-book) it fails to tell us where rumour and innuendo ended and serious misbelief began. There is nothing to suggest that the lives of the Spensers, or the Randals, John Knight or John Groser, were in any way affected by the heretical cloud that hung over their parish. But that charge can be pressed somewhat closer, through the fugitive alleged to have been harboured by the Randals – Thomas Man.

[60] Knight seems to have been close to the Belches. In 1528 he was co-executor with George Belch of the will of George's brother Richard, and three years later he appears again witnessing a will with George. His service with Thomas Spenser as executor for Thomas Baker in 1536 is indicative of working friendships (and the three of them were Henry Evelyn's executors in 1536). HRO, ASA 2 AR, fos. 204 v, 216 v, 237 v, 238 r; 5 AR, fo. 77.

[61] Given the controversial nature of preambles, it would be unwise to rest too much on these phrases. (None of these wills seems to have had clerical witnesses.) HRO, ASA 2 AR, fo. 216 v, 5 AR, fo. 77, 6 AR, fos. 175 v-6 r, 1 AW 10, fos. 1-2, and above n. 27.

[62] Another piece of Foxe's evidence which could have some bearing on Rickmansworth is John a Lee's denunciation of John a Weedon, Foxe, *A & M*, iv, p. 239. Various John Wedons are listed in the 1524-5 subsidy rolls at Rickmansworth (where the family seems to have been extensive), at Watford, and also in Buckinghamshire, PRO E 179/120/114, m. 4 v, E 179/120/134, m. 5, E 179/120/143; HRO, ASA 2 AR, fos. 80 v, 186 r; 3 AR fo. 77 r. See *The Certificate of Musters for Buckinghamshire in 1522*, ed. A.C. Chibnall (Bucks Rec. Soc. xvii, 1973), pp. 82, 237-40, 272-3, and *Subsidy Roll for the County of Buckingham*, ed. A.C. Chibnall and A. Vere Woodman (Bucks Rec. Soc., viii, 1950 for 1944), pp. 16, 29, for Wedons in Chesham and Wycombe.

Thomas Man, 'the manly martyr of Jesus Christ', in Foxe's words, was burned at Smithfield at the end of March 1518.[63] He was a missionary teacher who had enjoyed a wide range of influence, stretching from Billericay, Chelmsford and Colchester to Henley-on-Thames and Newbury. He had also been in Oxford, where he was imprisoned after abjuring a series of articles in October 1511. The heresies for which Thomas Man was convicted included, besides denial of the real presence and attacking confession and extreme unction, outspoken views against images. One of the bishop of Lincoln's nine charges against him in 1511 was 'that he had believed that images ought not to be worshipped, and that he neither believed in the crucifix, nor yet would worship it'. At his later trial, before the bishop of London in 1518, this point featured again. Going back on his word, Thomas Man and his wife were said to have converted between them six or seven hundred people to his old errors. He was accused of recidivism, maintaining his earlier heresies 'both against the sacrament of the altar, against pilgrimages and worshipping of images: and had blasphemed our blessed lady, called her Mably'.[64]

Foxe, who is our main source for Thomas Man's career and prosecution, tells us that this proselytizer was based for a time at Amersham, which seems to have been quite a Mecca for Lollards in the early sixteenth century. Fleeing first from Colchester and then Newbury, Man was seemingly in some straits until, 'hearing of the brethren who were at Amersham, [he] removed thither, where he found a godly and a great company, which had continued in that doctrine and teaching twenty-three years'.[65] It may be, however, that Thomas Man's arrival in this temporarily safe haven was not so fortuitous as it sounds, for it is possible that he was returning to home country.[66]

The family of Man, or Manne, was firmly established in the parish of St. Peter's in St. Albans in the early sixteenth century. Their surviving wills reveal such a spread of them here that it is difficult to untangle the family relationships. At the time which concerns us, there were at least two branches. The year 1505 brought the deaths of Richard Man and William Man, yeoman, both of whom paid their customary respects to the church of St. Peter's, in whose

---

[63] Foxe, ibid., iv, pp. 208, 213.

[64] Ibid., pp. 209, 210. For Lollards disparaging images of the Virgin see M. Aston, *England's Iconoclasts*, i (Oxford 1988), pp. 107-9.

[65] Foxe, *A & M.*, iv, p. 213, cf. 211. Foxe's record of Man's second trial gives him as being of the diocese of London, but it is also made plain that, before that 'he fled the diocese and jurisdicition of Lincoln', pp. 209-10. For Man's excommunication in the diocese of Lincoln on 18 Aug.1511 see PRO, C 85/115/10. His excommunication for relapse was in the diocese of London, 1 Mar. 1518, PRO, C 85/126/28. For his career and influence see Thomson, *Later Lollards*, p. 87, 92-3, 137, 170-1, 243; J.F. Davis, *Heresy and Reformation in the South East of England* (London, 1983), pp. 57, 61; Claire Cross, *Church and People 1450-1660* (London, 1976), pp. 39-40, 70.

[66] Though it is not clear when Man settled in Amersham (after leaving Newbury), it certainly became his home base (where he had a house) some years before the proceedings taken by Bishop Smith in 1511, Foxe, *A & M*, iv, p. 211, 213, 228, 230.

churchyard they were to be buried. Both men had territorial interests in
Colney, a few miles south of St. Albans. Richard, who died in the spring,
evidently had several children, but the only one he named was his unmarried
daughter Alice. William, who died that autumn, likewise mentioned only
female offspring, in his case his daughters Margaret Kentish and Joan. William
divided his Colney land between William and Thomas Man, two sons of
Richard Man – the presumption being that they were close unmarried relatives, possibly nephews. This supposition is supported by the will of Thomas
Man *alias* Thaune or Chawne, a weaver of St. Albans, who died in July 1547.
Among the outstanding business debts listed in his will, two were owed on
work he had done, making a coverlet and working a piece of cloth for the
fuller, on behalf of Henry Kentish's wife.[67]

The heretical Thomas, if he did come of this family, would have known his
way round the safe houses of the neighbourhood, whatever the desirability – or
otherwise – of revisiting St. Albans itself. And he was not the only Man
mentioned as suspect in Foxe's account. We also find named there, in the list of
those who abjured in the diocese of Lincoln, William Man and Sabine Manne,
while a William Man of Boxted in Essex was alleged to have had a biblical
conference with William Sweeting, and to have been able to elucidate a
passage in the book of Daniel for William Brewster – two heretics who were
burned in 1511.[68]

Did the incumbent at Rickmansworth, who came into office at a time when
Henry VIII was grasping the opportunities of reform, have some sort of
Lollard past behind him? Quite apart from the changing flow of heretical
streams, twenty-four years was long enough for an aspiring cleric to put a
questionable past behind him. Like his two predecessors at Rickmansworth,
William Man had a long ministry and died in office in March 1559, a quarter of
a century after he succeeded Thomas Cotton. His will took no account of the
Protestant expectations of the new Elizabethan regime. Faithful to tradition

[67] HRO, ASA 2 AR, fos. 123 r, 127 v; 3 AR, fo. 78 r; 297 AW 15. Richard Man was probably
married to a Smart as he bequeathed land that had come to his wife from John Smart. The
Kentishes were numerous in St. Albans at this time. Other wills of the Man family in the same St.
Albans parish are those of Richard Man (d. May 1531 leaving bequests to William, Richard and
Robert Man) and the weaver John Manne, who died in 1539 leaving two sons, Stephen and
Thomas, ASA 2 AR, fo. 216 r, 3 AR, fo. 15 v, 4 AR fo. 26 r. The holywell ward of St. Albans
fielded for the 1524 subsidy Stephen Man (£10 goods). John Man of Cropthorne, and John Man
alias 'Chalney' (£8 goods), who had as two of his three servants Thomas and Stephen Man, PRO,
E 179/120/114, mm. 2, 3 r.
[68] Foxe. *A & M*, iv, pp. 206, 215-16. Thomas Man had reportedly taught in Essex, including
Colchester, and he was also said to have spirited suspects out of Amersham into East Anglia, ibid.,
pp. 211, 213, 214.

(or the restored beliefs of the Marian years), William Man bequeathed his soul to Almighty God, the Virgin and all the blessed company of heaven. The box for singing bread in his parlour, and the pieces of old copes in his bed chamber at the time of his death, are indicative of the religious reversal of his later years. Suggestive too, of how that reversal may have been received by some of his parishioners, is one of the desperate debts owed to the vicar: 'Item, by the executors of George Belch For a Mortuary, 10s'.[69]

A signpost to an earlier religious horizon is to be found in the bequest of books that William Man belatedly disposed of, leaving them in a codicil to his friend and overseer, Richard Alexander, gentleman. 'Item, I geve more to Rychard Alexander my wrytten Byble and my best volumes of Saint Austyne and the best boke of St. Jeromes worke.'[70] What sort of Bible was this? If it was an English manuscript it could scarcely have been other than a Wycliffite Bible, and though possession of such a book tells nothing of its owner's beliefs, it might, in the vicar's hands, have some bearing on the identity of the relative whom he had been subsidising in some kind of high life in London.

When he died William Man was owed over £17 by Robert Man of London, the debt including an unspecified sum laid out for this kinsman to a city draper. Could this have been an older spendthrift version of the Robert Man who, as serving-man, had been taken to task in the diocese of London in 1531? The sartorial interest makes the identification tempting. For the articles Robert Man had abjured included, besides denials of purgatory, papal power and the sainthood of Thomas Becket, an eccentric remark about the value of gloves.

He used commonly, to ask of priests, where he came, whether a man were accursed, if he handled a chalice, or no? If the priest would say, Yea: then would he reply again thus: 'If a man have a sheep-skin on his hands', meaning a pair of gloves, 'he may handle it'. The priests saying, Yea, 'Well, then', quoth he, 'ye will make me believe

---

[69] Besides his inventory, Man's will survives in both the original paper version and the registered copy, HRO, ASA 6 AR, fo. 184 r, 1 AW 75, A25/326. These show that he was well off. The total of his goods and chattels was £24 1s. 8d.; his well-furnished six-roomed house contained painted cloths decorating the hall, damask hangings, cushions and carpets in the parlour, a feather bed with down pillows and counterpane (valued at £4) and a desk with lock; the vicar owned four gowns and a vestment of white and red damask. There was 13s. cash in his house when he died.

[70] HRO, ASA 6 AR, fo. 184 r, 1 AW 75. Alexander inherited 10s. in money and £1 of the debt owed by Robert Man; he was also a beneficiary this year from the will of George Belch. For Bishop Bonner's ownership and citation of a Wycliffite Bible, see *The Holy Bible . . . in the Earliest English Versions*, ed. J. Forshall and F. Madden (Oxford, 1859), i, p. xlv no. 46; Aston, *England's Iconoclasts*, i, p. 396. In Mary's reign Richard Alexander was involved in a suit in Star Chamber against George Gonner, Edward Wedon and others, about the felling of wood in Newlands Wood, Rickmansworth, belonging to the bishop of London, PRO, STAC 4/10/2. Richard Alexander, esquire, of Rickmansworth, died in 1586, PRO, PROB 11/69, 11/70, 11/75.

that God put more virtue in a sheep-skin, than he did in a Christian man's hand, for whom he died'.[71]

Although the perpetrators of the Rickmansworth church-burning remain infuriatingly concealed, it is possible to arrive at some kind of picture of the religious complexion of the parish. Point by small point, like the dashes of different colours in a pointillist painting, we can assemble flecks of the Rickmansworth landscape around the time of the arson. Whether or not the apostate friar Thomas Hemingford (who was still an active presence at Rickmansworth in 1491) was ever touched by Lollardy,[72] whatever the nature of William Man's manuscript Bible, the individuals who set fire to the church images and wrapped tow around rood and organs, had plenty of native predecessors who had aspired to such things.[73] They also had near neighbours who had suffered from the recent battery of attention focused on Buckinghamshire Lollards.

Was the Rickmansworth incident an act of revenge for Bishop Longland's prosecutions? The interconnections between this village and the parishes to the west that featured so prominently in the bishop of Lincoln's enquiries certainly suggest this possibility. In 1521-2 Rickmansworth must have been abuzz with rumour and counter-rumour as the bishop's officials, picking their way through the thickets of heretical informers, took up their stand in the very heart of Lollard country, at nearby Amersham. After the start of a fresh offensive against heresy, which began with Wolsey's burning of Luther's books at St. Paul's in May 1521,[74] it did not take many months for the authorities to home in on the Chiltern villages that had already given cause for disquiet in the previous decade. On 20 October 1521 the protection of local secular officials was provided by the king for the bishop of Lincoln, in the expectation that he might run into physical danger bringing heretics to justice.[75]

For the heretics, their sympathizsers and fellow travellers, the dreadful climax to these proceedings came early the following year. On 28 January 1522

---

[71] Foxe, *A & M*, iv, p. 585 ('Much Cornard', the location of this Robert Man, is presumably Great Cornard near Sudbury); v, p. 33. The debts of the London relative had gone to court: 'Robert Man of London owyth him for certen money borowed of the sayd vycar at severall tymes as apperyth by one accon' dependyng in the kinges benche £17'; also 'Robert Man owyth him more for certen money layd owt for him to one Mr. Draper of London': HRO, 1 AW 75. The will also refers to the testator's cousin John Man (left a flock bed), and his goods were divided between Richard Man and Cicely Hodson. This conjuction of William, Richard and Robert Man might point to identification with the three beneficiaries of the 1531 will of Richard Man (n. 67 above).

[72] See above n. 37

[73] Aston, *Lollards and Reformers*, pp. 167-77.

[74] Carl S. Meyer, 'Henry VIII Burns Luther's Books, 12 May 1521', *JEH*, ix (1958), pp. 173-87, explains the diplomatic background to the change of attitude towards Luther and Luther's books that took place in 1520-1.

[75] Foxe, *A & M*, iv, pp. 241-2; D. Wilkins, *Concilia Magnae Britanniae* (London 1737), iii, p. 698. On Longland's proceedings see M. Bowker. *The Henrician Reformation. The Diocese of Lincoln under John Longland, 1521- 1547* (Cambridge, 1981), pp. 58-62.

two men of Amersham, Thomas Barnard and James Morden (a husbandman and a labourer, according to Foxe), were signified as excommunicate for relapsed heresy, and in the words of the martyrologist, 'they two were burned both at one fire' at Amersham.[76]

This execution would undoubtedly have shocked parishioners of Rickmansworth, some of whom were related by family connections with one of the condemned men. The link was Alice Morden, a cousin of the condemned James. Alice, the daughter of John Morden, was married to Richard Ashford, who was either the half-brother or brother-in-law of Thomas Tredway. Tredway was among the many who had given information to Bishop Longland.

Thomas Tredway [was] compelled by his oath to detect John Morden [uncle of James], of Ashley Green, and Richard Ashford, his brother. These were accused and detected because John Morden had in his house a book of the Gospels, and other chapters, in English, and read three or four times in the same; in which book his brother Ashford also did read once. Item, because James Morden spake against images, and said these words: 'Our Lord Jesus Christ saith in his gospel, Blessed be they that hear the word of God, and keep it', etc.

Tredway also detected Agnes Ashford, his own mother, for teaching him that he should not worship the images of saints.[77]

Several members of the Tredway family had holdings in Rickmansworth at the time of 1524-5 subsidy. Walter and John Tredway were both assessed at £6 worth of goods in the hamlet of West Hyde. Richard Tredway topped the subsidy list for Chorleywood with goods at £20 and had a son William on a wage of 20 shillings. It seems clear that the Tredways of Rickmansworth were

[76] Foxe, *A & M*, iv, pp. 124, 245. Foxe's accuracy is substantiated to the extent that the four he names (Barnard, Morden, Rave and Scrivener) were all signified excommunicate as relapsed heretics on 28 Jan. 1521. PRO, C 85/115/13. This was not the only burning to take place at Amersham, for Foxe (who misdates the event), reports William Tillesworth's death there. Foxe, *A & M*, iv, p. 123; this was in 1511, coinciding with Thomas Man's Lincoln diocese trial, Thomson, *Later Lollards*, pp. 87-91.

[77] Foxe, *A & M*, iv, pp. 224-5, 227, 230-1 (for quotation), p. 232. Agnes Ashford was said to have taught James Morden. The depositions also mention Alice and Richard Tredway and speak of Thomas as being of Chesham. Ashley Green, home of Mordens, was part of the parish of Chesham. Readings were also reported to have taken place in the house of Richard Ashford at Chesham. The family relationships linking Mordens, Tredways and Ashfords are intricate; cf. Thomson, *Later Lollards* pp. 90- 2; and Richard G. Davies, 'Lollardy and Locality', *TRHS*, sixth series, i (1991), pp. 191-212. Foxe speaks of Richard Ashford of Walton-on-Thames (who was tried in the diocese of Winchester in Nov. 1521, perhaps as a result of these proceedings), as having the aliases of Nash or Tredway; he also shows that James Morden's brother Richard and sister Marion (both of Chesham) were under suspicion. A Marion Morden of Ashley Green died in the autumn of 1521, making dispositions which indicate that the Mordens were closely related to the Wedons, as well as the Ashfords. Her executors were Robert Wedon and Thomas Harding – the latter name suggestive of Lollard complicity since Thomas Harding (who seems to have lived in both Amersham and Chesham), having abjured under Bishop Smith and been named to Longland in 1521, was finally sentenced and burned in Chesham in 1532; *Courts of the Archdeaconry of Buckingham*, pp. 329-30, no. 402; Foxe, *A & M*, iv, pp. 123, 126, 225, 234, 580-2; Thomson, *Later Lollards*, p. 92; Reg. Longland (Lincoln), i, fo. 228.

part of the Buckinghamshire family. Richard died in June 1527, leaving his stock and possessions to his wife and son Walter. Walter was a yeoman living in Amersham when he made his will twenty years later, but he also held lands at Rickmansworth and bequeathed the church there the large sum of 20 shillings.[78] Was this a legacy which involved some sense of atonement?

And what of the vicar of Rickmansworth himself? His years at Chesham would surely have given him some knowledge of the heretical families who were at the centre of these troubles. It might have been hard for him to keep his distance from the official investigations, whatever he chose to do with the English Gospels surrendered to him by John Knight.

Whether or not the Rickmansworth church fire was a riposte to the Amersham heretic-burning, it was surely an *auto-da-fé* of some sort. Wolsey's and Longland's response proves as much. If the iconoclasts regarded the fire as the final proof of the spiritual inertia of the 'dead' image, Cardinal Wolsey for his part proclaimed the church-burning as sanctioning the opposite belief. The blaze at Rickmansworth (presumably known to him in some detail through Thomas Cotton and the servants at the More) had destroyed neither the host nor the rood. Both had survived in one of those miraculous displays of holy power (for which fire was so often the agent in the tradition of medieval miracles). Despite the melting of the pyx the bread 'was found upon the high altar and nothing perished'. And 'the blessed image of Jesu Christ . . . was nothing hurt'. It was one of the last attempts to revive the devotions of the old regime. One wonders what effect it had.

It was more difficult to counteract the demonstrators' attack on baptism. That had not, however, prevented the indulgence from reciting this display of those who, 'in despite of the sacrament of baptism', had broken open the font and thrown the holy water around the church. 'Cruel opinions' of this kind were soon to receive more publicity from continental reformers, but there were enough antecedents among English heretics for it to be unnecessary to look for specific outside inspiration. Lollards had long been attacking baptism, along with other sacraments. Views like those of heretics in the diocese of Norwich in 1430, that the usual form of church baptism 'is but void and not necessary to be done nor had, for all Christ's people is sufficiently baptized in

---

[78] PRO, E 179/120/114, m. 4 v, cf. E179/120/134, m. 5 v; HRO, ASA 2 AR, fo. 201 r. Walter Tredway was churchwarden of Amersham in 1520, *Courts of the Archdeaconry of Buckingham*, p. 298, no. 278M. His will (of 3 Sept. 1546, Bucks RO, D/A/We/8/80) refers to his lands in Rickmansworth: I owe this reference to Derek Plumb, whose unpublished PhD dissertation, 'John Foxe and the Later Lollards of the Thames Valley' (Cambridge, 1987) (cited at p. 272), identified many of the suspects of Chesham and Amersham; see also idem, 'The Social and Economic Spread of Rural Lollardy: A Reappraisal', *Studies in Church History*, xxiii (1986), pp. 111-29. On the Chiltern Lollards see also Andrew Hope, 'Lollardy: The Stone the Builders Rejected?', in P. Lake and M. Dowling (ed), *Protestantism and the National Church in Sixteenth Century England* (London, 1987), pp. 12-17. For Buckingham Tredways (including Thomas at Chesham in 1522, but not in 1524) see *Certificate of Musters for Buckinghamshire*, pp. 82, 231, 236-8; *Subsidy Roll . . . Buckingham*, p. 15.

the blood of Christ and needeth no other baptism', still continued and might combine with hostility to 'all the conjurations and charms' associated with holy water.[79] Sixteenth-century heretics may have had deeper thoughts on this topic. Anne Watts, examined with her husband Thomas Watts of Dogmers-field (Hants.) by Bishop Fox in September 1514, confessed that the English books she had hidden in a ditch included 'a treatise of the sacrament of baptisme al translate in to english'.[80] And, on 10 June 1521, John Drake of Ogbourne St. Andrew (just north of Marlborough) abjured six articles before Bishop Audley of Salisbury, five of which concerned the sacrament of baptism. They included the view

> that water is but a prophane or hethyn thing and so is an infant or childe be for it be baptismed [*sic*], and that oon prophane and hethin thing can not helpe un to the sanctifying or halowing of an other lyke prophane or hethin thing, and specially when it don [*sic*] at home where women have no auctorite to blesse or halowe the water.[81]

John Drake repudiated the sacrament of baptism, whether performed at home by the midwife in time of need or by the priest in church. 'Also I have said . . . that false is the very substaunce of the sacrament of baptysme', and he thought that the law of the church on the form of water and words 'was never made by saynte Peter'. Christians were therefore not bound to keep it, and infants who died without christening in the church's 'wordes and waies' would be accepted by God and should be given Christian burial.[82] These views may sound idiosyncratic, but they were nevertheless in a direct line of descent from earlier Lollards.

Whatever the precise nature of 'cruell opynyons' that prompted the Rick-mansworth fire, it took place at a significant time. English heretics and English prosecutors alike knew enough of Lutheran reform for the religious atmos-phere to seem headily or threateningly freshened. Lollard iconoclasts, who had long nurtured ideas of image-burning, are not known ever before to have brought off so spectacular a bonfire as that at Rickmansworth, but such talk as there was of new reform must surely have been a more distant reality than the insistent presence of the bishop of Lincoln and his officials, tracking down and listing so many suspect men and women in the communities of the Chiltern Hills. It has not proved possible to identify any decisive connections, but

---

[79] *Heresy Trials in the Diocese of Norwich, 1428-31*, ed. Norman P. Tanner (Camden Society, 4th ser. xx, 1977), pp. 134, 146, 154.

[80] Hampshire Record Office, A1/19, Reg. Fox, 3, fo. 74; Thomson, *Later Lollards*, p. 89. The heretics in Fox's diocese were linked with those in other areas, including the Chilterns.

[81] Wiltshire Record Office, D1/2/14, Reg. Audley, fo. 183 v.

[82] Ibid. Drake had said that 'water is not of the substance of baptyme', and that God would not punish any infant named without water or the required form of words. Drake's sixth error was his assertion 'that sith the tyme that Adam and Eve were delyvered fro hell no saule descended thethir nether shall unto the daie of dome or universall Iugement'.

perhaps there is enough to suggest at least a likelihood that the Rickmans-worth arson was some sort of Lollard counterblast to the intensive recent heretical prosecutions, and possibly linked with the executions of local figures.

This was just one episode in the dramatic upheavals of these years. There are many loose ends, which may or may not seem to join up somewhere with the profuse details of Foxe's record. One such was an assertion which brought its maker into court at St. Albans, probably in 1520, that Mr. John Dormar, vicar of Hoxton, was a Lollard – a remark which apparently arose from the vicar's careless and irreverent treatment of consecrated hosts at Easter. It does not seem to have been a matter of great concern, but the names of the parties are suggestive. The accuser was Edmund Randal, and in 1521 an Edmund Dormer of Amersham featured prominently among Longland's suspects.[83] Behind the formulations of charge and denial lay associations that can no longer be retrieved. In 1527 another man was brought to justice, whose activities would certainly have come to the ears of his neighbours in Rickmans-worth. John Woodward of Watford, who appeared in the archdeacon's court at St. Albans on 27 April 1527, was said to have been infected with heresy for a long time. A year later, on 1 May 1528, he abjured two heresies before Wolsey's officials: the assertion that Christ's body was not present in the sacrament of the altar, 'but that it was oonly the figure of it in the memory and honour of hym'; and 'Also I doubtyd whether our saviour Crist was born of a virgyn or nott and said I was nott bounde to beleve it'. Woodward, questioned under penalty of relapse, denied that he had had any teacher or associate in holding these views. He was sentenced to penitential procession, bearing a bundle of faggots, in both Watford and St. Albans, and thereafter was to be committed to perpetual imprisonment in the abbey precinct, with prescribed limits of movement which included freedom to attend the church.[84]

The successive inquisitions of Bishops Smith and Longland disturbed the calm of an area that must sometimes have seemed almost a no-go haven for heretical sympathizers, accustomed in this southern corner of Lincoln's huge diocese to long periods of immunity from the prying eye of authority. The events of 1521, especially, poisoned the air in communities of the Lollard country of the Chilterns. Neighbour turned on neighbour, and the air was thick with charge and counter-charge. Foxe, predictably, stresses this aspect of the investigations and, on the evidence he printed, it seems not unfairly. 'This is one of them that make all this business in our town with the bishop; I pray God

---

[83] HRO, ASA 7/1, fo. 23 r. For the Rickmansworth Randals see above n. 58. Marion Randal was among Longland's suspects, and Dormer was one of the Amersham men who abjured. Foxe, *A & M*, iv, pp. 220, 232, 234. Another possible connection with our parish is Alice Holting, ibid., p. 228, as there was a Rickmansworth family of that name, HRO, ASA 2 AR. fos. 80 v, 231 v.

[84] HRO, ASA 7/1, fos. 42 v, 46 v, 47 r-8 r. These proceedings include the instrument of Woodward's submission, with his rather shaky sign of the cross, fo. 48 r. Woodward's sentence is on a par with those imposed by Longland six years earlier, Foxe, *A & M*, iv, p. 244.

tear all the bones of him'.[85] Hostilities ripened as the bishop's business grew more threatening. Many would have echoed this remark, made to one of Longland's informers, as it became more difficult to move from one safe house to another, protected by the traditional loyalties of the sect.

These loyalties – witness some of the individuals we have encountered in Rickmansworth, who featured in Foxe's record – did not necessarily amount to anything in the nature of doctrinal heresy. Passing contact with a Lollard Bible (perhaps listening to readings from it), or enhanced attention to the needs of the poor, could bring people together in special (possibly compromising) ways, while their behaviour remained otherwise conventional. Doubtless some who were dubbed Lollards would have been dismayed by the burning of Rickmansworth church.

Others, surely, would not have been displeased by that event. Whoever was responsible did better than the reluctant 'roodman', Henry Phip, of Hughenden, who passed up a trip to nearby Wycombe with Roger Dods of Burford in 1515, on the grounds that, having charge of the roodloft, it was his job to 'go and tind a candle before his "Block Almighty"'.[86] The blaze kindled at Rickmansworth in 1522 set light to all the devotional candles, challenging the 'Block Almighty' to heretical trial by fire. If it was also intended as a challenge to Thomas Wolsey it succeeded, at least to the extent that he was shocked, and helped to give the affair publicity by the issue of the indulgence. But those who wished the cardinal's over-mighty powers could be used for a reform of images needed patience. 'I wold to god I had my Lord Cardinalls auctoritie, and then wold I pull downe thes images which be sett up in the church for I fere me a great many of you synne in ydolatrye'.[87] The prayer of the parish priest of Steeple Bumpstead was to be answered from other quarters.

This exploration of a peculiarly ignored incident has taken us up some of the bypaths of a Hertfordshire parish. It is disappointing that this detailed acquaintance with Rickmansworth's village community has not brought us face to face with the guilty parties. If the arsonists did succeed in evading detection, perhaps that was because, despite all the hiatus of the time, enough lips remained sealed to close the circuit of local gossip. In this small, tightly meshed world, group solidarity may have been temporarily shaken, but the signs are that those at Rickmansworth whose names were entered in episcopal files, belonged to a trusted circle. We can only surmise the differing reactions of the baker, Thomas Spenser, at one end of the social scale, and John Groser at the other, as they awoke to discover what the 'flambynge fyre' had done to their

---

[85] Foxe, *A & M*, iv, p. 226 (words of Roger Squire, reported by Thomas Holmes, who detected the Rickmansworth group). See pp. 218, 242, 245, for Foxe's remarks on how kindred and neighbours were forced to incriminate each other under oath.

[86] Ibid., iv, pp. 237-8.

[87] BL, MS Harl, 421, fo. 28 r, from the 1528 confession of Edmund Tyball, reporting words of Richard Fox; Davis, *Heresy and Reformation*, p. 64. For the similar view of Robert Goldstone, glazier, see Foxe, *A & M*, v, p. 32.

church. It is easier to guess the feelings of the churchwardens. For all of them alike it was surely a night long remembered.

Rickmansworth Indulgence

Be it knowen to all crysten people which ioyeth in theyr hartes of ye power of god shewed by his owne precyous body in fourme of brede in ye chyrche of Rykmersworthe where wretched & cursed people cruelly & wylfully set fyre upon all ye ymages & on the canape y^t the blessyd sacrament was in & make ye fyre more cruell they put towe w^t baner staves bytwene ye sparres & brases of ye chaunsell thrughe ye whiche fyre ye sayd chaunsell was brent & ye pyx was molten & ye blessyd body of our lorde Jhesu cryst in forme of brede was founde upon the hyghe awter & nothynge perysshed. Also they brake into ye vestry & put fyre amonge all ye ornamentes & Jewelles & brent ye sayd vestry & all y^t was therin. Also in ye rode lofte they wrapped towe aboute ye blessyd rode & about apayre of organs & melted all ye wexe in ye sayd lofte conteynynge in weyght.xiiii. score pounde where as ye flambynge fyre was in ye sayd lofte about ye blessyd ymage of Jhesu cryst nother ye sayd ymage nor ye towe about it was nothynge hurte thrughe ye myght & power of our savyour Jhesu cryst. Also to maynteyne theyr cruell opynyons they wente unto ye fonte & brake it open & dyspoyled ye water y^t was halowed therin & cast it a brode in ye chyrche flore in dyspyte of ye sacrament of baptyme. And for as moche as ye substancyall men of ye sayd parysshe hath invewed ye kynges grace how honourably god was served in ye sayd chyrche in tyme past; & also that it pleased hym to shewe his grete myght and power.

Wherfore my lorde Cardynall and legate de latere hath graunted C. dayes of pardon releasynge of theyr penaunce in purg[atory]y[88] to all them y^t g[y]ve ony parte of theyr goodes to ye restorynge of ye s[. . . . . chy]rc[he . . .]

A[lso m]y lorde of Lyncolne hath graunted.xl. daye[s . . .]

---

[88] The bottom page is torn and some words are missing.

9

Iconoclasm in England: Official and Clandestine

Iconoclasm was a feature of the English Reformation from its very beginning.[1] It recurred intermittently and sporadically, from the 1530's to the 1640's, and made an important contribution to events at each significant phase of settlement. The influence of iconoclasts in England is comparable to that of iconoclasts abroad, but reflects the peculiar nature of English reform, which was both tightly controlled from the centre and also upsetting in its switchback course. The removal and return of images, and the prolonged process of attrition that bore on some categories of imagery, caused individuals to express themselves through iconoclasm much longer than was the case in most continental centres of reform.[2]

The work of European iconoclasts stood throughout as an inspiration – or deterrent – to the complete clearance of all imagery from all churches. There were individuals who looked ahead, even under Henry VIII, to the ultimate iconoclastic position that was reached a century later. But official policy moved in effect by stages, proscribing a wider range of imagery as time went on, with the result that iconoclastic reformers, jumping ahead to deal with further categories of idols, vented their dissatisfaction by acts of demonstrative destruction. Breaking an image might be a way of stealing a march on hesitant or procrastinating magistrates. Officials and policy-makers, iconomachs themselves, were repeatedly at odds with more radical iconoclasts. Iconoclasm, always declaratory of Reformation on the move, itself declared divisions in the movement of reform. It raised in an acute manner the question of authority.

The eradication of idols presented many reformers with their Catch 22. One could not achieve a purified rite while churches still flaunted traces of idolatry. But to sweep away all the trappings of idols and false worship without first

[1]   Earlier versions of this paper were delivered in 1980 at the London University Seminar of Michael Hunter and Bob Scribner, and in 1984 at Keith Thomas's graduate seminar in Oxford. I am grateful for the comments offered on both occasions.

[2]   For the continental experience, see Carlos M.N. Eire, 'Iconoclasm as a Revolutionary Tactic: the case of Switzerland 1524-1536', *Journal of the Rocky Mountain Medieval Renaissance Association*, 4 (1983). pp. 77-96, and *War Against the Idols: The Reformation of Worship from Erasmus to Calvin* (Cambridge, 1986).

securing the hearts and minds of believers might jeopardize the reforming process. Luther, faced by the hasty iconoclasm of Karlstadt and the 'Heavenly Prophets', saw this clearly. Until the idols of the mind had been dealt with, it was pointless (as well as dangerous) to start demolishing external idols. In Strasbourg Capito said much the same thing. The suppression of idols (which meant all sorts of objects regarded as sacred) before preaching had implanted the true faith would, he said, offend weak consciences and invite a reaction against reform.[3]

On the other hand, independent zealots found the destruction of images a useful lever to promote or accelerate reform. To demolish images – or to clear a church of sculptures, paintings, and reredoses – was a declaratory act of faith which presented a physical rupture with the past. It could amount to a challenge to cautious or conservative authorities who were proving dilatory over the implementation of doctrinal change. Another catch situation was created, for to replace the ousted images in such circumstances would itself inevitably be contentious, while to acquiesce amounted to capitulation.

We can see a kind of counterpoint developing between the private and public destroyers: between the official, publicized, propagandist acts of iconoclasm, and the spontaneous, clandestine, illicit breakings or burnings undertaken by private groups or individuals. Strange though it may now seem, the public iconoclastic spectacle became part of the repertoire of government propaganda almost as soon as Henry VIII decided, under Thomas Cromwell's guiding hand, to sponsor the process of reform. The nearest modern equivalent that comes to mind is the breaking up of statues and ripping down of photo portraits that has taken place in this century at changes in Eastern bloc regimes. But that is not an exact parallel, for the statues of Stalin (for example) were of recent vintage, and even those who erected them were familiar with the language of the image-breakers and the vulnerability of public icons of this kind. Reformation iconoclasts, on the other hand, though they likewise destroyed for the end of *renovatio*, were employing a method that, being known at the time only as a proscribed activity, was quite novel as a government procedure. Its very adoption declared such magistrates to be reversing the world they were changing.

The spectacular burning or dismemberment of idols served the purpose of winning support for religious change by calling crowds to witness the ritual dismissal of rejected cult objects. Corporately venerated objects were corporately eliminated. Iconoclasm was a social process, designed to give group solidarity to the inauguration of doctrinal change. But as all recent advocates or perpetrators of such deeds had been condemned or burned as heretics, it must have appeared to some observers that their world was veritably turning

---

[3] René Bornert, *La réforme protestante du culte à Strasbourg au XVIe siècle (1523-1598): approche sociologique et interprétation théologique* (Leiden, 1981), p. 88, considering this danger of creating 'un blocage contre la réforme', cites Capito's *Was man halten und antwurten soll* (of October 1524).

upside down. For some that would naturally not have been unwelcome. Individuals were ready to take their cue, and there were various occasions on which government iconoclasm was imitated or followed by illegal acts of destruction. The motives were doubtless mixed, ranging from conscience-stricken new belief to revenge on failed intercessors, youthful pranks or drunken demonstrations, and conscious efforts to challenge authority.

Only a few years before Henry VIII's volte-face, steps were taken to counter some quite daring acts of clandestine iconoclastic destruction. It was probably in 1522 that Cardinal Wolsey and John Longland, bishop of Lincoln, together issued an indulgence promising pardons to all those who contributed to the restoration of the church of Rickmansworth in Hertfordshire, which had been badly damaged by nocturnal arson. 'Wretched and cursed people cruelly and wylfully set fyre upon all the ymages and on the canape that the blessyd sacrament was in', and also set light to the church vestry, with the result that this building with all the ornaments in it and the chancel were burned. These undercover culprits remain unknown, though it seems quite probable that they were Lollards, or at any rate were in some way caught up in the recent anti-heretical proceedings that had disturbed the entrenched communities in the neighbouring Chiltern Hills.[4]

More deeds of this kind are reported to have taken place early in the following decade, when the likelihood of continental inspiration of some kind is greater though still not explicit. According to John Foxe, many images were 'cast down and destroyed in many places' in 1531-2.[5] In fact, the examples he cited were all in one area in Essex and Suffolk, from Ipswich and several villages around Colchester. The incident to which this report was attached, described in graphic detail that had been given to the martyrologist by one of the participants, belonged to the same region. This was the burning of the rood of Dovercourt, a village in Essex just south of Harwich – an episode dated by Foxe to 1532. Like the Rickmansworth incident, it was carried out under cover of darkness, though in this case the perpetrators were caught.

The Dovercourt image was revered for miraculous powers, which according to Foxe (whose evidence obviously leaves something to be desired) included the ability to prevent anyone shutting the church door. The four men who set out to disprove this 'idol', including Foxe's narrator who was called Robert Gardner, came from the villages of Dedham and East Bergholt some ten miles and more away to the west at the head of the Stour estuary. They were favoured by a 'wondrous goodly night, both hard frost and fair moonshine' for

[4] The indulgence which vividly describes this event survives in a single copy in the BL (*STC*, 14077 c. 68), and is printed in facsimile in K.W. Cameron, *The Pardoner and his Pardons: Indulgences Circulating in England on the Eve of the Reformation* (Hartford, CT, [1965]), p. 49. See above chapter 8, pp. 233, 260.

[5] John Foxe, *The Acts and Monuments*, ed. J. Pratt, 3rd ed. (London: G. Seeley, 1853-68), iv, p.707.

Fig. 22 'Three Martyrs hanged for taking down the Rood of Dovercourt' in 1532, showing the rood-burning beside the execution. Woodcut in John Foxe, *Actes and Monumentes* (London, 1570).

their exploit – as well as by the fact that there was no need to break into the church, since local belief was such that nobody dared to shut its door. The mere ability to remove the rood and to carry it a quarter of a mile away 'without any resistance of the said idol' seemed itself to negate its repute, but the marauders left nothing to chance and made a bonfire of the vanquished carving before returning home. Within six months, according to Foxe's circumstantial account, three of these offenders were indicted for felony and hanged. Only Robert Gardner managed to escape.[6]

But the tale does not end here, for Foxe also tells us of the involvement of another man, a cleric. This was Thomas Rose, rector of Hadleigh, a village in Suffolk, about eight miles northwest of Dedham and East Bergholt. Rose was a convinced supporter of reform who survived various troubles, including two flights abroad under Henry VIII and several examinations and another exile under Mary, to see his own life story published by Foxe in Elizabeth's reign, by which time he was well into his seventies, though still active as a preacher at Luton in Bedfordshire. Nearly half a century earlier, Rose's sermons at Hadleigh had attracted attention for their vehemence against images, and among those he inspired to plot destruction were the four Dovercourt icono-clasts. After their successful mission they handed over the coat that had been

---

[6]   Ibid., iv, pp. 706-7.

on the rood to Thomas Rose, and he duly proved his own convictions by burning it.[7]

Although, according to Foxe (who remains our sole source for these events), the four iconoclasts refused to implicate Rose, he did not escape scot-free. He had enemies at Hadleigh who complained in high places with the result that he was examined before the Council and imprisoned in Bishop Longland's house for several months. It was thanks to Cranmer that Thomas Rose's fortunes improved. After Cranmer's consecration in March 1533, the offender was moved to the custody of the archbishop at Lambeth, a change which may be ascribed to the fact that his living belonged to the patronage and immediate jurisdiction of the archbishops of Canterbury. This connection may also have helped to get Thomas Rose reinstated in his living, and in March 1534 Cranmer wrote to the parishioners of Hadleigh suggesting that they should let bygones be bygones and forget their old grudge against their rector.[8]

The Dovercourt affair took place at an interesting moment. While from May 1532 steps were being taken towards the unilateral action that would cut the knot of the king's divorce, there was little to indicate that Henry might be ready to support the image-breakers. All iconoclasts, still suspect and subject to the ancient proscription of church law as dangerous heretics, acted perforce by subterfuge. Anxiety about the heretical dimensions of the case against church images was increasing (witness the expanded 1531 edition of Thomas More's *Dialogue Concerning Heresies*), and in the minds of conservatives the aspirations of native critics were conflated with the challenge of continental reformers. A sermon delivered some time before 1534 by Henry Gold, vicar of Hayes in Middlesex, warned against the dangerous teaching of Karlstadt as the source of such horrific deeds as the recent burning of a crucifix.[9] Old Lollard objections to images and pilgrimages entered a new domain. Whatever the persuasions of those who attacked images, they would be judged at the bar of a

---

[7] Ibid., viii, pp. 581-90. This account was first published in the 1576 edition of the *Acts and Monuments*. In 1538 Thomas Rose made a name for himself as a reformer. He received a handsome testimonial (sent to Cromwell, whose chaplain he was, according to Foxe) for a preaching tour in Lincolnshire, and was invited to preach in London, where it became known that Mass was being celebrated in English at his old parish of Hadleigh. *LP*, xiii, pt. 1, nos. 704, 1492, pp. 267, 552; *Wriothesley's Chronicle*, ed. W.D. Hamilton (Camden Soc., n.s. 11, 20, 1875-77), i, p. 83; Susan Brigden, *London and the Reformation* (Oxford, 1989), pp. 235-6.

[8] Diarmaid MacCullough, *Suffolk and the Tudors: Politics and Religion in an English County, 1500-1600* (Oxford, 1986), pp. 155, 159, 161, 163; John F. Davis, *Heresy and Reformation in the South-East of England, 1520-1559* (London, 1983), pp. 111-12; *Miscellaneous Writings and Letters of Thomas Cranmer*, ed. Edmund Cox (Parker Soc., Cambridge, 1846), p. 280; John Strype, *Memorials of Archbishop Cranmer* (Oxford, 1848-54), ii, pp. 369, 374-76; Jasper Ridley, *Thomas Cranmer* (Oxford, 1962), pp. 88-89. Possibly Rose was placed in the bishop of Lincoln's custody at the time of Warham's death; despite Foxe's report, (*A & M*, viii, p. 582), he seems to have regained the living at Hadleigh for a time.

[9] *LP*, vii, no. 523, pp. 208-09: PRO, SP6/1, no. 14, fo. 64r; Brigden, *London and the Reformation*, p. 215. The development of the case against images in this decade is examined in Margaret Aston, *England Iconoclasts*, i, (Oxford, 1988), chap. 5.

new set of expectations, and by 1532 texts of continental reformers dealing with this topic had reached England.

If theology of some kind, at some remove, lay behind the Dovercourt destruction, it is difficult to say whose it was. What had Thomas Rose been reading? We do know of someone he had almost certainly been hearing. Thomas Bilney, whose opposition to images was one of the salient features of his teaching, had preached at both Ipswich and Hadleigh in 1527. And, according to reports of a sermon given in London, he had called for the destruction of images: 'as Ezechias distroyed the brasen serpent that Moyses made by the commanndement of God, even soo shuld kynges and prynces now a dayes dystroy and burne the Images of saynts sett upp in churches and other placys'.[10] The questions Bishop Tunstall prepared for examining Bilney and Thomas Arthur included one on whether it was more Christian to remove images of saints from churches than to permit them to remain to be gilded and honoured.[11] Bilney and Arthur recanted and abjured in 1527. But Bilney, after rethinking his position, was burned at the stake in Norwich in August 1531.

It seems not impossible that there was a connection of some kind between Bilney and this batch of East Anglian image-breakers. The link is established in one case. In 1533 two shoemakers of Eye in Suffolk (about twenty miles north of Ipswich) were examined and abjured certain heresies, including refusal to worship cross or crucifix. One of them, Robert Glazen, was alleged to have said that if he had the rood of Eye in his yard he would burn it. He confessed that the source of his views was a sermon preached by Thomas Bilney at Hadleigh in 1527.[12] Did Bilney's execution provoke some of his followers into demonstrations of support for his views? Is it possible that the Dovercourt bonfire was some kind of riposte, as the Rickmansworth blaze some ten years earlier may have been related to the local executions of Lollards? Such questions must be rhetorical, but we can be sure that the iconoclasts' psychology was complex. Combining with the conscious determination of the 'burdened conscience'[13] to free God from the blasphemy of the idol was a heady mixture of derring-do, personal loyalties and frustrations, and the intoxicating excitement of an illicit nocturnal fire.

The situation changed dramatically at the time of the Dissolution. Well before the second set of royal injunctions was issued in the autumn of 1538, the country as a whole had become alerted to the threat (or promise) of royal iconoclasm. Monastic dissolutions were accompanied by the suppression of

---

[10] Foxe, *A & M*, iv, p. 627, appendix vi (unpaginated), from Reg. Tunstall, Guildhall Library, London, MS 9531/10, fo. 133 v; Davis, *Heresy and Reformation*, p. 49. Bilney denied the charge as worded (negat ut ponitur).

[11] Foxe, *A & M*, iv, appendix vi; Reg. Tunstall, fo. 133 v.

[12] Davis, *Heresy and Reformation*, p. 82; Davis, 'The Trials of Thomas Bylney and the English Reformation', *Historical Journal*, 24 (1981), p. 785.

[13] Foxe's phrase for the Dovercourt iconoclasts, *A & M*, iv, p. 706.

cult images – parochial as well as conventual.[14] And those for whom the suppression of idolatry was an urgent priority saw to it that the reduction of celebrated 'idols' – that is, images that had been pilgrimaged and offered to – received the maximum publicity in their demise. Ritual disproofs of venerated statues, until recently so dangerous an undertaking, now became government stunts, part of an official campaign of propaganda and credal engineering.

In July 1538 there was a public bonfire at Chelsea of the celebrated Virgin statues from Walsingham and Ipswich and of other images collected for this purpose, which (duly denuded of their jewels and ornaments) were burned at the direction of Thomas Cromwell 'because the people should use noe more idolatrye unto them'.[15] Earlier in the same year another event of the same kind had attracted a good deal of notice and aroused the hopes of reformers abroad. This was the ceremonial destruction of the rood from the Cistercian house of Boxley in Kent that took place at St. Paul's on Sexagesima Sunday (also St. Matthias's Day), 24 February. It was a carefully stage-managed event, undoubtedly contrived to focus attention on the reformist cause. For though the numbers of pilgrims to Boxley were on the decline by the 1530's, it was a well-known centre beside the route to Canterbury. Henry VIII offered half a mark to the Rood of Grace soon after his accession, and the papal legate Lorenzo Campeggio stopped off for a night at Boxley on his way to London in 1518. The abbey's miraculous crucifix was (or had been) capable of responding physically to the entreaties of ailing supplicants. It could turn its eyes and move its lower lip, and may have been one of those jointed figure carvings (examples of which still survive abroad) which were able to move like puppets.[16]

It was as a puppet that the Rood of Grace was publicly exposed. After an initial disparaging display on market-day at Maidstone, for the benefit of Kent locals, the rood was taken up to London for ritual disproof at the most public of all England's pulpits. Bishop Hilsey of Rochester preached an edifying sermon at Paul's Cross, thundering against the blasphemous and fraudulent deceptions of images. He made full use of the set piece placed before his congregation by demonstrating the cords and devices of the revered crucifix as he denounced the manipulations of the 'engines used in old tyme' in this image. The climax was dramatic: 'After the sermon was done, the bishopp

---

[14] Recent helpful discussions of these events include Robert Whiting, 'Abominable Idols: Images and Image-breaking under Henry VIII', *Journal of Ecclesiastical History*, 33 (1982), pp. 30-47; idem, *The Blind Devotion of the People: Popular Religion and the English Reformation* (Cambridge, 1989); Ronald Hutton, 'The Local Impact of the Tudor Reformations,' in *The English Reformation Revised*, ed. Christopher Haigh (Cambridge, 1987), pp. 114-38.

[15] *Wriothesley's Chronicle*, i, p. 83.

[16] BL, MS Add. 21,481, fo. 10 v, records under 29 July 1509: 'Item for the kinges offring at the Roode of grace 6s. 8d'. See also BL, MS Harl. 433, fo. 293; *Letters and Papers*, ii, pt. 2, no. 4333, p. 1336 (Campeggio, on this first visit to England, stayed at Boxley on the night of Monday, 26 July, having spent the weekend seeing the sights of Canterbury); Ronald C. Finucane, *Miracles and Pilgrims: Popular Beliefs in Medieval England* (London, 1977), pp. 208-10. I have benefited from the critical assessment of J. Brownbill, 'Boxley Abbey and the Rood of Grace', *The Antiquary*, 7 (1883), pp. 162-65, 210-13. The movements attributed to the rood grew in the telling.

tooke the said image of the roode into the pulpitt and brooke the vice of the same, and after gave it to the people againe, and then the rude people and boyes brake the said image in peeces, so that they left not one peece whole'.[17] According to another contemporary, John Finch, who delightedly reported the rood's unmasking to a correspondent in Strasbourg, 'after all its tricks had been exposed to the people, it was broken into small pieces, and it was a great delight to any one who could obtain a single fragment, either, as I suppose, to put in the fire in their own houses, or else to keep by them by way of reproof to such kind of imposters'.[18] A second iconoclastically disposed bishop, Hugh Latimer, then made his contribution to the occasion. He carried a small statue to the door of St. Paul's and 'threw [it] out of the church, though the inhabitants of the country whence it came constantly affirmed that eight oxen would be unable to remove it from its place'.[19] This was probably the diminutive figure of St. Rumwold, which had also formed part of the devotions at Boxley.[20]

Euphoric reports such as Finch's radiated exaggerated expectations. The self-conscious theatricality of the occasion, so obviously framed to impress the 'simple people', can scarcely have had the instant success that he and others claimed. If some were already conscious that credulity was exploited by clerical manoeuvres (and a London crowd was likely to include such sceptics), one or two iconoclastic demonstrations were not going to bring a harvest of converted ignoramuses to condemn the clergy as 'mere conjurors' working

[17] *Wriothesley's Chronicle*, i, pp. 75-76. Wriothesley reports that the image 'was made of paper and cloutes from the legges upward; ech legges and armes were of timber', and it seems that during Hilsey's sermon it was placed where his auditors could inspect it for themselves. The account sent to Cromwell by his agent Geoffrey Chambers, who arranged the exposure of the rood at Maidstone, two miles away, described 'certen ingynes and olde wyer, wyth olde roton stykkes in the backe of the same', which (like Wriothesley) does not suggest recent use. *Original Letters Illustrative of English History*, ed. H. Ellis (London, 1824-46), iii, pt. 3, pp. 168-69.

[18] *Original Letters Relative to the English Reformation*, ed. H. Robinson (PS, Cambridge, 1846-47), ii, p. 607. Finch's report (unlike Wriothesley's) was far from first hand; he had the news from a German merchant who had English contacts. Other such accounts also stressed popular indignation against the impostures of monks and priests. See *Original Letters*, ed. Robinson, ii, pp. 604, 609-10, for those of William Peterson and Nicholas Partridge, sent respectively to Conrad Pulbert and Bullinger; for John Hoker of Maidstone's rhetorical letter to Bullinger, see Gilbert Burnet, *The History of the Reformation of the Church of England*, ed. N. Pocock (Oxford, 1865), vi, pp. 194-5, see also the account given by Henry VIII's representatives to the Marquis of Berghen *LP*, xiii, pt. 2, no. 880, p. 366. On John Finch of Billericay, see C.H. Garrett, *The Marian Exiles* (Cambridge, 1938), p. 153, postulating a possible connection with John Finch, a tiler of Colchester, who abjured Lollard heresies, including 'that no maner of worship ne reverence oweth to be do to ony ymages', in 1431; *Heresy Trials in the Diocese of Norwich, 1428-31*, ed. Norman P. Tanner (Camden Soc., fourth ser., 20, 1977), pp. 181-89, esp. p. 185.

[19] *Original Letters*, ed. Robinson, ii, p. 607; cf. p. 609.

[20] William Lambarde, *A Perambulation of Kent* (London, 1576), pp. 181-89, gives a disparaging account of the practices at Boxley, including the deceptions of the image of St. Rumwold, 'a preatie shorte picture of a boy sainct . . . small, hollow, and light' in itself, but capable of being fixed immovably in place by means of a wooden pin. Lambarde (b. 1536) had no first-hand knowledge, but based his report on what was 'yet freshe in mynde to bothe sides'.

despicable trickery on the people. The unprecedented nature of the events must have taken some members of Hilsey's congregation by surprise. It was indeed intended to be a ceremony that shocked by deliberate reversal of ancient assumptions. Latimer, chucking the sculpture out of the cathedral, was providing an ocular demonstration of the emptiness of its supposedly miraculous powers – just as the men who burned the Dovercourt rood had erased a spiritual claim together with a physical object. Throwing the image out of the church, out of a consecrated building into the open space outside, was also a symbolic action that stood for the process Hilsey was advocating. It was a matter of desanctification, or repositioning the central sanctum of the holy.[21] Idolatry would not be eradicated from believers' devotions until the images they misused had been removed from sacred places and tested in the world as the Boxley rood had been put to the test; images that had proved false must be put where they belonged and profaned in the most profane of secular places.

Native pride and sense of possession apart, it may be that the sheer act of removing the cult image from the place where it had stood time out of mind, shattered its miraculous power just as devastatingly as its physical breaking. Local beliefs bonded to localized saints, attaching the special mana of venerated relic or icon to a specific location. Holy images, like the bodily remains of holy persons, were believed to have evinced their supernatural power by choosing their place of abode and rendering their removal impossible. Just as St. James the Great or St. Edmund had, through the miraculous journeying or immovability of their mortal remains, identified their final resting-places, so – according to the Kent legend reported by William Lambarde – the Boxley rood, made by a skilful carpenter to help pay his ransom, had originally arrived in this village as the result of its own extraordinary horse-ride from Rochester.[22]

We should be chary of taking at face value the reformers' triumphant claims about the delighted reaction of crowds who saw holy images being execrated and destroyed. The true (and surely mixed) feelings about these events may be largely a matter of surmise, but one man who made known his grief at the treatment of the Boxley Rood was a London curate, Edward Laborne. He went on record for passing remarks about the example of St. Augustine, who had not been against converting the English with 'a crosse of wode and a

---

[21] A. van Gennep, *The Rites of Passage* (London, 1977), pp. 113-14. For examples of evangelical desecration of the previously holy by ritual inversion in profane space, see R.W. Scribner, 'Ritual and Reformation', in *Popular Culture and Popular Movements in Reformation Germany* (London, 1987), pp. 103-22.

[22] Lambarde, *Perambulations in Kent*, pp. 182-85. On 'automobile' relics, see Stephen Wilson, *Saints and their Cults* (Cambridge, 1985), pp. 11, 41, 69.

picture of christe', and in whose time 'so wyse men were as now be'.[23] If it was the unscripted illiterate whose misuses of imagery the literate were bothered about, by definition we only know half the story. Some believers might well have been fearful of participating in the dismemberment of holy statues, and maybe it is significant that on two of these occasions at St. Paul's, Wriothesley reports 'the boys' as doing the breaking.

Would the demonstration of the rood's 'engines' necessarily have undermined people's feelings for it? Mechanical imagery of this kind was not out of the ordinary, and if the locals at Boxley prided themselves on having the handiwork of a specially ingenious craftsman, there were plenty of other such clever devices to be seen in pageants and plays and ceremonial. Some of these were quite sophisticated, and must have added spectacularly to the illusions of dramatic performances. In 1433, the York Doomsday pageant, for which the affluent Mercers were responsible, included, besides 'A cloud and ii peces of Rainbow of tymber Array for god' and a heaven with red and blue clouds, an iron swing or frame pulled up with ropes 'that god sall sitte vppon when he sall sty vppe to heuen'. A cloud machine of this kind would also have made it possible to execute the stage direction of the York Transfiguration play: 'Hic descendunt nubes. Pater in nube'. At Lincoln Cathedral a contraption with cords enabled the dove of the Holy Ghost to descend at Pentecost. And, not far from Boxley, the Canterbury pageant of St. Thomas (which came to an end about the same time as the Rood of Grace) had a mechanical angel which – though perhaps less cunning than the golden angel that had bent down to offer the crown to Richard II in his coronation pageant – was nevertheless a moving figure. In 1515-16 a penny was spent 'for wyre for the vyce of the Angell', and two pence 'for candell to lyght the turnying of the vyce'.[24]

Popular experience of dramatic imagery was not divorced from the experience of statues of the saints in churches. Remembering this must caution us against falling in too readily with the cause-and-effect scepticism presented by the iconoclasts. John Hoker of Maidstone reported hearty laughter in the market-place of his town when the Rood of Grace went on show. But laughter had not been alien to the devotions at Boxley where the alternating weight and weightlessness of St. Rumwold caused merriment among visitors, seeing 'a great lubber to lift at that in vayne, whiche a young boy or wenche had easily taken up before him'. Not all laughter was derisive, and not all illusions were to

---

[23] He was curate of St. Benet, Gracechurch Street, and the parishioners who accused him of preaching contrary to the injunctions surmised that he made the remark about Augustine because 'it grevede hym to see the Rode of Ungrace with soche other not with out good consideracyon broken in peces of late at paules and abolisshede', *LP*, xiii, pt. 1, no. 1111, pp. 406-07; PRO E 36/120, fo. 214; SP 1/132, fo. 218 r; Brigden, *London and the Reformation*, pp. 281-2.

[24] *York*, ed. Alexandra F. Johnston and Margaret Rogerson, Records of Early English Drama (Toronto, 1979), i, p. 55; *The York Plays*, ed. Richard Beadle (London, 1982), p. 196; *Records of Plays and Players in Lincolnshire, 1300-1585*, ed. Stanley J. Kahrl, Malone Soc. Collections, 8 (1974), pp. xiii-xiv, 26-27; *Records of Plays and Players in Kent, 1450- 1642*, ed. Giles E. Dawson, Malone Soc. Collections, 7 (1965), pp. 192-93.

be equated with delusion. Those who watched a Resurrection play, or a carved Christ being elevated from an Easter Sepulchre on Easter Day, could both revere the miraculous and respect the limitations of physical enactment. But representation itself became different for those who tended to see the suspension of disbelief as akin to submission to misbelief.[25]

Iconoclastic demonstrations were to become familiar. But how would they have presented themselves at this time to those (the majority of believers) who did not share John Finch's views? What points of reference were there for such image-breaking? It may help somewhat to redress the imbalance in contemporary reporting if we consider the contexts in which the 'simple believer' might hitherto have encountered the phenomenon of iconoclasm.

In the first place he or she knew – or should have known – that breaking images and crosses was a most serious offence, subject to the severest penalties of church law. According to the sentence of the great curse, solemnly pronounced to parishioners four times a year, 'Alle arn acursed . . . that robbyn, brekyn, or brennyn, holy cherche violently, or chapel, or place relygyous, or othere placys halwyd or privylegyd, or brekyn crosses, awterys, or ymagys, in dyspyght and vyolens'.[26] Anyone who lived within range of Rickmansworth or Dovercourt would have known the grave consequences of breaking this law, and as recently as 1529 the sanction of secular authority supplemented the ancient provision when the Reformation Parliament excluded those who pulled down crosses in highways from its general pardon.[27]

There were depictions which showed the terrible punishments that fell on those who transgressed in this way. England has nothing quite so dramatic as the early sixteenth-century Florentine painting of the execution of Antonio di Giuseppe Rinaldeschi, delineated hanging from a window of the Bargello while angels and devils contended over the fate of his soul. Rinaldeschi's crime was the blasphemy of throwing horse dung at a painting of the Virgin.[28] A

---

[25] See notes 18 and 20 above, for Hoker and for Lambarde on St. Rumwold. For an example of an Easter Sepulchre image, see below p. 282; Pamela Sheingorn, 'No Sepulchre on Good Friday', in *Iconoclasm vs. Art and Drama*, ed. C. Davidson and A.E. Nichols (Kalamazoo, MI, 1989), pp. 145-63. Jonas Barish, *The Anti-Theatrical Prejudice* (Berkeley and Los Angeles, 1981), considers the growth of suspicions of the theatre in England; see also Clifford Davidson, '"The Devil's Guts": Allegations of Superstition and Fraud in Religious Drama and Art during the Reformation', in *Iconoclasm vs. Art and Drama*, pp. 92ff.

[26] *Jacob's Well*, ed. Arthur Brandeis (EETS, o.s. 115, 1900), p. 16. For the church's ruling on publication, see William Lyndwood, *Provinciale, (seu constitutiones Angliae)* (Oxford, 1679), p. 355.

[27] Stanford E. Lehmberg, *The Reformation Parliament, 1529-1536* (Cambridge, 1970), p. 91; *Statutes of the Realm*, iii, p. 283; 21 Henry VIII, c. I, vii.

[28] Samuel Y. Edgerton, Jr., *Pictures and Punishment: Art and Criminal Prosecution during the Florentine Renaissance* (Ithaca and London, 1985), pp. 47-58, and the same author's 'The Last Judgment as Pageant Setting For Communal Law and Order in Late Medieval Italy,' in *Persons in Groups: Social Behavior as Identity Formation in Medieval and Renaissance Europe*, ed. Richard C. Trexler, Medieval and Renaissance Texts and Studies, 36 (Binghamton, N.Y., 1985), pp. 89-90.

comparable scene appears among the late fifteenth-century paintings of miracles of the Virgin in Eton College Chapel and the Lady Chapel of Winchester
Cathedral. There (illustrating a story in Vincent of Beauvais' *Speculum
historiale*) a perfidious soldier, shown throwing a stone at a statue of the Virgin,
is immediately struck dead while the image miraculously bleeds.[29] Divine and
human law alike imposed the severest penalties on those who attacked images.

   There was, on the other hand, a context in which image-breaking was
recognized and legitimate. This too was represented in contemporary art
forms, which must have made it relatively familiar to believers.[30] The utter
destruction, by supernatural or divinely aided human agency, of the idols of
the heathen was a recurring theme in the lives of saints. It was recounted in
sermons, and it seems safe to assume that it also featured in the drama of the
saints. 'Then thay turnet hom to the mawmetes that weron yn the tempull, and
commawndet the fendes that weron yn hom forto come out, and schow hom to
the pepull, and then plucke the ymages al to powdyr; and soo thay dyd.'[31]
Mirk's *Festial* thus described the action against Persian idols by Sts. Simon and
Jude. The destruction of idols was also part of the story of St. George.

> Likewise Saynt George and Saynt Sebastian
> Despising ydoles which courtes used then,
> Suffered harde death by manifolde torment,
> For love and true fayth of God omnipotent.[32]

Though it was as a dragon-killer that St. George is chiefly remembered, he was
celebrated by Alexander Barclay and others as a 'most stronge confounder of

[29] M.R. James and E.W. Tristram, 'The Wall Paintings in Eton College Chapel and in the Lady
Chapel of Winchester Cathedral', *Walpole Society*, 17 (1928-29), pp. 1-43, esp., for this scene, pls.
xiv, xxi. In both cases the source is given in the accompanying inscriptions, that at Eton reading
'Qualitas ymago filii beate virginis a perfidis percussa sanguinem dedit. Vincentius'; for the story,
'De imagine que percussa sanguinem reddidit,' see *Speculum historiale fratris Vincencii ordinis
predicatorum* ([Strasbourg], 1483), i, book viii, c. cx. The two series of paintings are related. For a
sermon by the Durham Benedictine Robert Rypon, countering the Lollard case against images
and the early iconoclastic example of Epiphanius, see G.R. Owst, *Literature and Pulpit in
Medieval England* (Oxford, 1961), pp. 139-40.

[30] An apocryphal scene in the life of Christ which was frequently depicted in medieval art (and
which allowed artists to express their ideas of pagan idols) was a miracle that took place on the
Flight into Egypt: as Christ and his parents entered an Egyptian city, all the idols fell and broke
(fulfilling a prophecy of Isaiah). This story, deriving from the *Liber de infantia* or *Gospel of
Pseudo-Matthew*, passed into popular sources including the *Golden Legend* and the *Meditations on
the Life of Christ* attributed to St. Bonaventure, and was illustrated in many places, including
church windows (Great Malvern still has an example) and Bible pictures. On this topic see now
Michael Camille, *The Gothic Idol* (Cambridge, 1989), pp. 1-7 (on idols of Egypt); M.R. James,
The Apocryphal New Testament (Oxford, 1953), p. 75; Gordon McN. Rushforth, *Medieval
Christian Imagery as Illustrated by the Painted Windows of Great Malvern Priory Church,
Worcestershire* (Oxford, 1936), p. 287; Sandra Hindman, *Text and Image in Fifteenth-Century
Illustrated Dutch Bibles* (Leiden, 1977), pp. 55-56, fig. 21.

[31] John Mirk, *Festial*, ed. Theodor Erbe (EETS, e.s. 96, 1905), pt. I, p. 265.

[32] *The Eclogues of Alexander Barclay*, ed. Beatrice White (EETS, o.s. 175, 1928), p. 100.

Fig. 23a, b Exploits of St. George: above from a ballad of *c.* 1695 telling how 'while he in Persia abode, /He straight destroy'd each Idol-god': below from *The Life and Death of St George* (1750?), showing Princess Sabra, saved from the dragon, introducing the saint to the king her father.

fals ydolatry'. The second part of his life in the *Golden Legend* was taken up by the tale of how St. George refused to sacrifice to idols as commanded by the emperor, the climax of which is God's dramatic answer to the saint's prayer: a descent of fire from heaven, which destroys the pagan temple, with all its idols and priests. Barclay's version of Mantuan's life (which was published by Richard Pynson in 1515) gave a full account of this episode, 'and howe at the prayers of saynt George the great temple of the Idollys brast in sonder and sanke into the erth with horryble noyse and murdre of paynyms'.[33]

Whether or not this scene featured in plays of St. George, it was certainly recounted from the pulpit and appears, for instance, in an address for St. George's day in the early fifteenth-century *Speculum sacerdotale*.[34] The saint's arraignment for denouncing pagan idolatry was also one of the twelve images illustrating his life in a window at St. Neot in Cornwall.[35] Long after the Reformation, fossilized references to St. George's prowess against idols remained embedded in the chivalric farrago of his chapbook fame. The destruction of 'each Idol God' during his mission to Persia appears in *The Life and Death of the Famous Champion of England, St. George* collected by Samuel Pepys, which had some relationship with the Mummer's Play story of the saint, while another chapbook version of about 1750 recounts that: 'As he went he could not forbear taking notice of the idolatry of the Persians, and at last his zeal for the service of Christ transported him so far, that he went into their temples, overthrew their images, &c. which caused the whole kingdom to rise in arms against him'.[36] There is an inherent probability that St. George's iconoclasm featured in the many dramatic forms in which his story was presented in the fifteenth century, and a stage direction for a medieval French play shows the kind of scene that could have been enacted: 'The dragon must

[33] Jacobus de Voragine, *The Golden Legend* (Westminster: [William Caxton], 1483), fos. clvi v–clvii v; *Three Lives from the Gilte Legende*, ed. Richard Hamer, Middle English Texts, 9 (Heidelberg, 1978), pp. 65-74; *The Life of St. George by Alexander Barclay*, ed. William Nelson (EETS, o.s. 230, 1955), pp. 12-13, 90, 106; *STC*, 22,992.1.

[34] *Speculum sacerdotale*, ed. Edward H. Weatherly (EETS, o.s. 200, 1936), pp. 129-33. This account reverses the *Golden Legend* order and places the burning of the idols before the dragon-killing; see p. 130 for St. George's prayer at which 'there come downe a fyre fro heuen and sodeynly brande the temple with alle the godis and the maistris'.

[35] Gordon McN. Rushforth, 'The Windows of the Church of St. Neot, Cornwall', *Exeter Diocesan Architectural and Archaeological Society Transactions*, 15 (1937), pp. 175-76, pl. xlvi.

[36] *The Life and Death of St. George, The Noble Champion of England* (London, [1750?]), p. 13. For the Pepys text (of which there were several editions between 1660 and 1689, his being possibly of 1685), I cite the copy in the Pepys Library, Magdalene College, Cambridge (Penny Merriments, ii (6), p. 123), on which see Margaret Spufford, *Small Books and Pleasant Histories* (London, 1981), pp. 227-31. I am most grateful to Margaret Spufford for lending me a xerox of this chapbook. St. George's image-breaking also featured in a work which was in print for the best part of a century after its first appearance in 1596. In Richard Johnson's *The Most Famous History of the Seven Champions of Christendome* (London, 1608), p. 23, the Persians' solemn sacrifice to their pagan gods 'so mooved the impatience of the English Champion, that he tooke the ensignes and streamers whereon the Persian Gods were pictured, and trampled them under his feete'.

come out of the idol and not be seen again, and the idol must be broken in pieces by the son of the said bishop'.[37]

Medieval England did not lack knowledge, then, of legitimate iconoclasm, but this belonged to a completely different world from that of the images encountered in everyday devotions. Given the ancient separation of these worlds – the world inhabited by familiar saints, and the alien world of pagan cults – their sudden assimilation could only have been startling. A capricious switch of royal policy abruptly inaugurated a whole new outlook in which things formerly kept apart were suddenly associated. The proscribed became legal: two kinds of imagery that had not previously been placed in relation to each other were, almost overnight, equated. Christian images of saints were regarded in the same light as pagan idols and were destroyed just as Christian saints had once destroyed idols of heathen gods. In March 1538, a royal candle was still burning before the image of Our Lady of Walsingham.[38] Four months later the revered statue went up in flames. It is not surprising that some of Henry VIII's subjects began to talk of him as a Lollard.[39]

The inauguration of this extraordinary reversal was given a great deal of publicity as plays, ballads, and sermons produced by Thomas Cromwell's circle hammered home the 'fantasies' and errors of England's idolatry. But the situation, despite all the attacks on new-style 'idols' that were openly chastised in 1538, was far from clear. For by no means all church images were condemned as idolatrous, and the government, in attempting to distinguish between those that were inadmissible (conceived to have spiritual powers) and those that were valid (as a means of instruction), certainly never intended that

[37] Lynette Muir, 'The Saint Play in Medieval France', in *The Saint Play in Medieval Europe*, ed. Clifford Davidson, Early Drama, Art, and Music, Monograph Ser., 8 (Kalamazoo, 1986), p. 159. The idol in this Bourges *Actes des apôtres* was capable of special trick effects. Cf. Clifford Davidson, 'The Middle English Saint Play', in *The Saint Play in Medieval Europe*, pp. 37, 40, 48, on the possible dramatic role of idols in English plays of Sts. Eustace, Lawrence and Catherine. Destruction of the entire pagan temple with its idol of 'mament' is one of the spectacular effects of the Digby *Mary Magdalene*; see *The Late Medieval Religious Plays of Bodleian MSS Digby 133 and e Museo 160*, ed. Donald C. Baker, John L. Murphy, and Louis B. Hall, Jr. (EETS, 283, 1982), p. 76. The destruction by fire that would have been called for in this scene was also encountered in dramatic presentations of Doomsday; see *Coventry*, ed. R.W. Ingram, Records of Early English Drama (Toronto, 1981), p. 230, including a 1565 payment at Coventry for 'Settynge the worldes on fyre'.

[38] *LP*, xiii, pt. 2, no. 1280, pp. 529, 535; Finucane, *Miracles and Pilgrims*, p. 205. Cf. *LP*, ii, pt. 2, pp. 1442, 1449, and BL, MS Add, 21,481, fos. 23 v, 51 r, 52 v, for earlier payments for the king's candle and his priest singing before Our Lady of Walsingham (costing £4 13s. 4d. and £10 a year respectively) and for the king's offerings there in 1520.

[39] *LP*, vi, no. 1255, p. 514, for the views of Richard Panemore (1533) on Latimer's reported preaching that church images should be pulled down and that the *Ave Maria* was no prayer; J.F. Davis, 'Lollards, Reformers and St. Thomas of Canterbury,' *Birmingham Historical Journal*, 9 (1963), p. 13.

individual subjects should start taking initiatives on this matter.[40] This was, however, precisely what happened. The dangerous lead given by the official iconoclasts prompted some radicals to follow suit. Clandestine image-breaking was given a new spur.

Affairs in London illustrate very clearly this threatening interaction between officially sponsored destruction and imitative subversive reform. One incident in particular showed with immediate effect how government destruction could thrill individual enthusiasts. On 22 May 1538, three months after the breaking of the Boxley rood, the capital was treated to another iconoclastic spectacle. This was a double burning, designed to demolish two misbeliefs in one fire: support for papal authority, and trust in the miraculous powers of images. A large crowd, including various notables accommodated on a specially erected platform, was gathered on this day to listen to an edifying sermon preached by Hugh Latimer and to watch the simultaneous burning of the Observant Franciscan, John Forest – who had been confessor to Queen Catherine of Aragon, and was guilty of loyalty to the pope – and the large figure of St. Derfel, extracted against strenuous local opposition from the village of Llandderfel in Wales, where he was credited with powers to save souls from hell, and of whom it had been prophesied that he would one day set a forest on fire.[41]

There was another aspect of this *auto-da-fé* which would not have been lost on those who saw heresy and orthodoxy changing places. Friar Forest, who was about sixty-eight when he died, was the first person to be burned as a heretic, as well as executed as a traitor, for believing in the church of Rome and upholding the authority of the pope.[42]

The morning after this event, 23 May, the parishioners of St. Margaret Pattens in the city of London woke up to discover that their church's rood had been broken to pieces in the night. This was done, according to Wriothesley, by 'certeine lewde persons, Fleminges and Englishe men, and some persons of the sayd parishe'.[43] The rood may have been specially vulnerable because it had been placed in a tabernacle in the churchyard while the church was being rebuilt, offerings to the rood being allocated to the new work, which had at this

---

[40] Aston, *England's Iconoclasts*, i, pp. 225-36, attempts to explain the situation at this time rather more fully than was done by John Phillips, *The Reformation of Images: Destruction of Art in England, 1535-1660* (Berkeley and Los Angeles, 1973), pp. 58-62.

[41] *Wriothesley's Chronicle*, i, pp. 79-81; *Hall's Chronicle* (London, 1809). pp. 825-26; *Original Letters*, ed. Ellis, iii, pt. 3, pp. 194-95; cf. i, pt. 2, pp. 82-83. See below, p. 303.

[42] *Wriothesley's Chronicle*, i, pp. 78-79; *LP*, xiii, pt. 1, no. 1043, p. 385; Ridley, *Thomas Cranmer*, pp. 160-61. Forest was hanged before being burned.

[43] *Wriothesley's Chronicle*, i, p. 81; John Stow, *A Survey of London*, ed. C.L. Kingsford (Oxford, 1905), i, pp. 209-10.

time progressed as far as the steeple. As one of the more famous images in London, it had for some while been the butt of denigration and suspect invective. For instance, among the charges reported by Foxe as being brought in 1529 against William Wegen, priest of St. Mary at Hill, was 'that he being sick, went to the Rood of St. Margaret Pattens; and said before him twenty Paternosters; and when he saw himself never the better, then he said, "A foul ill take him, and all other images".' A few years later Jasper Wetzell of Cologne added his voice to such domestic dissent; 'being at St. Margaret Pattens, and there holding his arms across, he said unto the people, that he could make as good a knave as he is, for he is but made of wood'.[44]

Some of the iconoclasts were caught and brought to book. The same day, Thursday 23 May, recognizances were taken from eight men – all of different trades – in the court of the aldermen to which they bound over. The eight, associated 'by theyre owne confessyon', with twenty more (unnamed), and with James Ellys, pewterer, and John Gough, stationer, 'assembled togyther late yn the nyght tyme yester nyght last past pulled downe ther the Roode at Saynt Margaret Paten'. The accused were not without defence. They said that according to Mr. Edward Crome's report the bishop of Worcester (Hugh Latimer) believed it to be Cromwell's will that the said image should be removed.[45]

If the blend of native and imported dissent had been undermining the repute of the rood for some while, there was also a spearhead of underground reforming initiative contributing to its demise. For the stationer named in this list had long been helping to publicize the evangelical case. John Gough was a publisher with a consistent record of sponsoring reforming books. He had been in trouble for such during the previous decade, and – particularly interesting in the context of the St. Margaret Pattens affair – he may have had a hand three years before this event in the production of the first book that openly canvassed the cause of iconoclasm in English: a translation of Martin Bucer's *Das einigerlei Bild*. Given what we know of the background to all these events,

---

[44] Foxe, *A & M*, v, pp. 28, 32. The king offered 6s. 8d. to the rood in 1511; *LP*, ii, pt. 2, p. 1449; BL MS. Add. 21,481, fo. 52 v.

[45] Corporation of London Rec. Office, Repertory 10, fo. 34 v: 'as they say M' Cromer reportyd by the report of ye bysshopp of Worceter that ye lorde prevy seales [commaundet?] that ye seid Image shuld be removyd'. I owe this reference to Susan Brigden, *London and the Reformation* (Oxford, 1989), pp. 290-1. The matter was of immediate concern to the court of aldermen, who, as patrons of the living, had two months earlier presented John Grene. He held St. Margaret Pattens until July 1542, when he resigned (Repertory 10, fos. 25 v, 267 v; cf. *LP*, xiii, pt. 1, no. 866, p. 319; PRO, SP 1/131/242, for a John Grene who petitioned Thomas Wriothesley for advancement to a living, having failed in his expectation of promotion through service to Chancellor Audley).

it is scarcely surprising that the accused iconoclasts pleaded the belief that Cromwell had ordered the removal of the rood.[46]

The effects of these affairs were felt far afield. Five months later, in the autumn of 1538, Cromwell was sent a letter from Lifton in Devon, written by William Dynham, gentleman. It reported a conversation that had taken place at a supper party at the priory of St. Germans in Cornwall, during which Alexander Barclay, the poet and ex-Benedictine, had been unwise enough to suggest that the removal of images was getting out of hand. 'I thinke menne are to besye in pullinge downe of Ymages, without especiall commaundement of the Prynce', he said. Dynham, who was keen to expose Barclay's 'kankrid harte', egged him on. 'I knowe none then pulled downe but sutche as Idolatrye was commytted unto', he replied, adding provocatively that there was much scriptural support for such action. The example of St. Margaret Pattens came up, adding to the heat of the argument, since Dynham advanced the view that although these iconoclasts were 'some what dispraised', they had a godly end in view and their doings were therefore tolerated. Barclay demurred. He suggested contrariwise that the serious fire that had taken place in the parish after the rood-breaking, burning many tenements and some people, represented divine vengeance for a great offence.[47]

The official policy regarding the reform of images at this time was dangerously ambiguous. The second set of royal injunctions, issued the day before Dynham wrote his letter, marked the advent of authorized iconomachy in every parish subject to the supreme head (in theory). For the first time there was an open assault on images and pilgrimage as unscriptural, superstitious, and idolatrous; and for the first time parish clergy were instructed to take down images. This order was, however, limited to a particular category of images. It was those that (in the words of Injunction 7) were 'abused with pilgrimages or offerings' which, for the avoidance of idolatry, the clergy were 'to take down and delay'. The problems were: how to decide – and who would decide – when an image was abused and, if the word *delay* meant simply to bear away, what

[46] The outcome of these proceedings is not known, but Gough was very much in business a few years after and was imprisoned in the Fleet for printing seditious books in 1541; see Margaret Aston, *Lollards and Reformers: Images and Literacy in Late Medieval Religion* (London, 1984), pp. 229-30, 242, 251, and *England's Iconoclasts*, i, p. 203.

[47] *Original Letters*, ed. Ellis, iii, pt. 3, pp. 112-15. This letter was dated 12 October; *LP*, xiii, pt. 2, no. 596, p. 232. Barclay, who had preached the previous day in honour of the Virgin, was under pressure from Dynham who was determined to exploit the situation. Stow, *Survey of London*, i, pp. 209-10, reports the fire in the parish of St. Margaret Pattens on 27 May 1538: 'amongst the basket-makers, a great and sudden fire happened in the night season, which within the space of three hours consumed more than a dozen houses, and nine persons were burnt to death there'.

suitable redress was there when enthusiasts took the injunction to mean not simply removal but also destruction?[48]

The months and years that followed showed that the iconoclastic reformers had opened up quite a hornet's nest. If on one side it seems remarkable that central government directive could erase with such speed so much ancient observance and ritual, there are, on the other side, plenty of examples of local controversies. Taking down an image was not the same at all as destroying it, and action of either sort might be challenged under the existing law. Although activists, especially those in dioceses whose bishops were iconoclastically inclined (or ready to let the image- reformers take over), could take advantage of the lack of clarity in the new law, they might find themselves up against vociferous resistance. At Salisbury, quite a stir resulted from the officious attempt by the city's under-bailiff, John Goodall, to prevent worshippers in the cathedral from kneeling before and kissing an image of Christ on Easter Day, 1539.[49] In Cranmer's own diocese considerable differences of opinion over interpretations of the 1538 injunctions were revealed by the inquiries set in train by the Prebendaries Plot of 1543, and, while two of the archbishop's deputies seem to have been earnestly bent on curtailing idolatry, others were busy opposing the removal of images. For instance, one Bartholomew, surgeon, was alleged to have said to Cranmer's apparitor, William Burges, 'Thou art he that would have pulled down our St. George, but your master lyeth by the heel, and we have showed the taking down thereof to the King's Council and were bid set it up again'.[50] In some cases images removed for

---

[48] There is a problem over the meaning of the word 'delay', for which the *OED* and *MED* do not give obvious analogous examples, the temporal meaning of the word (related to the Latin *differre* and English *defer*) being dominant. Ann Nichols suggests that since 'delay' and 'defer' could be used synonymously with the sense of 'postpone' (*OED* gives example from John Palsgrave's *Lesclarcissement de la Langue Francoyse* [1530], 'I delaye one, or deferre hym, or put hym backe of his purpose'), possibly 'delay' could be used synonymously for 'defer' in the meaning of 'to put on one side, set aside' (*OED* cites Lydgate, *Minor Poems*: 'Grace withe her lycour cristallyne and pure / Defferrithe vengeaunce off ffuriose woodnes'). The word 'defer' with this obsolete non-temporal sense of set aside, carry down, convey away, was synonymous with another obsolete form 'delate' (derived from the Latin *deferre*). An example cited in the *MED* of the verb 'delaien' used in this same sense is the Wycliffite Bible's translation of Psalm 21:20 (Tu autem Domine ne elongaveris auxilium tuum a me) as 'But thou, Lord, delaie not thin help fro me'. It seems likely that the injunction's 'delay' bore such a meaning (*elongare*, to remove, make distant), and this interpretation is supported by the proclamation of November 1538 against Becket imagery, ordering it to be 'put down and avoided' from churches. See *Visitation Articles and Injunctions of the Period of the Reformation*, ed. W.H. Frere and W.M. Kennedy, Alcuin Club Collections, 14-16 (1910), ii, p. 38; *Tudor Royal Proclamations*, ed. Paul L. Hughes and James F. Larkin (New Haven and London, 1964-69), i, p. 276; Aston, *England's Iconoclasts*, i, p. 227.

[49] Aston, *England's Iconoclasts*, i, pp. 230-2. Possibly this image, which held the host, was an Easter Sepulchre image: cf. H.J. Feasey, *Ancient English Holy Week Ceremonial* (London, 1897), pp. 134-37, and Pamela Sheingorn, *The Easter Sepulchre in England*, Early Drama, Art, and Music, Reference Ser., 5 (Kalamazoo, MI, 1987), pp. 58-59.

[50] *LP*, xviii, pt. 2, no. 546, p. 295.

alleged abuse were indeed subsequently reinstated. The rector of Milton near Canterbury, it was said, 'had in his church . . . an image of St. Margaret, to which was a common pilgrimage, and caused it to be taken down. And upon St. Margaret's day last past Mr. John Crosse, sometime cellarer of Christ-church, came to the same church and did set the same image again with a garland of flowers on the head of it, and did strowe the church and said mass there'.[51]

Such were the dangers of dicing with these differences of opinion that the authorities themselves sometimes went clandestine. In September 1547, when Edward VI's council was increasingly worried by disputes over the removal of images, the London authorities directed each alderman 'in the moste secrette discrete and quyette manner he can devyse', to visit the parish churches in his ward with the incumbent and churchwardens, and having 'shutt the churche doores' so that no crowds could gather, to make a record of the images – which were offered or prayed to and which not, who had taken them down and what became of them, what misdemeanours had been committed in this process, and what images still remained.[52]

On two occasions when images were removed from St. Paul's, the risk of disturbance in the city was obviated by taking action overnight. The famous rood at the north door of the cathedral, together with the image of St. Uncumber, were taken down by the dean of St. Paul's (acting on orders sent through the mayor, Sir Richard Gresham) on the night of 23 August 1538.[53] Likewise in November 1547, when the royal visitors – anticipating the action that in the rest of the country took place the following year – were pulling down all images in London's parish churches, the works in St. Paul's were under-taken by night. This proved difficult, and there was an accident as the large rood in the centre of the cathedral was dismantled in the darkness. The labourers let the great cross fall to the ground, killing one or two workmen and hurting others. Naturally there were those who drew a moral like Alexander Barclay: God had spoken.[54]

[51] Ibid., xviii, pt. 2, p. 297. On John Crosse, see Emden, (O), *1501 to 1540*, p. 153. For affairs in Kent at this time, see Michael L. Zell, 'The Prebendaries' Plot of 1543: A Reconsideration', *JEH*, 27 (1976), pp. 241-53; Peter Clark, *English Provincial Society from the Reformation to the Revolution: Religion, Politics and Society in Kent, 1500-1640* (Hassocks, 1977), pp. 38-66.

[52] Corporation of London Record Office, Repertory 11, fo. 349.

[53] Brigden, *London and the Reformation* (Oxford, 1989), pp. 10, 291; PRO, SP1/135, fo. 247; *LP*, xiii, pt. 2, no. 209, p. 81; *Wriothesley's Chronicle*, i, p. 84. A call for this action was sent to Cromwell a month earlier by George Robinson, who in a letter of 16 July described how he had visited St. Paul's: 'I went to powlles where I ffound sent Uncombre stonddyng in hyr old place and state with hyr gay gowne and sylver schews on and a woman kneelying beffore hyr at xi of the cloke.' It was for the king to be Josiah and take all such images away. *LP*, xiii, pt. 1, no. 1393, p. 515; PRO, SP 1/134, fo. 183r.

[54] *Chronicle of the Grey Friars of London*, ed. J.G. Nichols (Camden Soc., 1852), p. 55; *Wriothesley's Chronicle*, ii, p. 1.

Fig. 24 St. Wilgefortis and the Fiddler. 1513 woodcut by Hans Springinklee, illustrating the story of how an image of the saint miraculously shed a golden shoe to help a destitute fiddler.

Waverers and opposers of this kind were answered by another iconoclastic display. Ten days after the accident over the rood, a sermon and demonstration at Paul's Cross on the first Sunday in Advent (27 November 1547) announced to the capital – and to the rest of the kingdom – that the young king was taking up the mantle of Josiah that had been donned by his father in 1538. The sermon was preached by Bishop Barlow of St. David's (who had his own iconoclastic record), and he had exemplary specimens on hand to drive home his moral. In front of his pulpit was exhibited an image of Our Lady which the clergy of St. Paul's had vainly tried to conceal from the royal visitors. Barlow also had a jointed Easter Sepulchre figure of Christ, which likewise may be assumed to have been familiar to a number of his auditors. The moral was double; 'the great abhomination of idolatrie in images'; and the great sin of harbouring idols. To those of Barlow's mind, there was a world of difference between removing images from churches and destroying them. Idolatry could only be defeated by annihilation. 'After the sermon the boyes brooke the idolls in peaces.'[55]

Henry VIII, sensing the perils of Cromwellian policy, had retreated in the 1540s from the spectacular iconoclasm of 1538. Reform of images continued, but the supreme head, who did not see eye-to-eye with his archbishop on this score, was readier to complete the termination of major pilgrimage shrines than to undertake the eradication of idolatry desired by a number of his subjects. Some of these evangelicals went abroad when the brakes were applied at the execution of Cromwell. Others found ways of continuing to work for the cause on their own. One such was William Forde who, as usher of Winchester College between *c.* 1543 and 1547, managed – not without personal cost – to execute an iconoclastic manoeuvre in the college chapel. The story was recorded for John Foxe by John Louth, archdeacon of Nottingham (d. 1590). Forde, who was himself a scholar at Winchester in the 1530s, returned as usher in his early twenties, having been converted into a 'greate enemye to papisme' while at Oxford.

> Ther was many golden images in Wykam's colleage by Wynton. The churche dore was directly over agaynste the usher's chamber. Mr. Forde tyed a longe coorde to the images, lynkyng them all in one coorde, and, being in his chamber after midnight, he plucked the cordes ende, and at one pulle all the golden godes came downe with *heyho Rombelo.* Yt wakened all men with the rushe. They wer amased at the terryble noyse and also disamayd at the greevous sight. The corde beinge plucked harde and cutt with a twytche lay at the church doore.

---

[55] *Wriothesley's Chronicle,* ii, p. 1; Millar MacLure, *The Paul's Cross Sermons, 1534-1642* (Toronto, 1958), pp. 40-1; Sheingorn, *The Easter Sepulchre,* p. 61. The second of these images belonged to the execrated class of moving figures, like the Boxley one; 'the resurrection of our Lord made with vices, which putt out his legges of sepulchree and blessed with his hand, and turned his heade'. See also P. Sheingorn, ' "No Sepulchre on Good Friday": The Impact of the Reformation on the Easter Rites in England', in *Iconoclasm vs. Art and Drama,* ed. Davidson and Nichols, pp. 152-4.

Forde, naturally, was suspect. He was found in bed, but that scarcely absolved him. After doing this good turn to his *alma mater*, his life was made a misery. He was railed at by masters and scholars and mugged at night in the town, though (according to a Catholic reporter) he did succeed in converting the head boy.[56]

The iconoclastic purges carried out under the direction of royal visitors early in the reigns of Edward VI and Elizabeth I swept away much of what reformers objected to as idolatrous 'popish peltry'. And at Elizabeth's accession, when the restored roods and saints' images of the intervening Catholic years challenged the indignation of returned exiles, Londoners again witnessed ceremonial public image-burnings not unlike those of 1538. By the time of the issue of the Second Book of Homilies in 1563, with its long tripartite homily expounding the intolerable dangers of allowing any images to be set up publicly in churches, it might seem as if the iconoclasts had run their course. 'Alas, gossip, what shall we now do at church, since all the saints are taken away, since all the goodly sights we were wont to have are gone, since we cannot hear the like piping, singing, chanting, and playing upon the organs, that we could before.'[57] Churches surely looked bare, empty, denuded – 'scoured of such gay gazing sights', as the homilist, here rebuking the 'unsavoury' objections of tattling wives, scathingly put it. What remained for the iconoclasts to reform – apart from the fond memories and hoarded relics of the unconverted?

But the see-saw balance between public destruction and private enthusiasm was by no means over. Regional diversity apart, there still remained a range of objects that for long tested the initiative of committed purifiers. The imagery of church windows, crosses in churchyards and other public places, maypoles, and organs, were all grist to the iconoclastic mill. We can briefly see how this process continued by looking at the development of cross-breaking.

Disputes over the use of the cross took place on various levels during the reign of Elizabeth. Besides all the controversy aroused by the use of the sign of the cross in baptism, there was a campaign of attrition against the freestanding crosses in churchyards and other public places. Such monuments were defaced or destroyed officially on the grounds that they were sources of idolatry. For instance, in October 1571 rural deans in the diocese of York were ordered 'to se that no reliques of crosses remayne in any churche or chaple yard within there severall Deanryes'. Seven years later reports in the diocese of Chester suggest considerable lack of uniformity, some parishes still having their churchyard crosses while in others these had been reduced to stumps or

---

[56] *Narratives of the . . . Reformation*, ed. J.G. Nichols (Camden Soc., 77, 1859), pp. 29-30; Emden (O), *1501 to 1540*, pp. 208-9; Nicholas Sander, *Rise and Growth of the Anglican Schism*, trans. D. Lewis (London, 1877), pp. 207-8. 'Golden Gods' (a scriptual phrase) would have been especially provocative; see above Chapter 7, pp. 224-6.

[57] *Certain Sermons or Homilies to be read in Churches* (Oxford, 1844), p. 311, from the Homily of the Place and Time of Prayer.

headless monuments.[58] Discrepancies of this kind maddened the purists, and a number of open-air crosses were defaced or felled by individuals who took the law into their own hands.

At Durham, Neville's Cross was destroyed by nocturnal iconoclasts in 1589. This 'most notable famous and goodly larg cross' had been erected to commemorate the victory of 1346 at which the Scots had lost to Lord Neville and the English their celebrated black rood, and its carvings included a Crucifixion as well as the four evangelists and Neville's arms. It apparently remained intact until thirty years after Elizabeth's accession when 'in the nighte tyme the same was broken downe and defaced'.[59]

Other less conspicuous activists went to work on parish crosses. In 1603 charges were brought in the quarter sessions at Chester against a group of offenders in Bishop Vaughan's diocese. Seven men were accused, and confessed that they had one Sunday thrown down with staves a stone cross standing in the churchyard of Wharton, Cheshire, and the same night two of them had broken panels of glass representing St. Andrew and Lazarus in the chancel window at Tarvin some ten miles away. These nocturnal iconoclasts were the servants of John Bruen, who earned praise for his reform of 'painted puppets and popish idols' in the church at Tarvin. Doubtless it was the example set by this leading light of the godly in Cheshire that was being followed.[60]

Particularly celebrated examples of cross-breaking were those of Banbury and Cheapside. There could hardly be a more focal Puritan centre than Banbury (whose fame became linked with its cross), but even here iconoclasm was divisive and its proponents, aware of the contentiousness of the issue, tried to present the town with a *fait accompli*. Two stonemasons were set to work to hew down the Banbury High Cross at first light on the morning on 26 July 1600. This dawn endeavour was halted by a townsman who disliked the project, and before long a crowd of over a hundred had assembled, demonstrating for and against the work. There were enough supporters to see the demolition work completed, but also enough opponents to result in a case against a clique of the town's aldermen being taken to Star Chamber.[61]

The example of Cheapside Cross is illuminating. As one of the best-known crosses in the country, cherished and restored by generations of Londoners and a focal point in all city processions, it long withstood a battery of

---

[58] *Tudor Parish Documents of the Diocese of York*, ed. J.S. Purvis (Cambridge, 1948), pp. 177, 202.

[59] *Rites of Durham*, ed. J.T. Fowler (Surtees Soc., 107, 1903), pp. 27-8. This regretful account, outspoken in its condemnation of the 'lewde and contemptuous wicked persons' responsible for this deed, was written about 1593, and gives a full description of the cross.

[60] R.C. Richardson, *Puritanism in North West England* (Manchester, 1972), pp. 122-23, 158. (Since there is no Warton within range of Tarvin, I have taken the reference on p. 123 to relate to Wharton, Cheshire).

[61] P.D.A. Harvey, 'Where was Banbury Cross?' *Oxoniensia*, 31 (1966), pp. 83-106; William Potts, *Banbury Cross and the Rhyme* (Banbury, 1930); *A History of the County of Oxford*, ed. Alan Crossley, Victoria History of the Counties of England (London, 1972), x, pp. 7-8, 23, 98.

objections. This central public monument came to be viewed by some as the central idol in the land, and there were voices calling for its reform more than two generations before this was finally accomplished. One such advocate made known his view of the matter in a very well-read text.

The *Short Catechism for Householders* by John More and Edward Dering, issued in many editions between 1572 and 1634, was one of the more influential texts of its kind in the period. Edward Dering wrote the preface to this *Brief and necessary instruction, very needful to be known of all householders*, invoking readers to purification from 'the idolatrous superstition of the elder world'.[62] It was the world of popular literature he specifically had in mind: the dangerous 'spiritual enchauntmentes' and 'dreames and illusions' of the past that readers found in the tales of Robin Hood, Bevis of Hampton, and Arthur of the Round Table as well as saints' lives and satanic texts 'Hell had printed' – the chapbooks stocked by peddlers and chapmen alongside more edifying texts; those 'pleasant histories' which, as Margaret Spufford has shown, perpetuated the old world of monks and friars and priests with a timeless disregard for the changes effected by the Reformation.[63] We have seen how St. George lived on in this literature, attached to some of the assumptions of medieval iconography. Dering's solution was simple. All such books, with songs and sonnets, fables and tragedies, should be burned as publicly as possible in London's main thoroughfare so that (as he put it) 'the chiefe streete might be sanctified with so holy sacrifice. The place it selfe doth crave it, and holdeth up a gorgeous Idoll, a fyt stake for so good a fire'.[64] A bonfire of vanities at Cheapside Cross: Dering's wish was to be granted, but not during his lifetime.

Whatever the inspiration on Dering's readers there were individuals who tried to do something about the egregious idol, Cheapside Cross. The first serious attempt took place in 1581. John Stow described what happened one midsummer under cover of darkness: 'The 21 of June in the night, certaine young men, drawing ropes thwart the streete, on both sides the Crosse in Cheape, to stop the passage, did then fasten ropes about the lowest Images of the said Crosse, attempting by force to have plucked them downe, which when they could not doe, they plucked the picture of Christ out of his mothers lap, whereon he sat, and otherwise defaced her, and the other Images by striking

---

[62] *A briefe & necessary Instruction, Verye needefull to bee knowen of all Housholders* (London, 1572), sigs. Aii r-Aiii r. On this work (*STC*, 6679-6682.3, 6710.5-6724.5), see Patrick Collinson, *Godly People: Essays on English Protestantism and Puritanism* (London, 1983), pp. 297-98, 321-22.

[63] Spufford, *Small Books and Pleasant Histories*, pp. 219-20, 240-1, 250-1. Dering's proscribed books would have included lives of St. George like those mentioned above.

[64] *A Briefe & necessary Instruction*, sig. Aiii (with reference to the 'zealous Ephesians' of Acts 19).

off their armes'.[65] Despite the issue of a proclamation offering a reward for identification of the offenders, these iconoclasts were not discovered. But the matter was taken to the highest authority. On 4 July the city aldermen appointed a committee who were forthwith to 'conferre togeather and consyder what course ys best to be taken concerninge the repayringe of the great crosse in Cheapesyde'. They were to take advice from the bishop of Salisbury or some other learned divine on the repairs and also 'for thanswearynge of her majesties commaundement in that behalfe'. Five days later a deputation of aldermen had to keep a Sunday morning appointment at court 'touchinge the crosse in Cheapesyde'.[66] The queen was evidently concerned about the state of the city monument, though Stow's account suggests that it was a long time before some perfunctory restoration to the damaged Virgin and Child was completed.

The City authorities were in no hurry to improve their ancient monument, and differences of opinion between them and Queen Elizabeth became all too clear at the turn of the century. The removal of the cross at the top of the Cheapside monument, on the grounds of its dangerous state of decay, led to troubles over its replacement. Bishop Bancroft thought that a cross should be put back, and he had the queen behind him. Others, who had the support of the vice-chancellor of Oxford, George Abbot, were wholly opposed to this and thought that a religiously neutral object, such as a pyramid should be placed there instead. In the end, Cheapside Cross got back its cross, despite the iconomachs' learned censures. But only twelve days afterwards the nocturnal iconoclasts struck again, once more defacing Virgin and Child.[67]

Crosses and crucifixes were very much in the news after the opening of the Long Parliament – thanks in part to their increased visibility in the 1630s. Crosses came under attack from many directions, and the monument in Cheapside became the topic of a small library of pamphlets in 1642-3. Most of them aimed at its demise, and it comes as no surprise to find that the final destruction of the cross was the work of private as well as public iconoclasts. In January 1642 surreptitious image-breakers launched a new attack, scaling the iron railing that had enclosed the monument since 1603 and breaking several statues, including the figure of Christ. After this, trained bands were set to keep nightly watch on the cross, though it was clear to some that it could not last long.[68] Its obsequies were penned and published. The end came on 2 May 1643 when, with an attendant force of mounted horse and foot companies, with drums beating and trumpets sounding, in the presence of a huge crowd of

[65] John Stow, *Annales, or, A Generall Chronicle of England* (London, 1631-32), p. 694; cf. Stow, *Survey of London*, ed. Kingsford, i, p. 266, and ii, p. 331, which records the lowest tier of images as including the Resurrection, the Virgin Mary, and King Edward the Confessor.

[66] Corporation of London Record Office, Repertory 20, fo. 216.

[67] Stow, *Survey*; ed. Kingsford, i, pp. 266-67; [G. Abbot], *Cheapside crosse censured and condemned* (London, 1641); *Acts of the Privy Council of England*, n.s. 1542-1631 (London, 1890-1964), xxx, p. 27, and xxxi, p. 44.

[68] *The crosses case in Cheapside* ([London], 1642), pp. 1-2; *CSPD, 1641-43*, i, p. 274.

Fig. 25 Cheapside Cross pulled down to 'a greate shoute of people with joy', on 2 May 1643, and the burning of the Book of Sports on the same site. Engraving by Wenceslaus Hollar.

spectators, Cheapside Cross was finally haled to the ground. A print by Wenceslaus Hollar commemorated this dramatic occasion, and play was made with the coincidence of date with the Invention of the Holy Cross (3 May) in the Catholic calendar.[69] It was an event comparable to the scenes of 1538. Once again, despite the alteration of circumstance and the changed conception of the source of idolatry – Rome – spectacular official iconoclasm was a great propagandist rite of dismissal. The vanquishing of the 'idol' was a declaratory ceremony designed to sweep idolators into the purified space created by the destroyers.

Ironically – and somewhat inconsistently, given their own view that God was no respecter of places – the iconoclasts dedicated the site of the demolished idol to further ceremonies of the same kind. Hollar delineated the burning of the Book of Sports 'in the place where the Crosse stoode' beneath his etching of its destruction. Both in 1644 and 1645, on days of public thanksgiving, ceremonial bonfires of popish books, pictures, and crucifixes took place on the empty site of Cheapside Cross.[70] Edward Dering would have been delighted.

Extremist purifiers, aiming to free believers from the religious clutter that had endangered their forebears, found spiritual meaning in blank walls and silence. The militant iconoclasts who, in the course of a century, managed to annihilate so much of England's artistic heritage, in the shape of religious sculpture, painting, stained and painted glass, organs, bells, plate, and vestments, may only have been a small minority of activists. Their influence was none the less for that. As Sir Thomas Gresham's agent reported of the destruction in Antwerp on the night of 20-21 August 1566, it was incredible that 'so few pepell durst or colde do so much'.[71] Overnight image-breaking by the few could alter the course of reform and affect the future beliefs of the many. Such actions played a critical part in the politics of reformation, and through this physical alteration, separating the faith from so much familiar scenery, Christians were ushered into a reshaped spiritual world. God was to be heard, not seen. In learning to live by the Word, people gradually learned to find in their Bibles the compensation for that huge deprivation of their century, the enforced withdrawal of the 'goodly sights' that had accumulated over generations. Many had regrets, but those schooled in the meaning of defilement increasingly found themselves at home in their bared and whitened

[69] John Vicars, *A Sight of ye Transactions of these latter yeares* (London [1646]), p. 21; *True information of the beginning and cause of all our Troubles* (London, 1648), p. 17; Richard Pennington, *A Descriptive Catalogue of the Etched Work of Wenceslaus Hollar, 1607-1677* (Cambridge, 1982), p. 75 (no. 491a).

[70] Vicars, *A Sight*, p. 21; Bulstrode Whitelocke, *Memorials of the English Affairs* (Oxford, 1853), i, pp. 326, 482.

[71] J.W. Burgon, *The Life and Times of Sir Thomas Gresham* (London, 1839), ii, p. 139; cf. ii, p. 137.

churches. Some felt cleansed and were thankful, even able, like a preacher to
Parliament in 1645, to echo the Elizabethan homilist:

> I am glad for my part, they are scoured of their gay gazing, and I marvelled a great
> while since, how, and why the Organs grew so many and blew so loud, when the very
> Homilies accused them for defiling God's house.[72]

---

[72] Thomas Thorowgood, *Moderation Justified, and the Lords Being at Hand Emproved*
(London, 1645), p. 16; quoted by R.W. Ketton-Cremer, *Norfolk in the Civil War* (London, 1969),
p. 262.

Fig. 26 Catholic satire of Protestant image-destruction. Thomas Murner's *Great Lutheran Fool*, for whom the image has become an 'empty book', uses a wooden saint as firewood.

10

Rites of Destruction by Fire

In England the destructive process of iconoclasm was intermittent and prolonged, affecting the development of reform and politics for well over a
century – indeed for nearer three centuries, if one takes into account the legacy
of Wycliffe. This protracted development (which stands in stark contrast to
continental centres of reform) has the advantage of making it possible to see on
the ground in phases of conflict, the whole gamut of differing views on the
treatment of church images.

England, with its peculiar flair for domesticating divergent viewpoints,
continued – long after events in Europe had sealed this route – to accom-
modate simultaneously a Lutheran tolerance and a Calvinist intolerance of the
visual image. The tensions reverberated for decades between iconomachs,
who opposed religious images but were prepared to see them removed rather
than destroyed, and the more radical iconoclasts who regarded all images as
potential idols and for whom reform was of necessity a matter of physical
elimination. The spring-cleaning or slum-clearance of churches (and for some
extremists this included the razing of churches as places contaminated by their
polluting idols), was on some individuals' agenda from the earliest stages of
English reform, but overall purification proved a more problematic objective.
Events in England also demonstrate the strength of opposition to image-
breaking. Fears of old idols and old idolaters died hard. Throughout the
sixteenth century reformers expended vast efforts in catechising, and produced mountains of texts in order to indoctrinate coming generations with true
understanding of the sins of idolatry and the all-embracing meaning of the
second commandment.[1]

England's reforming theology may have been composed of borrowed plum-
age, but it did ultimately yield an indigenous hybrid. The doctrine that lay
behind the assault on idols was firmly grounded on the writings of leading
continental reformers, and some of the more important texts relating to
European iconoclasm infiltrated England at an early stage. Luther's *Lectures
on Deuteronomy* and Zwingli's *Commentary on True and False Religion* had

---

[1]   This aspect of the matter is explored in M. Aston, *England's Iconoclasts*, i (Oxford, 1988).

reached London by 1532.[2] Between the mid-1530s, when Bucer's *Das einiger-lei Bild* appeared in an English version, and the 1580s, when a translation of Bullinger's *Decades* became official reading for the ministry, England took to heart and absorbed the reformed churches' stand against images.[3] At key phases of religious change under Henry VIII, Edward VI and Elizabeth (1537-1538, 1547-1548, 1558-1559), the achievements of Strasbourg, Zurich and Geneva had a significant influence on English treatment of imagery. It is only necessary to open the 1563 book of Elizabethan Homilies for a glance at the long tripartite 'Homily against Peril of Idolatry, and superfluous Decking of Churches' (which borrowed largely from Bullinger's *De origine erroris*[4]) to realize the importance attached to the issue.

Almost as soon as the revised text of the decalogue, with the image-prohibition as an independent commandment, was adopted abroad, there appeared in England unofficial manuals of religious instruction that surreptitiously popularized this all-important change. This textual reform, though it emerged after, not before, Reformation iconoclasts had set to work, was critical for the entire movement.[5] It gave fresh and conspicuous prominence to the scriptural authority that powered a radical change of outlook. The image-prohibition, detached from its subordinate position in the traditional decalogue, became the iconomachs' manifesto. Iconoclasm in the sixteenth century – like all earlier iconoclasm – was firmly premised on Old Testament ground, though reformers of this period had the edge on Byzantines and medieval heretics, in their increased knowledge of Hebrew.

However, we should pause to notice that this central role of the image-prohibition itself opened the door to differences. The commandment text itself is *not* a charter for destruction. Rather, one might think, it supported the position of those who considered that the reform of images was completed by the removal of conspicuous objects of worship, such as the pilgrimage statues on which Henry VIII chose in the end to adopt a view not unlike that of Luther. Taking down abused carvings, and disposing of them so that they would not provoke the wrong sort of veneration, was a process that did not necessarily entail destruction. On the other hand there was obvious logic, reading the decalogue text in context, in attaching it to the numerous other Old Testament

---

[2] Guildhall Library, London, MS 9531/10, Reg. Tunstall (London), fo. 144 r (129r) misdated by John Foxe, *The Acts and Monuments of John Foxe*, ed. J. Pratt (London, 1977), iv, pp. 667-8; Aston, *England's Iconoclasts*, i, p. 201.

[3] *Zwingli and Bullinger*, ed. G.W. Bromiley (Library of Christian Classics, 24, 1953), pp. 284-5; P. Collinson, *Godly People* (London, 1983), p. 433. On Bucer see below.

[4] The debt of this Elizabethan homily to Bullinger's *De origine erroris, in divorum ac simulachrorum cultu* (of which there were three sixteenth-century editions) was pointed out by John Griffeths in *The Two Books of Homilies Appointed to be Read in Churches* (Oxford, 1859), i, pp. xxx-xxxii; book 2, p. 180ff.; Aston, *England's Iconoclasts*, i, p. 321. On Bucer's text see below.

[5] M. Stirm, *Die Bilderfrage in der Reformation* (Gütersloh, 1977), shows the stages by which this change took place abroad, and I have traced its occurrence in England in the work referred to above.

proscriptions of idols, which most clearly did enjoin extinction. The methods of image-reform formed part of the whole great issue, which divided Luther from Karlstadt and which resurfaced in an acute form in England during the Interregnum, of the standing of Old Testament law in a Christian community.

The differing ways of interpreting the commandment were already discernible in the two earliest Reformation publications devoted to image reform: Karlstadt's *Von Abtuhung der Bylder* (1522) and Ludwig Hätzer's *Ein Urteil Gottes* (1523). Both trailed the image prohibition – at this stage still regarded as part of the first commandment. But while Karlstadt focused on the dangers of images in churches (specially when placed on altars) and the need to remove them, Hätzer, gathering to his argument an anthology of biblical texts – including those that enjoined destruction as well as those forbidding worship – emphasized the divine cause of elimination. 'God', he wrote, 'calls for the destruction of the image and the punishment of those who have and worship it'. The correct fate for the idols was burning. 'Away with them to the fire: that is where the wood belongs'.[6] It is this prescription, the injunction to burn the idols, that I want to consider here, as a way of exploring England's iconoclastic experience.

A series of Old Testament texts from Exodus, Deuteronomy, and Numbers could be set beside the second commandment to show that God intended idols to be destroyed as well as shunned.

Ye shall destroy their altars, and break down their pillars, . . . and burn their graven images with fire (Deut. 7:5).

And ye shall overthrow their altars, and break their pillars, and burn their groves with fire; and ye shall hew down the graven images of their gods, and destroy the names of them out of that place (Deut. 12:3).

Destroy all their pictures, and destroy all their molten images, and quite pluck down all their high places (Num. 33:52).

These and other passages conveying the same message were put together by Calvin, as supplements to the second commandment, in the *Harmony of the Last Four Books of Moses* which he completed during the last year of his life.[7]

---

[6] 'Gott heisst die bild zerbrechen, und von der straff deren die sy habend und eerend'; 'Sind die bild und ölgötzen nit mörder so sy die seelen töden und sy von got irem eegmahel abfüren? Huss mit inen in ein fhür, da gehört das holz hin'. Hätzer, *Ein Urteil Gottes unsers Eegmahels wie man sich mit allen Götzen und Bildnussen halten sol* (Zürich, 1523), sigs. A ii v, Bv r. For Karlstadt's pamphlet, *Von abtuhung der Bylder und das keyn Betdler unther den Christen seyn sollen* (to which Hätzer was indebted), see the edition by H. Lietzmann (Kleine Texte für theologische und philologische Vorlesungen und Übungen, 74, Bonn, 1911), and *A Reformation Debate*, trans. B.D. Mangrum and G. Scavizzi (Toronto, 1991). C.M.N. Eire, *War against the Idols: The Reformation of Worship from Erasmus to Calvin* (Cambridge, 1986), pp. 57-8, 79-80.
[7] *Mosis Libri V, cum Johannis Calvini Commentarius* (Geneva, 1563), pt. 2, pp. 303-4; John Calvin, *Commentaries on the Last Four Books of Moses, arranged in the Form of a Harmony*, ed. C.W. Bingham (Edinburgh, 1853), 2, p. 386.

By this time the commandment in question had come to be regarded as a precept to destroy, not merely to refrain from the worship of idols. Sung in metrical form it prompted and accompanied corporate iconoclasm. The sacking of the abbey of Marchiennes in the province of Tournai in August 1566 took place after the singing of Marot's version of the second commandment, and in France five years earlier at Montauban idols were ceremonially burnt in the market-place while choirs of children chanted the metrical decalogue.[8]

A whole generation before this – in England and elsewhere – many opponents of images assumed that the scriptural code against idolatry called for the abolition of idols: pulling them down, breaking them up, at best reducing them to dust and ashes. The Old Testament rulers who became prototypes for reforming monarchs were those who had served God most faithfully in this respect. They were repeatedly cited as models for the Tudors, and if Edward VI was able to rejoice in his role as the new Josiah, his sister Elizabeth was less than enchanted by invocations to emulate Hezekiah. Hezekiah's achievement lay in having broken the brazen serpent and other images to pieces; Josiah had burned all the vessels made for Baal, beaten down the altars, broken the images and burnt the groves and high places. The brazen serpent, prototype of the cross in medieval typology, became the prototype of the properly destroyed idol for this new generation of aniconic Christians.[9] (Elizabeth, whose obstinacy over the retention of the cross caused a prolonged rumpus at the beginning of her reign, would not have missed the allusion). Misused to perdition, the brazen serpent had gone the way of the golden calf which Moses in his anger had burnt in fire, ground into powder and forced the children of Israel to ingest. To reforming iconoclasts, such as William Fulke, all religious images deserved such treatment.

> Though they were as ancient and as goodly monuments as the brasen serpent was, [he wrote in 1583], which no images at this day can be, it is to the great honour of God that they should be despised, defaced, burned, and stamped to powder, as that was . . .[10]

[8]   See the vivid description in J.L. Motley, *The Rise of the Dutch Republic* (London, 1896), 1, p. 503; S. Deyon and A. Lottin, *Les 'casseurs' de l'été 1566; l'iconoclasme dans le nord de la France* (Paris, 1981), pp. 51, 170, 177; Owen Chadwick, *The Reformation* (Harmondsworth, 1964), p. 163; cf. N.Z. Davis, *Society and Culture in Early Modern France* (London, 1975), pp. 179-80, 183; *Histoire ecclésiastique des églises réformées au royaume de France*, ed. G. Baum and E. Cunitz (Paris, 1883-89), 1, pp. 929-31.

[9]   *The Catechism of Thomas Becon*, ed. J. Ayre (Parker Society [hereafter PS], Cambridge, 1844), p. 69 on the brazen serpent which, though originally set up by God's commandment, Hezekiah properly 'plucked . . . down, burnt . . . and utterly destroyed': cf. also the Elizabethan homily against idolatry on this precedent; *Certain Sermons or Homilies* (Oxford, 1844), pp. 173, 210, 225. See Aston, *England's Iconoclasts*, for Old Testament prototypes and the Tudors.

[10]   W. Fulke, *A Defense of the sincere true Translations of the holie Scriptures* (London, 1583), ed. C.H. Hartshorne (PS, Cambridge, 1843), p. 191.

Reformation destroyers were fully conscious of the persuasive, propagandist value of iconoclasm. Besides being obsessed with the need to ensure that idols ceased to be such, they were concerned with the effects that purifying actions could have on idolaters – actual or potential. 'To show our detestation of the idol', wrote Robert Parker early in the seventeenth century, 'we must either destroy him, or in keeping him for private use, so alter and change him that . . . all the honour which the idol gaineth by him or giveth to him, may be turned upside down'.[11] Erstwhile holy objects could either be eliminated or defiled. Both methods had advantages and disadvantages.

Turning venerated images and consecrated objects to degrading secular use was designed to shock by deliberate inversion. What had been falsely sanctified and elevated was to be most thoroughly debased. 'That is, you must deal with it, as with the vilest, filthiest, most contemptible thing that your eye can look upon'.[12] The objects of spiritual pollution were themselves to be physically polluted. Though William Fulke was advocating an uncommon extreme when he suggested (on the example of Jehu) using an altar as a jakes, plenty of altar stones and holy water stoups (like those at Durham, converted into kitchen sinks by Dean Whittingham) found their way into domestic use.[13] The effect of such degradation was calculated. Making parishioners walk over their old altar-stones, which had stood in the holiest of places for the holiest of rites, was a kind of advertisement that coerced them into participation in the new order of priorities. Unlike the short-lived bonfire, this procedure had the advantage of presenting continuous reminders of the errors of old ways. But of course with this went the hazard that surviving banned objects might, even in a damaged state, curry hopes of a return to use.

Burning could be regarded as the proper and most desirable method. 'Ye shall burn their graven images with fire'. This, as we have seen, was the approved prescription of the old law, used by Moses and Asa and Josiah. The examples of Josiah and Jehu, who always 'rooted out and destroyed all monuments of superstition and idolatry', burning the idol cities 'so that none of that dammed thing that is in them shall cleave unto the hand', was held as the

[11] R. Parker, *A Scholasticall Discourse against Symbolizing with Antichrist in Ceremonies* (London, 1607), pp. 10-11.

[12] *The Crosses Case in Cheapside* (London, 1642), p. 30. This was more than transferring objects from sacred space into the profanest of profane places; it was aimed at annihilating supposedly immaculate purity by inversion. For ritual treatment of this kind see Davis, 'The Rites of Violence', p. 157ff; R.W. Scribner, 'Ritual and Reformation', in *Popular Culture and Popular Movements in Reformation Germany* (London, 1987).

[13] W. Fulke, *D. Heskins, D. Sanders, and M. Rastel . . . overthrowne* (London, 1579), pp. 574-5 (alluding to 2 Kings 10:26-7); *The Rites of Durham*, ed. J.T. Fowler (Surtees Soc., 107, 1902), p. 61: 'two holie water stones was taken awaie by Deane Whittingham and caryed into his kitching and put unto profayne uses; and ther stoode during his liffe in which stones thei dyd stepe ther beefe and salt fysh'. After her husband's death Mrs. Whittingham followed suit, removing one of the sometime holy water stoups for her kitchen, and building gravestones into her house – a happy combination of dogma and domestic convenience.

biblical pattern by Anthony Gilby.[14] The lesson was often repeated. External annihilation served the process of inner purification, and the finality of the fire was irreversible. An image reduced to dust and ashes could never rise again in its old form. It was consigned to everlasting oblivion. On the other hand there were dangers in the rite of burning: the danger of hostile reactions and also the danger of over-enthusiastic mimetic destruction.

The call to destroy images – as completely as possible – was sounded in England from early stages of the Reformation. One of the first works to appear in English advertising the case against religious imagery was a version of Martin Bucer's *Das einigerlei Bild* of 1530. The Latin version of this text seems to have reached London by 1532, and three years later a translation was in circulation, bringing home to vernacular readers the urgent need to do away with ecclesiastical imagery. It was a reform that (as was made clear) demanded total destruction.

> For if we were disposed to take away images, after such a manner and fashion as scripture teacheth and commandeth . . . we ought to break them, yea, and that all to powder, that they might never be made whole again.[15]

A generation later this teaching reached all ears by being incorporated in the Elizabethan homily against idolatry. This text gave prominence to the argument that, since to have any images at all in churches introduced the intolerable risk of false worship, the necessary course must be the removal and destruction of *all* images. Citing the words from Deuteronomy that I have already quoted ('. . . cut down their groves . . . burn their . . . images . . . ') the homilist continues: 'Here note, what the people of God ought to do to images, where they find them'. Destruction and burning were divinely ordained. 'God grant', prayed the homilist about church images, 'they may in the end be destroyed'.[16]

English believers were left in no doubt that in the Old Testament exhortations to abolish idols were on a par with the injunction of the second commandment against worshipping graven images. Thomas Rogers (d. 1616), a chaplain of Archbishop Bancroft, whose exposition of the Thirty-Nine Articles went through numerous seventeenth-century editions, and who was outspoken in censuring puritan 'demi-Jews', listed the following scriptural proofs of the divine censure of images.

---

[14] *The Seconde Parte of a Register*, ed. A. Peel (Cambridge, 1915), 1, p. 140.

[15] *A treatise declaryng and shewing . . . that pyctures and other ymages . . . ar in no wise to be suffred in . . . churches* (London, [1535]), *STC* 24238, sig. F vii v. For Bucer's text (dated Strasbourg, 6 March 1530) see *Martin Bucers Deutsche Schriften*, ed. R. Stupperich (Gütersloh, 1960), 4, pp. 161-81. For its arrival in England (in a Latin translation) see Foxe, *A & M*, iv, p. 669, and Aston, *England's Iconoclasts*, i, p. 204ff.

[16] *Certain Sermons or Homilies* (Oxford, 1844), pp. 165, 198, from the first and third parts of the 1563 'Homily against Peril of Idolatry, and superfluous Decking of Churches'.

Images are such an abomination to the Lord, as to make them among all men odious: . . . they are the doctrine of vanity, the work of errors, the teachers of lies, silver and gold . . .

2. He giveth a strait commandment, Not to bow down to them, nor worship them, not to make them, to fly from them, yea, to destroy both the images themselves, the idolaters, and the enticers unto idolatry.

3. He commandeth greatly and praiseth such men as have destroyed images, and not bowed unto idols.[17]

Bishop Jewel said no less. 'Neither doth God throughout all his holy scriptures any where condemn image-breakers; but expressly and every where he condemneth image-worshippers and image-makers'.[18]

Doubtless there was an important proviso here. It was the godly prince, the magistrate, whose duty it was to set the home fires burning. But this repeated harping on the divine sanction for such destruction, drummed into the ears of ordinary believers as they were catechised into the rejection of images, tended to diminish the impact of such qualifications. The importance of elimination loomed larger for many than the precise manner of accomplishing it. 'That all images of God, of Christ, of angels, and of saints, should be taken out of churches, and *burnt openly*' (as Thomas Becon wrote in his 1560 *Catechism*),[19] was an obligation of kings and bishops which others also took upon themselves to accomplish.

Let us now turn to consider some examples of these image-burnings. They fall into various categories, and I shall start with two instances of unofficial, indeed illegal fires, lit by private initiative, one at the time when Lutheran teaching was first prohibited in England, and the other just before the start of the Civil War. Some time before November 1522 (probably earlier that year), a fire badly damaged the chancel and vestry of the church of Rickmansworth in Hertfordshire. This was no accidental blaze. It was started deliberately by people who had set fire to all the images and the rood, wrapping tow around them and using tow and banner staves to act as fire-lighters in the chancel. The arson seems to have destroyed, along with most of the images, the organ and the rood-loft and all the ornaments in the vestry. We do not know the names of these iconoclasts, but they were duly castigated by Cardinal Wolsey, and

---

[17] T. Rogers, *The faith, doctrine and religion, professed . . . in . . . England . . . Expressed in 39 Articles* (Cambridge, 1607), pp. 125-6; ed. as *The Catholic Doctrine of the Church of England*, J.J.S. Perowne (PS, Cambridge, 1854), p. 221-2. (This comment forms part of the discussion of Article 22, 'Of Purgatory'). On this semi-official 'commentary' on the 39 Articles see Nicholas Tyacke, *Anti-Calvinists: The Rise of English Arminianism*, c. *1590-1640* (Oxford, 1987), pp. 25-7.

[18] *The Works of John Jewel*, ed. J. Ayre (PS, Cambridge, 1845-1850), ii, p. 668 (from the controversy with Harding).

[19] *Catechism of Thomas Becon*, p. 69 (my italics).

indulgences were granted to everyone who contributed to the restoration of the church.[20]

A century later the connotations of such a parochial blaze were very different – though the underlying premises remained the same. This is how Nehemiah Wallington described the goings-on at Radwinter in Essex one fast day in 1640, when soldiers impressed for service in Scotland made known their views of Laudian church furnishings.

> The Solgers went into the Church and pulled up the rayls & pulled down the Images (which as I heere Cost the parson to set up thirty pound) they tyed the Images to a tree and whiped them then they carryed them 5 mile to Saffarn Walden and burnt them and rosted the rost and heated the oven with it & sayd if you bee gods deliver your selves . . .[21]

There was a direct challenge to authority in the burning of the Radwinter images, as there had been in the firing of the Rickmansworth ones, but the intervening century provided many precedents and arguments to encourage the belief that iconoclasm of this kind was divinely sanctioned. The burning of church images construed as idols, even on the private initiative of lay persons, seemed defensible to many by the outbreak of the Civil War, and Wallington's report, with its echoes of Isaiah and Baruch, reflects consciousness of the biblical sanctions.

These two blazes shed some light on the manifold implications of image-burning. For fire, destruction by fire, held some unavoidable associations – soteriological and eschatological. Though this is obviously too vast a domain for exploration here, we cannot leave aside those beliefs in the fires of hell and purgatory that certainly had a bearing on the mundane burning of Christian

---

[20] The indulgence was printed in facsimile by K.W. Cameron, *The Pardoner and his Pardons: Indulgences Circulating in England on the Eve of the Reformation* (Hartford, CT, [1965]), p. 49. See above, Chapter 8.

[21] BL, MS Sloane 1457, fo. 60 r. I owe this reference to Gerald Aylmer. Richard Drake, rector of Radwinter since 1638 (who escaped the soldiers as he was away at the time), had erected a screen with carved cherubim, and the various articles for which he was condemned by the Grand Committee on Religion in 1641 show that parishioners objected to these images as 'intended for the resemblance of Christ'. Drake himself believed the soldiers' destruction was instigated by some of his parishioners. Harold Smith, *The Ecclesiastical History of Essex Under the Long Parliament and Commonwealth* (Colchester [1932]), pp. 69, 77-8, 82-4, 180. Cf. Isaiah 44: 14-17, 'he maketh a god and worshippeth it . . . He burneth part thereof in the fire; . . . he roasteth roast, and is satisfied . . . ': Baruch 6: 12, 15, 49, 55, 'Yet cannot these gods save themselves from rust and mothes . . . cannot deliver himselfe from warre and theeves . . . they be no gods, which can neither save themselves from warre nor from plague . . . they themselves shall be burnt asunder like beames'. Cf. *Certain Sermons or Homilies* (Oxford, 1844), pp. 164-5 for the citation of this chapter of Baruch in the Elizabethan Homily against idolatry. Also one cannot rule out crucifixion parody ('He saved others, himself he cannot save') and here it is worth recalling Foxe's (now discredited, but evidently once believable) story of the 'tree of Troth' in More's garden at Chelsea. 'Jesu's tree', to which suspect heretics were allegedly tied and then whipped. Foxe, *A & M*, iv, pp. 689, 698; Richard Marius. *Thomas More* (New York, 1985), pp. 404- 6.

Fig. 27 Woodcut in John Foxe's *Acts and Monuments* of the 1552 execution in Portugal of William Gardiner, an English merchant who had trampled on the sacramental host. Foxe, who describes Gardiner having his hands cut off before he was burned, considered him comparable to early church martyrs: 'what do . . . these great fires, and other horrible torments of martyrs, but upbraid unto us our slothful sluggishness . . .?'

idols. For the flames that tested images, like the flames that tested souls, were purgative, probatory, and punitive.[22]

Fire was purgative in various contexts, personal and social, as well as spiritual. The use of burning to deal with physical infection (both of people and livestock)[23] had long had its religious parallel in the burning of heretics and heretical texts. Fire eliminated the contaminating elements, freeing Christian society from pollution. In the words of Bernard Gui, the early fourteenth-century Dominican inquisitor: 'Heresy cannot be destroyed unless heretics are destroyed'. In the case of spiritual infection, publicity was part of the process; the cancer must be *seen and known* to be eliminated, since this was part of the cure. 'In the sight of men they shall be burned alive, committed to the judgement of the flames', ran Frederick II's decree for the death penalty for heretics.[24] Likewise when heretical books were burned, crowds were present to see the errors turned to ashes. Burning was the most effective method of cauterizing the poisoned limb, and society – the corporate body whose health was at risk – had to participate in the healing process. Idols, like heretics and heretical books, had to be banished in an open forum, in the face of the community.

Fire was also probatory in the sense of the ordeal. Just as an individual might prove his or her innocence by emerging without ill-effect from the blaze or hot iron, so holy objects proved their sanctity in tests of fire.[25] Many medieval miracles rested on the inexplicable survival through an otherwise consuming fire, of some revered item, particularly the eucharistic host. One well-known example is the holy blood of Wilsnack, which became a popular objective of pilgrims after a fire in 1383 burnt the church, leaving three consecrated hosts

---

[22] Here see Jacques Le Goff, *The Birth of Purgatory*, trans. A. Goldhammer (Chicago and London, 1990; orig. edn. Paris, 1981): C. – M. Edsman, *Ignis divinus: Le feu comme moyen de rajeunissement et d'immortalité* (Lund, 1949); Herbert Freudenthal, *Das Feuer im Deutschen Glauben und Brauch* (Berlin and Leipzig, 1931), pp. 449-69.

[23] Fire as protection against plague infection was used early on (Pope Clement VI's precaution in 1348 was to station himself between two large fires), and the burning of livestock to check cattle disease was common in Tudor England. Stuart Clark and P.T.J. Morgan, 'Religion and Magic in Elizabethan Wales: Robert Holland's Dialogue on Witchcraft', *JEH*, 27 (1976), p. 36. A variety of beliefs existed about the prophylactic value of St. John's Day fires (below n. 57), on which see Freudenthal, *Das Feuer*, pp. 212-13, 291ff.

[24] H.C. Lea, *The Inquisition of the Middle Ages: Its Organization and Operations*, introd. W. Ullmann (London, 1963), pp. 31, n.1, 292. In the case of heretics, not only the houses they had lived in were considered contaminated (and ordered to be razed in the thirteenth century), but even the sites might be regarded as unfit for habitation; (ibid., pp. 236- 37). In the Reformation, as a kind of inversion of this theory, we find places where outstanding idols had been destroyed being regarded by iconoclasts (with some inconsistency) as specially suited to further iconoclastic activity.

[25] Robert Bartlett. *Trial by Fire and Water: The Medieval Judicial Ordeal* (Oxford, 1986), pp. 21-22 gives an example of relics being tested in this way.

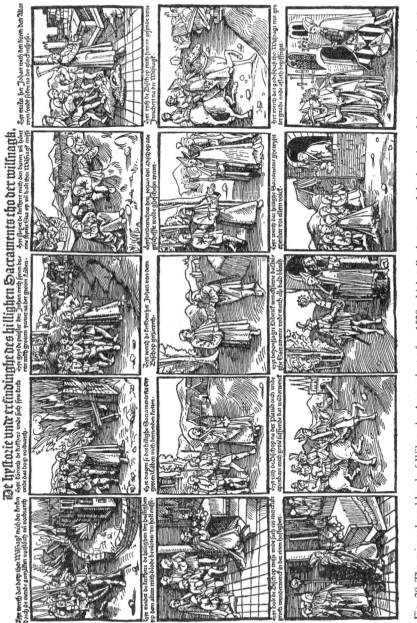

Fig. 28 The miraculous blood of Wilsnack. A woodcut of c. 1520 which tells the story of the burning of the town and church, the discovery of the blood-stained hosts on the altar, and the bishop's endorsement of the miracle.

unharmed in the tabernacle, sprinkled with blood.[26] An occurrence of this kind was claimed to have taken place when the arsonists burnt Rickmansworth church, and Wolsey's promised indulgence was attached to the story that although the chancel had been burnt and the pyx melted, yet 'the blessed body of our lord Jesu Christ in form of bread was found upon the high altar and nothing perished'.[27]

Auras of the miraculous clung to iconoclastic pyres, though the nature of the miracle was turned on its head. From the point of view of the image-burners (who were assured in their own piety), theirs was a miracle in reverse, an anti-miracle:[28] a holy object, to which unaccountable powers were attributed, might be destroyed and disproved without anything extraordinary or untoward taking place. The supernatural was discredited by inertia. The element of bravado that seems so often to accompany the most daring iconoclastic exploits surely masks some half-acknowledged fears that God *might* react – a nervousness lest, despite all assertions to the contrary, there might be some residue of power in things revered as holy. Phyllis Mack Crew cites an incident that illustrates this when, in the course of the midnight destruction of the crucifix in the church at Hasselt, the iconoclasts' torches and the bonfire lit to burn the ornaments suddenly and inexplicably went out, to the terror of those present.[29] Fears of this kind are usually screened by the triumph of achieved demolition. But the iconoclasts took pains to ensure that their disproving fires discredited as fully as possible old claims to the miraculous, showing images for what they were – lifeless, senseless, speechless blocks.

The dead idol was also punished for the falsity of its pretensions, for the seductions and delusions practised on its devotees. Those who had pilgrimaged and offered to an image in the hopes of a cure, who had believed in its miraculous movements, when these were the manipulations of false priests, were to see the offending idol receiving its just reward through the process of elimination. It was no accident that when the Wilsnack pilgrimage was discredited and terminated in 1552, the hosts once rendered miraculous by survival through fire, were given their disproof by the penalty of burning.

[26] E. Breest, 'Das Wunderblut von Wilsnack (1383-1552): Quellenmässige Darstellung seiner Geschichte', *Märkische Forschungen*, 16 (1881), pp. 131-301; L. Meier, 'Wilsnack als Spiegel deutscher Vorreformation', *Zeitschrift für Religions- und Geistesgeschichte*, 3 (1951), pp. 53-69; H. Boockmann, 'Der Streit um das Wilsnacker Blut. Zur Situation des deutschen Klerus in der Mitte des 15. Jahrhunderts', *Zeitschrift für historische Forschung*, 9 (1982), pp. 385-408.

[27] BL, C. 18. e. 2(96); *STC*, 14077 c. 68 (above p. 260).

[28] Devon and Lottin, *Les 'casseurs'*, p. 199; ' . . . le miracle se produit là où on ne l'attendait pas, à rebours, c'est l'antimiracle, et l'iconoclasme devient une gigantesque démonstration pédagogique . . . '.

[29] P.M. Crew, *Calvinist Preaching and Iconoclasm in the Netherlands, 1544-1569* (Cambridge, 1978), p. 25, n. 83; idem, 'The Wonderyear: Reformed Preaching and Iconoclasm in the Netherlands', *Religion and the People, 800-1700*, ed. J. Obelkevich (Chapel Hill, NC, 1979), pp. 192-3, 312, n.6.

In England a notorious and rather gruesome event of this kind was carefully stage-managed in the first iconoclastic campaign of this country's Reformation. This was the double burning that took place at Smithfield in London on 22 May 1538, of the Observant friar John Forest, and the huge image of Derfel Gadarn. Forest, who had been confessor to Catherine of Aragon, was burned as a relapsed heretic, his chief offence being his loyalty to the pope.[30] The large wooden figure of Derfel the Mighty had been specially brought up to London from Wales, where this image of an armed rider was credited with great powers to protect both man and beast. It was also prophesied of it that Derfel Gadarn would one day set a whole forest on fire. The dignitaries who – including members of the king's council, the mayor and bishop of London, and various aristocrats – assembled on a specially erected platform (with an enormous attendant crowd) to see this spectacle, and listen to an edifying sermon by Hugh Latimer, were present to witness what was in effect a reforming exposure of popular faith.[31] Derfel Gadarn set the wrong sort of Forest on fire. He was supposed to be able to rescue souls from hell, but he could not save himself from fire. If an image could not rise from the flames, what power could it have? Was it not just a log? As William Gray's ballad, composed at this time to impress the 'Fantasy of idolatry' on the people, put the case:

> But now may we see,
> What Gods they be,
>   Even puppets, maumets and elves:
> Throw them down thrice
> They cannot rise,
>   Not once, to help themselves.[32]

Perishing in the fire proved idols, to the iconoclasts' satisfaction, to be dead stocks and stones. 'They have sceptres and swords in their hands, but they are not able to defend themselves', wrote Thomas Becon, paraphrasing Baruch.[33]

---

[30] On Forest, who had been in prison, in fear of execution in 1534-36, see Emden (O), *1501-1540*, p. 209; M. Dowling, *Humanism in the Age of Henry VIII* (London, 1986), p. 56, and above p. 276.

[31] The image of St. Derfel, described by Wriothesley as an 'idol . . . of wood like a man of arms in his harness, having a little spear in his hand and a casket of iron about his neck hanging with a ribbon', was popularly believed to have power to fetch those who offered to it 'out of hell when they be damned', and this claim was posted in large letters on the gallows. Pilgrimage to this image was reported to be still flourishing, and there was strenuous local resistance to its removal, the parson and parishioners offering £40 to the commissioners to prevent its being carried off to London. *Wriothesley's Chronicle*, ed. W.D. Hamilton (Camden Society, 20-1, 1875-77), i, pp. 80-1; *Hall's Chronicle* (London, 1809), pp. 825-6; *Original Letters Illustrative of English History*, ed. H. Ellis (London, 1824-46), III, iii, pp. 194-5; cf. I, ii, pp. 82-3; *Three Chapters of Letters Relating to the Suppression of Monasteries*, ed. T. Wright (Camden Soc., 26, 1843), pp. 190-1; G. Williams, *The Welsh Church from Conquest to Reformation* (Cardiff, 1976), p. 497.

[32] Foxe, *A & M*, v, p. 409; cf. p. 408 on Derfel Gadarn. ('Maumet', from *mahumet*, Mahomet = false god, idol).

[33] Becon, *Catechism*, pp. 61-2; cf. Baruch 6: 15.

'If you be gods, deliver yourselves. The challenge of the soldiers at Saffron Walden in 1640 was much the same as that of the earliest known Lollard iconoclasts who, in the 1380s, had beheaded an image of St. Catherine and used it to cook their dinner.[34] The lack of physical response negated claims to spiritual power.

The purgatorial refining effect of fire, an ancient criterion for isolating the holy, was redirected by the reformers, much of whose work amounted to a redefinition of the sacred.[35] Objects as well as people could be put to the ordeal and tried by fire. Abused images could be chastised, punished by flames, at the same time as a reforming bonfire could be used to correct supporters of idols. And a purging fire (*ignis purgatorius*)[36] could be the instrument to signalize the purification of a Christian community, cutting itself off from the contaminated past, crossing the threshold to spiritual regeneration. If we look at some of the bonfires of idols lit by English reformers we can see how they have the character of initiation rites of the new regime.

There were several different kinds of reforming fires, of which I shall here consider three. First there was the grandiose official spectacle, like the Forest affair, designed as an instrument of government propaganda. Second, there were parish burnings, which might be either authorized (and perhaps enforced by local or central officials on a resistant community), or – like the Rickmansworth example – spontaneous and wholly illegal. Third, there were domestic burnings, which too might reflect either legal or illegal iconoclasm.

From 1538 on, the ceremonial iconoclastic bonfire was an accepted part of the official reforming process in England. Thomas Cromwell was the first to exploit it to the full, as part of his multi-faceted campaign against idolatry. Two months after the burning of Friar Forest and Derfel Gadarn, Cromwell supervised the burning of some of the most famous of England's pilgrimage statues. The images of the Virgin from Walsingham and Ipswich, together with other cult images sent up to London for this purpose were burnt publicly at Chelsea in the presence of the Lord Privy Seal in July 1538. Bishop Latimer, who had already the previous year taken steps to unmask his own 'great Sybil' (as he disrespectfully called the Worcester Virgin, which was discovered to be the dolled-up effigy of a medieval bishop), had advocated just this course that June. He wrote to Cromwell suggesting that all these deceiving sisters – the revered Virgins of Worcester, Ipswich, Penrice in Glamorgan, and Doncaster – who had (as he put it) been the devil's instruments to take men to eternal fire,

---

[34] M. Aston, *England's Iconoclasts*, i, p. 133, cf. p. 136 on the 'burnt arse', of Our Lady of Willesden which, Susan Brigden has pointed out to me, is denigration by fire of another kind, since to be 'burnt' then had the meaning of suffering from venereal disease, and hence this implied doubts of the Virgin's virginity.

[35] A topic that can be approached from various angles: see John Bossy on 'Migrations of the Holy' in *Christianity in the West* (Oxford, 1985), pp. 153-71.

[36] Le Goff, *The Birth of Purgatory*, pp. 133-53, 244- 5, 247-8, 260-1.

would 'make a jolly muster in Smithfield', and would not take all day to burn.[37] As with Derfel the Mighty, there was seen to be apt justice in consigning to flames, images believed to help rescue souls from flames.

Twenty years later, at the accession of Elizabeth, large bonfires of idols in the capital once again advertised the arrival of a reformist regime. St. Bartholomew's day, 1559, was celebrated with great blazes in St. Paul's churchyard, in Cheapside by Ironmonger Lane and at St. Thomas Acon, in which roods with their statues of the Virgin and St. John were 'burned with great wonder'. Other church goods also 'were sent to Terra Santa in this fiery sacrifice': rood-lofts, sepulchres and censers; copes, vestments and altar-cloths; banners, crosses and books. Such fires continued into September, as the royal commissioners in London and elsewhere interpreted their brief as covering the destruction of imagery in general.[38] Mary's attention during the previous reign to the restoration of roods, may have given the destruction of these images a special prominence, but besides the crucifix Elizabeth's visitors took in hand all kinds of images. And the articles of enquiry for the royal visitation of 1559, on which this action was based, seem to spell out quite clearly the terms of reference that allowed for such destruction. All images were to be regarded as themselves *ipso facto* causes of idolatry, and accordingly to be done away with.

In 1559, as in 1538, observers abroad took readings from these smoke signals. Sir Richard Shelley, who at this time was visiting Antwerp on business, decided not to return home, since the news of crucifix-burning made him fearful of popular disturbance. Similarly, Sir Thomas Chaloner, worried by the reception of these doings in the Low Countries, wrote to ask Cecil what construction he should put on them.

> The burning of the images in Bartholomew Fair [he wrote from Antwerp] is here much spoken of with divers constructions, some esteeming it done of purpose to confirm the Scottish revolt; others not marvelling at the plucking down of them, seeing it is a consequent of our religion reformed, do yet think that public burning, through the novelty, a matter rather envious than of necessity.[39]

As this report clearly shows, there was a world of difference between dismantling images and destroying them, especially in public. Such public bonfires (and particularly those that included crucifixes and crosses) held special meaning. They were taken as declarations of intent, displays of commitment to

[37] Wriothesley, *Chronicle*, i, p. 83; cf. *Hall's Chronicle*, p. 826. *Sermons and Remains of Hugh Latimer*, ed. G.E. Corrie (PS, Cambridge, 1845), p. 395; *LP*, 12, ii, p. 218, no. 587; 14. i, p. 155, no. 402.
[38] *The Diary of Henry Machyn*, ed. J.G. Nichols (CS, 42, 1848), p. 207; H.N. Birt, *The Elizabethan Religious Settlement* (London, 1907), p. 510; Aston, *England's Iconoclasts*, i, p. 302.
[39] Birt, *The Elizabethan Religious Settlement*, pp. 172-3, 510-11.

Fig. 29 Antipapalism was fuelled by Henrietta Maria's Catholic observance and her efforts to help Charles I by pawning the crown jewels. Cross and crucifix – here burnt with pictures of friar and bishop, and 'papistical books' – were regarded as papal emblems long before 1643.

reforming extremism. They also spelt potential disorder and revolt, and carried inevitable reminders of earlier alarming events at Basel, Münster and elsewhere. The events in England in 1559 showed, as had already happened to a lesser extent under Henry VIII and was to recur in 1640-1641, how spontaneous iconoclasm could harass authority. To dispose of an image by fire was not only the most effective way of ensuring that it could not be put back in position: it could also be a daring invocation to the government to change the law.

For the architects of a reformed polity, it was of supreme importance that the people should become positive participants as soon as possible in the great change they were inaugurating. To witness the disgrace and punishing of holy statues, to see them exposed as tools and dolls of fraudulent priests, was expected to produce disillusion with the past. The crowds at such public ceremonies were also sometimes given an active role in the dismembering of idols. For instance, at the destruction of the famous rood of Boxley in Kent (another example of an image brought to London for propaganda purposes in 1538), Bishop Hilsey preached an iconoclastic sermon, and then, it was reported,

> After all [the rood's] tricks had been exposed to the people, it was broken into small
> pieces, and it was a great delight to any one who could obtain a single fragment,

either, as I suppose, to put in the fire in their own houses, or else to keep by them by way of reproof to such kind of imposters.[40]

A similar thing happened in Edward VI's reign when, at the urging of a fanatical preacher, the parishioners of St. Andrew Undershaft in the city of London were persuaded that the huge maypole that hung from year to year under the eaves of their houses, was an idol. Householders and tenants gathered together, fortified by dinner on a Sunday afternoon, and with great labour took down the pole and sawed it into pieces, dividing it up amongst themselves. Thus, as John Stow reported it, the preacher's condemned idol was 'mangled and after burned'.[41] The domestic fire could be the follow-up of the public iconoclastic ceremony.

Whereas in the fervid world of relic collecting, believers were avid for morsels of saint's bones, in the enthusiastic demoting of the holy, fragments of images might be collected as evidence of fallen idols. In Geneva the boys who had helped to destroy the images in the cathedral offered them to bystanders. 'We have the gods of the priests; would you like some?'[42] Obviously one cannot be sure that those who went in for this kind of collection did so for the right reasons. One man who certainly did was Nehemiah Wallington. He saved some stained glass fragments from the idolatrous images removed from London churches in October 1641 'to keep for a remembrance to show to the generation to come what God hath done for us, to give us such a reformation that our forefathers never saw the like'.[43] This was model behaviour, precisely of the kind intended by those who structured these ceremonies of demonstrative destruction.

There is another ecclesiastical parallel here. The portions of broken idols taken home for domestic burning (allowing participants to complete under their own roofs celebration of the communal rite they had attended) were comparable to the pieces of holy bread which were taken home from church. That this is not a fanciful analogy is indicated by Thomas Walsingham's description of what happened at St. Albans in 1381. Anger over the abbey's long-standing dispute with its tenants over rights of milling was expressed in the revolt by the insurgents' breaking up the millstones which had been used to pave the abbot's parlour. The stones were taken up by the invaders, who broke them into small pieces and handed them out to the commons,

giving a piece to each person, just as holy bread is customarily broken and distributed in the parish churches on Sundays, so that the people, seeing these pieces

[40] *Original Letters Relative to the English Reformation*, ed. H. Robinson (PS, Cambridge, 1846-1847), 2, pp. 606-7, cf. 604, 609-10. The deceptions of the rood had already been displayed in the market-place at Maidstone in Kent; Wriothesley, *Chronicle*, i, p. 74. Above pp. 267-69.

[41] John Stow, *A Survey of London*, ed. C.L. Kingsford (Oxford, 1908), 1, pp. xxvi-xxvii, 143-44. This was Stow's parish church (in which he was buried) and he witnessed this event.

[42] Eire, *War Against the Idols*, p. 145.

[43] Paul S. Seaver, *Wallington's World: A Puritan Artisan in Seventeenth-Century London* (London, 1985), p. 151.

would know themselves to have been once avenged against the abbey in that cause.[44]

Breaking became a shared ceremony, broken fragments symbols of corporate triumph. Relics salvaged from the shattered past could act as valuable reminders to the recently redeemed.

Let us now consider parish bonfires. Image-burnings in local communities far from the centre of affairs shared some of the characteristics of the city ceremonies. They too exemplified to believers the dismissal of old idolatries. There are many examples of local officials kindling a fire in order to give the rejected images of their parish church the correct quietus.

Authorized fires of this kind started to be lit in earnest during the reign of Edward VI, when iconoclasm at a parochial level was first fully endorsed by the government. The orders to the clergy in the 1547 Injunctions to 'utterly extinct and destroy' all shrines and monuments of superstition and idolatry in their churches, 'so that there remain no memory of the same', were accompanied by directions to parishioners to deal similarly with misused images in their houses.[45] This was followed in February 1548 (after a period of growing differences over imagery) by an order for the removal of *all* images from churches and chapels throughout the realm. Though this fresh order did not (perhaps significantly) say anything about destroying, as opposed to removing, images, those who sought to do so seemed to have received the all-clear. The churchwardens of Ashburton in Devon (to take just one example) duly recorded in their accounts of 1549-50, the expenditure of 3s. 8d 'for le takyng downe the images and tabernaclez and burnyng the same'. Others found it possible to comply with the government's instructions by more moderate action. At Ludlow, for instance, the churchwardens sold off images of Jesus, St. Catherine, St. George and his dragon, with the tabernacles that housed them, and at Long Melford in Suffolk the church 'gear' taken down at the command of the royal visitors in 1547-1548 was likewise disposed of by sale (some of the largest and best images being bought by the local squire, Mr. Clopton).[46] But the parish bonfire held advantages that were not missed by the keenest reformers.

---

[44] R. Faith, ' "The Great Rumour" of 1377 and Peasant Ideology', in *The English Rising of 1381*, ed. R.H. Hilton and T.H. Aston (Cambridge, 1984), p. 66; Thomas Walsingham, *Gesta abbatum monasterii Sancti Albani*, ed. H.T. Riley (RS, London, 1867-9), iii, p. 309.

[45] *Visitation Articles and Injunctions of the Period of the Reformation*, ed. W.H. Frere and W.M. Kennedy (Alciun Club Collns., 14-16, 1910), 2, p. 126, no. 28; Aston, *England's Iconoclasts*, i, p. 254ff.

[46] *Churchwardens' Accounts of Ashburton*, 1479-1580, ed. A. Hanham (Devon and Cornwall Record Soc., NS 15, 1970), p. 124; *Churchwardens Accounts of the Town of Ludlow*, ed. T. Wright (Camden Soc., 102, 1869), pp. 36-7; William Parker, *The History of Long Melford* (London, 1873), pp. 91-5. (I owe this last reference to Eamon Duffy). For a valuable survey see Ronald Hutton, 'The local impact of the Tudor Reformations', in : *The English Reformation Revised*, ed. C. Haigh (Cambridge, 1987), p. 119ff. on the reign of Edward VI.

The Ninth Book , containing the Acts and things done in the reign of King E D VV A R D the fixth.

Fig. 30a, b Bonfires for ending images and bishops: above, part of a woodcut in Foxe's 1641 *Acts and Monuments* illustrating the 'purging of the temple' at the beginning of Edward VI's reign; below the scene in Chelmsford in 1641 or 1642 celebrating the Commons' vote against episcopacy – 'all usual expressions of an exulting joy . . . bonfires were kindled in every street'; detail from title-page of *Mercurius Rusticus* (1685).

In the diocese of Lincoln, where two returned exiles (Nicholas Bullingham and John Aylmer) held office as bishop and archdeacon at the beginning of Elizabeth's reign, parish fires were lit to serious effect. The returns of an enquiry of 1566 into the fate of popish ornaments in the churches of this diocese, tell of many parish fires, in which care seems to have been taken to give the maximum publicity to the burning of instruments of the old religion. At Grantham, 'the rood, Mary and John and all other idols and pictures, mass books, legend books and all other papistical books and ceremonies [serymonyes] was *openly burned* at the cross called market cross', in 1558-9. At Market Rasen the rood, with Mary and John, and 'the rest of the idolatrous images belonging to the abominable mass' were burnt in the market place in the presence of parishioners. Elsewhere roods, with the attendant Maries and Johns were reported as 'burnt before the parish', or 'made away and burnt . . . by the whole parish'.[47]

The churchwardens who arranged these events were surely conscious of the public impact of the changes they were implementing. These were officially directed fires, intended to involve the entire parish as witnesses and participants in the process of purification: open idol-burnings of the kind Thomas Becon advocated. It was not simply a question of eliminating a whole range of idolatrous objects from future use. People were to be welded to the new religious settlement by being personally involved in the ceremonial destruction of ritual objects of the old religion. Objectors might be ordered to attend. At Throwley in Kent, when the royal order for altering rood lofts was implemented in 1561, Richard Goteley 'was warned [by the ancients of the parish] to be at the pulling down of the rood loft, as well as others, for that he was an accuser in Queen Mary's time'.[48]

The parish bonfire was a rite of dismissal. After this community funeral pyre of old 'superstitions' it was time to make good for the future; to plaster over the scars where statues and their supporting corbels had stood, to whitewash church walls, and see to the provision of pulpit, communion table, lectern, poor box, and commandment tables.

Of course the accomplishment of such change was uneven in the extreme. There were still parishes that housed rood-lofts years after Elizabeth's accession. The instrument of the bonfire long continued to serve a useful purpose in places where local diehards were discovered harbouring images, resistant to reform. At Askrigg in Yorkshire the curate and churchwardens alike were found negligent and lacking 'circumspection' when images and vestments were discovered in their church in 1571. For this offence they were fined and ordered to 'carry the images to the fire and put the fire with their own hands to them till

[47] *English Church Furniture, Ornaments and Decorations . . . a List of the Goods destroyed in . . . Lincolnshire Churches . . . 1566*, ed. E. Peacock (London, 1866), pp. 37, 40, 87-8, 124, cf. 61, 69, 110 (my italics).

[48] Collinson, *Godly People*, p. 406; A.L. Rowse, *The England of Elizabeth* (London, 1950), p. 417, n. 1. The source is Canterbury Cathedral Archives and Library, X.i.3, fo. 133 v.

the images be consumed'. This was done on market days at Middleham and Richmond, where the conflagrations were assured of publicity.[49] A few years before this another Yorkshire parish (Aysgarth in the North Riding), seems to have been united in its opposition to iconoclasm. Those placed under orders by the ecclesiastical commissioners in 1567 included the curate and two members of the Metcalfe family (whose most distinguished member in the previous generation was Nicholas, chaplain to John Fisher and Master of St. John's College, Cambridge).[50] The church's harboured images – which included the large figures of Mary and John from the rood – had been shifted from one hiding-place to another: from a vault in the rood-loft to a lime kiln, till they finally fetched up in Sir Christopher Metcalfe's house. The penalty for this illicit hoarding included barefoot penance in Aysgarth churchyard, public confession of concealing idols, and then the offenders had to 'burn all the images before so many of the parishioners as shall be there assembled'.[51] The parish bonfire punished idolaters as well as idols.

By no means all such parish fires received official sanction. From the beginning of the Reformation there were individuals who realized that iconoclasm was a powerful lever. If an activist took it on himself to destroy imagery in his parish church it was unlikely, given the risks of security involved, that it would be restored. Three of the four men who, about 1532, undertook the nocturnal exploit of abducting the pilgrimage rood of Dovercourt and burning it, are reported to have been hung, but there is no evidence that the rood was restored.[52] The opportunities of stealing a march on the law were seized by a number of enthusiasts in Archbishop Cranmer's diocese in Kent, in and after 1538. At Walmer the priest and clerk were reported to have taken down images still permitted by law (as not abused by worship) and to have burnt them. One George Wyborne beheaded, quartered, and then burnt an image of St. Stephen. And the town clerk of Canterbury (Christopher Levins) was said to have violently pulled down images in various churches.[53]

Finally, there were the domestic fires, by which these ritual conflagrations were continued or completed indoors. It was a process that, as we have seen, was envisaged by the government in 1547, and carried out by the London parishioners who sawed up their maypole in 1548. In general (not surprisingly) we have less information about this kind of fire. I do not know of any English example of an image-donor turned image-burner, like the case of Frau Göldli

---

[49] *Tudor Parish Documents of the Diocese of York*, ed. J.S. Purvis (Cambridge, 1948), p. 152; cf. pp. 146-8 for exemplary burnings, including 'in open market'.

[50] On Nicholas Metcalfe, described by Roger Ascham as 'a papist indeed', see Emden (C), p. 403; Dowling, *Humanism in the Age of Henry VIII*, pp. 91, 99; *Humanism, Reform and the Reformation: The Career of Bishop John Fisher*, ed. B. Bradshaw and E. Duffy (Cambridge, 1989), pp. 26, 36, 39, 40, 41, 72; *DNB*.

[51] Ed. Purvis, *Tudor Parish Documents*, pp. 144-6, 225-7, cf. 36.

[52] Foxe, *A & M*, iv, pp. 706-707. See above pp. 263-5

[53] *LP*, 18, ii, pp. 300, 308, 309, 312, no. 546. On Levins see Peter Clark, *English Provincial Society* (Hassocks, 1977), pp. 39-41.

early in the 1520s (cited by Charles Garside), who having given – to promote a cure – a votive statue of St. Apollinaris to a Beguine church in Lucerne, became so conscience-smitten at this misconceived act that she herself removed the image and burnt it.[54] But we do know of individuals in England whose conscience provoked them to deal thus with other people's images. The coat taken from the destroyed Dovercourt rood was handed over to a sympathizer, Thomas Rose, curate of Hadleigh, who himself had the pleasure of burning it.[55] The iconoclastic city clerk of Canterbury whom I have just mentioned, burnt the bones of St. Blaise in his own house. And Mrs. Whittingham, diehard wife of the diehard dean of Durham, whom we have also already encountered, took it on herself to burn the famous banner of St. Cuthbert.[56]

There are some other important associations of fire which I cannot pursue here. There was the conviviality of fire, which undoubtedly belonged even to the purposeful destruction we have been considering. Reforming bonfires were occasions of joy, just as much as the customary midsummer fires of St. John's Day, which were referred to in Bishop Bossuet's 1690 catechism for the clergy of Meaux as 'fires of joy'.[57] Even Bishop Joseph Hall, who found little to rejoice over in the 1643 bonfire at his cathedral of Norwich, remarked on the 'zealous joy' that attended this event.[58] Ancient folk ways had anciently been converted to religious ends, and the St. John's day bonfires reflect some complicated interweaving between time-honoured habits and the upheaval

[54] C. Garside, *Zwingli and the Arts* (New Haven, CT, and London, 1966), p. 99.

[55] Foxe, *A & M*, iv, p. 707; 8, p. 581, above pp. 264-5.

[56] *LP*, 18, ii, pp. 312-13; *Rites of Durham* (see n. 13 above), pp. 26-27.

[57] J.B. Bossuet, *Catéchisme du diocèse de Meaux* (Paris, 1690), p. 363, includes the following exchanges. '*Est- ce pour cela* [the birth of St John Baptist] *qu'on alume des feux de joye?*' 'Oui, c'est pour cela'. '*L'Eglise prend-elle part à ces feux?*' 'Oui, puisque dans plusieurs Dioceses, et en particulier dans celui-ci, plusieurs Paroisses font un feu qu'on appelle Ecclésiastique'. '*Quelle raison a-t-on eû de faire ce feu d'une manière Ecclésiastique?*' 'Pour en banir les superstitions qu'on pratique au feu de la Saint Jean' [sic]. These superstitions included (p. 364) dancing round the fire, singing indecent songs, and condemned practices with herbs. On this ritual see P. Burke, *Popular Culture in Early Modern Europe* (London, 1978), pp. 229-30, and on the activities involved see Freudenthal, *Das Feuer*, pp. 288-327. The convivial bonfires, like love-feasts – though associated with other frowned-on practices – had an ancient history, well remembered long after the Reformation. The early fifteenth- century *Speculum sacerdotale*, ed. E.H. Weatherly (EETS., OS 200, 1936), p. 166, alluded to the 'joying' of the occasion, including foolish 'makyng of grete fires in stretis'; 'Sires, in the nyght of Seynt John ben bones i-brenned, wheles ben lappid up, fire is brennyd to askes, churches and howsus ben honowred with herbes and leves and viriditees'. In Elizabeth's reign both John Stow and Roger Martin looked back with some nostalgia on these old summer ceremonies. Stow, *Survey of London*, 1, p. 101, described the bonfires made in the streets at dusk, called bonfires 'of good amity', at which neighbours feasted and enemies were reconciled; Martin recalled more patriarchal occasions in his grandfather's hall at Long Melford, with friends and poor neighbours in to share the fare, again with bonfires and lights to honour the image of St. John the Baptist. J.P. Neale and J. Le Keux, *Views of the Most Interesting Collegiate and Parochial Churches in Great Britain* (London, 1824-5), 2, on the church of Holy Trinity, Melford, Suffolk.

[58] J. Hall, *Hard Measure* (1710), p. 16 (this was written in 1647). Aston, *England's Iconoclasts*, i, pp. 68-70.

inaugurated by the iconoclasts. Lighting fires in what Bossuet called an 'ecclesiastical manner' was an activity of Catholics as well as of reformed Protestants, and Lutherans too knew the propaganda value of flames.[59] The old association of a purifying bonfire with the purifying season of Lent was given a new dimension by the image-burners. And in England some new days of bonfire lighting were added to the post-Reformation calendar.[60] Besides Queen Elizabeth's Accession Day (17 November), there was Gunpowder Day (twelve days earlier) which became linked with iconoclastic activity.

The reformers took over rituals of fire and turned them to their own uses. Of course they could only burn the combustible, and though stone cracked and metal melted in the greatest pyres, it was wooden statues and carvings that formed the main fuel for these iconoclastic demonstrations. If the destroyers could scarcely innovate, dealing with an elemental force and such timeless modes of behaviour, they did discover some fresh dangers by sponsoring the official holocaust. Burning is a dangerous art, and though they played with fire for the most earnest ends, it sometimes threatened the very objectives it was intended to serve.

Fire was the ultimate destroyer, the agent of the expected conflagration that would end the world, and the sight of long-revered holy objects vanishing in the flames prompted thoughts of last things.

> If you had seen the general dissolution of the world, and all the pomp and glory of it consumed to ashes; if you saw all on a fire about you, sumptuous buildings, cities, kingdoms, land, water, earth, heaven, all flaming about your ears; if you had seen all that men laboured for, and sold their souls for, gone . . . what would such a sight as this persuade you to do? Why, such a sight thou shalt certainly see.[61]

In these words Richard Baxter expressed a common assumption. Everyone was conditioned to think of the consummation of the world by fire, and the iconoclasts, who set out to reduce a whole world of impurities to ashes, impressed the finality of flames on their generation. Theirs was an idealistic vision: renewal by obliteration.

---

[59] R.W. Scribner, 'Incombustible Luther: The Image of the Reformer in Early Modern Germany', *Past and Present*, 110 (1986), pp. 38-68.

[60] On this see David Cressy, *Bonfires and Bells: National Memory and the Protestant Calendar in Elizabethan and Stuart England* (London, 1989).

[61] R. Baxter, *The Saints Everlasting Rest* (London, 1653), pt. 3, p. 124. On the eschatological aspect of iconoclasm see A. Chastel, 'L'iconoclasme', in *Von der Macht der Bilder*, ed. E. Ullmann (Leipzig, 1983), pp. 264, 268, 269.

Index